Occupation in the East

OCCUPATION IN THE EAST

*The Daily Lives of German Occupiers
in Warsaw and Minsk, 1939–1944*

STEPHAN LEHNSTAEDT

Translated by dbmedia

berghahn
NEW YORK • OXFORD
www.berghahnbooks.com

Published in 2016 by
Berghahn Books
www.berghahnbooks.com

Published in cooperation with the German Historical Institute in Warsaw

© 2010 Oldenbourg Wissenschaftsverlag, GmbH, München. All rights reserved.
English edition © 2016, 2019 Berghahn Books
First paperback edition published in 2019

Originally published in German in 2010 as
Okkupation im Osten. Besatzeralltag in Warschau und Minsk 1939–1944.
All rights reserved.

Except for the quotation of short passages
for the purposes of criticism and review, no part of this book
may be reproduced in any form or by any means, electronic or
mechanical, including photocopying, recording, or any information
storage and retrieval system now known or to be invented,
without written permission of the publisher.

Library of Congress Cataloging-in-Publication Data
Names: Lehnstaedt, Stephan, 1980- author.
Title: Occupation in the East : the daily lives of German occupiers in Warsaw and Minsk,
    1939-1944 / Stephan Lehnstaedt ; translated by Martin Dean.
Other titles: Okkupation im Osten. English
Description: English edition. | New York : Berghahn Books, 2017. | "Published in
    cooperation with the German Historical Institute, Warsaw"—Title page verso. |
    "Originally published in German in 2010 as Okkupation im Osten : Besatzeralltag
    in Warschau und Minsk, 1939-1944"—Title page verso. | Includes bibliographical
    references and index.
Identifiers: LCCN 2016024749 | ISBN 9781785333231 (hardback : alkaline paper) |
    ISBN 9781785333248 (ebook)
Subjects: LCSH: World War, 1939-1945—Social aspects—Poland—Warsaw. | World War,
    1939-1945—Social aspects—Belarus—Minsk. | Poland—History—Occupation, 1939-1945.
    | Belarus—History—German occupation, 1941-1944. | Germans—Poland—Warsaw—
    History—20th century. | Germans—Belarus—Minsk—History—20th century. | Warsaw
    (Poland)—History—20th century. | Minsk (Belarus)—History—20th century.
Classification: LCC D802.P6 L42513 2017 | DDC 940.53/43841—dc23
LC record available at https://lccn.loc.gov/2016024749

British Library Cataloguing in Publication Data
A catalogue record for this book is available from the British Library.

ISBN 978-1-78533-323-1 hardback
ISBN 978-1-78920-498-8 paperback
ISBN 978-1-78533-324-8 ebook

Contents

List of Figures and Tables	vi
List of Abbreviations	viii
Introduction	1
Chapter 1. Germans on Duty in the East in Warsaw and Minsk	20
Chapter 2. Daily Life Prescribed by Norms	75
Chapter 3. Transgression of Norms	122
Chapter 4. The Attitude of the Overlords	161
Chapter 5. Violence in Everyday Life: The German Occupiers and the Local Population	209
Conclusions	269
Bibliography	281
Index	302

List of Figures and Tables

Figures

1.1.	Palais Brühl, Official Residence of the Distrikt-Governor in Warsaw	39
1.2.	Map from the Official Guide to Warsaw for German Soldiers in 1942	54
1.3.	A Modern Apartment Block on Karowastrasse in Warsaw	56
2.1.	The Residential Hostel on Karowastraße: Single Apartment	82
2.2.	The German House in Warsaw (Radziwiłł Palace)	85
2.3.	The Dining Room in the German House in Warsaw	86
2.4.	Scene from *Iphigenie auf Tauris* in Łazienki Park	99
2.5.	The Home of the Sports Club Palais Brühl, Warsaw	102
3.1.	Warsaw in the Winter of 1939–1940.	124
3.2.	An Entrance to the Ghetto in Warsaw	139
4.1.	Funeral of Franz Kutschera, February 4, 1944	181
4.2.	German Weddings in Warsaw, 1941–1944	184
5.1.	The Public Hanging of Twenty-seven Prisoners of the Pawiak Prison in Warsaw on Gerichtstrasse (now Lesznostrasse), February 11, 1944	219
5.2.	The Connecting Bridge between the Halves of the Warsaw Ghetto	223
5.3.	Jews from Warsaw Are Forced to Board a Train for Treblinka in the Summer of 1942	236

5.4. The Burning of the Warsaw Ghetto during the Uprising in 1943 — 241

Tables

1.1. Germans Working in the Civil Administration of Distrikt Warschau — 39

1.2. German Births in Warsaw, 1940–1942 — 49

3.1. German Tourists in Warsaw, 1933–1937 — 126

3.2. Black-Market Prices in Warsaw as a Percentage of the Official Price — 137

5.1. Official Daily Rations of Required Forms of Nutrition in Warsaw (in percent) — 211

5.2. Deportations of Jews from the Reich to Warsaw — 228

5.3. Deportations of Jews from the Reich to Minsk — 229

LIST OF ABBREVIATIONS AND ACRONYMS

AAN	Archiwum Akt Nowych [Archive of New Documents]
AK	Armia Krajowa [Polish Underground]
APW	Archiwum Państwowe m.st. Warszawy [State Archive of the Capital City of Warsaw]
BAB	Bundesarchiv Berlin [German Federal Archive Berlin]
BAL	Bundesarchiv-Außenstelle Ludwigsburg [German Federal Archive-Ludwigsburg Branch]
BALAA	Bundesarchiv-Lastenausgleichsarchiv, Bayreuth [German Federal Archive-Burden Sharing Archive]
BAMA	Bundesarchiv-Militärarchiv [German Federal Archive-Military Archive]
BayStA	Bayerisches Staatsarchiv [Bavarian State Archive]
BAZAH	Bundesarchiv-Zwischenarchiv Berlin-Hoppegarten [German Federal Archive-Intermediate Archive Hoppegarten]
Bd.	Band [Volume]
BDC	Berlin Document Center
BDM	Bund Deutscher Mädel [(Nazi-organized) League of German Girls]
BdO	*Befehlshaber der Ordnungspolizei* [Senior Commander of the Order Police]
BdS	*Befehlshaber der Sicherheitspolizei und des* SD [Senior Commander of the Security Police and the SD]
BfZg	Bibliothek für Zeitgeschichte [Library for Contemporary History]
BStU	Die Bundesbeauftragte für die Unterlagen des Staatssicherheitsdienstes der ehemaligen Deutschen

Demokratischen Republik [The Federal Representative for the Documents of the State Security Service of the former German Democratic Republic]

CdZ	*Chef der Zivilverwaltung* [Head of the Civilian Administration]
DDR	Deutsche Demokratische Republik [German Democratic Republic, or East Germany]
DTA	Deutsches Tagebucharchiv [German Diary Archive]
DVP	Deutsche Volkspartei [German People's Party]
ERR	*Einsatzstab Reichsleiter Rosenberg* [Operational Staff of Reich Leader Rosenberg]
FDP	Freie Demokratische Partei [Free Democratic Party]
GDR	German Democratic Republic (East Germany)
Gestapo	Geheime Staatspolizei [Secret State Police]
GG	Generalgouvernement Polen [General Government of Poland]
GK	Generalkommissariat [General Commissariat]
HBD	Haupteisenbahndirektion [Railway Main Office]
HSSPF	Höherer SS- und Polizeiführer [Higher SS and Police Leader]
ID	Infanteriedivision [Infantry Division]
IfZA	Institut für Zeitgeschichte, Archiv [Institute for Contemporary History, Archive]
IPN	Instytut Pamięci Narodowej [Polish Institute of National Remembrance]
KdG	*Kommandeur der Gendarmerie* [commander of the gendarmerie]
KdO	*Kommandeur der Ordnungspolizei* [commander of the Order Police]
KdS	*Kommandeur der Sicherheitspolizei und des* SD [commander of the Security Police and the SD]
MBliV	Ministerialblatt des Reichs- und Preußischen Ministeriums des Innern (previously Ministerialblatt der inneren Verwaltung) [Ministerial Publication of the Reich and Prussian Interior Ministry (previously Ministerial Publication of the Interior Administration)]
MfS-HA	Ministerium für Staatssicherheit der DDR, Hauptabteilung [GDR Ministry for State Security, Main Department]

NCO	noncommissioned officers
NL	*Nachlass* [legacy of collected papers]
NSDAP	Nationalsozialistische Deutsche Arbeiterpartei [National Socialist German Workers' Party]
NSV	Nationalsozialistische Volkswohlfahrt [National Socialist People's Welfare Organization]
NTN	Najwyższy Trybunał Narodowy [Highest National Tribunal]
Ober Ost	Oberkommando Ost [High Command in the East]
OFK	Oberfeldkommandantur [Senior Field Commandant's Office]
ÖGZA	Österreichischen Gesellschaft für Zeitgeschichte, Archiv [Austrian Society for Contemporary History, Archive]
OKH	Oberkommando des Heeres [High Command of the Army]
OKW	Oberkommando der Wehrmacht [High Command of the Armed Forces]
POW	prisoner of war
RFSS	*Reichsführer* SS [Reich leader of the SS]
RGVA	Российский Государственный Военный Архив [Russian State Military Archive]
RKFDV	Reichskommissar für die Festigung des deutschen Volkstums [Reich Commissioner for the Consolidation of German Ethnicity]
RKO	Reichskommissariat Ostland [Reich Commissariat for Ostland]
RMbO	Reichsministerium für die besetzten Ostgebiete [Reich Ministry for the Eastern Occupied Territories]
RMdI	Reichsministerium des Innern [Reich Ministry of the Interior]
RONA	Русская Освободительная Народная Армия [Russian People's Liberation Army]
RSHA	Reichssicherheitshauptamt [Reich Security Main Office]
RVD	Reichsverkehrsdirektion [Reich Transport Head Office]
SA	Sturmabteilung der NSDAP [Storm Troopers of the Nazi Party]
Schupo	Schutzpolizei [Defense Police; urban branch of the Order Police]

SD	Sicherheitsdienst des Reichsführers SS [Security Police of the Reich leader of the SS]
SiPo	Sicherheitspolizei [Security Police]
Slg.	Sammlung [Collection]
SS	Schutzstaffel der NSDAP [Protection Squad of the Nazi Party]
SSPF	SS- und Polizeiführer [SS and police leader]
StAM	Staatsarchiv Münster [Munster State Archives]
Stasi	Staatssicherheitsdienst der ehemaligen DDR [Office of State Security of the former GDR]
UdSSR	Union der Sozialistischen Sowjetrepubliken [Union of the Soviet Socialist Republic]
US-NARA	U.S. National Archives and Records Administration
VfZ	*Vierteljahrshefte für Zeitgeschichte* [Quarterly Journal for Contemporary History]
VtH	Villa ten Hompel, Archive
WHW	Winterhilfswerk (Winter Aid Drive)
YMCA	Young Men's Christian Association
YV	Yad Vashem Archive
ZAH	Zentralarchiv zur Erforschung der Geschichte der Juden in Deutschland [Central Archive for Researching the History of the Jews in Germany]
ZSL	Zentrale Stelle der Landesjustizverwaltungen [Central Office of the Regional Judicial Administrations]

INTRODUCTION

On September 1, 1939, the Third Reich started World War II by attacking the Polish Republic. A few days later Wehrmacht (German armed forces) reached the Polish capital, Warsaw, which capitulated on September 28, following a siege of just three weeks. This marked the start of German occupational rule; it lasted until the arrival of the Red Army on January 17, 1945, and cost the lives of more than 600,000 of the city's original population of 1.3 million.[1] In the Generalgouvernement Polen (General Government of Poland), which Hitler established in October 1939, the local population paid a high toll in blood for the military defeat inflicted by the aggressor from the West. The policies of General Governor Hans Frank, who established his capital not in Warsaw, but in Krakow, together with those of the other institutions of the Nazi regime, resulted in the deaths of at least 4.5 million inhabitants of Poland, two-thirds of them Jewish.

There were more victims during the war in the Soviet Union than in Europe, which was invaded by German troops on June 22, 1941. The Soviet Republic of Belorussia was one of the first regions to come under German rule, and with 2.2 million dead from a prewar population of 10.6 million, it was also one of the most severely hit.[2] The Generalkommissariat Weißruthenien (General Commissariat of Belorussia), which was created by Berlin from parts of the Belorussian Soviet Republic and parts of prewar Poland, was directed by General Commissar Wilhelm Kube in Minsk. The capital, which was captured on June 28, 1941, and liberated on July 3, 1944, had some 240,000 inhabitants, of which more than half perished during the three years of occupation.[3] Nazi policies resulted not only in the destruction of a large part of the population, but also in the destruction of both cities that form the subject of this work; these cities by the end of 1944 lay almost completely in ruins and had scarcely any districts left that were still habitable.

In Warsaw and Minsk German occupational rule also entailed the near complete extinction of the indigenous culture and way of life. Educational institutions were closed down; theaters and museums largely shut their doors, or at least reduced their presentations and displays to a poor standard; sports and the media were subjected to strict controls and regulations. The social life of the population took on completely different forms than before the war since material shortages forced people first and foremost to secure their own existence. By contrast, the Germans created a wide range of cultural activities to meet their own needs, reflecting almost all aspects of life. This was the basis for a German society of occupiers that soon became established in the East—strictly segregated from the local population—and with its own distinctive norms.

This society of occupiers comprised many thousands of Germans, who, as soldiers, members of the German administration, policemen, or private individuals, secured and organized German rule and thereby also facilitated the genocide of the Jews, the mass murder of actual or supposed resistance fighters, the starvation of the local population, and the destruction of the two cities. The concept of genocide is understood here as a descriptive category, whose essential elements are the planned and actual destruction of an ethnic group; in this sense the German treatment of the Poles—at least in Warsaw—can also be characterized as genocide.[4] Beyond this, violence here also includes the indirect use of force against noncombatants by individual and state actors, including, for example, the effects of enforced malnutrition and sickness.

This book aims to present a history of daily life (*Alltagsgeschichte*) for the German occupiers in Warsaw and Minsk. The German edition was published in Munich in 2010. In the years since, several relevant publications have appeared that also deal with the history of other cities under occupation during World War II, without, however, examining the perpetrators in close detail.[5] Now as ever, the urban living space, with all its intertwined conflicts and tensions, remains a rich field for historical study. Increasingly, the traditional German–Polish dividing lines are being blurred and academics are reading the sources and literature in the respective other languages. Yet the regime change in Eastern Europe in 1989 is still setting the research agenda: the files of the Nazi occupiers held in the Eastern European archives and the history of Nazi crimes in Poland and the occupied Soviet territories are of much greater interest in Germany than they are in Poland. Polish academics had concerned themselves with this topic from the 1950s and published many studies that received recognition only decades later in the West. The newly acquired access to specific archives has been exploited by the historians east of the Elbe and the Oder mainly to focus on Stalinist crimes.

For future research, the comparative study of Stalinism and German National Socialism will prove to be an especially fruitful topic.[6] Yet the history of daily life during just one occupation can offer a new perspective because it not only facilitates the detailed description of crimes based on many facts, but also emphasizes the people involved and the nature of their lives. This presents also an opportunity to describe the fate and the actions of those who until now have often been characterized as passive victims, or—in the case of the occupiers—as an undifferentiated band of murderers. Furthermore, the history of daily life examines the significance of those structures that provide the framework within which people make decisions. And it can offer new perspectives, by including contemporary interpretations that make it possible to describe both normality and exceptional events. Especially in the East, where *Reichsdeutsche* (Reich Germans) and *Volksdeutsche* (ethnic Germans) were brought together in a new society, the question was also raised of what makes up the *Volksgemeinschaft* (people's community).[7] The powerful influence of this concept can be seen more clearly in the East than anywhere else.

Such a perspective is also possible because the chronology and dimension of the crimes in both cities and regions have now been quite thoroughly researched. For Minsk the studies of Bernhard Chiari[8] and Christian Gerlach[9] are available, although these studies are not directly concerned with the city, but rather with Generalkommissariat Weißruthenien as a whole. Both books, with their wealth of information, also fill a large gap in research on Nazi occupation policies; prior research had scarcely taken any interest in this Soviet republic.

The state of research regarding Warsaw is quite different: here Polish academics have conducted the major studies of German crimes—some of which are available also in translation—while historical research in the country of the perpetrators has hardly produced anything. The classic study is still the book of Tomasz Szarota,[10] which, moreover, is mainly devoted to the daily life of the local population. This reveals a key tendency that is still valid for Polish historians: they remain focused on their own compatriots as victims while describing the course of events, facts, and details accurately and comprehensively. Their knowledge about the occupiers usually remains limited. This explains why Czesław Madajczyk's comprehensive history of German occupation policy in Poland,[11] which in the original Polish version dates from 1970, still provides a convincing overview with respect to the occupiers.

The most important findings of the German research conducted since 1990 have not yet been integrated into a synthesis covering the entire *Generalgouvernement*: examples are research done by Dieter Pohl on Distrikt Lublin and Distrikt Galizien, or on the German civil administration by Bogdan Musial, Robert Seidel, and Jacek Andrzej Młynarczyk.[12] Surprisingly there have been no recent studies on Distrikt Krakau or the capital itself, or on Warsaw, the largest city in the General Government. For Warsaw many older works exist that cover various aspects of German occupational rule; almost always, however, these works are written from the perspective of the Polish victims and not the perpetrators. This applies also to the conditions facing the Jews in Warsaw, which have been thoroughly researched.[13] In these studies the Germans are confined to the role of organizing the Jews' destruction, but no detailed analysis of the personnel involved has taken place. Despite certain changes in recent years, research has concentrated mainly on the role of the state and its mobilization of individual groups. The racist ideology of the Nazis and the central role of Berlin in planning the genocide are both heavily emphasized in these works; historians, especially the German historians, focus on the Jews mainly as victims in their studies of Eastern Europe.[14]

Research on the perpetrators that examines the personalities of the Nazi criminals as well as the specific causes that turn men into murderers has been in vogue ever since Christopher Browning's pioneering work in this field.[15] Browning, who chose *Ordinary Men* as the title for his book in 1992, produced an interpretation of the crimes committed by members of Reserve Police Battalion 101 that assumed that under certain circumstances almost everyone is capable of becoming a murderer. Although this thesis has found general approval and individual studies have attempted to define these conditions more precisely, the majority of German researchers have concentrated on the biographical particularities of individuals[16] or, in collective biographies,[17] of groups, and uncovered thereby the disposition to commit murder not of "ordinary men," but rather of senior Nazi office holders and leaders.

However, purely in terms of numbers, these groups composed only a small part of the German occupation force in the East, and the other Germans, who also contributed to securing German rule and thereby the commission of genocide, have been researched to a much lesser extent, if at all. An exception is the senior postal official in Warsaw, Hermann Beyerlein, whose daily life has been documented together with many photographs.[18] Yet despite the upsurge in academic activity resulting from the Wehrmacht Exhibition in Germany, not a single monograph has been produced, either on Poland or on Belorussia, that looks at the German troops stationed there. It seems to be little better with regard to the ethnic Germans, whose significance, especially in the General Government, can scarcely be underestimated, both in terms of their numbers and their contribution to the functioning of the German occupation regime.[19] The same applies also to German women, who were deployed to the East in considerable numbers.[20] The available studies on the civil administration are concerned mainly with their administrative activities, but largely neglect biographical aspects and the question of freedom of action in the local context.

Another significant topic, the public nature of the violence and the extent to which Germans were aware of the genocide, has also received much attention recently, notably in the book by Peter Longerich.[21] His study is based on official reports on the mood of the population, propaganda, press manipulation, and other official assessments of German public opinion, but does not include any analysis of the flow of information within Eastern Europe itself. The overarching character of the book, therefore, does not provide the in-depth view of a local study. While Longerich pursues a mainly chronological approach to this question, Bernward Dörner, in his study of public opinion and the Holocaust proceeds thematically, and explains, using examples, the various possible ways that existed for Germans to become aware of the genocide.[22]

Questions Posed and Methodology

There still remain many gaps in the research on German occupation of the East. Nevertheless, several recent collective-biographical studies, based mainly on the postwar criminal investigations of the Federal Republic of Germany (West Germany) by the Zentrale Stelle der Landesjustizverwaltungen (Central Office of the Regional Judicial Administrations, or ZSL) in Ludwigsburg, have considerably expanded our knowledge of the Nazi state and the personnel that implemented its criminal policies. Addressing the question of how the regime was able to turn so many people into murderers has, however, often been left by the historians to academics from other disciplines. Sociologists, in particular, have formulated wide ranging and stimulating interpretations concerning the situational aspects of violence that frequently, however, have not been secured by a sufficiently broad source basis.[23]

From all these conclusions researchers have distilled out a wide variety of motivations among the perpetrators. On the one hand, there were people who believed in what they were doing on the basis of their ideological convictions or a corresponding socialization, and on the other there were also the "ordinary men," for whom a variety of motives need to be considered. Alongside the bureaucratic implementation of orders, the pursuit of personal gain, careerism, and the anti-Semitism that was widespread in German society during the nineteenth and twentieth centuries, there are also the effects of group dynamics. All of these causes have been identified as keys to understanding the Holocaust and the actual source of the violence.[24] However, the interrelations between these various factors, which have been seen usually as mono-causal answers, still have to be examined in detail. This applies also in large measure to the relations between the occupiers and the occupied, which have scarcely yet been examined in academic studies.

Furthermore, no one has yet attempted to combine in one study various methodological approaches such as biographical, the history of daily life, and comparative history in order to reveal deeper insights into the intentions of the perpetrators. It is especially the formative experiences of those present on the spot and the interrelations between perpetrators and victims have yet to be incorporated within historical monographs. However, real progress can only be expected, given the already high standard of the academic works on German occupation and genocide in Eastern Europe, if an integrative approach is pursued. Perpetrator research has to combine the polar opposites of disposition and situation, examining them together, just as the commission of crimes was embedded within the daily life of the occupiers and the society they lived in.[25]

In order to identify the conditions that first made possible the implementation of violence, we have to go beyond questions of plans and intentions. Only in this way can we even start to comprehend the complex nature of the genocide. There was more than one direction for the violence because various groups were targeted in turn. There was more than one group of perpetrators because all members of the society of occupiers were necessarily involved to a greater or lesser extent. There was more than one motive for the violence: economic, ideological, and behavioral factors were linked to state orders and norms that developed their own intertwined dynamic, with fateful consequences for the local population.[26] The causes of mass murder lie within the society in which it takes place— or that produces it—and have deeper roots than just state policy, although that policy sets many of the conditions under which genocide occurs. But structures explain at most *how* people act, not *why* they act.[27]

The genocide in the East was a "collective enterprise marked by the division of labor."[28] The participants included not only those people who directly ordered the murders or physically carried them out, but also those who prepared them, who created the organizational framework, who contributed to maintaining German occupational rule, or those—such as wives—who supported the social and emotional stability of the perpetrators. Almost all Reich Germans and ethnic Germans that spent time in Minsk or Warsaw during the war made their own contribution, one way or another, to enforcing the occupation, and thereby became implicated in the crimes of that occupation. As research has now clearly established, there was no ethical or social background, no age, religion, nor level of education that could protect one from becoming a perpetrator.[29] Exactly for this reason the question must be posed: What were the conditions that made so many Germans active participants in the occupation, and thereby in the violence that it necessarily entailed?

This study attempts to answer this question using the cities of Warsaw and Minsk as examples, and thereby to make a contribution to understanding Nazi genocide.[30] The first chapter examines the various groups that composed the society of occupiers, such as the Wehrmacht, the Schutzstaffel der NSDAP (Protection Squad of the NSDAP; SS), the police, the civil administration, as well as Reich and ethnic German civilians. It presents an overview of those Germans who were present, their backgrounds, and also their functions, while also explaining why those individuals travelled to the East. The spectrum of causes ranges from those who headed directly to Warsaw as volunteers, through civil servants sent on official duty, on to the soldiers doing military service who were stationed there more or less by chance. Special attention has been given also to the spatial presence of the Germans in both cities, which not only influenced the relations within the group, but also the relations of the group with the local population.

Chapter 2 turns next to the question of what rules and patterns shaped the lives of the occupiers. Not only do we examine their official duties, but we also look at communal life in their shared quarters and the various forms of organized leisure activities. Political indoctrination in its various forms will also be taken into account. In view of the highly regulated nature of the occupiers' daily lives, the amount of freedom they enjoyed needs to be carefully weighed and contrasted with the extent to which their lives were determined for them by external forces. That the occupiers accepted such conditions reveals the potency of political instructions in the East and how much this differed from the Nazi penetration of daily life inside the Reich. It reveals the real circumstances under which the occupation took place and how they were experienced by the occupiers. What dividing lines—actual or only perceived—were drawn by the war between the home front and those Germans deployed outside the Reich?

This approach would be incomplete if the nonregulated aspects of daily life were excluded. Chapter 3 deals therefore with those activities that the Germans in Warsaw and Minsk developed that did not correspond to the wishes of the regime, or at least lay outside the framework of organized leisure. Prior to this, however, we will take a glance at the self-perceptions of the occupiers to clarify how they related to their own existence in the East; individual actions are determined in large part by whether someone is satisfied with or rejects the situation they find themselves in. Most important for one's subjective evaluation of things are the options that exist outside of the given norms: foremost among these is the area of supplies—also in the form of plunder—but especially supplies on the black market, in which most occupiers gladly participated. But even religion or alcohol alleviated their daily existence. When dissatisfaction nevertheless emerged, most conflicts took place within the circle of comrades. It is important to measure the extent of this kind of adaptation to daily life, to name the likely reasons and consequences, and, in addition, to assess the reactions of those in power, in order to show the full spectrum of options for action.

The investigation of daily life makes it possible to illuminate those aspects of the society of occupiers that represent the special nature of deployment to the East, things that were not present in other places, and that proved fertile ground for excessive violence and genocide. Arising from these special conditions, there emerged a repertoire of behavioral patterns that distinguished the occupiers. It was expressed particularly in relations with the local population and in the appearances of the German occupiers outside their own closed society. We will sketch out the demands posed on individuals—not only by the offices and institutions, but also by colleagues and comrades—their practical effects, and the picture the occupants had of the Polish or Belorussian population. Here, the relations between the sexes—above all between German men and local women—are significant because access to sex was a yardstick for the Germans to measure their own position and their own self-perception within a starkly hierarchical rank structure that segregated them strictly from the occupied peoples.

From acceptance of their position and, above all, denigration of the local population, it was only a small step to violence against the occupied. Moreover, precisely this development demands very careful analysis so we can examine the legitimation of violence, as well as its presence in the public sphere. The evaluation of systematic repression, individual hangings, massacres, and finally mass murder and genocide depended considerably on its visibility; nevertheless, reports and rumors were discussed among colleagues. Therefore, the flow of information about these events is important, but the channels and content of communications are also important and play a key role. It has to be asked how the respective violence was viewed and how the occupiers judged themselves and their own contribution, especially toward their family members at home. The crimes and the course of events in Minsk and Warsaw are comparatively well-researched and therefore are not the subject, but rather the starting point for this study: What role did violence play in the life of the occupiers and how did people justify the violence of the occupation as well as the violence of the roles played by individuals? Or asked in another way: Was it not disturbing and terrifying for the Germans deployed to the East to live in an environment where mass murder was taking place?

In order to help explain and assess the issues outlined above, this study is based on the following methodological concepts.

1. Conditions in the cities of Warsaw and Minsk will be examined using a comparative approach. This makes it easier to identify local specificities and commonalities. Comparisons also protect historians from overemphasizing individual issues that under slightly different circumstances may have led to a different outcome. In addition, by studying two cities the relevance of the results is increased and—with great caution—their universal validity can be assessed more easily. The case studies of Warsaw and Minsk reveal initially the high degree of heterogeneity that distinguished the administration of the occupied territories, both regarding the formal relations with the authorities in the Reich and with respect to internal structures. This study excludes countries in Western Europe due to the comparatively low levels of violence there and focuses instead on the East. In the occupied Soviet territories, the drastic practices of the various civilian and military offices brought the Führer state to the fore, both with regard to its personalization and to its unpredictability. Conditions in the General Government were clearly different because Hans Frank, at the head of the administration, was the personification of the Nazi lawyer. In both Eastern European regions the occupiers committed crimes of excessive violence. Because rurally dominated regions are hardly suitable for study due to the small number of occupiers, the available sources encourage the study of one major city in Poland and one in Belorussia because there were plenty of Germans to be found there. Compared to the capital city of Warsaw, with more than a million inhabitants and the largest Jewish population in Europe, Minsk was a considerably smaller city with some 240,000 inhabitants. In order to remain focused, the study concentrates more on Warsaw; on the one hand there are more sources in Warsaw, and on the other it has been more intensively studied. Given the central importance of the city for German rule in Eastern Europe, the large number of occupiers living there, and especially the scale of the crimes, this focus appears justified. Minsk is placed alongside it as a comparative yardstick and as a contrast. In order to bring out the specific qualities of the East, reference will also be made to the Reich because it to some extent represents the normal case for German living conditions and daily life.

2. Central to the approach are concepts from the set of tools called *Alltagsgeschichte* developed in Germany mainly by Alf Lüdtke,[31] which permit access to how the occupiers perceived the world around them because they sorted and internalized the experiences and uncertain meanings of daily life. On the one hand we can question the significance of the given norms. On the other hand, we need to assess the

extent to which these norms were really accepted; that is, the adaptation, relativization, softening, and ignorance that rules always undergo. With this approach, the conventional duality of personal and political—that is, private and public—will be dissolved, and thereby the horizon of structural history and perpetrator research opened to a complex and at the same time integrative understanding of Nazi rule in the East. If this makes it possible to avoid simply contrasting the public sphere, politics, and ideology on the one side against daily experiences on the other, then the mutual interdependencies can be shown, by which politics shapes daily life, and daily life also influences politics.

3. The experience of daily life had a direct influence on the still-forming attitude, which we call habitus, of the occupants. The concept of habitus developed by Pierre Bourdieu[32] describes patterns of perception, thinking, and action that help people to demonstrate their social position in situations where those social positions are not clearly defined by the contextual relationships, as is the case, for example, among a circle of friends. A constitutive element of Bourdieu's hypothesis is that actions cannot be derived primarily from laws and rules because the actors themselves do not apply those types of theories, but rather develop their own adaptation of social behavior. Here there are overlaps with the idea of adapted daily life or the *Eigensinnkonzept* (concept of self-will) used by historians of daily life. Put more generally, the occupiers' attitude offers rules of interpretation under which the environment is ordered and classified, and that provide a basis for action. For Warsaw and Minsk the concept of self-will concerns first interactions with other occupiers who did not belong to the same group, but above all it concerns the contacts with the local population that frequently involved violence. In the course of its development and adaptation, attitude, which essentially is based on daily life, becomes something natural, taken for granted, and the internalized structures become second nature.[33]

Attitude therefore makes social necessity into a virtue and becomes an expression of recognition for the ruling order. However, attitude is not determinism; rather it only delimits those practices that are possible and impossible. Yet it does not set the process in stone, but rather determines the manner in which it is implemented.[34] These practices are matched to the present and the expected near future. A study of daily life can show whether social structures have merely been reproduced or whether they were also transformed. In order to measure the role of violence in the occupiers' daily lives, we will not only describe its forms and consequences, but also will make an assessment of how public it was. In connection with attitude, this will show how "normal" and legitimate it seemed to the occupiers to be constantly surrounded by violence and even to be personally involved. Therefore, we must analyze the degree of knowledge about those crimes that were not directly visible and how they were reported and evaluated within the public sphere of the occupiers.

In a central article on the public space in dictatorships Adelheid von Saldern proposed five models, including two that are particularly relevant for the circumstances of an occupation: closed public spaces and informal public spaces.[35] For the special conditions in the East, we identify a hybrid type that we will designate occupation public space. It is distinguished by daily communication, and at the same time by the maintenance of strict secrecy toward those outside the occupation circles.[36] This kind of public space cannot be simply shut down by the ruling elite; it can only be limited, for example, by using the deterrence of setting severe examples, if the circle of people aware of crimes becomes too great. It is possible to set the limits of what is permitted and what is forbidden by drastic measures, but also by informal and largely unspoken agreement, established through the mechanism of habitus.

Within a closed group like the society of occupiers certain topics of the internal public sphere reinforced the exclusivity of membership against those outside the group, even when the latter were in the majority. At the same time, it was possible for this small group via the mail or through visits home to expand the area of its public space in terms of both localities and people. In Warsaw and Minsk crimes of violence took place almost every day, but much of the killing was not conducted in public. Therefore, the manner and extent people communicated with each other regarding the violence are key elements in the functioning of occupation public space in these cities.

Sources and Source Problems

In order to answer the questions outlined above, a historian must examine a much wider range of sources than merely the classic official administrative records. In particular, the history of daily life demands an expansion of perspectives to include the ego documents of the actors. To reach these intimate documents we have used diaries, memoirs, and above all letters, such as those held in the Sammlung Sterz in der Stuttgarter Bibliothek für Zeitgeschichte (Sterz Collection of the Stuttgart Library for Contemporary History). This is the largest collection of letters from the front in the German language; other institutions have much smaller holdings. However, even the more than forty available letters concerning Warsaw and Minsk can provide at best only snapshots of life in the East; detailed chronologies, complete pictures, or impressions that changed over time, cannot be found here.

Of the 30 billion to 40 billion letters sent home from the front, on average 430–570 postal dispatches per Wehrmacht member, just a tiny fraction has survived. There are also considerable methodological problems involved in using these letters because they contain only those things the writer considered worth mentioning and what they were able to describe. Clearly more important than the official censor were those restrictions imposed by the writers themselves, especially their consideration for the sensitivities of the recipients.[37] Previous investigations have revealed also that war crimes are mentioned only rarely, and hardly ever are described in detail.[38] The murders were not, however, banished into a taboo zone; the letters reveal above all the specific perceptions of the writer—the ghetto as revenge on the Jews or as German cultural shame, their motives for action, and especially how the writer viewed the victims of German war crimes. They provide some hints about certain patterns of behavior because they remain very personal documents.

With certain reservations most of these comments apply also to diaries and memoirs. For the history of daily life they are first rank sources, for here the experiences and views that an individual considered worth reporting are recorded over a longer period. This kind of complete record on the micro level is almost never found with other types of documentation. The situation for the German occupation in Eastern Europe is, nonetheless, quite desperate: even for very large cities, such as Warsaw, only a few personal diaries are available. It is likely that many occupiers kept diaries, but most have not been preserved or were never handed over to the archives. The important exceptions have mostly been published.[39] Still, in the Deutsches Tagebucharchiv (German Diary Archive) in Emmendingen and in the Sammlung Primavesi (Primavesi Collection) in the Staatsarchiv Münster (Münster State Archives; StAM), a few diaries and memoirs were discovered, and a number of fragmentary collections have been preserved in other places. It should be noted that the authors are all soldiers or members of the police who were quartered in barracks. Apart from the sheer size of these groups, one can only speculate about the reasons for the absence of diaries kept by others. A circular letter sent to around fifty German and Austrian non-professional history research groups also produced no useful results.

Extensive ego documents can, however, also be found in the numerous investigative files of the postwar judicial authorities. Among these, the trials in Poland are of less interest because there the statements, apart from those of the defendants, are limited mainly to the victims. Instead it is the proceedings in East or West Germany that are useful. In the German Democratic Republic (GDR), the investigations were conducted by the Staatssicherheitsdienst (Office of State Security), which often used coercion against those being questioned.[40] The central West German collections, now preserved in the Ludwigsburg branch of the *Bundesarchiv* (Federal Archives), have increasingly become a central focus of interest for historians over the past fifteen years. These investigations were conducted in accordance with proper legal principles and previously were relevant mainly for examining the course and conduct of mass crimes.[41] Less considered, on the other hand, is the use of these sources beyond merely reconstructing the course of historical events or the attempts by the perpetrators to justify themselves; the aim of historians previously was mainly to repersonalize history by demonstrating individual guilt, moving from an impersonal account to one focused on the actions of individuals. However, the interrogations tell you much more. Precisely because many of those questioned had no genuine interest in conceding any guilt at all, they gladly talked about seemingly unimportant details. The investigators mainly asked the accused, but much more rarely the witnesses, specific questions, and they enquired only routinely after certain names and events; in this way they facilitated a largely unrestrained recall in which very often people talked about the daily life of the occupiers.

The protocols from the former GDR differentiate themselves in the way the investigations were conducted. In contrast to those in West Germany, the investigators often confronted witnesses repeatedly with the same or similar allegations. The sort of unrestrained recall that took place in the Federal Republic of Germany (West Germany) was not likely to result from this interrogation technique. Therefore, there are scarcely any useful references for the history of daily life in these files. The same applies for the files in the Instytut Pamięci Narodowej (Polish Institute of National Remembrance; IPN) in Warsaw, the Polish authority responsible for investigating both Nazi and communist crimes, similar to the Birthler Authority in Germany, which now holds the records of the Staatssicherheitsdienst. The files of the investigations of German officials serving in Warsaw during the occupation contain mainly statements by the victims.[42]

Nevertheless, numerous insights can be gained from this material, precisely because those affected personally always present a subjective view of events. Thus the sheer frequency of certain comments speaks volumes for their plausibility, especially if specific details are perceived by many to be common practice. On the other hand, if the aim is only to verify certain key facts within the specific context of the interrogation, particular details often prove not to be reliable, or only partially correct. If one takes into account the time elapsed between the events and their retelling, nonetheless, significant discoveries can sometimes be made: an example might be when marriage partners are questioned and touch on aspects of marital life during the occupation, information that cannot be found in other sources. These statements because they reveal subjective perceptions and moments from that time that were important for those concerned, are of considerable relevance and their value should not be underestimated. Against this, some adventurous stories have to be dismissed as improbable if they are simply too fantastic to be true.

It has to be stressed that many assessments and perceptions are highly subjective and one encounters also some excessively positive or highly misleading impressions of the East in these postwar recollections. Therefore, it is essential to treat this material with caution because it concerns the reception of impressions that only subjectively approach the truth. The human tendency to cover up events in the past and to push away unpleasant memories must be taken into account, especially when the dominant social values between the time of experience and the time of retelling are diametrically opposed.[43] Clear guidelines for assessing what is accurate and what is not cannot be given here. Ultimately the historian has to evaluate the plausibility of each account by applying knowledge of the context and comparing it to similar events.

Problematic in this respect are reports about the public nature of violence. This was not usually the subject of questioning during interrogations. Furthermore, testimonies that do mention it are usually very fragmentary because they can easily become self-incriminating. If they are made, nevertheless, together with other sources they increase our knowledge of how the violence was seen by the occupants. In such cases, it is usually difficult to decide whether the witness is describing something that happened every day or something unusual. Of course exceptional perceptions are also a part of daily life, but assessing this can only be done with caution.

While remaining aware of the numerous pitfalls, this source can at least partially plug an important gap that needs to be filled due to the lack of other ego documents. The roughly one hundred statements by eighty-eight witnesses used for this study, taken from numerous files, tell the history of daily life in an unconventional, new way. More than one thousand other protocols were not taken into account because they did not contain any substantive information about daily life or perceptions of it. In accordance with German data protection regulations and archival laws, the names have been rendered anonymous, insofar as they do not concern persons in prominent positions.

It is of course difficult to determine how representative the sources are. Among those questioned by the public prosecutors there were only a few civilians and members of the civil administration; the majority were from the ranks of SS and police units, and for this group at least, a fairly representative sample can be assumed, simply because the numbers of people questioned were so large. Equally, it was by no means intended to question a cross section of the society of occupiers. The available material, therefore, can only partially satisfy the ideal of universal validity; the questions posed by the history of daily life, however, are less interested in social statistics. Instead they are focused much more on the individual, whose life is observed in the context of his (or her) own self-evaluation. For this purpose, these sources are very well suited.

Next to this, daily newspapers take on an especially high relevance. Both cities possessed such publications; there was a *Minsker Zeitung* (Minsk newspaper) as well as a *Warschauer Zeitung* (Warsaw newspaper), although the latter appeared only until the turn of 1940–1941, at which time it was subsumed within the *Krakauer Zeitung* (Krakow newspaper), which included a regional section with numerous reports from Warsaw. Research on the occupational press has so far only really been conducted in detail with regard to Poland.[44] Nevertheless, with more than four hundred newspaper reports for Warsaw and almost six hundred for Minsk, it is clear that a significant body of text for the local perspective of the occupiers is available. In view of state control and the censor there are of course no critical commentaries or reports of crimes against the local population to be found; the news is distinguished rather by its trivial character. Sports reports, reviews of ongoing cultural and entertainment activities, mass and Nazi Party events, and reports on the exemplary constructive work of the Germans dominate the content.

The newspapers also reported on those things the occupiers experienced all the time and that greatly impacted their stay in the East. Even if it is not possible to speak of objectivity because the texts were shaped by ideology, the reporting of most events does correspond with accounts in other sources, even with those of the local resistance. If that were not the case, the newspapers would have risked losing their readership, since too great a divergence from one's own observations, which could easily have happened with local news, would have driven readers away. If one takes into account the intention to indoctrinate that was clearly present, nonetheless significant information concerning the realities of daily life for the occupiers can be found,[45] showing that newspapers can serve as an important supplement to the available ego documents.

In the Polish archives, it is mainly the voluminous reports of various German military and civilian offices that prove most relevant for answering the questions posed by the history of daily life. Here the monthly reports for Distrikt Warschau stand out as a key source for life in the city because they not only describe numerous events with attendance numbers and other details, but they also present insights into the mood of the occupiers. In addition, they also demonstrate the perception of Poles by the Germans. On the other hand, despite regular reports under this heading, they actually tell us very little about the real mood among the Poles since these reports are based excessively on wishful thinking.

Another key source for this work were the surviving official collections, which for Warsaw can mainly be found in the Archiwum Państwowe m.st. Warszawy (State Archive of the Capital City Warsaw; APW).[46] Admittedly, complete records are not available for a single German office, but the amount of material preserved is very extensive: for example, for Distrikt Warschau, when the files of the *SS und Polizeiführer* (SS and police leader; SSPF) are included, we have around forty disciplinary files. Especially this type of source involving investigative files can tell us much about the individual occupiers and also about breaches of the regulations while on duty and the ensuing sanctions, which can help us to answer the questions posed by the history of daily life. This applies also to the extensive court records: the documents of the Sondergericht (Special Court) served as a central collection in this study for the question of norms and deviation from the norm in the behavior of the occupiers. Of the roughly 1,800 files, not quite a hundred—that is, about 5 percent—were evaluated including all those that were concerned with Germans and ethnic Germans. This gives us a complex picture of the forbidden and tolerated modes of conduct. Although no administrative documentation of the court has survived, the collection permits a central insight into those spheres of daily life that are only very rarely touched on in letters, diaries, or even newspapers. Especially those acts of violence against the local population not carried out while on official duty—and their limits—can thereby be exposed. The collection cannot, however, make any claim of being statistically representative because it is not clear how many files were destroyed during the Warsaw Uprising and the hasty evacuation of the German authorities in the fall of 1944. Nevertheless, on account of the large number of cases, a certain critical mass is achieved that makes it possible to describe certain patterns of behavior. These sources are in any case at least sufficient to document certain decisive events and turning points in the lives of individuals.

Finally, it is necessary to make a few comments regarding the terminology used by the perpetrators that is dominant in the sources. In view of the frequent intention to cover up or at least render harmless, above all, mass murder, this linguistic distancing from events sometimes reaches its limits. The choice of completely different words is not always possible and occasionally quotation marks have to be used. Problematic also is the use of the word "Jew." It cannot always be avoided and for the occupiers it had in most cases an arbitrary definition; the most significant characteristic of these Jews was that the Germans did not count them among the "Poles" or "Belorussians" or "White Ruthenians", as the Christian population was called.[47]

Before the publication of this book, I undertook several years of intensive research and discussions in Poland and Germany. I believe it was especially fortunate that I was able spend several months in Warsaw and not only read paper sources there, but also move among the historic sites mentioned in this work, insofar as they were still extant. In January 2010 I returned to Warsaw to take a position as an academic researcher at the Deutsches Historisches Institut (German Historical Institute), which had already provided me with accommodation during my previous research visits to Warsaw, and that has now also provided the financial support necessary for this English translation. I owe for this a debt of gratitude to the institute's directors Klaus Ziemer, Eduard Mühle, and Miloš Řezník.

Without Piotr Wróbel (Toronto) and Steven Feldman (Washington, DC) this English edition would not exist. The German edition was made possible primarily by my supervisor Hans Günter Hockerts (Munich), whose guidance and suggestions contributed considerably to the success of the work. The role of second adviser was warmly accepted by Horst Möller (Munich), and additional key tips and stimulating advice were received from Dieter Pohl (Klagenfurt). Peter Lieb (Sandhurst and Potsdam) generously made available to me his transcript of Carl von Andrian's diary. Representative for the support of all the archival staff and librarians over the years, I would like to recognize especially here Jan Bańbor of the Archiwum Akt Nowych (Archive of New Documents) in Warsaw, who has supported this—and more-recent projects—with access to files and professional advice. Editors of the German edition were Petra Weber and Angelika Reizle of the Institut für Zeitgeschichte (Institute for Contemporary History) in Munich; in Poland Jürgen Hensel and Patrycja Pieńkowska-Wiederkehr provided additional editorial services. And without my parents, of course, the book would never have been written.

Notes

1. Borodziej, *Aufstand*, pp. 16, 189–190.
2. Gerlach, *Morde*, p. 11.
3. Schlootz, *Propaganda*, p. 75; Cerovic, *Paix*, pp. 78–79.
4. On the definition and problematic nature of this concept, see Gerlach, *Societies*, pp. 455–456.
5. Cohen, *Smolensk under the Nazis*; Czocher, *W okupowanym Krakowie*; and Mick, *Kriegserfahrungen*.

6. Böhler and Lehnstaedt, *Gewalt und Alltag*; see also Snyder, *Bloodlands*.
7. On this, see Steber and Gotto, *Visions of Community*.
8. Chiari, *Alltag*.
9. Gerlach, *Morde*.
10. Szarota, *Warschau*.
11. Madajczyk, *Okkupationspolitik*.
12. Pohl, *Judenpolitik*; idem, *Judenverfolgung*. Musiał, *Zivilverwaltung*. Seidel, *Besatzungspolitik*. The book reflects largely the structure adopted by Musiał, but deals with Distrikt Radom rather than Distrikt Lublin. Apart from a chapter on forced labor, there are no significantly different insights to be gained. Młynarczyk, *Judenmord*, examines the murder of the Jews in Distrikt Radom, but also takes into account the perspective of the victims.
13. Gutman, *Jews*; Sakowska, *Menschen*; Engelking and Leociak, *Warsaw Ghetto*.
14. On this general tendency in genocide research, see Gerlach, *Societies*, p. 466. A recent and instructive overview of German research on Poland can be found in Pohl, *Ermordung*.
15. Browning, *Männer*.
16. There is an extensive literature, and we list only a few of the more recent (and short) biographies of German perpetrators in Warsaw and Minsk: on Curt von Gottberg, see Klein, *Gottberg*; on Wilhelm Kube, see Zimmermann, "Ehrenbürger"; on Georg Heuser, see Matthäus, *Heuser*; on Ludwig Hahn, see Kur, *Sprawiedliwość*; on Ludwig Leist, see Walichnowski, *Rozmowy*.
17. The most prominent example is certainly Wildt, *Generation*. For Eastern Europe see Birn, *Polizeiführer*; and Birn, *Sicherheitspolizei*.
18. Jaworski and Peters, *Alltagsperspektiven*.
19. Stimulating and instructive on this issue are Bergen, "Volksdeutschen"; and ibid., "Concept." For the period immediately after the start of the war, see Jansen and Weckbecker, *Selbstschutz*. See also Lehnstaedt, "Volksdeutsche."
20. Harvey, *Women*; Schwarz, *Frau*.
21. Longerich, *Gewusst*.
22. Dörner, *Deutschen*.
23. See, e.g., Sofsky, *Traktat*; and Sofsky, *Prinzip*. Specifically focused on Nazi crimes and the "very ordinary men" is Welzer, *Täter*. In 1967 the lawyer and criminologist Herbert Jäger published a study that examined the causes and conditions for individual guilt on the basis of judicial records: Jäger, *Verbrechen*.
24. On these typologies, see Mann, "Perpetrators," pp. 332–333; Paul, *Psychopathen*, pp. 61–62.
25. Longerich, "Tendenzen," p. 3; Herbert, "Vernichtungspolitik," p. 31.
26. Gerlach, *Societies*, p. 458.
27. Bauer, *Rethinking*, p. 30.
28. Paul, "Psychopathen," p. 15.
29. Ibid., p. 62.
30. On the "explicability of the Holocaust," and whether this can ever be achieved, see Bauer, *Rethinking*, pp. 14–38.
31. Lüdtke, *Alltagsgeschichte*. A new collection of essays is Geschichtswerkstatt, *Alltagskultur*; the best overview examining the problems involved is: van Laak, *Alltagsgeschichte*. Detailed methodological remarks can be found in this volume, chapter 2,
32. Bourdieu, *Theorie*, etc. pp. 165 and following.
33. Bourdieu, *Rede*, p. 84.
34. Schwingel, *Bourdieu*, pp. 69–70.
35. From Saldern, "Öffentlichkeiten," pp. 451 and following. For a discussion of both models, see chapter 5, this volume.

36. On the ambivalence of communication between public space and secrecy, see Westerbarkey, *Geheimnis*.

37. Latzel, "Feldpostbriefe," p. 172.

38. Ibid., p. 175.

39. E.g., on Warsaw see Hosenfeld, "Retten."

40. Leide, *NS-Verbrecher*, pp. 112, and 120 and following.

41. On the trials, see Rückerl, *NS-Verbrechen*. Historians working with the statements recently include, e.g., Pohl, *Judenverfolgung*; Musiał, *Zivilverwaltung*.

42. In addition, IPN also holds a collection of original documents that we have used quite extensively in this study.

43. In general, on the problem of people self-adopting modes of interpretation, see Jureit, *Generationenforschung*, esp. pp. 12–13.

44. Jockheck, *Propaganda*, esp. pp. 99–114. See also Kołtunowski, *Strategia propagandy*.

45. On the value of occupation newspapers as sources, see Lüdtke, "Fehlgreifen," p. 68.

46. Important publications for this work include the official diary of Hans Frank (Präg and Jacobmeyer, *Diensttagebuch*); the war diary of Police Battallion 322 in Warsaw (Leszczyński, *Dziennik*); the reports of the *Einsatzgruppen* in the Soviet Union (Klein, *Einsatzgruppen*); a collection of documents on genocide in *Reichskommissariat* Ostland (Benz, Kwiet, and Matthäus, *Einsatz*), as well one on Nazi rule in Eastern Europe (Röhr et al., *Europa*).

47. On the linguistic problems, see Friedländer, *Kitsch*, pp. 78 and following; and Pohl, *Judenverfolgung*, pp. 21–22.

Chapter 1

GERMANS ON DUTY IN THE EAST IN WARSAW AND MINSK

The German society of occupiers in the cities of Minsk and Warsaw was not homogeneous. First one must differentiate between those Germans that volunteered for the East, and those who were transferred or posted there. The employees and civil servants, who in the public sector all wore uniforms, fall into both of these categories. Most Reich German civilians were in the former, whereas soldiers and members of the police were mainly in the latter. Then there were the *Volksdeutschen,* or ethnic Germans, many of whom had lived as a minority in the East for several generations, but who only now discovered the advantages of joining forces with the occupiers.

The respective professional duties of the Germans made up a large part of their identities and led to the fragmentation of the society of occupation along institutional lines. But even these segments were only ever rarely homogenous. For example, the employees and officials came from very disparate authorities, such as the municipalities, ministries, the Deutsche Reichsbahn (German Railway), or the Reichspost (Reich Post Office). Differences began with the respective mentalities of the individuals' home regions, as well as the varying requirements of the employing agencies, their level of education, social background, and parental home environment; in other words, differences were rooted in the variable socialization of the individual occupiers. The intention here is not to create a group biography; that would be quite impossible for the 10,000 Reich and ethnic Germans in Minsk[1] and the 30,000 in Warsaw;[2] not to mention for the 5,000 and 40,000 Wehrmacht personnel stationed respectively in the two cities and their vicinity.[3]

Although there were also groups of people with similar backgrounds in the society of occupation, overall a disparate picture emerges that broadly reflected German society as a whole. Nevertheless, it would be a mistake to make a direct comparison with the Reich because there were two key differences: The number of German women among the occupiers, at around 15 percent, was much less than in the German population as a whole, and people under age eighteen, as well as those over fifty, were scarcely represented. Yet a much broader spectrum of the population than just the wartime (World War I) youth generation served as the main foundation of the society of occupation.[4] Even though those born between 1900 and 1910 provided the leadership corps for the civil administration, the police, and the SS, the realities of daily life during the occupation were determined by them only to a limited extent. The ordinary members of the Wehrmacht, the police, or the civil administration can certainly not be fully described by such generalizations. As Bernd Rusinek has observed, National Socialism cannot be reduced simply to a "generational project."[5]

1. Wehrmacht

The first German occupants entering a new city were always units of the Wehrmacht. On September 30, 1939, they captured Warsaw and, almost two years later, on June 28, 1941, they entered Minsk. Of all Germans present in the two cities during the war, soldiers made up at least half. In August 1941 around 5,000 Wehrmacht members were stationed in Minsk and roughly 40,000 in Warsaw.[6] Due to considerable fluctuations, precise numbers can be given only with difficulty. Both cities were key staging areas and transit points for the front; almost all trains carrying soldiers to the Eastern Front departed from or arrived at Warsaw or Minsk. In any case, the troops passing through usually had stopovers lasting several days, which they viewed as a welcome break from combat. The troops generally greeted these visits to Warsaw enthusiastically since the entertainment and refreshments available in the rear area were equally attractive as the chance to go sightseeing.[7] Precise numbers are difficult to ascertain because even units stationed there were generally reassigned after much less than a year. Therefore most soldiers remained in the two cities for just a short period, from just a few weeks to several months; exceptions to this were mainly those units with few personnel engaged in supplying the larger Wehrmacht units. In addition, the area around Warsaw became a rest and recuperation area for troops returning home from the front or being redeployed to other war theaters. Nonetheless, the military presence was considerable in both cities. It stood continuously at around 3 percent of the total population, and it was seen as a constant threat, since Wehrmacht troops, in addition to those of the police, always performed security and guard duties.

Soldiers were an ever-present sign of occupation. German *Landser* (slang for soldiers) were always on the streets, some off duty in small groups, others officially on patrol or parade. However, the visible Wehrmacht personnel made up just a part of the overall total. Some units were stationed permanently in the city, such as armaments detachments, intelligence units, repair and construction squads, as well as numerous military hospitals and Luftwaffe (German air force) units.[8] Eighteen teachers taught around six hundred soldiers, who had been released from their units, in several occupational training programs in Warsaw.[9] In July 1943 almost 23,000 Heer soldiers, 6,230 members of the Luftwaffe, and 15,000 wounded men receiving medical care were registered in the city,[10] which was probably the highest number attained, apart from the periods of initial occupation and retreat. By no means did all of these people take an active part in the life of the society of occupation: about half of them probably never saw anything of the city other than their barrack or the military hospital.

Generally the soldiers felt a sense of familiarity and protection within their units, even in a foreign environment. This was due mainly to Wehrmacht recruitment practices that called up and trained conscripts regionally according to *Wehrkreisen* (military districts), establishing battalions, regiments, and later even divisions in this way. With the exception of certain specialized smaller units, such as the military administration whose personnel comprised officials of the financial, communal, and judicial administrations,[11] this promoted the units' homogeneity and coherence. This homogeneity and coherence was not always apparent at the divisional level, but could be significant for smaller groups, such as companies or platoons with up to a hundred men, especially if the superiors looked out for their men. Traditionally, officers were expected not only to accompany their men in combat, but also to engage themselves in their private concerns in order to bond with them more closely. These measures helped to compensate for the fact that none of the men had volunteered for service in Warsaw or Minsk, but rather were sent there with their units for reasons of military necessity. This shared regional background—although it declined steadily as the war went on and the number of deaths rose—as well as being together for a longer period of time, sharing almost all aspects of life, and the experience of training and combat, all created a strong spirit of comradeship.[12] This established group loyalty that made any contact with the defeated enemy appear suspect. At the same time, it also created strong friendships and bonds that reduced the locals to the level of a completely foreign other, to be stared at collectively but that could never be accepted as an equal conversation partner, still less a friend. This perception was definitely reinforced by ideological indoctrination. The average soldier who had been a child or a youth on Hitler's seizure of power, had spent a great portion of his life under Nazism. In addition to his schooling, the Hitler Youth had a considerable influence on the soldier's socialization. While the transmission of ideology was not the main priority at school, and its intensity could also vary from one school to another, it was an essential element in the Hitler-Jugend. There the soldiers were imbued with an ideology that stressed German superiority and an aversion that bred hatred toward the Eastern Europeans and especially toward the Jews.[13] The Wehrmacht was not far behind in its efforts to indoctrinate through its training and care for the troops, but the role of ideology remained firmly subordinated to the main military purpose.[14] If this education's actual effectiveness can scarcely be measured, its implications for the youngest sector of the society of occupation must not be underestimated. This was especially true when superior officers and generals aggressively transmitted the images of "overlords" and "subhumans"–directed partly against sentient beings.[15]

The Wehrmacht took over administrative authority for a few weeks on capturing the respective cities,[16] an authority that it exercised until a civil administration had been established. Immediately after the occupation *Ortskommandanturen und Feldkommandanturen* (local and field commandants' offices) were established,[17] centrally, on the main streets: in Warsaw for example between Krakauer Vorstadt and Adolf-Hitler-Platz in what became—for this reason—Kommandanturstraße.[18] They were in charge of the billeting office and the military police for all military units stationed within the city limits; all troop detachments had to report here on arrival and were instructed how to conduct themselves, assigned their accommodation, and informed of their duties during their stay. The commandants' offices also assigned soldiers to guard various objects of military importance, even though from the end of 1939 this was partially a police responsibility. Nevertheless, numerous *Sicherungs- und Landesschützenbataillone* (security and home defense battalions), each of around three hundred men, were deployed in the two cities in turn throughout the occupation only for this purpose, and were subordinated to the commandants' offices.[19] Since their sites of deployment were in Warsaw and Minsk, they remained for a number of months, and were stationed there longer than the other military units.

Given the large number of soldiers, it is not surprising that members of the Wehrmacht often considered themselves the real masters of the city. They, or rather their comrades, had conquered the city, defeated the enemy, and by their presence ensured that the Germans remained the rulers of the country and that the population did not rise up. Therefore, the troops usually showed little enthusiasm for paying much respect to the civil administration or the SS and police units, who were direct competitors as guarantors of security. Alongside disputes between individuals, conflicts also took the form of institutional battles over the distribution of accommodation and offices, which the military did not want to release for others to use.[20] In addition, military units requisitioned flowers and grass as horse food from city gardens and parks without permission, or simply allowed their horses to graze there.[21] The relationship between the Wehrmacht and the civil administration was much tenser in Minsk than it was in Warsaw because in Belorussia (*Weißruthenien*) the Wehrmacht's role and presence was much more important owing to the serious nature of the partisan threat. Despite numerous exhortations on both sides, there was no smooth, almost invisible, cooperation. Many soldiers viewed the civilians as lazy, scared, and mainly interested in enrichment.[22] They were therefore not seen as equal partners, and especially not accepted as the political authorities in the occupied territories. This was true also in Poland, where cooperation was somewhat better. Here there were even organized events at which, the—in fact still quite bad—cooperation was celebrated. In Warsaw in 1941 General Governor Hans Frank emphasized the equality of members of the administration with the troops using this comparison: "The men of the Administration are also the Führer's soldiers here in the East, who must contribute to victory by their intense activism and diligence at their posts."[23]

But the soldiers were involved not only in numerous conflicts with their own countrymen, but also to no small degree were active participants in the crimes and murders committed against the local population.[24] During the first days after the conquest of a city, initially this comprised everyday plundering and requisitioning, which in many cases involved brutal violence.[25] Robbery was continued, primarily in the ghettos, for a long time after the end of hostilities. In addition there were multiple cases of rape,[26] and in Minsk next to the establishment of the ghetto by the *Feldkommandantur* on July 19, 1941,[27] a prisoner of war (POW) camp[28] was also set up for around 100,000 Soviet soldiers and an additional 30,000 male inhabitants of the city aged between eighteen and forty-five.[29] These male civilians were taken into preventive custody immediately after the Germans' arrival and detained in the *Stalag* (short for *Stammlager* or main POW camp) that later became infamous for its high death rate. The civilians were mostly released only after a lengthy period. Men of the 354th Infantry Regiment together with the *Feldgendarmerie* (Field Gendarmerie), the *Geheime Feldpolizei* (Secret Field Police) and action squads of the *Kommandeur der Sicherheitspolizei und des* SD (commander of the Security Police and the SD) in Warsaw [sic] shot several thousand Jews in this camp in July 1941.[30] The units stationed in and around Minsk were also involved in a bitter struggle against Belorussian partisans immediately after they occupied the city.[31] The Jews from the city and its surrounding area were often simply lumped together with the partisans, and therefore the Germans demanded their destruction.³² Admittedly, violent battles were not fought directly in the city, but soldiers were conducting murder in close cooperation with the Security Police and the Sicherheitsdienst des Reichsführers SS [Security Service of the Reich leader of the SS; SD) in the immediate vicinity. The frequent *Aktions* demonstrate that the *Bandenkampf* (struggle against the bandits)—that is, the war against the partisans—formed a considerable part of their official duties and therefore also influenced their experience of daily life. On the present-day territory of Belarus, the Germans attempted to wipe out the entire population of 628 villages during the occupation, murdering 83,000 people.³³ Elements of the 707th Infantry and the 286th Security Divisions distinguished themselves particularly by their brutality. The 707th Infantry Division, under its commander Gustav von Bechtoldsheim, together with other subordinated units, had killed 20,000 people by the end of 1941, among them 10,000 Jews.³⁴ *Aktions* such as Unternehmen Kormoran (Operation Cormorant), from May 25 to June 17, 1944, resulted in only around a hundred German casualties against 7,700 Belorussians killed, with just a few more than three hundred weapons captured, showing clearly that no actual combat had taken place, but that instead it had been the mass murder of local inhabitants.³⁵

In these operations the Wehrmacht in Minsk cooperated very effectively with the Security Police and the *Einsatzgruppen* (operational groups) in killing Jews; not infrequently, the Geheime Feldpolizei did this on its own.³⁶ The exploitation of the labor force, which consisted primarily of Jews, must also be considered: for example, there were thirty-one firms using Jewish labor that were directly subordinated to the Wehrmacht in Warsaw, even before the Germans established the ghetto.³⁷ The around fifty German military officers, officials, and soldiers of the Rüstungskommando (Armaments Command) in Warsaw also cooperated directly with numerous companies in the ghetto and oversaw their production—primarily of clothing items—that were produced cheaply to meet orders from the Wehrmacht. The men serving under Wilhelm Freter had less of a problem with the working conditions of the Jewish prisoners than with their deportation to the Treblinka extermination camp in September 1942, since that entailed a loss of production. The Rüstungsinspektion (Armaments Inspectorate) criticized the "loss of materials, machines, and time," due primarily "to the overhasty clearance of the ghetto." The Wehrmacht did nothing to oppose the implementation of genocide, but instead organized alternatives to enable production to continue close to the extermination centers.³⁸

Wehrmacht soldiers were recruited from all classes and regions of Germany. Their deployment to Warsaw or Minsk was not of their own choice, but was ordered by their senior commander. The latter was also the reason for the high turnover, which meant that most soldiers had left the city after a few months. Nevertheless, numerically they formed the largest group within the society of occupation, even though the individuals were never members of that society for long and rarely came into contact with the other occupiers or local inhabitants since most were housed in barracks. The troops viewed themselves as the guarantors of German rule in the East because they secured military superiority; the soldiers were the first occupiers to enter a city and the last to leave it.

2. SS and Police

Markedly smaller than the forces of the Wehrmacht were the SS and police units, which in Warsaw numbered a maximum of eight thousand[39] and in the whole of Weißruthenien Mitte (central Belorussia) in 1943 comprised just slightly more than three thousand men.[40] Alongside offices like the SS and police leader with his staff, or the commander of the Security Police and SD, this also included units of the Ordnungspolizei (Order Police) made up mainly of the Schutzpolizei [Defense Police; urban branch of the Order Police] in the cities), as well as police battalions and detachments of the Waffen-SS (armed wing of the SS). Stationed in Warsaw, for example, were the Waffen-SS Totenkopf-Standarte 8, as well as a cavalry training and replacement unit.[41] In terms of pure numbers, members of the Waffen-SS made up more than half of all the personnel of the SS and police. They contained mainly selected volunteers with long-standing membership in the Nazi Party or the SS. In the SS units, much value was placed on ideological training, with special attention given to anti-Semitic and racial indoctrination. During the invasion of Poland, these units participated in numerous murders and other crimes: for example, in Warsaw they took part in mass murders in the garden of the parliament and at Palmiry, close to the city.[42] However, because of their close personal and organizational ties with the other SS and police troops, they could hardly be compared with regular Wehrmacht units.

Within the society of occupation, the SS and police were responsible for the security of the other Germans. More than even the Wehrmacht they embodied supervision of the local population because they exercised considerably more direct control over them. Their self-identification was on the one hand as "normal" policemen, but on the other hand as the guarantors of German life in the East, precisely because, in contrast to the soldiers, they were not only a protective force, but also (and primarily) served as an instrument of control and punishment. From their own perspective, they were the ones that made the maintenance of German rule possible.

The police detachments were recruited in a similar manner to the Wehrmacht units, although the volunteers joined the police mainly to avoid an impending call up to the military.[43] By contrast, most of the officers and noncommissioned officers (NCOs) had joined the police before the war had started. Because the police organizationally was also part of the SS, its requirements for membership were more stringent than for the Wehrmacht. In addition to political checks by the Nazi Party chancellory, suitability for the SS was assessed by strict achievement tests, as well as documented proof of heredity and health, which went far beyond the mustering process of the Wehrmacht. Those that met the criteria for acceptance entered a unit formed by region and were then usually sent to the East. Before they were mustered out the men received a general police, but mainly a paramilitary training, which was combined with ideological elements and was as well-suited for police guard duty as it was for combat duty, or as preparation for the struggle against racial opponents. The above-average proportion of Nazi Party members in the police detachments indicates that the selection was not left to chance and some attention was given to choosing politically reliable men.[44] In the Totenkopf-Standarten, more than 80 percent of the men were born between 1909 and 1923, and more than 30 percent were ethnic Germans from all parts of Europe. For those units in particular, service in the SS was the expression of an ideal and not a merely subsidiary aspect of being a soldier.[45] Nevertheless, it can be said for the majority of policemen, as with the Wehrmacht, that Germans of all classes, from all parts of the country, and—with certain qualifications—of all convictions were present.

Much greater attention was paid to unit composition in the other SS and police units than in e.g. the administration. In particular the leadership, especially that of the HSSPF[46] and SSPF, was characterized by a high degree of alignment to the Nazi world view. It was notable for a general agreement with the anti-Semitism of the regime.[47] No "very ordinary men" like those in the police battalions served in these positions, but rather an ideologically convinced leadership elite that favored radical solutions for the germanization of the East.

Exemplary for the leaders who ordered and supervised the crimes against the local population in Minsk were men like Georg Heuser and Eduard Strauch, officers in the Security Police. Heuser was born on February 27, 1913, in Berlin and completed his studies in law. In the 1920s this subject was already distinguished by a legal positivism that was used increasingly as an instrument against the Weimar Republic.[48] In December 1938 Heuser joined the police as a trainee detective. In the Polish campaign he served as an officer in Einsatzgruppe I. In December 1941 he was attached to the office of the KdS in Minsk, where he was head of the Geheime Staatspolizei (Secret State Police; Gestapo), and from the fall of 1943 until June 1944 he was with the *Befehlshaber der Sicherheitspolizei und des* SD (Senior Commander of the Security Police and the SD; BdS) in Minsk, where he was in charge of Section N, responsible for antipartisan warfare. In 1954 he was appointed as *Kriminaloberkommissar* (detective chief inspector) in Rheinland-Pfalz, and in 1958 became head of the Landeskriminalamt (State Office of Criminal Investigations) there. In 1961 an investigation was opened against him that on May 21, 1963, resulted in a sentence of fifteen years in prison for murder and complicity in murder. On December 12, 1969, Heuser was released from prison; he died on January 30, 1989 in Koblenz.[49]

Eduard Strauch was from Essen, where he was born on August 17, 1906. Like Heuser, he was also a lawyer and employed by the SD of the SS from 1931. In March 1942 he took up his office as KdS in Minsk, from which he was transferred in 1944 to become KdS Wallonien in Belgium. On April 10, 1948, he was sentenced to death in the *Einsatzgruppen* trial, but subsequently he was handed over to Belgium for crimes committed in Wallonia. There his death sentence was not carried out, due to his mental illness. Strauch died on September 15, 1955, in the hospital in Uccle.[50]

Strauch and Heuser are linked not only by their study of law, but also by their generational experiences. Beyond the rejection of the democratic system promoted within this discipline that students of the nationalist populist milieu saw manifested in parties like the Nazi Party,[51] Strauch and Heuser were also united by a shared belief in the radical ideas of the SS with its contempt for humanity.

In Warsaw this can be observed in men such as SSPF Jürgen Stroop or at the KdS in Josef Meisinger and Ludwig Hahn. Jürgen (until 1941, Josef) Stroop was born on September 26, 1895, in Detmold and joined the Nazi Party and the SS in 1932. In 1939 he reported for service in Poland as a leader of the *Selbstschutz* (a local ethnic German paramilitary force). He served only from April to August 1943 as the SSPF in Warsaw, but led the suppression of the Warsaw Ghetto Uprising of April–May of that year. As a reward for services rendered, in September 1943 he was promoted to become HSSPF in Greece, and from November 1943, he served as HSSPF Rhein-Westmark inside the Reich. On March 21, 1947, he was sentenced to death by the U.S. Military Tribunal in Dachau for murders committed against Allied pilots inside the Reich. Nonetheless, he was extradited to Poland, where he was also sentenced to death; he was executed on March 6, 1952, in Warsaw.[52] Stroop does not completely fit the picture of an homogeneous academic elite, although his fanatical hatred of Jews, suppressing the uprising until the death of the very last Jew, was typical for the leadership personnel of SS and police units in the East.

Like Stroop, Josef Meisinger distinguished himself by joining the SS at an early stage. Meisinger came from Munich, where he was born on September 14, 1899. From 1934 he was active in the Reichssicherheitshauptamt (Reich Security Main Office) or rather its predecessor organization, the Geheimes Staatspolizeiamt (Central Office of the Gestapo; Gesatapa), and from 1936 he was head of the Reichszentrale zur Bekämpfung der Homosexualität und Abtreibung (Reich Central Office for Combating Homosexuality and Abortion). In 1939 he advanced to deputy head of Einsatzgruppe IV, and then from October 1939 to October 1940 to KdS in Warsaw. In 1943 he was transferred to become the police attaché at the German Embassy in Tokyo. After the war he was extradited by the Allies to Poland, where he was sentenced to death on March 3, 1947, and executed the same day.[53]

Dr. Ludwig Hahn, born on January 23, 1908, in Eitzen, like Meisinger was a lawyer. He entered the Nazi Party in 1930 and joined the SS in 1933; the latter employed him in the SD-Hauptamt (SD Main Office). In 1939 he was the head of Einsatzkommando (Task Force – a subdivision of Einsatzgruppen) 1 of Einsatzgruppe I in Poland and from January 1940, he was assigned to KdS in Krakow. In August 1940 he became Himmler's special representative in Bratislava, it appeared that his stay in Poland had come to an end. However, just one year later, in August 1941, he was transferred to become KdS in Warsaw and held this office until the German retreat in August 1944. The legal authorities of West Germany became interested in him quite late, such that he was only sentenced to life in prison on July 4, 1975, in Hamburg. He died in prison on November 10, 1986.[54]

Seen as a generation, this leadership corps of mass murderers was remarkably homogeneous, since almost all of them were born after the turn of the century between 1900 and 1913, and did not participate in World War I.[55] In the General Government, of twelve commanders of the Security Police with an average age of thirty-six, eleven had completed a university education and nine were lawyers.[56] Yet being members of a generation was much less important for the behavior of these men than how they viewed themselves. Those who thought that they were members of a specific generation also adopted patterns of perception and interpretation that conformed with those of their age cohort. Conduct that appeared to be cohesive was thereby encouraged and at the same time attributed to membership of a specific generation.[57] This is reflected in the opinion that specific actions—such as the destruction of the Jews—were the result of world views and attitudes toward life. But even here it would be a simplification to assume a direct causal relationship between conduct and generation. Next to situational factors, such as direct contact with the Eastern Jews defamed by the regime's propaganda, it was primarily their careers and training in the SS that played a very important role in the mass murders.[58]

Because an almost limitless hatred of Jews and Bolsheviks, but also of Poles, propelled these young academics upward in their careers in state, Nazi Party, and SS offices, the personnel section of the Reich Security Main Office deliberately selected them to serve in Eastern Europe.[59] There the new office heads tried to integrate their hatred of the so-called subhumans into the training for the lower ranks: in numerous classroom lectures a mentality of racism and superiority was imbued into policemen—mostly successfully—thereby promoting the goal of an ideological police force.[60]

This leadership made possible the full implementation of Nazi plans to govern the East. The SS and police units became the most important instruments engaged in the destruction of the local population. In Warsaw, between 1939 and 1944 the SS and police units killed almost 500,000 Polish Jews by organizing their deportation to the extermination camps.[61] Within the city limits alone, they shot some 27,000 people—including many Catholic inhabitants.[62] The numbers of victims in Minsk are almost as horrendous: for a start, there were at least 106,000 Jewish victims of the Maly Trostenets extermination camp, located just fifteen kilometers (9.4 miles) from Minsk. Soviet postwar estimates mention a larger total of some 200,000 deaths by also counting the victims at the surrounding execution sites in these overall numbers. Both estimates include 39,000 of the close to 100,000 inmates of the Minsk ghetto, who unlike most of the others were sent to Trostenets, and therefore were not murdered directly in the city.[63]

The non-Jewish inhabitants became the victims of mass shootings in the course of "reprisal measures," and were also subjected to mass deportations to Germany for forced labor.[64] Like the Jews, they found themselves defenseless and at the mercy of SS and police violence, such as in the infamous Pawiak Prison in Warsaw. During the entire occupation, almost 100,000 people of all confessions passed through this prison, of which some 37,000 were murdered and 60,000 dispatched to concentration camps.[65] Similar mass crimes were committed against the non-Jewish population in Minsk, where shortly after the occupation of the city a squad from Einsatzkommando 8 (part of *Einsatzgruppe* B), consisting of only eight or twelve Germans, organized regular killings in Stalag 352 that lasted for weeks, claiming more than two hundred victims per day.[66]

The RSHA established the offices of the SS and police in Warsaw and Minsk by drawing on the leadership and core personnel from the mobile *Einsatzgruppen* that had passed through these cities earlier.[67] In contrast to the police battalions, the other police posts in the East did not contain reservists. Instead, these units were staffed mainly by officials and employees of the Reich that had been called up for the duration, and were transferred to the East.[68] Like those serving in the civil administration, they represented a wide variety of social backgrounds.[69] Volunteers were an exception because they already held positions in the Reich that excused them from military service. The career prospects for middle- and high-ranking officials were scarcely improved by transfer to the East. The footsloggers, therefore, seldom had any great ambitions packed in their luggage, or brought any special qualifications to their posts in Warsaw or Minsk, but career possibilities opened up mainly for the leaders in the higher echelons of state service.

In Warsaw, all police troops and offices were subordinated to the SS and police leader[70] and had their headquarters on Polizeistraße. This modern building dating from the 1930s, located in the German residential quarter just a short distance from the city center, had previously housed several Polish ministries. Almost all police offices were located here; only the Criminal Police (*Kripo*) resided on Siegesstraße, while the local stations of the Order Police (Schutzpolizei, or Schupo) were scattered throughout the city. Their patrols gave them a constant presence in the city; they also had guard posts stationed on the following streets: Krochmalna (North), Willowa (South), Krakauer Vorstadt (Center), and Targowa (East). Each guard post itself commanded one or more subordinate outposts with up to twenty policemen.[71] The Pawiak Prison was on Dzielnastraße in the ghetto. Here the Nazis used—more for practical than symbolic reasons—an infamous institution from the Tsarist period, whose very construction had come to represent the suppression of Warsaw's population. Additional prisons were located in the Mokotów district of the city on Rakowieckastraße, on Daniłowiczowkastraße, as well as on Gänsestraße—also in the ghetto. These prisons were all run by German officials who served as guards, but who also, at times, tortured many of the prisoners.[72]

The police units were subordinated either to the *Kommandeur der Ordnungspolizei* (commander of the Order Police, KdO) or the KdS. The SS and police leader, a position established only in 1939, was responsible for the coordination of specific police tasks that involved both Order and Security Police units. In addition, he also had authority over stationary units of the Waffen-SS. The subdivisions of the KdS office were based on those within the Reich Security Main Office: Sections I and II were responsible for the administration and personnel issues of the KdS; Section III comprised the SD; Section IV carried out the functions of the Gestapo, under the name Opponents and Counter-Operations, while the detectives of the criminal police were organized within Section V. In Warsaw, there was also Sonderkommando Spilker (Special Force Spilker, named after SS-Hauptsturmführer Alfred Spilker), another police unit assigned to Section Intelligence and Investigation, which was directly subordinated to the BdS in Krakow. From the start of 1942 Sonderkommando Spilker attempted to observe activities of the Polish underground.[73]

For KdS in Warsaw, the following numbers are available regarding its personnel: in 1943, more than 400 people were working in the institution, of which 332 were in the individual sections, another 74 in the Pawiak Prison, while a few more worked in the *Kasino* (officers' mess), the stables, and the motor pool.[74] Among them were more than a few women, typically employed as contractors in subordinate positions as typists and telephone operators, with no realistic chance of promotion or of ever achieving the status of civil servants.

For most of the policemen the barracks were the only quarters they would ever get to know in Warsaw or Minsk. The men were distributed around the city and as a rule stationed in public buildings that had been converted for this purpose. In Warsaw, for example, the police battalions lived in the Polish parliament building, the Sejm, but some were also billeted in the buildings of the Polska Akademia Nauk (Academy of Sciences) and the Muzeum Narodowe (National Museum).[75] Most of these accommodations were in the German residential quarter, but a few others were located further out, such as on the right bank of the Vistula in the Praga district. Below the senior ranks, generally two or three policemen had to share one apartment comprising several rooms.

The institutional structure of the German occupational authorities in Minsk differed only slightly from that in the Polish metropolis. The main difference was that in Weißruthenien the police forces mainly spent their time fighting the partisans. The central leadership in Berlin approved of SSPF, Curt von Gottberg's uncompromising approach to breaking resistance, so that he was seen as the best-suited candidate to replace Wilhelm Kube, when he was assassinated by a female resistance fighter. Gottberg, who was born on January 11, 1896, in Preussisch-Wilten, started his career as a farmer, then in 1933 he became a professional SS leader. In 1937 he was appointed as head of the SS-Rasse- und Siedlungs-Hauptamt (Settlement Office in the SS Main Office for Race and Settlement, RuSHA), and in October 1940 he was transferred to become head of the Erfassungsamt (Registration Office) in the SS-Hauptamt (SS Main Office). Only in the fall of 1942 did he arrive in Minsk to assume the post of SS and police leader; subsequently he was promoted to become the HSSPF Russland-Mitte (central Russia). From September 1943 he then served as general commissar in Weißruthenien. In the face of the German defeat and the threat of being captured, he committed suicide on May 31, 1945 in Flensburg.[76] His remarkable career was thanks mainly to the high esteem in which the SS and police forces in Minsk were held; it makes clear which institution the Nazi leadership in Berlin trusted to break resistance in Weißruthenien. This sign of favor, which was clear for all to see, was never achieved by the SS in Warsaw, despite the uprisings that took place, first in the ghetto in 1943 and then in the entire city in 1944.

Their ongoing task of suppressing the partisans meant that the police troops in Minsk spent most of their time in the surrounding area. In the city itself there were relatively few policemen in comparison with Warsaw; the office of the HSSPF Russland-Mitte, for example, had only fourteen administrative officials stationed in Minsk.[77] They worked in very small offices and lived by no means as comfortably as their colleagues in Warsaw. The office building of the HSSPF was the former city Registration Office. It was a sturdy construction comprising two stories with central heating, but far too small. The construction office of the Waffen-SS and police therefore erected four barracks next to the building in order to meet the urgent need for more space. Because of their light construction, however, they offered inadequate protection from the weather except during the summer. Plans were drawn up for additional apartments and living barracks to house all of the men, but there is no evidence these were ever built.[78]

Beyond the terror it directed against the local population, the German police also carried out authority and security tasks customary for police work everywhere. Detectives of the Criminal Police operated in conjunction with the regular police on patrol; assignments to guard important buildings and people were just as common as those to check and observe suspicious persons, which here were primarily the responsibility of the Gestapo and the SD. But simply due to a lack of manpower—as apart from the battalions there were only 467 members of the Schutzpolizei and 272 gendarmes to maintain order throughout all of Weißruthenien—the German police were unable to meet all of their obligations without assistance. Therefore, alongside the German police the occupational authorities also established an indigenous local police force; in September 1942, in addition to the 739 German members of the Order Police, there were another 10,132 locals serving as police auxiliaries.[79] In all the territories of the East, the indigenous forces were responsible for routine matters that the Nazi rulers assigned a low priority, and that could be delegated without sacrificing any security or control. For the Poles and Belorussians, a local policeman remained in most cases the only person they could approach to deal with petty crime involving non-Germans; the German Criminal Police became involved only with respect to crimes that carried the death penalty.

There was also collaboration that went much further than traditional policing tasks, namely with regard to the mass shootings conducted in the German-occupied Soviet Union. Local helpers, organized into *Schutzmannschaft* (Auxiliary Police) units, assisted especially the police battalions with their killings. However, these murder squads were not recruited from their deployment areas, but were sent there as organized units from outside. The 12th Schutzmannschaft Battalion, consisting of some 250 Lithuanians, was sent to Minsk, where it that participated in several massacres in October 1941. At the mass shootings these auxiliaries herded together the victims, cordoned off the killing sites and afterward killed any Jews who escaped from the grave or who emerged from hiding places.[80] Additionally, in the General Government a small auxiliary police force recruited from ethnic Germans existed until 1943; it was trained in Warsaw and known as the Sonderdienst (Special Services).[81] But even here a language barrier remained because most of them scarcely knew any German and, as contemporary investigations revealed, due to their limited intellectual level, they were hardly able to acquire these skills. Only a few men of the *Hilfspolizei* could be used as translators.[82]

Of all the Germans in Warsaw and Minsk, the men of the SS and police were subjected to the greatest political influence regarding the selection of their personnel. Despite their numerical inferiority to the Wehrmacht and relatively high turnover, they played a decisive role in the occupation by serving as the executive arm of repression and upholding the New Order. For these reasons, they saw themselves as the spearhead of German rule in the East. Above all, they were the ones who implemented the violence against the local populations and set about establishing the occupiers as the masters over life and death.

3. Administration and Offices

After the Wehrmacht's invasion in the late summer of 1939, several *Chefs der Zivilverwaltung* (heads of the civil administration; CdZ) introduced a German administration in the conquered territories of Poland.[83] On September 25, 1939, a Hitler decree placing Poland under military administration[84] initially did not affect their jurisdiction and the CdZs continued their work. Following the proclamation of the Generalgouvernement Polen on October 26, 1939, General Governor Hans Frank, who resided in Krakow, became responsible for setting up the new administration in the central and southern parts of the country.[85] It was his cherished hope to bring to the East an "ideal type of the decisive political civil servant." Frank did not want "tired, dusty paper-pushers, bureaucratically-corrupted fellows," but rather a "cast of genuine hard-workers" among his staff. Above all he sought to employ "*Recken* [ambitious young men], who were absolutely determined to destroy the Poles."[86] In the administration, initially he took over personnel from the military offices that the Reich Interior Ministry had seconded from their regular posts. As the highest central authority, it could order the seconding of personnel from all subordinate offices, such as from the presidents of the regional governments (*Regierungspräsidenten*), or from the *Landkreise* (county) and *Kommunen* (local community) administrations. The instrument of seconding meant, for those affected, that their work location had changed, but formally they still belonged to their original institutions, to which—after an undetermined period—they would ultimately return. Transfers, on the other hand, meant that the official was deliberately handed over to a specific office, without the possibility of returning to his prior institution. In the case of seconding, the official was only placed at the disposal of the General Governor, or farther west, in one of the newly incorporated *Reichsgaue* (regions of the Reich), where the *Regierungspräsident* (Regional Governor) would then determine his specific posting. In the General Government, therefore, there were more than 17,500 Germans active in the administration in 1943—not including those working for the Ostbahn (Eastern Railway) or the Post Office.[87] The majority of them were employees, workers, or civil servants from the Reich; only a part of the administrative personnel had been recruited as volunteers from among the local ethnic Germans. The administrative officials were significantly older than the soldiers. This was because only those civil servants born before 1910 were exempted from military service.[88]

The top positions in the General Government and in the occupied territories of the Soviet Union were deliberately filled with Nazis, who had earned the gratitude of the Nazi Party through loyal service.[89] Yet even below the top level, this no longer applied. The Reich Interior Ministry, the central coordinating office that selected civil servants and employees for deployment to the East, was not primarily interested in Nazi Party loyalists, but rather sought first those people qualified for all sectors of public service. In this regard, technical ability was the most important criterion for selection, although the nominations made by the authorities were, just occasionally, scrutinized—for example, by the Nazi Party Chancellory.[90] In any case, of the 70,000–80,000 secondments—including postal and railway workers—to Poland from the public service by the end of November 1939,[91] by no means all were from the Interior Ministry and its subordinate institutions. They came also from a variety of other specialist administrations, such as the Finance Offices or the Ministry of Justice.

If one considers all these factors, it is hardly surprising that overall there was no uniform policy of secondment: a different procedure applied to employees in public service than for civil servants. The home institutions in both cases listed the names and passed them on, but here—different from on the Reich level—a negative selection was made because the offices only reluctantly released competent personnel from among their constantly thinning ranks. Only during the course of the war did the Interior Ministry itself deliberately go over to using transfers and secondments into the General Government and the occupied Soviet Union to rid themselves of officials with poor assessments or who were subject to disciplinary measures.

In contrast to the seconded civil servants, the interior administration usually checked volunteers very carefully. Especially those people that were not already in public service were frequently motivated by a love for adventure or careerism, and in many cases they were seeking refuge from failure in the Reich or being called up to the Wehrmacht. Among them were some criminals, as well as underaged applicants, men subject to military service, or even pensioners (retired persons). As opposed to the local institutions in Poland that from mid-1940 could recruit their employees themselves—which they did in large numbers—the Interior Ministry also tried to filter out unsuitable candidates. The number of such people hired was correspondingly small, and, as a result, the search by the offices in Poland for men already in service became more intense and against the intentions of the Interior Ministry no genuine selection took place, because almost everyone was accepted that sought a position there.[92] The practice with regard to applications to the Reichsministerium für die besetzten Ostgebiete (Reich Ministry for the Eastern Occupied Territories, RMbO) that was responsible for Weißruthenien and thereby also Minsk, differed very little from that in Frick's Interior Ministry.[93] Just like their colleagues in the interior administration, Rosenberg's institution initially turned down many volunteers and valued qualified personnel,[94] but as the war progressed, they were unable to maintain these high standards.

Overall, it must be said that there was no uniform, minimum absolutely required qualification for service in the General Government or Weißruthenien. In the Reich, the Interior Ministry considered for jobs in the East only those people who were already in state service or, at the least, were qualified to work in the civil service. In Poland, on the other hand, the administration took on almost every volunteer; the leadership positions—as in Weißruthenien—were generally occupied by men the *Distrikt-Governors* trusted personally. The bulk of the personnel, however, could not by any means be described as a group of carefully selected "*Recken*, who were absolutely determined to destroy the Poles." Inside the Reich—and also with regard to recruitment in the General Government—there were only a few cases in which the applicant's vision for the East, his reliability as a Nazi, or his attitude toward the local population served as the main yardstick for selection.[95]

The civil administrations in Warsaw and Minsk differed from each other much less on the local level than was the case with regard to the overall organizational structure. Whilst in Poland, the Warsaw *Stadthauptmann* (City

Governor), Ludwig Leist,[96] was subordinated only to the Distrikt-Governor Ludwig Fischer and the General Governor and Reich Minister Hans Frank, Minsk *Stadtkommissar* (City Commissar) Wilhelm Janetzke, had a chain of command passing through the General Commissar of Weißruthenien, Wilhelm Kube, then the Reich Commissar for Ostland, based in Riga, Hinrich Lohse, and finally, in Berlin, Reich Minister for the Eastern Occupied Territories Alfred Rosenberg. This organization applied different degrees of control (or latitude) from above over time,[97] while the tasks on the ground remained mainly the same.[98] Clearly the purely administrative exercise of rule in the Warsaw metropolis entailed much greater difficulties than in Minsk. In both places the respective powers of the City Governor and the City Commissar remained limited due to the superior authorities also residing in each city; this was especially the case in Warsaw. In addition, questions of competency were in many sectors not clearly delineated, or varied from case to case. In Warsaw, for example, supervision of the so-called Jewish residential district (ghetto) lay directly in the hands of Distrikt-Governor Fischer, while the ghettos in the other towns of Distrikt Warschau were administered by the respective *Stadthauptmänner* or *Kreishauptmänner* (city or county governors).[99] Cliques and networks at the leadership level deserve careful scrutiny because they determined to a large extent the realities of how the administration operated.[100]

Ludwig Leist was born on March 14, 1891, in Kaiserslautern and served as a lieutenant in World War I. In his largely unspectacular career, he had reached the rank of *Oberzollinspektor* (Senior Customs Inspector) and Sturmabteilung der NSDAP [Storm Troopers of the NSDAP; SA) *Oberführer* by the outbreak of war in 1939, before he finally became the City Governor of Warsaw from March 16, 1940, until July 31, 1944. For his crimes during this period, he was sentenced in Warsaw to eight years in prison on February 24, 1947.[101] Leist received his position in Poland only thanks to his Nazi Party connections to the *Distrikt-Governor*, Ludwig Fischer because Fischer was also from Kaiserslautern, where he was born on April 16, 1905. But in contrast to Leist, Fischer was a lawyer and had joined the Nazi Party in 1926, as well as the SA in 1929. His good contacts to Hans Frank helped him to achieve the position of deputy leader of the *NS-Rechtswahrerbund* (Nazi Association for Legal Professionals) in 1931. Then in 1933 he was promoted to *Regierungsrat* (a mid-level government official), and in 1937 he became a member of the *Reichstag* (German Parliament). Frank called on his deputy in the Nazi lawyers' association immediately after the establishment of the General Government and entrusted him on October 24, 1939, with the important Distrikt Warschau. The Polish Supreme Court in Warsaw sentenced Fischer to death on February 24, 1947, and he was executed on March 8, 1947.[102]

In Minsk similar conditions prevailed, if the selection of Wilhelm Kube as General Commissar also came as a surprise to his contemporaries. Kube studied German and was born on November 13, 1887, in Glogau. He joined the Nazi party very early and was a member of the *Reichstag* from 1924 to 1928 and again in 1933, as well as being the head of the Party delegation in the Prussian parliament. In 1928 Kube was already *Gauleiter* (a regional leader of the Nazi party) of the Ostmark (Eastern March)—known after its fusion with Gau Brandenburg in March 1933 as the *Kurmark* (Electoral March). When he also took over the office of *Oberpräsident* (the highest level of regional governance in Prussia) of Brandenburg-Berlin in 1933, it appeared that he was destined for an outstanding career in the Nazi state. But in 1936 he was dismissed from all his posts due to allegations of corruption, as well as, and especially, due to rivalries within the Party. In order to obtain rehabilitation, in 1940 he entered service as an SS-*Rottenführer* (senior lance corporal) in the Dachau concentration camp, and then unexpectedly, on July 17, 1941, he was appointed General Commissar of Weißruthenien, where he continued to use the title *Gauleiter*. This office was to be his last: on September, 23, 1943, Kube was killed by a bomb that exploded underneath his bed in Minsk.[103] Just as Fischer had brought Leist to Warsaw in 1939, Kube also had called on a trusted subordinate, bringing to Minsk Wilhelm Janetzke, born in 1911, who had been the mayor of Falkensee, which lay in Kube's former Gau Ostmark. Janetzke remained City Commissar of Minsk from November 1941 until October 1943, when he had to leave on the arrival of Kube's successor, General Commissar Curt von Gottberg.[104]

The administration directed by these men dealt with similar tasks to those in the Reich. In Warsaw these included, among others, internal administration, food supply and the economy, finances, health, culture, forestry, schools, as well as *Volksaufklärung* (education of the German people) and propaganda, construction, and employment offices.[105] There were even registration offices for births, marriages, and deaths, as well as a section for libraries and archives.[106] These institutions, insofar as they were part of the *Distrikt* government, were housed in Palais Brühl, the seat of the former Polish Foreign Ministry, directly on the Adolf Hitler Platz (see figure 1.1). The city administration resided in Palais Blank on Senatorenstraße. In addition, there was the judicial administration, consisting of the Obergericht (German High Court) with the Special Court on Lesznotraße,[107] as well as a Staatsanwaltschaft (State Prosecutor's Office), in the former Polish Interior Ministry on Neue Welt.[108] All of these institutions were housed outside the German residential quarter in the most representative sector of Warsaw and demonstrated by their choice of location their claim to be the legitimate successors to the Polish government. In terms of the number

Figure 1.1. Palais Brühl, Official Residence of the Distrikt-Governor in Warsaw
Source: Gollert, *Warschau*, p. 14.

of personnel, they remained, however, behind the former Polish capital. In Distrikt Warschau between five hundred and seven hundred officials, employees, and workers were responsible for the administration (see table 1.1); in the city administration there were only fifty-four Germans.[109]

By comparison, Generalkommissariat Weißruthenien, with similar powers and responsibilities, had to get by with only two hundred personnel. Like almost all of the German institutions in Minsk, the offices of the General Commissar were housed in the large Soviet Tower Block directly in the city center.[110] Before the war the building had been used as administrative offices and for the staging of public events. Both city administrations were united in that they continuously complained about a shortage of personnel.[111] This applied also to the other German institutions, such as the Post Office and the German Railway. In 1942 around 130 Germans were working in the Warsaw-based head office of the Ostbahn on Chalu-

Table 1.1. Germans working in the civil administration of Distrikt Warschau

	Jan. 1, 1941	April 30, 1941	Dec. 12, 1941	Jan. 1, 1943	Oct. 10, 1943
Officials	52	57	56	57	52
Employees	380	382	430	578	515
Workers	60	60	77	74	55
Total	492	499	563	709	622

Source: The actual numbers are from the budget plan of the GG; figures for 30.4.1941, are from IPN, NTN/281, "Bericht des Distrikts Warschau für April 1941", 12.5.1941.

binskistraße.¹¹² The railway administration employed about 450 workers altogether in the city.¹¹³ Two years earlier, in the entire General Government the Ostbahn had employed 6,293 Germans just for administrative tasks, of which about one-quarter were based in Warsaw because it was a key railway junction.¹¹⁴ In this region the German Post Office had at its disposal more than 2,390 Reich German and 600 ethnic German employees.¹¹⁵ The Reichsverkehrsdirektion (Reich Transport Head Office, RVD) in Minsk, which was responsible for 5,700 kilometers of railway track, 379 stations, and 1,050 locomotives, could call upon 21,000 Germans in the whole of Weißruthenien: 7,500 officials and 13,500 workers, including 406 women.¹¹⁶ Although the number of employees continued to rise until around the start of 1943, thereafter it declined in all sectors of the civil administration, owing to men being called up into the Wehrmacht. During the course of 1943, 120 officials, employees, and workers from the administration of Distrikt Warschau were sent to the front—that is, about 15 percent of the total working there at the start of the year.¹¹⁷

Although many thousands of Germans were working in the administration of the East, they still remained dependent on the local workforce to a large extent. For this reason, they retained the prewar administration at the village level, as well as in the railway and the postal services. The task of the German organizations of occupation was confined in these cases mainly to direction and supervision, while the implementation of German decrees and the everyday running of the administration were conducted by local inhabitants.¹¹⁸ In terms of pure numbers, therefore, the locals in public service vastly outnumbered the occupiers; in Minsk and Warsaw there were several tens of thousands of Poles and Belorussians that continued working in the public administration. In the Stadtsteueramt (Warsaw City Tax Office) No. I on Bombrowskiplatz, for example, 825 Poles were working under twelve Germans on December 1, 1941.¹¹⁹ In the General Government, however, the competencies of the local administration were very restricted, such that—in contrast to Weißruthenien—it is not possible to speak of state collaboration.¹²⁰ The Polish offices, as mere recipients of orders, were only responsible for their own compatriots.¹²¹

The majority of the Germans working in the administration, unlike the Wehrmacht or the SS, were not quartered in separate barracks or hostels, but instead lived in the German residential district. Usually two or three civilians shared an apartment in a building in which only Germans could reside. Each person would have his or her own room, but only senior officials and employees had their own apartments. Those working in the administration were much better off than their comrades in the barrack accommodations, and when they first arrived in Warsaw it was not uncommon for them even to be put up into hotels that the German authorities had requisitioned for this purpose. For example, in 1939 the propagandist Theo L. stayed initially in the Hotel Bristol and the Hotel Europeiski. Later he moved into a house occupied by several families close to the Dreikreuzplatz and lived there with two other Germans in an apartment, in which each person had their own room and everyone shared the living room. After getting married in Warsaw, L. moved with his wife into an apartment within a building reserved for German civilian employees.[122]

After the Germans began construction of the walls enclosing the Warsaw ghetto on April 1, 1940,[123] the persecution of the Jews was concentrated in a specially created office, known as the Kommissar für den jüdischen Wohnbezirk (Commissar for the Jewish Residential District), led by the fanatical Nazi Heinz Auerswald. Directly responsible for the process of ghettoization was Waldemar Schön, who was in charge of the Abteilung Umsiedlung (Resettlement Division). Born on August 3, 1904, in Merseburg, the lawyer Schön had known Governors Frank and Fischer before the war because he had joined the Nazi Party in 1930. In that year he became the training director of the *Ortsgruppe* (Nazi local group) in his home town, and in 1932 he served also as *Kreisschulungsleiter* (county training director). In his career as a Nazi, he also became *Kreis* (county) speaker in 1930, *Gau* speaker in 1932, and after that even *Reichsredneranwärter* (Reich speaker in waiting). The Nazi seizure of power made it possible for him to rise to director of welfare in the Sachsen-Anhalt provincial administration in the fall of 1933. From 1934 he was active in the Nazi Party leadership's *Hauptamt Kommunalpolitik* (Main Office for Local Politics) and was promoted to the rank of *Reichsamtsleiter* (Reich Office Leader) in the NSDAP. He arrived in Distrikt Warschau on January 19, 1940, as director of the Abteilung Umsiedlung, where he was responsible for the ghettoization of the Jews. In March 1941 he became acting director of the Innenverwaltung (Department for Internal Administration). After the war he lived in Munich without coming under the scrutiny of the judicial authorities.[124] Auerswald, who came from Berlin, was also a lawyer. He was born on July 26, 1908. He joined the SS in 1933, and six years later he also joined the Nazi Party. He took part in the Polish campaign as an officer in the Schutzpolizei and after that became director of the Abteilung Bevölkerungswesen und Fürsorge (Division for Population and Welfare) in Distrikt Warschau. From April 1940 until November 1942, he was the German organizer of the ghetto as Commissar for the Jewish residential district. On the dissolution of this office, he became *Kreishauptmann* in Ostrow, but he was soon called up to the Wehrmacht in January 1943. After the war, he worked as a lawyer in Düsseldorf, where he died on December 5, 1970.[125]

These men not only set the delivery quotas for taxes and economic products from the ghetto, but also were responsible for the grossly inadequate supplies of food and medicine. In 1940 each Jew in Warsaw received on average only 413 calories per person per day; one year later each received just 253 calories, and yet in 1936 the League of Nations had set the physiological minimum for nourishing a full-grown person at 2,400 calories.[126] The death rate was correspondingly high, mainly due to the pressure exerted by the civil administration.[127] Until the start of deportations to the Treblinka extermination camp in the summer of 1942, more than 70,000 people died in the ghetto. In this way, the civil administration made its own particular contribution to the Holocaust.

The German administration did not personally inflict violence on the Jews. During the occupation, very few German officials looked directly into the eyes of their victims. Yet many of their decrees had life-threatening consequences for the local population. The rationing of food, for example, applied not only to Jews, but also to the Polish and Belorussian populations, for whom it was also much too low. In Warsaw, the official calorie ration in 1943 was only 30 percent of the physical requirement.[128] As the occupiers intended, the local population had to rely on its own production and—against their intentions—also on the black market. In addition, the civil administration ordered the deportation of forced laborers into the Reich; that deportation was implemented by the SS and police. As a rule, during the day a street would be blocked off without warning and all those not already working for the Germans in the East were deported to the West.[129] Then, the judicial authorities, in the form of the Special Courts, were responsible for many deaths[130]—among Poles, Belorussians, and Jews. The Sondergericht in Warsaw convened twice a week in a former Polish court building, which formed part of the ghetto boundary, and it issued around thirty verdicts on each occasion. The accused were mostly young men and women who had left the ghetto illegally in search of food. They were sentenced to death; the total number of verdicts is estimated at between 1,000 and 1,500 in one year. The Special Court was occupied with these cases from November 1941 until the middle of 1942. At that point the SS assumed this task without conducting legal proceedings. They either shot those captured on the spot or sent them to Treblinka, where they were murdered.[131] Less final, but also with severe consequences for those affected, was the material plunder that plunged many local inhabitants into indigence. Even German school policy impacted their lives because it aimed to confine education for the local population to only the most basic schooling, leading to the closure of the universities and all institutes of higher education.[132]

In Warsaw, Friedrich Gollert and Otto Gauweiler, departmental heads in the Distrikt administration, were also charged with promoting their own achievements. In contrast to most of the officials and employees, they were carefully chosen for these leading positons on the basis of their previous experience. They were supposed to promote a picture of the Nazi administrative leader that corresponded to the ideals of Hans Frank and could serve as a model for their subordinates. Friedrich Gollert, who had a doctorate in law, was born on December 2, 1904, in Neuruppin and worked there after his studies as a lawyer. From 1930 to 1933 he was a member of the Deutsche Volkspartei (German People's Party, DVP). He joined the SS in 1933 and then the Nazi Party in 1941. As a *Wachtmeister der Reserve* (private of the reserve), he arrived in Warsaw with a police regiment in 1939 and in 1940 he was transferred to the Justizabteilung (Justice Department) of the Distrikt. In 1941 he took up a position as the personal assistant of Ludwig Fischer and was promoted in March 1942 to head of the *Raumordnungsamt* (Spacial Planning Office). He finished his career in Warsaw in 1944 as director of the Justice Department.[133]

Dr. Otto Gauweiler was also a lawyer and came from Gommershausen in the Palatinate, where he was born on April 25, 1910. In his Nazi Party career he reached the rank of *Reichsamtsleiter*, from October 1939 he was head of the interior administration in Distrikt Warschau.[134]

4. Civilians and Ethnic Germans

The members of the groups outlined above were an integral part of the institutions of occupation. But in Warsaw and Minsk there were also other Germans present. The Wehrmacht, the police, and the civil administration employed more than a few women, mostly as telephone operators or typists, or otherwise as workers in the field of social welfare. Among the Nazi Party organizations, there were branches of the Nationalsozialistische Volkswohlfahrt (National-Socialist People's Welfare Organization; NSV), kindergartens, welfare offices for ethnic Germans, railway station canteens, advice centers for mothers, and services for the care of the wounded. In all of these, mainly women who had been sent from Germany were deployed.[135] In addition, there were also jobs in hospitals or in old people's homes,[136] as well as in *Frauenarbeit* (women's work), that is, taking care of the German women.[137] Until recently, historical research has paid little attention to the contribution women made to German rule in the East, despite the fact that these tasks were essential to the successful conduct of the occupation.[138]

However, it is known that almost all of the mostly young and single female helpers volunteered to go to the East and only a few of them were obliged to go as part of their jobs. The term "*Mädel*" (girl), used so frequently in contemporary sources, testifies convincingly to the average age of the female volunteers, who in many cases went straight to the East as soon as they had outgrown the (Nazi-organized) League of German Girls (Bund Deutscher Mädel; BDM).[139] The women made an important contribution by taking over jobs from men, thus making male manpower available for military service and other so-called male occupations. Because service in Poland and Weißruthenien was not compulsory, mainly young, adventure-seeking women applied; to them this distant deployment offered a degree of independence and freedom that would have been unimaginable at home. The female helpers saw in the East a much greater career opportunity than, for example, the older men subjected to compulsory secondment, who would much rather have stayed in the Reich with their families. They could—quite in contrast to Nazi ideological precepts—cross some gender-specific boundaries and considerably expand their otherwise limited freedom of action—great tasks awaited them. Because the women had volunteered, they generally had a positive attitude to their work; otherwise they would have had to wrestle self-critically with their own decisions. The East was viewed from the perspective of a conqueror, or, rather, a conquering woman; dissatisfaction with such a woman's own situation was comparatively rare.[140] Thereby the women developed a self-perception that was not dependent on their type of employment, but rather consisted of the fighting woman in the East; they were acutely aware of their special status as female soldiers.

Differences among the women according to field of deployment can scarcely be detected because the respective activities at the various offices and institutions were very similar. In addition, they lived in shared accommodations, and experienced the same organized entertainment programs that were aimed at them primarily as women, and not as members of the Wehrmacht, the civil administration, or the SS.[141] This did not preclude them from being seen, in the eyes of the Nazis, as irreplaceable linchpins of German rule. Without their support of the men and their irreplaceable assistance in the administration of the respective units, the crimes in the East would hardly have been possible on such a massive scale, even though they did not personally take up arms and become hands-on killers.[142] The young women were not, as in the Reich, seen primarily in the role of future mothers,[143] but as the "female comrades of the men," who would support them as much as they could with "bravery of the heart."[144] They were therefore an integral part of the society of occupiers and of its daily life, even if there were clearly fewer women than men. In Minsk, for example, at the beginning of 1942 there were around 1,800 female German occupiers—including some ethnic Germans—of which 850 were employed.[145] For Warsaw no figures are available, but it was probably a number about five times this, or around nine thousand, including ethnic Germans. This would represent about 15 to 20 percent of the society of occupiers, in which ethnic German women outnumbered those from the Reich considerably.

In both cities, the female employees lived separated from the men in apartment blocks and hostels that were in part organized by the respective offices they worked for.[146] In Minsk, for example, there was a women's hostel for 130 female railway workers of the Reichsbahndirektion Mitte (Railway Directorate Center) located in a wing of a railway-owned towerblock. There were facilities for washing and ironing in the building, dormitories with four to six beds in each, and a common room. In 1942 the general commissar's office in Minsk had a total of fifty-two female employees, of which twenty-two were to be accommodated in a new house, so that those under twenty years of age could live together under one roof.[147] Apartment blocks in which women could have a room for themselves were available only in small numbers in Warsaw. The reason why the women were always quartered together, especially in the occupied territories of the Soviet Union, was due to the dangerous security situation. For example, the Post Office—as in the Reich—initially did not envisage deploying any women to the East. Only later, once shared accommodations and supervision by older female officials had been secured, did they start sending them. The supervisors were required to be at least age thirty because it was firmly believed that especially young women should not live alone on moral grounds.[148]

Most of the German women from the Reich formed part of the society in uniform in the East, for as female Wehrmacht auxiliaries, or employees of the SS and the administration, they also wore uniforms or at least service badges that clearly indicated that they belonged to the institutions of German rule. The women were members of the society of occupiers, in which almost everybody signaled their membership, as one of the new holders of power, with a uniform. At the same time, the uniformed Germans could view themselves as protectors of the few compatriots who were not clothed like them. These were primarily the wives who had followed their working husbands to Warsaw and Minsk and did not have any employment there. In Weißruthenien, however, female civilians remained an exception because the practice of families coming out East to join their menfolk was not desired, on account of the endangered security. In the General Government this was not a problem, although women were not allowed in barracks. In Warsaw, in addition to those housewives accompanying their husbands, more than a few couples were engaged in state service and frequently employed together in the same office branch.[149]

A large section of the society of occupiers consisted of ethnic Germans. In Warsaw there were well over 10,000 in 1943,[150] in Minsk around 2,500. In both cities around half were men and half women.[151] The Nazis defined as *Volksdeutsche* all people whose language and culture had German roots, even if they were not *Reichsbürger* (citizens of the Reich).[152] In order to acquire formal membership in this group, it was sufficient to be on the *Deutsche Volksliste* (German people's list) that, once the applicant's details had been checked, led to the granting of German citizenship. The germanization of the applicants was run by the Volksdeutsche Mittelstelle (Office for Ethnic German Affairs), which was subordinate to the Reich Commissar for Strengthening the German People (Reichskommissar für die Festigung des Deutschen Volkstums; RKFDV), Heinrich Himmler. During this process, the applicants were first assigned to various groups that reflected their suitability for germanization. In Group 1 were those people whose membership in the Nazi Party was desired because they had acknowledged their German origins before 1939. People assigned to Group 2 had German roots without making any public display of this; being a member of either of these two groups was sufficient to ensure that citizenship would be granted. In the next category were those who had family ties with Poles, but for whom it was believed that they would find their way back into the German fold. Among them were non-German spouses and people who had a Slavic mother-tongue, but who were recognized as having at least had German ancestors. People in this category could receive only provisional citizenship and only after a racial examination. The last categorization was assigned to all other applicants. They were subjected to the normal process of applying for citizenship.[153] The Nazis did not make a strict selection for being put on the list, but in Warsaw in the years from 1942 to 1944, all the same, around 12 percent of the applicants were denied.[154] Farther east, since only around 5,000 ethnic Germans were present in Weißruthenien,[155] it hardly made sense to apply the *Deutsche Volksliste* in this region. Due to these small numbers, neither RKFDV nor VoMi were active in Weißruthenien, and ethnic German affairs were left to the civil administration.[156]

Membership in the *Deutsche Volksliste* was not only linked to an ID card that promised work, benefits, and preferential treatment from the authorities, but also entailed entitlement to additional food rations far above the levels of the Poles or Belorussians. More than a few people applied for this status on purely opportunistic grounds; they belonged to categories 3 or even 4 and by their names, or above all according to their language, were scarcely identifiable as Germans. Since almost 90 percent of the applicants were workers or according to official records at least did not belong to the middle class,[157] it is possible that the applicants for ethnic German identity cards were in some cases suffering from material shortages. Numerous court files from Warsaw show ethnic Germans who were not able to follow proceedings in the German language, such that the discussions could only be conducted in Polish. Many language courses were offered at German schools for these people—50 percent of whom lived in alien marriages with Poles,[158] because they had great difficulty integrating within their chosen role in the society of occupiers.[159] To the regret of the rulers, there was little interest in these four-hour classes that were given by teachers from the German high school especially in winter, and attendance was at best sporadic.[160]

The Nazis had a great interest in the ethnic Germans because their status of alleged victims of the Slavs partly legitimized the war of aggression. In addition, they were a kind of Fifth Column who knew the local population and its specific character very well. They were the object of German settlement planning that was supposed to secure German rule in the East for centuries. There were many reasons to make an effort for these people and at the same time not to set the standards too high.[161] In Poland, Hans Frank set an example and participated—also in Warsaw—in the celebrations in their honor,[162] which were held every year on the anniversary of the "liberation" —or rather capitulation—of Warsaw.[163] In 1941 alone, the Nazi Party conducted six recruiting campaigns, in which they completely filled meeting halls with interested people who supposedly had applied for the German people's list and thereby became "full members of the German community."[164] The *Warschauer Zeitung* and its successor, the *Krakauer Zeitung*, also published many articles addressed specifically to the ethnic Germans, and in the *Deutsche Gemeinschaft* they even had a newspaper that aimed to serve them exclusively. It appeared from the end of 1942 in Distrikt Warschau and Distrikt Radom. With its linguistically simplified articles, mostly digested from pieces in the *Krakauer Zeitung*, it achieved a circulation of 15,000.[165]

For ethnic Germans, possession of the ID card, alongside the numerous advantages it offered, also resulted in their exclusion from previous Polish social circles because in the eyes of their compatriots they were now collaborators. Particularly in Warsaw, but also in Minsk, a separate ethnic German society developed that existed in the space between the locals and the occupiers. Genuine integration with the Reich Germans was possible for only a small number of those who worked for the German authorities. Those who had the necessary German language skills—and that was not many—mostly chose this path because it promised the best financial rewards. That did not mean, however, that the ethnic Germans enjoyed the same material conditions as the Reich Germans, who oversaw their service in the East.[166]

Nonetheless, the ethnic Germans should still be considered as a part of the society of occupiers, and in any case should not be counted among the occupied. Their voluntary acknowledgement of their German roots speaks for itself. In addition, one must consider their active participation in the exercise of German rule. Many ethnic Germans—who were trusted more than Poles or Belorussians—were employed as guards; some in their spare time were even active as members of the *Selbstschutz*. In this organization as well as in the guard units, they belonged to the uniformed sector of the society of occupiers. The *Selbstschutz*, in the General Government and in the Reich *Gaue* (provinces) of Wartheland and Danzig-West Prussia, was responsible for numerous crimes against humanity.[167] Up until their disbandment in August 1940,[168] the *Hundertschaften* (*Selbstschutz* squads) were constantly visible in Warsaw, demonstrating their allegiance to the new regime. At the same time, the *Selbstschutz* served also as a symbol of the Volksdeutschens' changed self-perception, which raised the ethnic Germans as victors clearly above the defeated Poles. Naturally this force received its own *Kameradschaftsheim* (club home), in which apart from relaxed social gatherings, German nationalist and Nazi indoctrination were conducted. For this purpose, SS-Standartenführer Wilhelm Gunst, in charge of the unit, installed a "dining room in the style of the Black Forest. The wood-paneled walls, along which benches were lined, the beams under the roof, the chairs and tables, all magically transported from home a piece of Germany out to Warsaw. On the lead-glass windows four runes represent the four Distrikt-cities of the General Government—for Warsaw the 'Tyr-rune,' the rune of victory."[169]

Alongside those who spent their spare time in the *Selbstschutz*, there were also full-time members of these units: in Warsaw alone there were four hundred men stationed in one barrack, where they received paramilitary training.[170] They were based in barracks partly with the intention of germanizing the men so that after their service in the *Selbstschutz* they could be transferred quickly for use in the Wehrmacht and *Hilfspolizei*, or in the formations of the SS and SA. Nonetheless, in the General Government only 20 percent of *Selbstschutz* members met the requirements for joining the SS—as opposed to 40 percent in the western Polish regions.[171] Among them, it was mainly the professional members of the *Selbstschutz* who became Holocaust perpetrators: their units were deployed as auxiliaries during the deportations and mass killings,[172] and served as perimeter guards around the ghettos.

Their clear acknowledgement of German identity required that the ethnic Germans be fully integrated into daily life; this was facilitated through numerous training and support programs conducted by Nazi organizations.[173] Ideological indoctrination formed a part of these programs because especially among the ethnic Germans there were considerable deficits in this respect. Among the topics covered were, for example, "Our great goal in the East" or "the life story of the Führer."[174] In addition, the *Volksdeutsche Gemeinschaft* received its own communal building on Siegesstraße in Warsaw, known as the Albert-Breyer-Haus, where there was not only a hall for large-scale events, but also two coffee rooms, a library, a games room, a smoking room, and a ladies room.[175] The naming of the building was also highly symbolic: the ethnic German teacher and *Siedlungsforscher* (settlement researcher) Albert Breyer was a celebrated propagandist for the long-term presence of Germans in Poland who was killed as a Polish soldier on September 11, 1939, in a German air-raid.[176] In the clubhouse that bore his name, the ethnic Germans were not only separated from their previous Polish surroundings, but also indirectly from the Reich Germans, who had their own clubhouses. In 1941 the Nazis converted this ethnic German community into a German community comprising Germans that were not Nazi Party members and had been in the General Government for more than three months.[177]

The institutions of occupation introduced many welfare measures for ethnic Germans and their families because they were the German population in Warsaw and Minsk—the administration did not need to take care of members of the Wehrmacht or the SS.[178] Since in the Polish metropolis there were few Reich German children, the NSV ran two aid centers for mothers and children with a total of eleven employees, primarily for the ethnic Germans. In addition, there was a nursing home for infants (for German births in Warsaw see table 1.2) on Professorskastraße with twelve employees,[179] and also three kindergartens.[180] The ethnic Germans benefitted most from these facilities, and their children also went to the *Volksschulen* (general schools)[181] and *Gymnasien* (advanced schools),[182] for which many teachers were recruited from the Reich. The number of general school teachers in Distrikt Warschau rose from forty-six at the start of 1940 to eighty-eight two years later; at the high schools (*Oberschule*) there were still seventeen teachers at the start of 1942.[183] In the educational sector, it was possible to portray Nazi rule as especially beneficial because this degree of support had not existed under Polish rule. The sight of German children attending German schools was a visible measure of the success of the occupation in attaining its goals. In the language of the Nazis, they had

Table 1.2. German Births in Warsaw, 1940–1942

Period	Total	From Warsaw	From outside Warsaw	Reich German children	Ethnic German children
May 1, 1940–December 31, 1940	70	57	13	4	66
January 1, 1941–December 31, 1941	230	196	34	40	190
January 1, 1942–March 31, 1942	56	49	7	2	54

Source: Leist, *Bericht*, p. 54.

created a "citadel of German culture and a spiritual 'Ordensburg.'" Even General Governor Hans Frank was pleased to be seen at the opening of a school, as the "symbol of a new period in history," which was described in the press as a "moving rally of all the Germans in Warsaw."[184] In school, the ethnic German children were to be shaped in terms of ideology, which is why the educational institutions were subordinated to the Reich Commissar for Strengthening the German People, but were paid for by the General Government.

Forty-eight teachers were sent to Poland from the Reich to teach at the ten *Oberschulen* in the General Government. In the 311 *Volksschulen*, 5 *Hauptschulen* (main schools), 17 *Internaten* (boarding schools), and 20 *Berufsschulen* (vocational schools), on the other hand, mainly ethnic German teachers were appointed.[185] In October 1939 the first general school with eight classes was opened in Warsaw. In the *Distrikt* alone, the number rose to fifty-two general schools by the summer of 1944; in the city itself there were two with sixteen and two with eight classes. Six thousand children were being taught in Distrikt Warschau, whereby the schools outside the city had boarding houses, so that the children did not grow up in a Polish environment. At the high school, which also had a boarding house that was later handed over to the Hitler-Jugend (Hitler Youth; HJ) or the BDM, there were more than four hundred students in 1944. The vocational school taught eight hundred young people in twenty-two classes, with only eighteen primarily ethnic German, nonacademic teachers.[186]

Many adult ethnic Germans worked as tradesmen or craftsmen; these people benefited considerably from German rule in terms of their upward social mobility. Now they had the opportunity to advance rapidly in—frequently confiscated—former Polish and, above all, former Jewish businesses.[187] The need to be able to negotiate with the Nazi authorities required a business manager who spoke German. Because sudden promotion to a leading position was often the result of simple threats to denounce or discredit the previous owners, not only able candidates received such a chance. Nevertheless, by no means all holders of ethnic German ID cards profited from the new conditions. Precisely those opportunists, who were hardly competent in the German language, were in many cases also unable to improve their social position. They remained suspect to the occupiers. The verdict issued by the Commander of the Security Police in Warsaw against a drunken, rampaging, ethnic-German guard, reflected a widely shared prejudice among Reich Germans: that most ethnic Germans, to judge by their "whole behavior both on and off duty, belonged to those elements, which only sought personal advantage, but otherwise had remained Poles."[188]

Therefore, many ethnic Germans continued to pursue the same jobs and occupations as before the war. The new holders of power did not have any positions for them because the Reich German companies in particular could afford to select their personnel according to competence. For Reich German businessmen, the ethnic Germans filled the role of translators for communication with the Polish employees; they also entrusted some with assessing local business conditions. As a survey by the Hauptgruppe Handel, Wirtschaft und Verkehr (Warsaw Main Group for Business, Economy, and Transport) of Germans employed by German companies in Warsaw revealed in 1942, around two-thirds of these people were ethnic Germans. The survey showed also that for all of the businesses in German hands, usually only the owners or business managers were German.[189] In several cases, however, businesses had brought all of their own personnel with them from the West. One example is the textile company Dirksen, operating in the Hotel Bristol, Warsaw, whose more than thirty employees—like the owner—all came from Danzig.[190]

Hardly any sources are available on those people who went to Warsaw or even to Minsk as private individuals from the Reich. Despite the caution this situation demands, one has to describe the majority of them as adventurers, who, conscious of the risks, were still attracted by the opportunities offered by the new economic areas; only very few of them are likely to have been sent there by their previous employers. The general shortage of manpower in Germany meant that companies were desperately looking for German workers who were not subject to military service. For this reason, one must assume that the average age was well over thirty years. This was not necessarily the case for the wives that some of these men brought with them to Warsaw. Since as a rule they did not take up any employment until the start of 1943, when the obligation to work was introduced also for women in the General Government,[191] even less is known about them than about the male civilians. Like most of the ethnic Germans, these occupants were housed in the German residential quarter, where there were enough apartments to accommodate them.

The East offered the Reich Germans, both economically and financially, a very lucrative new area of activity into which German businesses quickly expanded—if much more into Poland than into Weißruthenien. Thus the only German notary in Warsaw, Albrecht Eitner, in the six weeks between November 15 and December 31, 1940, took in almost 16,000 Złoty—or 8,000 Reichsmark—in fees. Even though he earned another 15,000 Złoty from the end of 1940 to the end of May 1941, daring to make the move to the East still paid off handsomely for him.[192] His monopoly position, as well as his knowledge of Polish, made him the first person many Germans approached regarding various legal issues. Precisely because the new holders of power were very happy to avoid doing business with the locals, profits were easy to come by, especially for orders requiring a lot of manpower because here the local population could be called upon—quite often in the form of forced labor. In both cities the companies profiteered from the criminal Nazi state, supported it, and had a stake in maintaining it. In Minsk, for example, twelve construction companies were working for the Organisation Todt (Todt Organization), and all of them utilized numerous forced laborers.[193] Production using Jewish workers was practiced on a large scale, especially by German firms operating in the Warsaw ghetto. The largest of these firms working for the Wehrmacht, which especially included textile firms, were the shops of Walter C. Toebbens with six thousand to ten thousand Jewish workers, and Fritz Schultz with two thousand to three thousand Jewish workers.[194]

Other German businesses that did not use any forced laborers mainly met the occupiers' needs for luxury and diversion. There was always demand for these and the occupiers were prepared to pay good money for high quality. Many businessmen had recognized this and made good profits. At the end of 1939 the largest nightclub in Warsaw, the Adria Variety, came into German hands. With several bands and 135 permanent employees, it was very popular with the Germans.[195] Julius Meinl ran four grocery and luxury food shops in which locals were not allowed to shop.[196] In Warsaw in 1942 there were fifteen food shops in addition to Meinl's that were reserved for the occupiers.[197] The Deutsche Industrie- und Handelskammer (German Chamber of Commerce and Industry), which was established on Siegesstraße just after the start of the occupation,[198] also listed as members those companies that only had new owners, and no longer had pre-occupation owners. The Polski Bank Przemysłowy (Polish Industrial Bank), the Asid Instytut Serologiczny (Asid-Serum Institute), or the Fabryka Kabli Ożarów (Ożarów Cable Factory), were now just as German as the Warsaw branch of Siemens or the local office of Steyr Daimler Puch had been before 1939.[199]

These companies employed many ethnic Germans because it was not possible to get workers from the Reich, and they generally viewed the Poles with suspicion. A typical career is that of Eitel-Friedrich Bonk with the Junkers-Werke (Junkers Company), which had taken over the Fabryka Silników i Traktorów URSUS (URSUS Factory) in Warsaw. He was initially employed as a factory guard and was soon promoted to a position in the economic section, where he was entrusted with purchasing food for the factory canteen. However, Bonk could not resist the large sums that had been placed in his trust and squandered at least 38,000 Zloty in various nightclubs; in addition, he was also able to sell 422 kilograms of butter, 300 kilograms of margarine, as well as 3,585 packets of saccharine on the black market. It was indicative of the shortage of suitable German workers that he managed to reach this position at all because even the usually unbending Special Court granted him the extenuating circumstance that his assigned tasks were beyond his intellectual abilities.[200]

It is difficult to describe systematically as a group the German men and women who went to Warsaw or Minsk as private individuals. The overriding common feature is that they all came to the East voluntarily. This unites them with the ethnic Germans who had pledged their allegiance to the occupiers of their own volition, and who, despite this—or precisely because of it—were always viewed with suspicion. This was also due to the fact that they never gave up their roots completely and continued to maintain contacts with Polish friends. All the same, the ethnic Germans were one of the sources of legitimation for German rule because now they finally had received the status that allegedly before the war had been denied to them. In comparison with other sectors of the society of occupiers, they and the German civilians from the Reich profited the most from German rule.

5. The German Residential Quarter and Contacts with the Local Population

When the Wehrmacht entered Warsaw in the Fall of 1939, it found a city severely damaged by aerial and artillery bombardments; around 15 percent of the buildings had suffered during the fighting,[201] and some 66,000 apartments with 102,800 individual rooms were destroyed.[202] Just two years later the Germans witnessed even more serious damage in Minsk, although their impressions were affected by the poverty of many of the houses and the fact that many were built of wood and had been seriously damaged by fire. This degree of war damage was unknown to the occupiers prior to this because their homeland had not yet been scarred by Allied bombing. Correspondingly, Warsaw and Minsk were "heaps of ruins,"[203] and the soldiers even discussed whether responsibility for this lay with the Wehrmacht or with Germany's enemies.[204] Even the official occupation newspaper in Minsk still referred in 1942 to the "ruined city."[205]

For the new rulers the destruction meant that there were very few intact apartments available. Because they were interested in modern and comfortable quarters, immediately after their conquest they started to confiscate suitable apartments. Initially this was done unsystematically and without any geographical preference decided pragmatically, according to the quality of the accommodation, but soon the men started to concentrate themselves in specific quarters of the city. Not able to choose were of course the units in barracks—and that means a large part of the society of occupiers—that, for reasons of security, were scattered not only in the city center (see figure 1.2), but across the entire area.

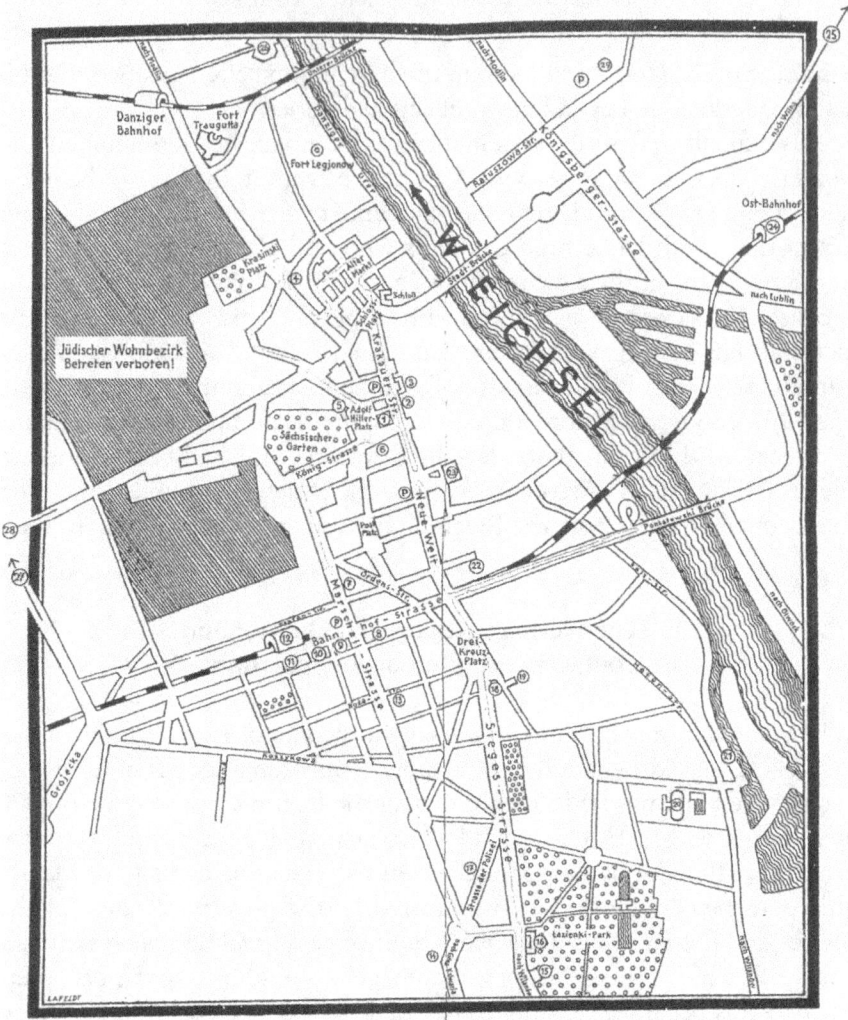

Figure 1.2. Map from the Official Guide to Warsaw for German Soldiers in 1942
Source: Meier, *Soldaten-Führer,* appendix.

Note: The German residential quarter is not marked here; it comprised roughly those streets shown south of Bahnhofstraße. Key: 1. *Oberfeldkommandantur* (Senior Field Commandant's Office); 2. Hotel Bristol; 3. Deutsches Haus (German House); 4. *Kath. Garnisonkirche* (Catholic Garrison Church); 5. Palais Brühl (Brühl Palace); 6. *Soldatengaststätte* (soldiers' restaurant); 7. *Wehrmacht-Lichtspiele* (Wehrmacht Cinema); 8. *Quartieramt für Offiziere* (quartering office for officers); 9. Hotel Reichshof; 10. *Quartieramt für Mannschaften* (quartering office for other ranks); 11. *Frontleitstelle* (front coordination office); 12. *Hauptbahnhof* (main railway station); 13. *Wehrmacht-Theater* Viktoria; 14. *Ev. Garnisonkirche* (Protestant Garrison Church); 15. Magdeburger Haus; 16. *Schloss* Belvedere (Belvedere Palace); 17. *Sitz des KdS* (seat of the KdS); 18. *Soldatenheim* (soldiers' home); 19. YMCA; 20. *Wehrmacht-Stadion* (Wehrmacht Stadium); 21. *Wehrmacht-Bootshaus* (Wehrmacht Boat House); 22. *Wehrmacht-Schwesternheim* (Wehrmacht Nurses' Home); 23. Theater der Stadt Warschau (City Theater of Warsaw); 24. *Ostbahnhof* (Eastern Railway Station); 25. Zum Ehrenmal General Fritsch (To the Memorial for General Fritsch); 26. Zitadelle (citadel); 27. Zum Heldenfriedhof (To the Heroes' Cemetery); 28. und 29. *Entwesungsanstalten* (delousing facilities). P: *Bewachte Parkplätze* (guarded parking lots).

In Minsk the Germans lived in the city center that was built in a socialist style, close to the central administration building. In the so-called tower block, a multistory Stalinist construction, next to the offices of the general and city commissars, there were also numerous apartments for the employees of these institutions. The city, which was viewed by the occupiers as very impoverished,[206] consisted in large part of damaged wooden houses; they did not want to live in those, and considered as livable only the few intact stone buildings from the Soviet period. The fifty Norwegian wooden houses, erected in the city park in May 1942, formed a unique feature. Each had eighty-six square meters of living space, and were reserved for those occupiers that moved to the East with their families.[207] There was no genuine German quarter, in the sense of a more-or-less separate and closed-off area only for Germans; they tended to concentrate in the center of Minsk, however. Therefore, Germans that decided to move into secure and half-decent accommodations were not subjected to strict regulation, on account of the general shortage of living space. General Commissar Kube wrote to City Commissar Janetzke, "After the Volga Germans refused to take over from you the listed apartments [in the former ghetto area], further efforts to find accommodation for this obstinate group are no longer required."[208] This also shows, alongside the low esteem with which Reich Germans held the ethnic Germans, why there was no separate quarter for Germans in Minsk, as was the case in Warsaw: they lived wherever it was possible and pleasant. The demarcation of the Germans from the locals, nonetheless, took place in a similar manner as occurred in Poland; because of the alleged better racial quality of the Belorussians, however, it was not regulated to the same extent in Minsk as it was in Warsaw.

In Warsaw, by contrast, there was a geographical separation between the working and residential areas: the administration moved into the representative buildings in the center of the Polish capital. The offices were located between the ghetto, which was established only shortly afterward, and the River Vistula, around Krakauer Vorstadt and Neue Welt. The palaces and villas, which had been built mostly at the end of the eighteenth and the start of the nineteenth centuries, were well-suited to the new rulers' need to demonstrate their importance. It was significant, however, that Distrik Governor Fischer did not reside in the Zamek Królewski (Royal Castle) or even in the unfinished Pałac Saski (Saxon Palace) of the Wettin dynasty, but consciously shunning Warsaw the capital, moved instead into the Palais Brühl, which was the former Foreign Ministry building.

The private quarters of Warsaw's occupiers were located mainly about two kilometers (1.2 miles) south of the government district in the Mokotów section of the city and all around Park Łazienkowski (Łazienki Park).[209] While barriers separated this German quarter from the rest of the city, the government offices resided in individual buildings outside the old town. Later, during the 1944 Warsaw Uprising, this proved to be a serious mistake because it rendered impossible a systematic and solid defense against the local population.[210] In 1940, though, the selection of the area for the German residential quarter was easy because the houses there dated mostly from the 1920s and 1930s, and met the then-current standards for modern living (see figure 1.3).

The occupiers who wanted to live in this part of the city were registered by the civil administration and the Nazi Party and were assigned to suitable apartments.[211] After some initial voluntary changes of residence, occupiers were only allowed to live outside the German residential quarter with special permission. In February 1943, after several requests that had little effect,[212] the administration issued a decree that prescribed resettlement.[213] This had been posted on placards by the Polish Underground: disguised as an official German announcement. The aim was to promote fear of the local population among the Germans because the text read, "The Police cannot guarantee the personal security of these compatriots and their families [outside the German quarter] to the extent that is possible inside the German residential quarter. For Reich Germans, who have their families here, the continued presence of their family members is prohibited."[214] The

Figure 1.3. A Modern Apartment Block on Karowastraße in Warsaw This early example of German living quarters is actually outside the German quarter.
Source: Gollert, *Warschau*, p. 264.

paranoia this appeal aimed to inspire, however, did not achieve its goal until the start of 1944, when the occupiers not only patrolled the streets, as before, but also even fenced in the German quarter with barbed wire.[215]

The Wohnungsverwaltungsamt (German Accommodation Office) was responsible for managing relocation within the city. Initially it had to ensure that the apartments and buildings used for business purposes that were being claimed by Germans had been vacated by their Polish owners and officially assigned to their German successors. Yet even before the establishment of the residential quarter, the needs of the Germans had already driven many Poles from their apartments. Locals were no longer permitted to reside in those apartment blocks reserved for the occupiers and were also being driven out of the quarter more generally. Only friendly foreigners, such as Hungarians and Finns, could remain there, but people from neutral countries were permitted only if no German needed the living space.[216]

By July 1942 the Accommodation Office was had assigned around 11,000 people to 3,572 apartments in the German quarter; each apartment thus held, on average, three people. Just one month later, the occupiers had more than 4,179 apartments at their disposal, and by the end of the year it was already 6,342.[217] The official statistics for May 1943 report 14,132 Aryan and 120,000 Polish inhabitants in the quarter.[218] Initially, the resettlement of Germans into the quarter went fairly smoothly due to the availability of newly constructed apartments in no need of repair. But from August 1942, the assignment of accommodation started to encounter serious difficulties: "Those apartments still available require not only serious renovation, but they also need to be disinfected, if they are to become habitable for Germans." That also meant that the Poles living there would be driven out of the residential quarter more drastically than before, while now there were no replacement accommodations for them elsewhere in the city. The office therefore introduced a measure for "concentrating the Poles by quartering tenants compulsorily in extra-large apartments." In such apartments every room was to be occupied by at least two people.[219] A similar process of displacing the locals was applied also in Minsk.[220]

The occupiers' plans for Warsaw's future were continued with the same radical intensity with which they were begun. They intended to transform the metropolis into a small town with around 40,000 German inhabitants for which, in accordance with the model of the future *Gau* capitals, numerous insignia of German rule in the East, such as towers and *Foren* (forums) were being designed. This plan entailed a reduction of the physical stock of buildings, which among other things would have got rid of the previous German residential quarter.[221] The goal was not only the creation of an Aryan settlement, but above all the destruction of Warsaw and its meaning as the capital city and center of Polish identity. For example, Jürgen Stroop, who laid to waste the ghetto, leaving only rubble and ashes in 1943, confirmed these politics to a fellow prisoner in Polish captivity after the war.[222] According to a memorandum the head of the *Raumordnungsamt*, Friedrich Gollert, wrote in early 1944, Warsaw had lost half a million inhabitants since 1939, mostly due to the murder of the Jews. However, this was not enough for him; he also spoke about a German center in which no Poles at all would reside.[223] To this end, in May 1942 they were already forbidden to move into the city or its surroundings.[224]

From 1939 the occupiers spurred on the germanization of the subjugated cities. In June 1940 many names of streets in Warsaw were changed.[225] On the one hand, no national Polish symbols were permitted to remain, and, conversely, the Germans wanted to give clear expression to their own rule. In most cases the renaming was limited to literal translations into German, but the administration also chose some names for political reasons. Pilsudskiplatz (Piłsudski Square) therefore became Sachsenplatz (Saxon Square)—on which, however, initially celebrations in honor of Piłsudski continued to be held. Poniatowskibrücke (Poniatowski Bridge) received the ingenious designation Neue Brücke (New Bridge), and Napoleonplatz (Napoleon Square) was converted into Postplatz (Postal Square). Many similar examples could be given, and in later years some names were changed again. For example, after only three months Saxon Square was changed to Adolf-Hitler Square, and Ujazdowski Allee, which in the meantime had become the Lindenallee, now became Siegesstraße.[226] Minsk differentiated itself from Warsaw in that there one did not get rid of the cyrillic letters, but only replaced the Soviet names with national Belorussian ones in combination with a German translation.[227] There were also some genuine Nazi names, such as the Gauleiter-Kube-Platz (Gauleiter-Kube Square), which commemorated the murdered general commissar.[228]

Not only street names publicly symbolized Nazi rule: A large number of swastika flags gave the impression of a city in the Reich, large propaganda placards were put up for the locals and the occupiers, and signposts were maintained only in German.[229] A modern loudspeaker system installed in Warsaw in April 1942 was intended to have the same impact as it had in Germany. Its fifty public loudspeakers broadcast speeches and especially German news reports five times per day.[230] To maintain German order, for example, it was forbidden to post death notices on house walls.[231] The legitimation of German rule was attained through self-representation. Therefore, the alleged constructive achievements of the occupiers were constantly trumpeted. When the main railway station in Warsaw was provisionally completed, this was declared to be a great accomplishment.[232] The Germans also celebrated the reopening of the devastated city parks as a reversal of the uncivilized Polish conduct of the war, which allegedly had led to the destruction of these cultural sites.[233]

The shops, which were soon opened all over the cities, also provided comfort to the occupiers. Thus in Warsaw there was not only a German pharmacy, which accepted payments from health insurance plans in the Reich,[234] but also a department store[235] and several food shops.[236] While some of the latter at least could be found in the German residential quarter, the pharmacy, the department store, and most other shops were on Krakauer Vorstadt, and therefore outside the German quarter. In the eyes of the rulers, shops required special designation so the nationality of the owner would be immediately visible. German shops had to put up special signs in German, but were also allowed to have signs in Polish. This rule also applied to Polish shops: they were allowed signage in both Polish and German. Jewish businesses, however, were not permitted to have signs in German; by decree the company name had to be written in Hebraic script—that is, in pseudo-Hebraic latin characters.[237] The practical consequence was that, especially those ethnic Germans who had owned a business before the war, put up large signs saying German Business that could be seen from afar. Of course this mainly served their economic interests, but at the same time the occupiers also knew immediately where they could shop without encountering any language barriers.

If the occupiers were in Warsaw only for a short time or simply had not yet found a fixed abode, they could initially move into one of the many requisitioned hotel rooms. The Germans administered many hotels, such that in May 1943, 4,430 hotel rooms with around 5,550 beds were occupied.[238] These accommodations were mainly available to the Wehrmacht, and offered officers passing through the city a comfortable place to stay. But these accommodations were also very popular with members of the civil administration because they offered many amenities and were centrally located.[239] Most hotels were located in the city center, not the German residential district, and there were no great differences in standards. This had the advantage that sleeping quarters, work, and especially the opportunities for nightly amusement were all close together: restaurants, cinemas, theaters, and similar facilities were not located in the residential areas, but in the city center.[240] A further advantage of a hotel room was the low cost. All new members of the civil administration quartered in hotels paid a rate in accordance with their income: senior officials paid 3 Reichsmarks per day, the middle ranks paid 2.50 Reichsmarks, and all others paid 1.50 Reichsmarks. Up to 75 percent of these costs could be reimbursed, however, up to 24 Reichsmarks per month.[241]

The distances that the Germans had to overcome in both of these large cities brought certain problems with them. Walking distances of between two and four kilometers (1.2 and 2.5 miles), such that from the German residential quarter in Warsaw to Palais Brühl or other offices in the government quarter, could not be reconciled with the self-image of the occupiers. Such long walks through the city did not project the desired air of superiority. In addition, questions of security also played a key role because pedestrians offered an easy target for attacks and assassination attempts. Therefore, the Germans were very keen to expedite improvements in the efficiency of public transport. In July 1942 they attempted to increase the electricity supply in Minsk by burning peat in order to get the badly worn-out streetcar system running again.[242] However, the streetcars did not work properly until almost one year later, when in May 1943 a test service was able to start up, running every twenty minutes—but the shortage of electricity continued to cause problems.[243] Prior to this prestigious project of the city administration the city had to rely on the help of the Ostbahn (Eastern Railway); the Ostbahn ran a bus every two hours that linked together all the most important institutions in the city.[244]

The situation in Warsaw differed from that in Weißruthenien considerably. The Polish capital had an excellent streetcar network before the war that had suffered only minor damage in 1939. The last repair work took until 1940 to complete, but public transport was more or less fully working before this.[245] Since the streetcar was also the favored means of transport for the locals, it was important for the occupiers to be able to keep their distance while travelling. Allegedly on account of the danger of infections being spread, the local people were not permitted to use the seats in the cars of the occupiers, but were only permitted to stand on the rear platform.[246] This honorable but still uncomfortable regulation then became obsolete with the introduction of cars only for Germans. The occupiers thereby achieved their separation from the rest of the population also in local transport because they had previously enforced it against the Jews. The segregation reached its apogee in the establishment of a streetcar line only for Germans, on which no Polish streetcars were allowed to run. The cars ran every seven and a half minutes across Warsaw and linked the residential quarter with the government district. Clearly the government offices were concerned about the attractiveness of this service, as in announcements about it they stressed that all Germans should now use this line, to ensure that it was not unprofitable.[247]

Since the occupiers had their own businesses, places of amusement, and means of transport, it was actually possible for them not to have any contact with the Polish population at all. Many possible opportunities, such as visits by local doctors, were in any case explicitly prohibited.[248] On top of that, especially at night, when the occupiers were not engaged in their official duties, there was a rigidly enforced curfew. The local population faced severe sanctions for any breach of the curfew regulations; they could get around the regulations only by obtaining a special permit, for example, for performing one's job. The curfew times varied according to the season. In Minsk in summer 1943 they were as follows: April 1–30, 8:00 P.M. to 5:00 A.M.; May 1–August 31, 9:00 P.M. to 5:00 A.M.; and September 1–March 31, 7:00 P.M. to 5:00 A.M.[249] In Warsaw the city administration ordered very similar restrictions for the Polish population,[250] so that, generally, after dusk only Germans were still supposed to be on the streets. By contrast, for the Wehrmacht and the SS and police—that is, for all those units housed in barracks—there was also the nightly *Zapfenstreich* (retreat), blown at 10:00 P.M.; for NCOs it was blown at 11:00 or 12:00 P.M. For officers and all German civilians, however, there were no such restrictions.[251]

Even during the officially permitted times, it was difficult to communicate with the local Poles or Belorussians because very few of the occupiers could speak these languages. If a conversation did take place, it was usually with residents of the city, who spoke a few words of German. The Nazis promoted this speechlessness precisely because contact was not desired. In Minsk, the German railway workers, for example, received only a teach-yourself Russian book with the title *1,000 Words of Russian* in March 1944—that is, almost three years after the initial conquest.[252] If conversation took place, then it was conducted by higher ranks at work, or by officers of the Wehrmacht, who spoke with business people. In official circumstances or when accompanied by subordinates or colleagues, it was scarcely possible to discuss private topics at all, let alone strike up a friendly relationship. Such relationships were discouraged by numerous prohibitions, in any case, which were often repeated, put on posters, and also carefully controlled: members of the Wehrmacht were not permitted to be seen with locals—especially not female locals—or even to visit a restaurant and socialize with them.[253]

Nevertheless, the women were an attractive distraction, and their proximity was sought, given the sexual deprivation among the troops.[254] But overall the contacts of the soldiers with locals were limited. The various prohibitions, language difficulties, and very restrictive and closely controlled curfews all led to the creation of special alternatives, mainly for the Wehrmacht: if you wanted to visit a restaurant, you could go to an establishment that was registered for the Wehrmacht and run by ethnic Germans, in which contact with the locals was neither possible nor necessary, but where only other comrades could be found. In addition, all the cultural and entertainment offerings available to the Germans were forbidden to the Polish population; the Belorussians, however, were at least partially tolerated.[255]

In order to meet with local inhabitants in their free time, soldiers had to leave the protection and familiarity of their barracks, where apart from a few local auxiliary workers, non-Germans could not be found. They rarely ventured out alone, but rather in small groups. In any case, leaving the barracks was usually strictly regulated for the ordinary soldiers. Those who wanted to make contact with the local population needed not only a dose of curiosity, but also a willingness to take risks because serious punishment loomed, including loss of trust and exclusion from the circle of comrades. The officers—in Warsaw there were around two thousand[256]—had it considerably easier in this respect because they could move more freely around the city and were subject to fewer restrictions.

Especially the more educated among the officer class, such as Udo von Alvensleben, for example, were inclined to take advantage of local cultural events, such as Polish concerts. Alvensleben liked to play the role in Warsaw of a cultivated nobleman, and thought it natural to interact with Poles and their culture, mixing especially with members of the Polish aristocracy.[257] This example is rare, but not unique. Germans met with Poles, Belorussians, and Jews, usually without being seduced or viewing themselves as heroes. In 1944 Captain Wilm Hosenfeld, a school teacher before the war, helped save Władysław Szpilman, whose story was depicted in the film *The Pianist*, by Roman Polanski. However, this act is not even mentioned in his letters or diaries; before this event he had already met with Poles and established friendships with them.[258] Other members of the occupation forces chose girlfriends from among the locals, whom they often supplied with food or money. In general, however, Poles and Belorussians did not come into contact with most German soldiers and officers; the Germans viewed the locals with a degree of suspicion, and of course the feeling was mutual.

Even a friendship among comrades was scarcely imaginable with ethnic German auxiliary policemen, and not at all with non-Germans because the authorities paid so much attention to segregating ethnic groups. Contacts and opportunities for contact were slender after work hours because the respective parties usually returned to their own group environment. The occupiers in Weißruthenien who supervised the local auxiliary police, viewed their job as a burdensome "educational task," and they feared at any moment a "reversion to Soviet practices," such as breaches of discipline or alcoholic excess.[259] A particular "indignity" was the necessary cooperation with the *Jüdischer Ordnungsdienst* (Jewish Order Service) that initially guarded the Warsaw ghetto with 2,400 men and served as a kind of police force toward the other Jews. It required, of course, a fair degree of supervision from the Germans and Poles, who also guarded the ghetto externally.[260]

Problems also arose in the interactions of Germans with the local civilian population, and it was policemen that locals were most likely to encounter. In view of the perceived and experienced harsh treatment of the Eastern Europeans by the Germans, abuses were inevitable, especially as police orders stressed the need to be as decisive as possible. Any confrontations were mostly distinguished by one-sided brutality. The Germans often took the foreign language of the Poles and Belorussians simply as a sign of their reluctance to cooperate—and in such cases they quickly resorted to the use of force. Accordingly, such contacts remained brief and confined themselves only to the most essential matters. In any case, private conversations with the locals were no more tolerated among the policemen than among the soldiers of the Wehrmacht.

Communications with the Polish and Belorussian populations were also rare for members of the civil administration and encountered the same linguistic barriers as for the Wehrmacht and the police. Negotiations with the local administration were usually initiated by the occupied; they deliberately sent German-speaking representatives to the occupiers, as the latter, due to the language difficulties involved in issuing orders, often reacted as if they had been provoked and generally were inclined to resort to repression. German was much more widely known among the educated classes in the East than were Slavic idioms in the West.[261] For example, in the Generalkommissariat Weißruthenien, there was only one Reich German official who spoke Belorussian at all—and he was soon transferred to the General Government.[262]

In dealings with the Jews, even official communications were restricted to the most essential matters. The Jewish councils, which received their orders from German officials, served as a compulsory administration to facilitate Nazi control over their main ideological enemies. Yet at the same time they also managed to deflect the hatred of the ghetto dwellers to a large extent against their own administration.[263] Nevertheless, in transmitting German orders the authorities' main aim was to overcome language barriers. This could be achieved in some unusual ways: the chairman of the Jewish council in Warsaw, Adam Czerniaków, reports, for example, in his diary on a conversation conducted in Russian with the female secretary (an ethnic German from Riga) of the Commissar for the Jewish Residential Area. She was not only Auerswald's secretary, but also his wife.[264]

The German residential districts and the associated organization of the occupiers' daily lives served many functions. First, the Nazis were interested in segregating the occupiers as much as possible from the locals. Living in a foreign environment was to be accomplished without Germans having much contact with Poles or Belorussians at all. This division was combined with the creation of a community that defined itself by living together in a common space. Second, this self-imposed separation was an important element in German security policy because where there were no locals, there could also be no threat to the occupiers. Third, the establishment of their own city within a city provided visible evidence of the supposed superiority of the German race and its historical mission as rulers of the East. The residential district was therefore a prestige-laden model for the future reign of the Aryans. Fourth and finally, the specific buildings chosen presented a modern, contemporary style of living with maximum comfort, so that the quarter also fulfilled a very pragmatic need that the city's new rulers could also realize at the local population's expense.

Nonetheless, the residential quarters did not prevent the splintering of the German society of occupation along institutional lines. During the entire war the Germans remained divided into groups, comprising the Wehrmacht, the SS and police, the civil administration, private individuals, and ethnic Germans. Very little interaction took place between these separate segments because the Germans spent most of their time with their own colleagues. Yet here there was still a key difference compared to back home in the Reich; among the occupiers of Warsaw and Minsk only a certain age spectrum was represented, such that younger and older people, as well as women, were strongly underrepresented. The large numbers of people in uniform, the privileged standard of living, and the fact that mainly those engaged in work were stationed in Poland and Weißruthenien, also differentiated them starkly from conditions at home. Furthermore, the occupiers saw themselves as part of a coerced community because only a few of them had volunteered for life in the East or had even been specially selected for it. Yet precisely from this circumstance, there emerged a high degree of cohesion because the occupier's mutually shared fates created strong bonds. For the Germans living in the cities of Warsaw and Minsk, there were no familiar surroundings, no old friends, and no habitual entertainments; even their former modes of behavior had now lost any validity, far from home. The conquerors had established their rule by the use of force—and now they had to bear the consequences.

Notes

1. Gartenschläger, *Stadt*, p. 65.
2. APW, 485/333, "Bericht des Wohnungsamtes Warschau", 15.7.1942. See also Szarota, *Warschau*, pp. 252–253, 257. Not accurate are the numbers given by Getter, *Środowisko*, p. 225.
3. For Minsk, see Gartenschläger, *Stadt*, pp. 65–66; for Warsaw, see Szarota, *Warschau*, p. 257.
4. Ulrich Herbert has called the generation of war-hardened youth, the "main support of the Nazi dictatorship ... [and] the administrative apparatus in the occupied territories of Eastern Europe." See Herbert, *Generationen*, p. 100.

5. Rusinek, *Krieg*, pp. 143–144.
6. Szarota, *Warschau*, p. 257; and Gartenschläger, *Stadt*, p. 65, esp. fn. 460.
7. For this reason, a special guidebook to Warsaw was published just for the Wehrmacht. Meier, *Soldaten-Führer*.
8. Tessin, ed., *Verbände*. Stationed in Warsaw were the Intelligence Regional HQ (Nachrichtenabteilung 542 des Militärbefehlshabers GG) from December 1942 until August 1944 (vol. 11, p. 114), the Kriegslazarettabteilung (Reserve-Military Hospital Section) 515 from October 1942 until October 1942 (vol. 11, p. 48), and the Grosse Kampffliegerschule (Main Combat Flight Training School) no, 3 of the Luftwaffe (vol. 2, p. 210); the Wehrwirtschaftskommando (Military Economic Command) was based in Minsk from July 1941 until June 1944 (vol. 4, p. 167); and the Nachrichtenkommandantur (Intelligence Commandant) no. 305 from September 1941 until August 1944 (vol. 9, p. 92).
9. IfZA, MA 679—6/273ff., "Monatsbericht der Oberfeldkommandantur Warschau für die Zeit vom 16.2.–15.3.1943", 21.3.1943.
10. BAB, R 102 I/23, S. 1, "Schreiben der Oberfeldkommandantur Warschau an den *Distrikt*gouverneur", 20.7.1943.
11. Gerlach, *Morde*, p. 136.
12. Bartov, *Wehrmacht*, pp. 52ff.
13. Ibid., pp. 167ff.
14. Rass, *Menschenmaterial*, pp. 312–317. On the Nazi socialization of a Wehrmacht division, see ibid., pp. 121–134.
15. Bartov, *Wehrmacht*, pp. 318–327.
16. For the Polish campaign, see Kettenacker, "Chefs"; and Umbreit, *Militärverwaltungen*. For Belorussia, see Gerlach, *Morde*, pp. 134ff.
17. Tessin, ed., *Verbände*. The identity numbers of the *Kommandanturen* changed frequently in Minsk. For a short period, each of the following *Ortskommandanturen* were used: 257, 352, 411, 436, 650, 850, and 906 (vol. 16, p. 3). In Warsaw in 1940–1944, among others the *Ortskommandantur* 907 was stationed (vol. 13, p. 113). The commandant was from 1.10.–10.10.1939, was Generalleutnant Conrad von Cochenhausen, commander of the 10th Infantry Division. His successor was Generalleutnant Karl-Ulrich Neumann-Neurode until spring 1940, then Generalmajor Walter von Unruh, from early summer 1943 Generalleutnants Fritz von Rossum and Werner Schartow, then from the end of July 1944 Generalleutnant Rainer Stahel. Szarota, *Warschau*, pp. 231–232.
18. From here the German street names as found on the city map (see chapter 1 section 5, this volume) will always be used. On that map the Polish designations can sometimes be found also. In Minsk the *Kommandantur* was also located on Kommandanturstraße.
19. Tessin, *Verbände*. In Warsaw this was above all the Wachregiment Warschau from April 1940 (vol. 13, pp. 197 and following); but also, e.g., Infanterieersatzregiment 601 from July 1941 to February 1942 (vol. 11, p. 263), the Sicherungsbataillone 944 and 945 in 1943 to 1944 (vol. 13, pp. 149–150), and Landesschützenbataillon 476 from 1941 to 1944 (vol. 10, p. 261). In Minsk there was the Infanteriedivision 707 from December 1941 until April 1942 (vol. 12, p. 156), Reserveinfanteriebataillon 312 from October 1942 until August 1944 (vol. 8, p. 24 and vol. 9, p. 116), and the Sicherungsregimenter 603, 609, and 611 in the years 1942 to 1944 (vol. 11, pp. 273, 292, and 298). Finally, with rotating deployments between 1941 and 1944, there was the Landesschützenbataillone 624, 653, 787, 791, 860, 915, and 975 (vol. 11, p. 333; vol. 12, p. 46 and 314; vol. 13, pp. 70, 122, and 175).
20. IfZA, MA 1790/12; 688–3–8, Internal "Schreiben des Stadtkommissariats Minsk," October 1942. On the one hand the Wehrmachtskommandantur did not want to hand over empty buildings to the civil administration or theNazi Party; on the other hand it demanded that the city administration clear a house for the needs of the Wehrmacht without offering any replacement to the city administration, and even threatened it with a directive from the OKH.

21. IfZA, MA 1790/3; 379-2-45, Kommandanturbefehl Minsk no. 18, 11.7.1942: "The city of Minsk is no longer to be viewed as enemy territory. From 1.9.1941, it is under civil administration and the same principles are valid here as at home. The unit commanders must again and again inform their subordinates of this, so that these attacks by individuals finally cease."

22. See, e.g., the diary of Carl von Andrian according to the transcript prepared by Peter Lieb, original in the Bayerisches Kriegsarchiv, hereafter cited as "Carl von Andrian diary/Peter Lieb transcript", entry of 30.1.1942; BfZg, Slg. Sterz, Letter of Unterfeldwebel Hermann Schilling from Minsk, 6.8.1944.

23. *Krakauer Zeitung*, no. 77, 4.4.1941: "Verbundenheit von Wehrmacht und Verwaltung."

24. Regarding the conclusion that the Wehrmacht participated in genocide rather than simply being caught up in the campaign against the Soviet Union, see, e.g., Pohl, *Wehrmacht*, p. 51. On the thesis of a war of destruction conducted by the Wehrmacht starting in 1939 during the Polish campaign, see Böhler, *Auftakt*.

25. Szarota, *Warschau*, p. 244. The Wehrmacht encountered great difficulties putting a stop to the plundering in Warsaw in 1939. US-NARA, RG 242, T 312, Reel 42/2471–2472, Letter of the Warsaw Stadtkommandant to the commanders of the 18. and 19. ID, 6.10.1939. [For providing a copy, I thank Mathias Irlinger.]

26. BAB, R 58/214, "Ereignismeldung UdSSR" [USSR] no. 23. This *Einsatzgruppen* report also describes the plundering in Minsk.

27. The order is published in Kohl, *Ich*, p. 218.

28. In Minsk *Stalag* 352. IfZA, MA 1790/3; 379-2-45, "Kommandanturbefehl Minsk" no. 51, 14.11.1942. Gerlach, *Kontextualisierung*, p. 85.

29. Gartenschläger, *Stadt*, p. 21.

30. Gerlach, *Morde*, pp. 506ff.

31. Gerlach, *Morde*, pp. 870–1054. An overview of recent research is offered by Brakel, "Wut der Bauern," esp. pp. 393–399.

32. Krausnick and Wilhelm, *Truppe*, p. 600.

33. Gerlach, *Morde*, p. 871.

34. Lieb, *Täter*; and Gerlach, *Morde*, pp. 617ff.

35. Gerlach, *Morde*, p. 904; and Krausnick and Wilhelm, *Truppe*, p. 236.

36. Gerlach, *Morde*, pp. 139ff., 152ff.

37. Sakowska, *Menschen*, p. 54.

38. BayStA, Staatsanwaltschaften 34865/18, "Kriegstagebuch des Rüstungskommandos Warschau", 6.2.1943. On the activities of the Wirtschaftsstab Ost (Economic Branch East) in Weissruthenien, see Gerlach, *Morde*, p. 142.

39. Szarota, *Warschau*, p. 257. Among the eight thousand men in June 1944 were four thousand members of the Waffen-SS. This figure should be seen as the largest point.

40. IfZA, MA 1790/4; 359-1-6, "Kräfteübersicht des HSSPF Rußland-Mitte", 20.7.1943.

41. Tessin, *Verbände*, vol. 3, pp. 120–121: The Totenkopf-Standarte 8 was formed on 11.11.1939 in Krakow from Totenkopf-Standarte 4, which originated in Linz. Abteilung (Section) II was stationed in Warsaw, as was the staff unit from 1.12.1940. The *Ausbildungsabteilung* (training unit) was in Warsaw from December 1941 until mid 1944; see ibid. and vol. 2, p. 79. See also Cüppers, *Wegbereiter*, pp. 28–29, 31.

42. Cüppers, *Art*, pp. 94ff.; on the mass murders, see p. 99.

43. Browning, *Männer*, pp. 25ff; Klemp, *Ermittelt*, pp. 67ff.

44. Klemp, *Ermittelt*, pp. 214–215.

45. Cüppers, *Wegbereiter*, pp. 75–89.

46. In 1941 and again from mid February 1943 the HSSPF Russland-Mitte was stationed in Minsk. BAB, R 70 SU/21, p. 87, "Tagesbefehl Nr. 1 des Bevollmächtigten des RFSS für Bandenbekämpfung", 17.3.1943.

47. In general, see Birn, *Polizeiführer*; Mallmann, *Mißgeburten*, p. 76. On the biography of the SS- und Polizeiführer in Warsaw, see Mix, "Organisatoren," pp. 131ff.
48. Ruck, *Korpsgeist*, p. 222.
49. Matthäus, *Heuser*.
50. StAM, Polizeipräsidien, Slg. Primavesi/208.
51. Herbert, "Generation," pp. 35ff.
52. Moczarski, *Rozmowy*.
53. Ramme, *Sicherheitsdienst*, p. 267; Sawicki, *Staatsanwalt*, pp. 243ff.
54. Młynarczyk, *Massenmörder*. In general, see Kur, *Sprawiedliwość*; Ramme, *Sicherheitsdienst*, p. 263.
55. Wildt, *Generation*, pp. 847ff.
56. Borodziej, *Terror*, pp. 50–51.
57. Jureit, *Generationenforschung*, pp. 11–12.
58. Ibid., pp. 12–13.
59. Wildt, *Generation*, pp. 546ff.
60. Matthäus, "Judenfrage."
61. Gutman, *Jews*, esp. pp. 197ff.
62. Bartoszewski, *Todesring*, pp. 357ff.
63. Kohl, *Trostenez*; Wankewitsch, *Fahrt*.
64. Quinkert, "Terror." More than 460,000 people were deported to work in Germany from the area of present-day Belarus during the war; only 5 percent or less of them are likely to have volunteered. One source reports as many as 82,538 forced laborers deported by the beginning of 1944: "every eleventh Pole from Warsaw." Gollert, "Grundsätzliche," as cited by Gutschow and Klain, *Vernichtung*, p. 128. For an overview of forced labor in the General Government, see Marszałek, *Obozy*.
65. Stawarz, *Pawiak*, p. 10.
66. Gerlach, *Kontextualisierung*, p. 89; Krausnick and Wilhelm, *Truppe*, p. 236.
67. In Warsaw this was Einsatzgruppe IV under SS-Brigadeführer Lothar Beutel, which was then taken over by Josef Meisinger. Biernacki,"Organizacja"; see also Mallmann, Böhler, and Matthäus, *Einsatzgruppen*, pp. 99ff.; Bartoszewski, *Todesring*, p. 335. In Minsk in December 1941 the German police was made up from parts of Sonderkommando 1b and of Einsatzkommando 8 under Walter Hofmann. Curilla, *Ordnungspolizei*, p. 476.
68. Borodziej, *Terror*, pp. 50–51.
69. Regarding the generally comparable office of KdS in Reval, see Birn, *Sicherheitspolizei*, pp. 42ff.
70. These were, in order, SS-Gruppenführer Paul Moder (1941), SS-Oberführer Arpad Wigand (1941), SS-Oberführer Ferdinand von Sammern-Frankenegg (1942–1943), SS-Brigadeführer Jürgen Stroop (April–September 1943), SS-Brigadeführer Franz Kutschera (October 1943–February 1944), SS-Oberführer Herbert Böttcher (February 1944), and SS-Brigadeführer Otto Geibel (March–August 1944). Bartoszewski, *Todesring*, pp. 336–337.
71. Bartoszewski, *Todesring*, pp. 337–338.
72. On the personnel of the Pawiak Prison, see Domańska, "Policja."
73. Bartoszewski, *Todesring*, pp. 338–342.
74. Borodziej, *Terror*, p. 60. On pages 58–59 and 61ff., the various detachments and sections within the KdS in Radom are examined, which were very similar to those in Warsaw and Minsk.
75. Battalions 6 and 301 found themselves in the Polish parliament building (Sejm); see Klemp, *Ermittelt*, pp. 84 and 231. In the Dom Akademicki (Academic House) on Krakauer Vorstadt were parts of Battalion 61. StAM, Polizeipräsidien, Slg. Primavesi/270, War Memoirs of the Oberwachtmeister der Schupo der Reserve Otto Nahlmann about his time with Police Battalion 61. In the National Museum on Bahnhofstraße were SS quarters for two

thousand men. APW, 482/1552, "Monatsbericht des Distrikts Warschau für Mai 1941", 10.6.1941.

76. Klein, *Gottberg*.

77. BAB, R 19/137, pp. 103ff., HSSPF Russland-Mitte to RFSS, 17.6.1943.

78. BAB, R 19/137, pp. 93–94, "Vermerk über die Dienstreise des Amtsrats Reimers nach Mogilew und Minsk Anfang April 1943", 22.4.1943.

79. Curilla, *Ordnungspolizei*, p. 398. The numbers come from a report dated 11.9.1942. Gerlach, *Morde*, p. 217, gives the figure of 1,400 German policemen on 1.10.1943.

80. Dean, *Collaboration*, pp. 43ff., 60ff.

81. *Warschauer Zeitung*, no. 209, 4.9.1940: "Ausbildung volksdeutscher Polizisten in Warschau."

82. Borodziej, *Terror*, pp. 41–42.

83. On Hitler's plans regarding the CdZ, which were subordinated to the relevant armies, the organization of the administration in the conquered and incorporated territories, as well as the legal status of the General Government, see Rebentisch, *Führerstaat*, pp. 169ff., as well as Alberti, *Verfolgung*, pp. 49ff.

84. See Moll, "Führer-Erlasse," Document 10, pp. 97ff.

85. On this Musiał, *Zivilverwaltung*, pp. 13ff. On the CdZ see, in general, Umbreit, *Militärverwaltungen*; Berenstein and Rutkowski, "Administracja."

86. As cited in Präg and Jacobmeyer, *Diensttagebuch*, p. 18, Frank's speech on the visit of Robert Ley, 7.11.1940.

87. Haushaltsplan des Generalgouvernements 1943. For 1943, Musiał gives the number of 13,820 Germans and does not include the 3,924 planned officials of the General Government in his statistics, Musiał, *Zivilverwaltung*, pp. 87ff.

88. RGVA, 720-2-46, p. 128, "Verfügung des OKW betreffend die Freistellung von Beamten vom Wehrdienst", 17.2.1940.

89. Roth, *Herrenmenschen*, pp. 90–92.

90. Lehnstaedt, "Ostnieten," pp. 719ff.

91. Rebentisch, *Führerstaat*, p. 186. The numbers are for the General Government and the territories incorporated into the Reich.

92. Roth, *Herrenmenschen*, pp. 110–111.

93. Zellhuber, *Verwaltung*, pp. 169ff. Nonetheless the Interior Ministry had special competencies that continued to secure it a key role: Rosenberg's ministry was not empowered to issue instructions to the internal administration in the Reich and therefore was unable to order secondments. If it wanted to send a specific official to the Soviet territories, it still had to obtain approval for his release via the Interior Ministry.

94. Chiari, *Alltag*, p. 60. The basis for the personnel in the occupied territories of the Soviet Union was the Führer Decree of 16.1.1942. On the formation of the administrative leadership corps in the occupied eastern territories, see Moll, "Führer-Erlasse," document no. 134, pp. 223ff.

95. On earlier interpretations, see Lehnstaedt, "Ostnieten."

96. Leist's predecessors were the following, in order: 1. From the end of September until early October 1939 Dr. Helmut Otto, born 15.3.1892, in Antwerp; lawyer and physician; BA in agriculture; SA-Standartenführer, 1933–1937; Oberbürgermeister in Solingen and later in Düsseldorf. 2. Dr. Oskar Dengel, born 27.12.1899, in Waldbüttelbrunn; lawyer, 1926 Regierungsassessor; Stadtpräsident in Warsaw from 4.10.1939 to 15.3.1940.

97. On Frank's exercise of power, see Madajczyk, *Okkupationspolitik*, pp. 85–86; Musiał, *Zivilverwaltung*, pp. 30ff.; Pohl, *Judenverfolgung*, pp. 75ff.. On the relative independence of GK Weissruthenien from Lohse and Rosenberg, see Gerlach, *Morde*, pp. 159ff. A comparative overview is offered in Oldenhage, "Verwaltung."

98. A description of the tasks can be found for the Soviet territories in BAB, R 43

II/685a, pp. 37ff., "Die Zivilverwaltung in den besetzten Ostgebieten (Braune Mappe)", Berlin April 1942.

99. Sakowska, *Menschen*, p. 46.
100. Roth, *Herrenmenschen*.
101. Walichnowski, *Rozmowy*; Sawicki, *Staatsanwalt*, pp. 246ff.
102. Compare Berg, *Raporty*.
103. Zimmermann, *Kube*; Heiber, "Akten."
104. Gartenschläger, *Stadt*, pp. 31–32.
105. *Warschauer Zeitung*, no. 20, 5.12.1939: "Die Verwaltung des Distrikts Warschau." A comprehensive description from within the administration is available in Gauweiler, *Berichte*. An overview of the structure of the administration is given in Adamska, "Organizacja"; and also in Roth, *Herrenmenschen*, pp. 74–77.
106. BALAA, Ost-Dok. 13/266, Interview with Wilhelm Witte, Bibliotheksverwaltung Warschau, dated 1–2.7.1957.
107. *Warschauer Zeitung*, no. 86, 13.4.1940: "Deutsches Obergericht in Warschau eröffnet."
108. *Warschauer Zeitung*, no. 153, 30.6./1.7.1940: "Die deutsche Staatsanwaltschaft in Warschau."
109. *Warschauer Zeitung*, no. 253, 25.10.1940: "54 Deutsche leiten Warschaus Stadtverwaltung"; Leist, *Bericht*, pp. 282ff.
110. IfZA, Fa 91/4, pp. 866ff., "Bericht Nr. 4 des Beauftragten des Reichsleiters Bormann im OKW, Albert Hoffmann, über Weissruthenien/Minsk", 26.5.1942.
111. Z.B. IfZA, MA 158-1, "Bericht des Distrikts Warschau für Oktober 1940", 15.11.1940: "In den Berichten der Kreishauptleute wird besonders über den Mangel an reichsdeutschem Personal geklagt."
112. BAB, R 5 Anh. I/127, pp. 459ff., "Geschäftsverteilungsplan der Zweigstelle Osten des Reichsverkehrsministeriums in Warschau, gültig ab 1. April 1942"; also *Krakauer Zeitung*, no. 107, 6.5.1943: "Jetzt drei Ostbahndirektionen im GG."
113. Pitschel, *Generaldirektion*, pp. 70ff.
114. Reimer and Kubitzki, *Eisenbahn*, pp. 29, 39ff., 130.
115. IfZA, ED 6-II/33, "Bericht über den Aufbau im Generalgouvernement bis 1. Juli 1940", p. 65.
116. BAB, R 5 Anh. I/144, pp. 1391ff., "Organisatorische und personalstatistische Angaben der RVD Minsk, Stand 1943".
117. AAN, 111/393/6, Internal letter, "Personalamts der Regierung des GG an das Referat Soziale Betreuung", 25.11.1943.
118. For Warsaw, see Kulski, *Zarząd*, pp. 117ff. The work of the Polish utilities for water, gas, and so on, and their "cooperation" with the Germans is described in Gajewski, "Urządzenia."
119. APW, 485/348, Voranschlag zu Einzelplan II Kapitel 1 des Entwurfs des Haushaltsplans des Generalgouvernements für das Rechnungsjahr 1942, Anlage 2.
120. Chiari, *Alltag*, pp. 96ff.; in general, see Rein, *Kings and the Pawns*.
121. Seidel, *Besatzungspolitik*, pp. 57ff.
122. BAL, B 162/AR 179/71, Bd. 8, pp. 1525ff., statement of Theo L. on 6.3.1972.
123. Szarota, *Warschau*, p. 44. On 27.3.1940, the Jewish Council was given a map showing the borders of the future ghetto, and on 1.4.1940 construction work started on the walls.
124. Berenstein, "Schön."
125. Browning, "Ghettoisierungspolitik."
126. Szarota, *Warschau*, pp. 111ff.
127. Browning, "Bürokratie," pp. 52ff.

128. Szarota, *Warschau,* p. 114. In other years the percentages were as follow: 1940 27.9%, 1941 29.7%, 1942 25.8%, 1943 28.6%, 1944 38.5%.

129. On Minsk, see Quinkert, "Terror."

130. On this, see Becker, *Mitstreiter,* pp. 47–69 and 184–185. There is still no study of the Special Courts in the *Generalgouvernement.*

131. On the *Sondergericht* in Warsaw, see BAL, B 162/AR 1391/62, pp. 16ff., "der Staatsanwaltschaft Lübeck", 4.10.1964. On the sentencing of Jews in Warsaw generally, see Grabowski, *Żyda,* pp. 24ff.

132. Sakowska, *Menschen,* pp. 129ff.

133. BAB, R 102 I/15, Personalakte Friedrich Gollert.

134. BAB, BDC, Partei-Kanzlei-file Otto Gauweiler.

135. *Minsker Zeitung,* no. 184, 7.8.1943: "Der NSV-Bahnhofsdienst in Minsk"; and no. 130, 13./14.9.1942: "NSV-Kindergarten in Minsk eröffnet"; *Warschauer Zeitung,* no. 276, 22.11.1940: "Deutscher Kindergarten in Warschau"; and, no. 27, 2.2.1940: "Mütterberatungsstelle in Warschau."

136. *Warschauer Zeitung,* no. 89, 17.4.1940: "Deutsches Krankenhaus in Warschau"; and no. 303, 25.-27.12.1940: "Das deutsche Altersheim in Warschau."

137. *Minsker Zeitung,* no. 84, 22.7.1942: "Die Aufgabe der Frau im Osten."

138. Harvey, *Women,* pp. 192–230.

139. Ibid., pp. 94ff.

140. Ibid., pp. 212ff.

141. E.g., women's sports. *Minsker Zeitung,* no. 84, 22.7.1942: "Die Aufgabe der Frau im Osten. Abteilung 'Frauensport' im Amt 'Wehrmannschaft' gebildet."

142. On the wives of SS-men, see Schwarz, *Frau,* p. 103.

143. Nonetheless the "cult of the mother" also existed in the society of occupation. *Minsker Zeitung,* no. 115, 18.5.1943: "Der Ehrentag der deutschen Mütter."

144. *Minsker Zeitung,* no. 40, 17.2.1943: "'Die deutsche Aufgabe im Osten.' Gauleiter Kube in der ersten Kundgebung deutscher Frauen." See also BAB, R 90/229, "Bericht über die Frauengrosskundgebung in Minsk am 15.2.1943", 20.2.1943.

145. Gartenschläger, *Stadt,* p. 65; Chiari, *Alltag,* p. 61.

146. For Minsk, *Mitteilungsblatt des Reichskommissars für das Ostland,* Nr. 36 vom 7.10.1942, pp. 158–159, Runderlass des RKO vom 29.9.1942.

147. BAB, R 90/229, GK Weissruthenien to RKO, 10.8.1942.

148. BAB, R 48/33, Reichspostminister to Generalpostkommissare, 18.8.1941.

149. See chapter 4, this volume.

150. The *Stadthauptmann* gives the figure of 9,130 ethnic Germans for March 1942; in view of the declining rate of increase one year later it would have been well over 10,000. Leist, *Bericht,* p. 51. On the numbers of ethnic Germans in prewar Poland, see Janusz, "Regelungen," pp. 133–134.

151. Szarota, *Warschau,* pp. 252 and 257; Gerlach, *Morde,* p. 124. In the latter can be found for 1.3.1943, the figures of 2,446 ethnic Germans in the city of Minsk and 1,627 in (Rayon) Minsk-Land. Also see *Minsker Zeitung,* no. 164, 23.10.1942: "Holz—Kartoffeln—Federbetten. Über 500 volksdeutsche Familien werden von der NSV für den Winter versorgt."

152. Bergen, "Concept," pp. 569–571.

153. Janusz, " Regelungen," p. 136.

154. IPN, 694/20. Applications received by the Stadthauptmannschaft Warschau for the issuing of ID cards for those with German roots for the letters A-B, D-F, H, J-M and O, June 1942 to July 1944. In total from this group 3,445 applications were received, of which 406 were denied, although not all cases bear a processing stamp. Thus the denial rate was 11.78 percent. A somewhat higher figure is given by Leist, *Bericht,* p. 51, but these numbers are for March 1942 and in the following years almost all applications were approved. The

generous rate of selection is generally valid; see Strippel, *NS-Volkstumspolitik*, pp. 122–125, 216–218; Wolf, *Ideologie und Herrschaftsrationalität*, p. 421.

155. Gerlach, *Morde*, p. 124.
156. Ibid., p. 125.
157. Leist, *Bericht*, p. 117.
158. Ibid.
159. AAN, 116/38, Rundschreiben no. 13/42, NSDAP-Distriktstandortführung Warschau, 6.3.1942.
160. APW, 482/1228, "Monatsberichte der Deutschen Oberschule", October 1941–May 1944.
161. Bergen, *Volksdeutschen*, pp. 72–73.
162. *Warschauer Zeitung*, no. 100, 30.4.1940: "Deutschtumsfeier in Warschau."
163. *Warschauer Zeitung*, no. 232, 1.10.1940: "Volksdeutsche danken der Wehrmacht."
164. *Krakauer Zeitung*, no. 154, 4.7.1941: "Starker Zulauf zur Deutschen Gemeinschaft."
165. Jockheck, *Propaganda*, p. 99.
166. Lehnstaedt, "Volksdeutsche," pp. 437–438.
167. Jansen and Weckbecker, *Selbstschutz*, p. 210.
168. Ibid., p. 195.
169. *Warschauer Zeitung*, no. 106, 8.5.1940: "Kameradschaftsheim der Selbstschutzmänner."
170. *Warschauer Zeitung*, no. 165, 14./15.7.1940: "Neues Heim des Warschauer Selbstschutzes."
171. Jansen and Weckbecker, *Selbstschutz*, pp. 74–75.
172. Bergen, *Volksdeutschen*, pp. 75ff.
173. *Warschauer Zeitung*, no. 36, 23.12.1939: "Volksdeutsche Fragen im Distrikt Warschau." On the necessity of providing support services for women, see *Warschauer Zeitung*, no. 146, 22.6.1940: "Deutsche Frauenarbeit im Distrikt Warschau." In general, see Lehnstaedt, "Volksdeutsche," pp. 433–436.
174. AAN, 116/38, "Rundschreiben Nr. 13/42", NSDAP-Distriktstandortführung Warschau, 6.3.1942.
175. *Warschauer Zeitung*, no. 99, 28./29.3.1940: "Das Albert-Breyer-Haus eröffnet."
176. Rogall, *Land*, p. 425. See, also, *Warschauer Zeitung*, no. 100, 30.4.1940: "Deutschtumsfeier in Warschau."
177. APW, 486/48, "Rundschreiben Nr. 12/41", NSDAP-Distriktstandortführung Warschau, 21.3.1941. *Krakauer Zeitung*, no. 58, 13.3.1941: "Volksdeutsche Gemeinschaft geht in NSDAP auf."
178. For Warsaw, see Leist, *Bericht*, pp. 88ff.
179. AAN, 116/17, "Personalaufstellung der NSDAP *Distrikt* Warschau", 1.6.1942.
180. *Warschauer Zeitung*, no. 276, 22.11.1940: "Deutscher Kindergarten in Warschau." On the role of the kindergartens in the germanization of the East and their personnel, see Harvey, *Women*, pp. 232ff.
181. *Warschauer Zeitung*, no. 21, 6.12.1939: "Erster deutscher Schultag in Warschau."
182. *Warschauer Zeitung*, no. 107, 9.5.1940: "Deutsche Oberschule auch in Warschau."
183. IfZA, Fb 63/29, "Monatsbericht des Distriktgouverneurs Warschau für Januar 1942", 10.2.1942. On the schoolsystem in Warsaw, see Leist, *Bericht*, pp. 144ff.
184. *Warschauer Zeitung*, no. 14, 28.11.1939: "Der Generalgouverneur eröffnet in Warschau die erste deutsche Schule".
185. Kleßmann, *Selbstbehauptung*, pp. 48ff.
186. BALAA, Ost-Dok. 8/830, pp. 2ff., "Bericht von Dr. Paul Gruschinske, Regierungsdirektor und Leiter der Abteilung Wissenschaft und Unterricht im Distrikt Warschau", n.d.
187. Dean, *Robbing*, p. 188; Lehnstaedt, "Volksdeutsche," pp. 441–446.
188. APW, 49/94, "Verfügung des KdS Warschau", 27.7.1940.

189. APW, 496/34. Various reports by German companies in Warsaw, August 1942.
190. BaySta, Staatsanwaltschaften 34761/10.
191. On the introduction of *Arbeitspflicht* (the duty to work), see *Krakauer Zeitung*, no. 76, 28.3.1943: "Was wollen sie denn arbeiten?"
192. IPN, 106/22, "Vermerk der Abteilung Justiz des *Distrikts* Warschau", 14.2.1941, and Eitner to Abteilung Justiz, 3.6.1941.
193. IfZA, MA 1790/3; 378-1-28, OT-Frontführung Weißruthenien to Wehrmachtskommandantur Minsk, 28.8.43.
194. BA-LAA, Ost-Dok. 8/828, pp. 4ff., Testimony of Wilhelm Freter, Kommandeur Rüstungsbereich Warschau, 12.10.1954. Additional companies are named in Sakowska, *Menschen*, pp. 255–256. On the most important ghetto factory, Toebbens, see Tusk-Scheinwechslerowa, "Fabryka."
195. BAL, B 162/AR 179/71, Bd. 4, pp. 863ff., Interrogation of Lothar S., 1.9.1971.
196. *Krakauer Zeitung*, no. 167, 19.7.1941: "Deutsche Lebensmittelgeschäfte in Warschau."
197. Leist, *Bericht*, p. 65.
198. *Warschauer Zeitung*, no. 20, 5.12.1939: "Die Verwaltung des *Distrikts* Warschau."
199. APW, 496/32, "Verzeichnis der dt. Aktiengesellschaften mit Sitz im Distrikt Warschau", n.d. [1939/early 1940].
200. APW, 643/1322 (new: 1105), "Urteil des Sondergerichts Warschau in der Strafsache gegen den *Volksdeutschen* Eitel-Friedrich Bonk", 20.7.1943.
201. Morawski, *1939*, p. 7. The photographs in the book give a good impression of the destruction in Warsaw as the Germans saw it at the time.
202. APW, 485/333, "Bericht des Wohnungsamtes Warschau", 15.7.1942.
203. For Warsaw, see DTA, 280/I, diary Franz Jonas, 3.8.1941 (the quote is from here). See also the pictures of Hermann Beyerlein in Jaworski and Peters, *Alltagsperspektiven*, pp. 43–46. For Minsk, e.g., see DTA, 884, diary Michael Ritter, 30.10.1943; BfZg, Slg. Sterz, letter by Hauptmann Hermann Göbel,13.8.1941.
204. BfZg, Slg. Sterz, letter by Leutnant Helmut Hänsel,14.7.1941: "What made a deep impression on me, was that Minsk was almost completely burned down. We are arguing among ourselves, whether the Russians had set it ablaze or our fliers had done it. Views differ on this point."
205. *Minsker Zeitung*, no. 146, 3.10.1942: "HBD richtet Omnibuslinie ein." There it reads, "Every two hours a bus drives through the ruined city.'"
206. See, e.g., BfZg, Slg. Sterz, letter by Hauptmann Hermann Göbel,13.8.1941.
207. *Minsker Zeitung*, no. 39, 30.5.1942: "Behebung der Wohnungsnot."
208. IfZA, MA 1790/11; NARB, 370-1-486, Kube to Janetzke,20.11.1942.
209. *Warschauer Zeitung*, no. 245, 16.10.1940: "Deutsches Viertel in Warschau." It is significant that the article, which also announced the establishment of the ghetto, depicted only the ghetto on a map; the borders of the German residential quarter were only very vaguely described in words, and were not included on the map.
210. BAB, R 6/260, pp. 2–3, Reichskanzlei to RMbO, 15.8.1944.
211. *Krakauer Zeitung*, no. 104, 2.5.1942: "Umsiedlung in den deutschen Wohnbezirk. Anträge sind beim zuständigen Warschauer Standort der NSDAP zu melden."
212. Szarota, *Warschau*, p. 252.
213. APW, 485/333, "Anordnung über die Bildung des deutschen Wohngebietes im Stadtgebiet Warschau", 6.2.1943.
214. APW, 485/332, placard appeal: "An alle Deutschen Warschaus," n.d. [1943].
215. Szarota, *Warschau*, p. 253.
216. APW, 485/334, Wohnungsamtes des Stadthauptmann to Distriktgouverneur, 15.5.1942.
217. APW, 485/333, report, Wohnungsamt Warschau, 15.7.1942; ibid., report, 31.12.1942.

218. APW, 485/333, "Bericht des Wohnungsamtes für den Monat Mai 1943", n.d.
219. APW, 485/333, report, Wohnungsamt Warschau, 15.7.1942.
220. *Minsker Zeitung*, no. 136, 20./21.9.1942: "Umsiedlungen in der Stadt."
221. Gutschow and Klain, *Vernichtung*, pp. 28ff.
222. Ibid., p. 121.
223. Gollert, *Grundsätzliche*, as cited by Gutschow and Klain, *Vernichtung*, pp. 129–130.
224. BAB, R 102 I/1, p. 45, "Erlass des Distriktgouverneurs Warschau", 4.5.1942.
225. *Warschauer Zeitung*, no. 129, 2./3.6.1940: "Deutsche Straßennamen in Warschau." See also *Mitteilungsblatt der Stadt Warschau*, no. 17, 30.5.1940, pp. 2–3: Bekanntmachung, 24.5.1940.
226. *Warschauer Zeitung*, no. 203, 28.8.1940: "Weihe der Adolf-Hitler-Plätze."
227. *Minsker Zeitung*, no. 78, 1.4.1944: "Alte Straßen—neue Namen."
228. *Minsker Zeitung*, no. 264, 9.11.1943: "Gauleiter-Kube-Platz in Minsk."
229. Szarota, *Warschau*, pp. 39–40.
230. *Minsker* [!] *Zeitung*, no. 13, 29.4.1942: "Lautsprecheranlage in Warschau." In 1940 a provisional system had already been erected in Warsaw, which, however, was not adequate for the Germans' demanding propaganda requirements, see *Warschauer Zeitung*, no. 176, 27.7.1940: "Warschau erhielt eine Grosslautsprecheranlage."
231. *Warschauer Zeitung*, no. 11, 14./15.1.1940: "Keine Todesanzeigen mehr an den Häusern."
232. *Warschauer Zeitung*, no. 135, 9./10.6.1940: "Ausbau des Warschauer Hauptbahnhofs."
233. *Warschauer Zeitung*, no. 79, 5.4.1940: "Warschaus Parks werden wieder hergerichtet."
234. *Warschauer Zeitung*, no. 267, 12.11.1940: "Warschau erhielt eine deutsche Apotheke." On the pharmacies in Generalkommissariat Weißruthenien, see *Amtsblatt des Reichsministers für die besetzten Ostgebiete*, no. 10, 23.10.1943, pp. 75–76, "Runderlass des Ostministeriums", 15.10.1943.
235. *Krakauer Zeitung*, no. 71, 28.3.1941: "Warschau erhielt ein deutsches Kaufhaus."
236. *Krakauer Zeitung*, no. 167, 19.7.1941: "Deutsche Lebensmittelgeschäfte in Warschau." See also chapter 1 section 4, this volume.
237. *Verordnungsblatt für das Generalgouvernement*, no. 8, 30.11.1939, pp. 61–62. The Hebraic script was of the type used whenever the Nazis wanted to defame the Jews. An infamous example is the poster for the film *Jud Süss*.
238. APW, 485/333, "Bericht des Wohnungsamtes Warschau", 31.5.1943.
239. APW, 485/333, "Aufstellung der dem Civil-Quartieramt zur Verfügung stehenden Zimmer, im Juli 1942". Only a few of the hotels listed here offered a room with a bath. It was customary at this time for toilet and bath facilities to serve residents of an entire floor.
240. APW, 496/114, "Verzeichnis der Lokale und Gaststätten in Warschau, die für Wehrmacht, SS und Polizei zugelassen sind", 1941.
241. APW, 482/13, "Merkblatt des Chefs des *Distrikts* Warschau", 8.12.1940.
242. *Minsker Zeitung*, no. 74, 10.7.1942: "Probefahrt der Straßenbahn."
243. *Minsker Zeitung*, no. 116, 19.5.1943: "Straßenbahn der Minsker Stadtverwaltung in Betrieb."
244. *Minsker Zeitung*, no. 146, 3.10.1942: "HBD richtet Omnibuslinie ein"; *Minsker Zeitung*, no. 150, 7.10.1942: "Der Minsker Omnibusverkehr."
245. *Warschauer Zeitung*, no. 122, 25.5.1940: "Täglich 800 Arbeiter, 120 Fahrzeuge eingesetzt."
246. AAN, T 501-228/901, Kommandanturbefehl Warschau no. 169, n.d. [August 1940].
247. APW, 482/794, "Rundschreiben des *Distrikts*", 21.4.1942.
248. AAN, T 501-228/1263, Kommandanturbefehl Warschau no. 43, 26.2.1940.
249. *Minsker Zeitung*, no. 77, 1.4.1943: "Neue Sperrstunden für Einheimische."
250. AAN, T 501-228/1166, Kommandanturbefehl Warschau no. 73, 4.4.1940; APW, 486/1165, "Anordnung des SSPF Warschau", 5.12.1942.

251. IfZA, MA 1790/3; 379-2-45, "Merkblatt für Soldaten und Einheiten im Standort Minsk", September 1941; AAN, T 501-228/1000-1001, Kommandanturbefehl Warschau no. 126, 25.6.1940.
252. *Amtsblatt der Reichsverkehrsdirektion Minsk*, no. 15, 20.3.1944.
253. The placards are in Blättler, *Warschau*, pp. 64ff.
254. Szarota, *Warschau*, pp. 247ff.
255. See chapters 2 section 3 and section 4, this volume.
256. Szarota, *Warschau*, p. 257. The number is for August 1941.
257. Alvensleben, "Abschiede," pp. 141ff.
258. In general, see Hosenfeld, "Retten."
259. *Minsker Zeitung*, no. 103, 13.8.1942: "'Nix ponemai' und trotzdem Ordnung. Kleiner Morgenbesuch bei der Minsker Stadt-Schutzmannschaft."
260. Sakowska, *Menschen*, p. 243; and in general Podolska, *Służba*.
261. Szarota, *Warschau*, p. 293.
262. BAB, R 93/1, p. 62, GK Minsk to Personalabteilung der Regierung des GG, 13.4.1943.
263. Trunk, *Judenrat*, p. 261.
264. Fuks, *Getto*, pp. 155–156, Tagebucheintrag vom 28.5.1941.

Chapter 2

DAILY LIFE PRESCRIBED BY NORMS

Chapter 1 demonstrates that, right up to the highest level of leadership, the Germans in Warsaw and Minsk came from all classes, backgrounds, and regions. Different combinations of all three could be found in their personal histories, and nothing in their personalities specifically and inherently qualified them for deployment to the East or predestined them to commit war crimes. The answer to the question of how the mass killing of the local population was nevertheless possible should therefore be sought in the processes and situations in the East that turned the occupiers into murderers.[1]

Sociological studies have shown that "in situations in which individuals experience significant social uncertainty, they reject their individual frames of reference and try to orient themselves according to predominant group norms. The greater this uncertainty becomes, and the more unaccustomed the circumstances are, the more fully they seek to conform with the group."[2] The disorientation that accompanied the new realities in the East was an essential part of the Germans' experience of being part of the occupation. None of these men and women had ever found themselves in such a situation before; it was in every way a unique and totally new experience. The familiar surroundings had been replaced by an alien-threatening environment, and there were new official duties and an unfamiliar social context. Their once-helpful beliefs and behavioral norms had lost, in these extreme circumstances, most of their utility. This demanded a new framework for decision-making, the reorientation of values, and adaptation to the changed realities.

Nonetheless, people's reactions to a given situation cannot easily be reduced to the implementation of laws and rules: individuals do not act on theories, but instead develop their own social adaptations. Their actions are determined less by logic or intention and more by the practical demands of reality. The social context and immediate circumstances set limits on action while providing behavioral patterns around which the actor orientates himself, and to which he is to a large extent bound. Social reality is, for this reason, not exclusively the result of individual will, but also the result of the structural conditions of society. Individuals act on the basis of these ongoing internal adaptations.[3] They were scarcely able to escape these rules because if they did they faced sanctions and exclusion from their social network.

These social structures and functions are, however, only relevant insofar as they have something to do with the real lives of the actors. Official laws that are ignored collectively, for example, have hardly any significance for how people act; on the other hand, the tolerated crossing of fixed written norms does have real consequences. It would be one-sided to try to explain the behavior of individuals in a given situation only from their social background. Much more important is how their understanding of their immediate circumstances causes them to act.[4] The present plays a much greater role in this situational behavior than previous experiences.

1. Official Duties

But how does the world change if the conditions for action, on the one hand, are given, and on the other hand are always being newly created and transformed? We can attempt to answer this question using insights from clearly defined categories such as norms and deviance from the norm, but the much more differentiated realities of everyday life remain predominant.[5] Even clearly defined roles in an office or a barrack were subject to adaptation: daily life at work is determined not only by a job's stated requirements, but also through relations with colleagues, the mood in the workplace, or even the office decor. All these aspects can be influenced by individuals and at the same time are strongly constrained by rules and superiors.

That thereby self-perceptions can completely coincide with the external prescriptions, comprised of the intentions and interpretations of Nazis, is scarcely surprising. Nazi propaganda focused mainly on praise and always emphasized its successes; at least in public no criticism was voiced of its own institutions. For example, in Distrikt Warschau the work done was described by General Governor Hans Frank as distinguished by the "greatness of that already achieved." He observed that the "comradely" Nazi spirit "would never be [stifled] by bureaucratic narrow-mindedness." In his opinion the occupiers conducted their work "as a proud duty," which is made possible by "nurturing the spirit as … self-education."[6] This kind of propaganda existed in various forms—sometimes much more subtle—for all parts of the society of occupation, including for the Wehrmacht.[7] The contents were similar and confined themselves mostly to characterizing service as "fulfilling duty to the last, absolute discipline, and honest comradeship."[8] In view of the alien environment, qualities such as comradeship or obedient service were values with which most Germans identified and had already assimilated,[9] even if they did not accept all the interpretations and consequences on which the local leaders based them.

In reality, one cannot put any special meaning on fulfilment of duty because it was much too imprecise a value. Most Germans claimed to have performed their service correctly and diligently. Here there was no difference to their previous work in the Reich, since it was naturally also expected of them there. A colonel, such as Carl von Andrian, deployed in Minsk, had, for example, a "lot of paperwork" to get done, work that clearly was less interesting to him than, say, inspections or commanding his subordinates.[10] His daily schedule was shaped by the routine of an officer who constantly had to deal with similar problems to his troops. For instance, the office rooms were lacking in furniture and ovens so he constantly had to improvise; especially in winter the cold made the daily service routine difficult.[11] The senior lieutenant and later captain, Wilm Hosenfeld, describes his service in Warsaw as a series of constant patrols, office work, and meetings.[12] Ultimately, on account of his previous training as a school teacher, he was able to rise to the head of soldiers' education, in which he was able to organize his training center relatively independently. A simple soldier, however, had no such possibility to avoid unwelcome activities or to take on responsibility in a leading position. He was mostly deployed in barracks in Warsaw or Minsk and there endured almost constant drill; in addition, he was responsible only for cleaning, cooking, and similar tasks. The signalman Franz Jonas was assigned in Poland to listen to enemy communications; as Warsaw was only a transit point for him, he experienced his time there mainly as a burden, waiting to see what would come next.[13] This uncertainty was typical for many soldiers in the two cities, where they spent a few months away from the front. Here they had a comparatively pleasant and, above all, safe life, but could never know how long this would last and where they would be sent next. So Franz Jonas envied his comrades who were sent to Brussels in the West, while he did not see as desirable deployments to the Eastern Front.[14]

Those deployed to Minsk or Warsaw as soldiers had little free time. The tasks conducted by the Wehrmacht consisted mainly of guard duty and patrols that took place at all times of the day and night. It was similar for units of the SS and police that were based in barracks. However, the work rhythm was different for the civil servants and employees who worked in the various administrative offices. In Distrikt Warschau German employees worked fifty-three hours a week. Work started every day at 7:00 A.M. and finished usually at 5:00 P.M., and at 4:00 P.M. on Wednesdays. There was a half-hour break for lunch. On Saturdays they worked only until 1:30 P.M. In winter, in order to save energy, the office buildings were generally open only until 4:30 P.M.[15] The leisure time of civil servants and employees was therefore much greater than that of the soldiers and policemen based in barracks. At least in the evenings and on Sundays the men regularly had the opportunity to escape from the strong influence of norms in government service and from their superiors.

During office hours there were also numerous meetings, roll calls, and other communal office events, such as *Werkpausenprogramme* (work-break programs)[16] that officials and employees had to attend. For example, the main office of the Ostbahn organized a concert in the large locomotive shed during the lunch break on September 17, 1943, for all those employed at the Ostbahnhof Warschau (Railway Station Warsaw-East). Germans and Poles listened together to a concert with waltzes and peasant dances from the opera *Halka* and a rhapsody by Liszt.[17] The presentation was counted as work time, and therefore it was everyone's duty to be present. This can be viewed as a disruption of the service routine ordered by the management; that this was perceived to be particularly pleasant is doubtful. Numerous signs that participation in the event was not voluntary confirm its compulsory nature[18]—and duty, unlike leisure time, does not permit one to determine one's own actions, but is perceived as being regimented and almost impossible to influence. Therefore, these ordered celebrations were only another variant of normed daily life.

In the overall picture, the significance of service duties for the daily lives of the occupiers should not be overestimated: for most people influences from outside of work were very important. Even in Warsaw and Minsk, leisure time, in contrast to work, offered the possibility to do things that each individual could largely decide for themselves. But in contrast to the Reich, in the society of occupiers one's work colleagues were mostly the same people with whom one spent one's free time. The relationships or animosities established there had consequences not only for service matters, such as the behavior of supervisors, but also for very banal things, like relaxation and distractions. This is shown in exemplary fashion in the memoirs of the policeman Otto Nahlmann. He reports that his guard duty at the Bank Polski (Bank of Poland) in Warsaw was "boring. The checks were always conducted very precisely."[19] The process was normed and subjected to strict regularity; a certain fear of the supervisors also came with it in his case. Here it appears that the conditions of service were considerably less important than the non-service-related framework: he remembers and communicates his experiences in a foreign city and with comrades in detail, but not his work routine. These comments apply for almost all ego documents, such that for the reconstruction and reception of daily life in service, at least in part, there is a problem with regard to sources. From this discovery it can be established at least that the events were not considered worth reporting, because they were routine and monotonous and because this sameness was not seen to be any different from in the Reich.

2. In the Residential Homes: Rooms, Canteen, and Comradeship Evenings

The daily lives of the occupiers were not only strictly regulated by norms during work hours, but also there were restrictions that applied to their time after work, especially if one considers how the Germans were accommodated. Only a few had their own apartments; most were housed in barracks or shared apartments in hostels. In these buildings, where the segregation according to service office was maintained, it was common for work colleagues to share a place to live. In addition, they ate together in canteens that were frequently located in the hostels. Beyond these conditions, which considerably limited one's self-determination over the time after work, there were also the *Kameradschaftsabende* (comradeship evenings) that brought colleagues together again in a more or less predetermined context.

Compared to the situation at work, the occupiers' individual wills played a greater role in the hostels; despite the presence of a certain group dynamic that made participation in the communal meals and comradeship evenings more or less compulsory, no regulations existed to enforce this. One could influence things and even express a certain degree of criticism, but the norms still outweighed self-will. Typical examples were the canteens, such as the SS canteen on Polizeistraße. Policeman Heinz M., who was deployed in Warsaw, reports that he and his colleagues ate breakfast, lunch, and dinner in this canteen; they also celebrated Christmas, New Year, and other holidays there.[20] Canteens catered exclusively for members of their own institutions; visiting another canteen was not permitted. The railwaymen-canteen in Warsaw-Praga issued large portions known as *Distrikt* rations to its workers, but for railwaymen from outside the local office there were the Wehrmacht-rations, which were also generous.

Patrons were permitted to exert a limited and carefully regulated influence on what was served in the canteen. The competence of the refectory committee, which consisted of five men of various ranks, was confined, however, mainly to planning the menu, which was not always easy due to food rationing. Apart from that, it was responsible for responding to complaints because the quality of canteen food did not always please everyone. *Amtsgerichtsrat* (Senior Court Official) Franz Wiesmann complained in February 1941 to the offices of the Distrikt Warschau administration about the quality of the food in the *Kasino* in the German House; he also criticized the slow and unfriendly service. Significantly, such initiatives, which were expressed in the form of a critical letter, were not welcome. After Governor Fischer had seen the letter, the Justice Department replied to Wiesmann two weeks later: "The Governor has ordered that, on account of the tone and contents of your letter, you are barred from the communal kitchen with immediate effect."[21] In an internal memorandum, however, Wiesmann's criticism was considered justified. The office followed up the complaint and effected an improvement; all the same, the case of the lawyer was seen as a problem. His divergence from the norm, which did not intend such an approach, led to further sanctions: Wiesmann was advised to ask for a transfer. His exclusion from the community and the resulting bad relations with his superiors caused the *Amtsgerichtsrat* to apply for a transfer in May 1941.[22]

In practice it would have been difficult for Wiesmann to meet Germans outside the refectory that could have provided him with company at mealtimes. To have one's own kitchen would also have been unimaginable, for this was available in only very few quarters—precisely because there were communal dining facilities. The canteens were very inexpensive, and on account of their semi-official status, they were the place where the occupiers ate almost all of their meals. Restaurants were not very common and the gastronomic offerings were restricted only to drinking and amusement houses, in which at best, and only in exceptional cases, food could be eaten—and certainly not before dinner in the evening. Here the prices were considerably higher; due to rationing, individuals had to use coupons, whereas in the canteen their charges would have been settled up automatically by their office. Therefore, the authorities' expectations, expressed mainly through the compulsion of group dynamics, as well as simple practicality, both spoke in favor of using the refectories. Precisely when eating without compulsion, one had the opportunity to make informal agreements and nurture contacts to other sections that were so vital within any office.[23]

Apart from encouraging solidarity among the Germans, canteens and hostels also had the important function of "binding them to the accommodation."[24] Especially in Warsaw this seemed necessary to the *Distrikt* administration and the Wehrmacht commandant's office because they viewed the city as a kind of den of iniquity, in which there were many possibilities for distraction that did not correspond with the moral precepts the regime sought to propagate. The interior decor of the refectories, therefore, had to be as pleasant as possible, in order to counteract other attractions, such as Polish women or alcohol, and thereby deter any contact with the local population.[25] For this reason, the KdO wanted to expand and renovate the lounges and dining rooms for his men so that they would spend their free time in their own hostel rather than elsewhere.[26]

At the Post Office staff usually had lunch in the dining room on the fifth floor of the employees' hostel on Chmielnastraße, but they picked up breakfast and dinner from the canteen to eat it in their rooms. In the postmen's house, too, originally built in 1936 for training Polish postal officials, the rooms were not to the satisfaction of the German head of the office. The kitchen was far too small because it was intended for the preparation of just one meal per day. It had to be expanded so that the men could be fed in their own hostel; this was the only way to ensure that they would gladly spend more of their time under the oversight of their supervisors.[27]

Precisely for this reason, the residential quarters were often equipped with other facilities, such as craft workshops or a shop. The Distrikt Warschau administration made it possible for its officials to buy soap, razors, and other items needed for daily use there, but also offered sweets, vegetables, and fruit.[28] The Security Police (Sipo) on Polizeistraße even went so far as to run a barber's shop. This became necessary when the Order Police refused to grant their colleagues in the Sipo access to their own hair salon. The main reason for this, however, was to ensure that the policemen did not visit Polish barbers. Significantly, the business was established in a former Jewish barber's shop which had been "secured for this purpose"—that is, confiscated.[29] As a result of all these measures, daily life in the East was subjected to norms to a much greater extent than had ever been the case in the Reich; the civilian and military institutions sought to organize the entire daily routine of the occupiers.

The number and configuration of the available rooms was especially significant because the men and women were supposed to spend all of their spare time here that was not taken up by group activities or sleeping. Most accommodations consisted of one completely furnished room, usually intended for at least two people (see figure 2.1). These rooms were equipped with beds, a table, chairs, and cupboards, but no cooking facilities or bathroom. The main differences compared to the barracks, where the Wehrmacht and most policemen were accommodated, lay in the number of occupants per room, usually between four and six for the lower ranks of civilian officials, as well as in the furnishing of the rooms. In addition, for civilians most of the norms did not take the form of written orders, but rather were of an informal character. The totalitarian claims made on a soldier's lifestyle could not be enforced for civil servants and other gov-

Figure 2.1. The Residential Hostel on Karowastraße: Single Apartment
Source: Gollert, *Warschau*, p. 265.

ernment employees; at least officially it was left up to them to decide how they were housed and spent their free time. Even if in practice the civilians still lived a daily life largely regulated by norms, the occupiers who lived in barracks were subjected to considerably more restrictions.

Yet despite many attempts to improve things, only rarely did it feel "almost like home."[30] When, for example, 127 postal officials were accommodated in rooms with two or more beds, this was nothing like a homely apartment—even for Hermann Beyerlein, the head of the Telegraphenamt (Telegraph Office), who subsequently shared with his wife a large official apartment that had three and a half rooms.[31] In the residential hostels there was constant observation by a supervisor who insisted on the maintenance of cleanliness, discipline, and order. The reality of such lodgings differed quite considerably from the propaganda-image of comfort that was announced during the unavoidable ceremonies on the completion of construction or their official opening.[32] Especially in Minsk, quarters that were too small and inadequately heated were the rule rather than the exception. For example, the SS moved into four wooden barracks in Minsk that were scarcely capable of offering adequate protection against the raw weather conditions in the winter.[33] In the *Haus des Generalkommissariats* (housing for officials of the General Commissar's Office) the heating was better, but the room furnishings were substandard.[34] In the Wehrmacht, Colonel

Carl von Andrian confided in his diary that he found his room—which in terms of size and equipment was of a considerably better standard than for ordinary soldiers—"extremely uncomfortable."³⁵

And yet the Germans lived luxuriously in comparison to the locals. For instance, the Distrikt Warschau administration looked after its employees in a model fashion, not only providing apartments, but also refurbishing them. The senior officials in residential hostels generally received a furnished apartment that had been decorated. The department heads in the *Distrikt*, the directors of independent offices, as well as several other senior officials, received two rooms. The Hauptabteilung Finanzen (Main Department for Finance) in the General Government ordered in April 1941 that the total costs for furnishing a room should not exceed 2,500 Złoty. For the second room, an additional 1,700 Złoty could be spent. In order to get around these restrictions, the free distribution of furniture was customary, especially in Warsaw. These items came from confiscated, mostly Jewish, property.³⁶

Much value was placed on the decoration of the residential hostels for female government employees. Their lodgings and protection was given special attention by the occupiers, because under no circumstances were single women to reside alone: this would have been irreconcilable with contemporary moral expectations. For this reason the houses were furnished by the relevant authorities in cooperation with the Nazi Party's *Frauenamt* (women's office), but only after the residential homes for men had been completed. The Eastern Railway, for example, did not open its house for fifty-one women in Warsaw, where everyone was to get a single room, until October 1943; the house had been used as a residential hostel prior to this, so renovations were mainly necessary only for the communal areas. These differed clearly from the lodgings for men because sewing machines formed part of the standard equipment designed to meet the special needs of women.³⁷

In Minsk the female railway workers lived in less comfort. In August 1942 there were 130 women there, employed by the Reichsbahn Hauptverwaltung (Main Office). They were accommodated in a wing of the Reichsbahn tower. They also had washing and ironing facilities, but in contrast to Warsaw, only shared dormitories for four to six women, and only one common room. The Nazi women's leader, Elisabeth Morsbach, wanted to improve the living conditions by hanging curtains in the rooms, since "the city offered no possibilities for sitting together in comfort" and much time was spent in the rooms. In another house, twenty-two women were to be accommodated, so that those born between 1917 and 1923 could all sleep under one roof. The female railway workers in Minsk had to be fed separately. For this a second manager of the hostel was requested because the difficulties in obtaining food otherwise required the preparation of communal meals.³⁸ A second hostel for women, however, was never opened. An *Oberregierungsrat* (senior official) in the Eastern Ministry (RMbO) commented in his report about a visit to Weißruthenien: "The female employees, some of whom have been in Minsk for more than a year [had resisted] being forced to leave the apartments in their current lodgings, which they had spent great effort in furnishing. Until now they have lived in the same building as the male employees of their office or section."³⁹ The women's stubbornness saved them from undesired changes in their lodgings.

The troops had a particular type of communal quarters. Their barracks provided only a limited degree of comfort. As a substitute, *Soldatenheime* (Soldiers' Homes) were established that did not contain lodgings, but that provided a safe place for eating and amusement. They were intended for soldiers who went for a stroll through the city in their free time and neither wanted to enter a private restaurant nor return to the barracks, just to get something to eat or meet with comrades. Like the residential hostels, the actual intention was to get the soldiers off the streets and offer them a leisure program circumscribed by norms under controlled conditions.

In Warsaw one of the two Soldiers' Homes was centrally located on the Drei-Kreuz-Platz in the representative building of a former girls' high school; this had become available once the occupiers had abolished advanced schooling for the local population in 1939.⁴⁰ The building contained not only a dining room that had been decorated by the Munich artist Helgo Pohle and that could seat 180 people, but also a games room, a reading room, and a separate café.⁴¹ The house was praised by one visitor as "wonderfully decorated" and as a "highlight" of the city.⁴² The second home had been established in 1939 directly next to the Commandant's Office on Adolf-Hitler-Platz—that is, also in the center of the city. Here there were similar facilities, but also an orchestra played daily during meal times. In addition, the home offered beds for three hundred individual soldiers in transit, who could thereby avoid using a hotel, where they might have escaped the social control of the Wehrmacht. The degree of comfort, however, left something to be desired: during the first years of the war there were no showers in the bathrooms.⁴³

In Minsk the Wehrmacht became heir to the Soviet Union, at least with regard to the rooms it inherited: on the conquest of the city it took over the Red Army House and renovated it for the use of its own soldiers; an additional home was added in 1943.⁴⁴ The intended functions of these buildings scarcely differed from those of their counterparts in Warsaw. Their propagandistic marketing, however, was somewhat different: in Poland it had stressed comfort and, above all, cleanliness, whereas in

Weißruthenien more was made of the Soviets' strict segregation of officers and men, providing no equal treatment for those who shared the same fate. In contrast to the supposedly egalitarian Soviet Union, the people's community of the Third Reich kept its promise of true comradeship. In addition, it was notable that as servers for the German soldiers, "70 fresh, young Belorussian girls" were waiting.[45] In view of the lower racial barriers compared to Poland, such an advertisement was acceptable—and promised success. In the General Government the authorities endeavored to employ only ethnic German waitresses.

Just as the soldiers' homes were open to all members of the Wehrmacht, for the other occupiers there were *Deutsche Häuser* (German Houses), which were always in representative buildings, but rarely as impressive as those in Warsaw.[46] There the Palais Radziwiłł, built in 1655, and prior to the war the Cabinet's Residence, had been selected (see figure 2.2). This imposing building, situated on Krakauer Vorstadt in the city center, had suffered some bomb damage in the fall of 1939, but the occupiers had immediately begun its restoration that same year. As this proceeded, the German House was opened for use section by section, starting with the left wing that had twenty-eight rooms and a café.[47] Most rooms were fully furnished and permanently in use for housing officials of the *Distrikt* administration, but in principle the Haus was open to all Germans from 8:00 P.M., so they could meet one another and spend time together, without having to rely on restaurants or visiting the Polish amusement houses. On account of the clearly stated claim made in its name, the *Distrikt* administration

Figure 2.2. The German House in Warsaw (Radziwiłł Palace)
Source: Gollert, *Warschau*, p. 39.

spared no expense or effort in refurbishing this highly symbolic palace. Therefore, it comes as no surprise that General Governor Hans Frank was present for the official opening in January 1941, and that he gave a speech explaining the building's function: "The bond of our common blood must unite all of the people here ... so the German House in Warsaw should set an example for the attainment of a Nazi sociability, it should serve the creation of a new social version of our shared community values."[48]

These far-reaching ideological claims could not be matched in reality. After its completion the building served mainly as the central canteen for all officials and employees in public service in Warsaw. The two dining rooms, as well as several clubrooms and cafés, catered to the physical well-being of the occupiers. Representative halls for banquets, concerts, and meetings stood next to simple rooms with facilities for the men to play billiards and table tennis, a small library, as well as beer and wine bars (see figure 2.3).[49] Here various programs for the occupiers' daily lives were available, but the leisure activities were conventional; the normed aspects of these offerings contained no particular ideological message, and differed from those in other residential hostels and communal housing only in terms of their number and scale. In Minsk the café had capacity for six hundred, and the dining room could seat four hundred,[50] which permitted a degree of anonymity.

The aim, however, was not independently organized leisure time, but rather socializing subject to the influence of given norms. The many evening events in the residential hostels and canteens were intended to

Figure 2.3. The Dining Room in the German House in Warsaw
Source: Gollert, *Warschau*, p. 263.

prevent individuals escaping from the enforced community. If the Schutzpolizei in Minsk permitted its men to play the accordion, or SS-men to put on a comedy, play pranks, or sing songs, this was not only to let them show off their talents and for collective entertainment, but also was rather an event for which attendance was compulsory for all policemen.[51] Particularly in Weißruthenien it was also common for local artists to appear on stage as part of the entertainment program for the Wehrmacht.[52] Undoubtedly many of the men were happy to be cheered up on command, in order to pass the time; this was demonstrated by the high degree of attendance. Yet there was scarcely any alternative because even when one's presence was not officially commanded, the effect of peer pressure remained strong.

The comradeship evenings were confined only to the men. These celebrations were organized by the offices and also partly subsidized. The Eastern Railway in Warsaw paid a subsidy of 8 Złoty for each attendee, so that participation was attractive merely on account of the cheap drinks.[53] Here there was no cabaret or other performances; people just sat together, drank, talked, and enjoyed themselves.[54] The organized events were intended to overcome one's individualism completely. For many occupiers this goal was attained. They drank happily and celebrated with gusto. Only a few individuals could resist this kind of group dynamic,[55] as described, for example, by the officer Wilm Hosenfeld in Warsaw. Even when he drank together with generals until 3:00 A.M., he still withdrew himself in good time, fully aware that this was the only way could he remain true to himself.[56]

3. Cinema, Radio, Reading

If the occupiers wanted to withdraw from the group bonding activities, there were still a few possibilities that were even tolerated and promoted by the state; among them were reading, going to the cinema, and listening to the radio. One pursued an individual interest and was not dependent on the company of others. Therefore, these activities—as opposed, say, to the theater, opera, or sports—were generally individual and not collective pursuits. At the same time, the content transmitted via these media was still subject to strict regulation and alignment with norms—if one excludes forbidden foreign broadcasts or propaganda sheets, which were much less common in the East than in the Reich.

Among the first things the German authorities set up in the newly conquered East were cinemas. In contrast to theaters or concert houses, very little in the way of personnel was necessary and at the same time the movies were much more popular. In Warsaw, therefore, the first cinema had already opened—in a house for the SS and police—at the start of 1940.

Situated centrally on Neue Welt, once the war damage to the building had been repaired by "large squads of Jewish auxiliary workers," it showed as its first film, *Schlussakkord* (*Final Agreement*), in what initially were closed screenings for the German troops.[57] This 1936 film by Detlef Sierck, who after emigrating became known as Douglas Sirk, celebrated the overcoming of distance by the radio and thereby addressed propagandistically a problem that directly affected the occupiers.[58] In the cinema, however, melodramas like *Schlussakkord* were not shown very often; instead, usually comedies were shown, such as those starring Hans Albers, who was supposed to convey the carefree atmosphere of the homeland as a contrast to the predominant mood in Warsaw. Despite prices of 40 Groszy—that is, 20 Pfennig—and only admitting members of the SS and police, the cinema was still very well attended.

In September of the same year, Helgoland, a former Polish film theater now under German control,[59] was opened to meet the needs of the soldiers and civilians and provide further variety. This thoughtful measure was deemed necessary mainly to dissuade Germans from attending the Polish cinemas in contravention of orders.[60] With the Kammerlichtspiele and the Schauburg in Praga on the right bank of the Vistula, additional venues were added, although the latter was closed in 1942 and in its place the Apollo was confiscated from its Polish owners in the German residential quarter.[61] Both were public film theaters, while most government offices also offered film shows for their own workers. Especially well-suited for this was the tower occupied by the general commissariat in Minsk, which had space to show films on its fifth floor. After the closing of what until then had been the public cinema Heimat, every Friday after work hours a film was shown there.[62] Things were similar in the Reich Transport Directorate (RVD), which also had a cinema-room in its office building—if the railway men wanted to take advantage of the screenings, however, they had to be in their office on Sunday or late on Saturday.[63]

The Wehrmacht made considerable efforts to supply films to its soldiers. In Warsaw, in 1941, it offered four or five free film programs every day in two cinemas, as well as three so-called sound-film vehicles, which were usually used in the military hospitals.[64] In addition, narrow-track film projectors were distributed to the troops, but for these there was no suitable film material to be shown.[65] These measures succeeded in raising attendance numbers, just for soldiers, from 56,000 in October 1941 to 70,000 in January 1942; to these numbers should be added 23,000 men, who attended those shows put on using mobile film equipment that in spite of continuous gas shortages were used mainly in the outskirts of Warsaw as well as in Distrikt Warschau.[66] These figures show that on average each member of the Wehrmacht went to the cinema two or three times per month. Especially for soldiers in transit, who only spent a few days in the cities, seeing a film was a must—particularly as its attractiveness had been enhanced by making it a free form of entertainment.[67]

The attendance figures were naturally subject to fluctuation because not all films were equally popular: especially large-scale productions, such as the anti-English drama about the Boer War, *Ohm Krüger*,[68] or the spectacular and not ideologically laden first German color film, *Münchhausen*,[69] were very popular, while the film *Ich klage an* (I Indict) that served as propaganda for the euthanasia program and was shown during the Deutsche Kulturtage (Days of German Culture), drew little interest.[70] The film preferences of the soldiers matched those of the home front; those responsible for selecting the films satisfied the demand by showing the same reels in the Reich and in the East.[71] In the East propagandistic works were certainly not any more popular than in the Reich and intensified attempts at indoctrination cannot be detected. Also for this reason, going to the movies was one of the occupiers' most favorite pastimes—and not just for the soldiers—as they created an indirect link to the Reich. In March 1942 the Filmvorführstelle (Nazi Film Office) in Warsaw registered 272 film showings with 98,011 civilian attendees,[72] such that the frequency of cinema-going, at more than three visits per month, was actually higher than for the Wehrmacht.

In comparison to Warsaw, Minsk's cinema programing was provincial. This was mainly due to the low standard of living there even before the war. There were no opulent film palaces in the city as in the Polish metropolis, where in contrast to communist countries, great value was placed on comfortable and representative places of entertainment. In order to put on a film program in Weißruthenien outside the former Soviet administrative buildings, it was necessary for the Germans to construct suitable buildings themselves. This was done using standardized prefabricated wooden-built cinemas: these fairly uncomfortable buildings had a capacity for 450 people, and apart from the foundations, all of the materials came from the Reich. Therefore, probably only the box office or the toilets reminded the occupiers of home. The presentations of the Zentral-Filmgesellschaft Ost (Eastern Central Film Company), the state-run operating company, had nonetheless the advantage that, due to the "lower racial bar" in comparison with Poles, Germans were able to visit the cinema together with Belorussians, although this was not always welcomed.[73] Nonetheless, in Minsk there was also the Heimat (Homeland) Cinema that was exclusively reserved for the occupiers, where they did not come into contact with the local population.[74]

The film program was strictly controlled. Of course only registered productions were shown, but even the selection from among these films was subjected to careful scrutiny. This applied also to the radio: the authorities used this medium to support and influence the occupiers. A popular instrument, therefore, were the community receptions that were organized mainly on state holidays. During the celebrations, the participants would gather together in a large hall to listen to speeches over the radio from Berlin or Krakow, while local musicians provided the background, underlining the festive nature of the holiday. Such events took place, for example, every year on the anniversary of the Nazi seizure of power on January 30; on this day in 1940, the speech of Hans Frank was relayed in the Helgoland Cinema and the Roma Theater in Warsaw, accompanied by speeches from *Distrikt* officials and a parade by the "ethnic German Selbstschutz."[75] These kinds of events cannot be compared to simply listening to the radio as an individual, but they do reveal the considerable importance placed on this medium.

The main function of the radio program was distraction from the hardships of life in the East, as well as promotion of German group identity and solidarity, mainly through traditional German music and spoken segments, for example, about different regions in the Reich.[76] In close cooperation with the local Propagandaamt (Propaganda Office), the officials running the radio station in Minsk sought to prevent those at the front from drifting apart from the homeland, and at the same time to encourage Belorussians, in their own language, to engage in hard-working collaboration under German direction. As with the cinemas, it was the Wehrmacht that also set up the first broadcasting station, sending a radio squad to Minsk in early August 1941, soon after the city's capture; it took over the Soviet station and broadcast from there. Almost a year after the establishment of the civil administration, the military radio was transferred in May 1942 to the Reichsrundfunk (Reich Radio Service), which established a so-called regional radio station headed by Erwin Jansen and later by Günter Koderisch.[77]

In Warsaw, by contrast, they did not have their own station; instead, the station was based in the seat of government in Krakow. In addition, the Germans could also receive Reich radio transmissions from Breslau; because its main broadcast area did not include the General Government, it was for the listeners a great event when in October 1940 the radio orchestra and its conductor came to Warsaw from Silesia to give several guest concerts there.[78] Overall though, radio played a lesser role in the Polish metropolis than in Minsk because there were no spoken segments specifically prepared for this city. It should also be noted that even in Weißruthenien there was little original programing and most of the programs were simply rebroadcast from the Reich.[79]

The importance of radio can hardly be overestimated, but it is difficult to measure. The number of radios in use and the number of listeners remain unknown, but there are clear indications that a constant demand for radio receivers existed. Despite continuous deliveries throughout the war, radios always remained in short supply in Warsaw.[80] Thus the Wehrmacht was scarcely able to supply its troops with enough receivers. Even a senior officer like Carl von Andrian commented regularly in his diary on his radio consumption—or, rather, he expressed irritation when no reception was possible.[81]

The radio station in Minsk regularly broadcast news in the Belorussian language; the news consisted more or less of the ritual announcement of the military triumphs from the official Wehrmacht report. In addition, it also broadcast many music programs that were adapted from the program in the Reich. This meant that entertainment dominated most of the transmission time.[82] It satisfied the listeners' demands because the familiar tunes from home represented not only pleasant memories, but also offered a pleasant distraction from daily life in a foreign environment. Classical music, by contrast, was played less often, but then in a sophisticated presentation that was celebrated as an outstanding cultural event. On these occasions, it was not uncommon for guest conductors to be brought from the Reich, such as Hans Hilgers from Cologne, who led the radio's own orchestra in Minsk several times in October 1943. The works of composers such as Beethoven, Haydn, and Brahms were not played in their entirety; instead, only excerpted passages were performed. Only Mozart's Violin Concerto in A Major was given a complete performance.[83] The generally low quality of the performances becomes clear, however, when the local production of selections from the opera *Der Freischütz*, as well as the staging of the audio play *Vienna*, were celebrated and "singled out as exceptional" events; the critic in the *Minsker Zeitung* heaped praise on this "culture transmitted via the ether."[84]

Lectures with ideological content were only rarely included in the programs, but this shows that indoctrination was nonetheless given some space. The tenor was aimed mainly at stressing the allegedly very positive influence of the Germans in the East. In February 1942 the regional radio station in Minsk made a series of broadcasts on this topic with the title "Land im Aufbau" (Country under Construction).[85] The occupiers' claim to their new living space was made in a series called "Volk im Osten" (Volk in the East) that used pseudohistorical arguments to legitimate German conquest of the Soviet Union as the liberation of this territory from the unproductive influence of the Slavs.[86] Preference was given, however, to influencing people indirectly via entertainment rather than through direct propaganda of this kind. By the start of the Russian campaign in the summer of 1941, programs designed for entertainment were strongly favored over classical heroic broadcasts. Next to the many news bulletins that reported on developments in the war, distraction from the harsh realities of the Russian campaign, promoted by Joseph Goebbels, predominated. The minister of propaganda had thereby clearly recognized the needs of the listeners.

After radio, the newspapers, local periodicals, and books were the most important media for the occupiers. In both Warsaw and in Minsk the Germans possessed, at least for a time, a daily newspaper, that carried the name of the city in its title. Yet by the time the *Minsker Zeitung* appeared in April 1942, the *Warschauer Zeitung* had ceased to exist. After just over one year, the last issue appeared on New Year's Eve 1940. After this, the Germans in Warsaw had to make do with the *Krakauer Zeitung*, which was met with little enthusiasm. Complaints about this are even recorded in some Gestapo reports ("Meldungen aus dem Reich" [Reports from the Reich]).[87] In the former Polish capital, one felt disadvantaged compared to the provincial city Krakow. Coverage in the *Krakauer Zeitung*, which even before the demise of the *Warschauer Zeitung* differed from it only in terms of local news items, was remarkably extensive. Between 1939 and 1944 the *Krakauer Zeitung* averaged ten printed pages and was considerably thicker than comparable publications in the Reich.[88]

All three newspapers included not only political news, but also had a large regional section with daily announcements and reports on events of relevance to the lives of the occupiers. However, in the *Krakauer Zeitung* the reports on Warsaw received only a small amount of space: one page had to cover the entire General Government. Only about 20 percent of the news was concerned specifically with occupied Poland—and the section on Warsaw was correspondingly small. The *Krakauer Zeitung* and *Warschauer Zeitung* informed their readers exhaustively about events in Germany. In contrast to the propaganda claims, they were newspapers intended for those for whom the East had still not become home.[89] Similar things can be said about Minsk, except that the regional section was exclusively focused on the city. As part of the local news there was always an extensive section devoted to sports reports in which not only major events such as soccer matches were discussed in detail, but also peripheral events, such as chess tournaments.

The high quality of the arts section made the *Krakauer Zeitung* especially interesting for demanding subscribers: prominent authors including Hermann Hesse and Werner Bergengruen frequently contributed consciously apolitical articles. This made the *Krakauer Zeitung* attractive not only for readers who kept their distance from the regime, but also for those who were looking for more than just entertainment.[90] Next to its—certainly political—demonstration of German cultural superiority, the newspaper aimed also to compensate for the hardships of the war and deployment to the East. Extravagant publications such as the irregularly appearing *War-*

schauer Kulturblätter (Warsaw Cultural Pages) served mainly the demonstration of German cultural dominance. Printed on shiny paper and including many pictures, Governor Fischer presented himself there, in competition with Hans Frank's similar publication *Generalgouvernement*, as a sponsor of German culture and intellectual life, as things that lay close to his heart. To this end, the topical pages contained extensive essays on recent theater productions or articles on the history of the Germans in Warsaw.[91]

Because the *Krakauer Zeitung* was one of the few newspapers with its own correspondents in friendly foreign countries, its political reports were of a reasonable quality, which was even acknowledged by the Polish Underground.[92] However, objectivity and detailed recording of the facts were completely absent in those reports concerned with the occupied territories. Thus the articles in the business section viewed the Polish economy only with regard to its utility for the Germans, just as all reports from the General Government were written only from the standpoint of the occupiers.[93] Joseph Goebbels and Hans Frank both agreed that propaganda should convince the Germans that they belonged to a "master race." With this consciousness, a sense of community and superiority would also be developed, so the occupiers would keep their distance from the locals.[94] In addition, the rulers wanted to stress the construction work that was being done and the extent to which National Socialism was modernizing the East.[95] Typical for this were stories underlining the contrast between the "dirty" and "primitive" cities under Polish—or, in Minsk, under Bolshevik—rule, set against the German ideals of "order" and "cleanliness." Especially in Belorussia this concept was emphasized repeatedly.

Even though in quality, circulation, and size, the *Minsker Zeitung* did not come close to its Polish cousins, nevertheless, it was a much-read publication. At the beginning of 1944, 22,000 copies were sold daily, produced by just a few more than fifteen fully employed Germans working as editors. More than two-thirds of the circulation was for the Wehrmacht at a reduced price, which were then distributed to the soldiers for free.[96] Against this, the *Krakauer Zeitung*, with a circulation of 50,000 at the end of 1939 and more than 130,000 by July 1942, was a genuine mass publication. However, not too much should be placed on these numbers because by contract the Wehrmacht was guaranteed one subscription copy for every ten soldiers stationed in the General Government.[97] This will have ensured a certain level of reception, but it is by no means certain that all of the copies were actually read by the troops.

Next to the widespread and subsidized reading of newspapers, books were also a popular and valued leisure activity. The first German bookshop opened in Warsaw at the end of 1939, with ethnic German assistants and around 12,000 titles. The shop's high standard is clearly demonstrated when one considers that in the other smaller towns of the *Distrikt* on average only 500–1,200 titles were available.⁹⁸ A few months later, Warsaw was able to expand considerably its selection. In the former Polish central library on Koszykowastraße—but independent of this institution—the *Distrikt* administration established two separate reading rooms, one for smokers and one for nonsmokers, as well as a newspaper room in which some 30,000 books were available to readers. These books came from the collections of the same Polish institutions where the Germans could now indulge their pleasure in reading. Characteristic for the provenance of the book collection, therefore, was the large scientific section. Access was permitted for Reich and ethnic Germans in return for a monthly subscription of 1 Złoty, while members of the Wehrmacht were admitted for free.⁹⁹

In the view of the rulers, the main weakness in the collection was the absence of genuinely Nazi books. Only thanks to a very large donation from the Reich was it possible to overcome this "deficit." It was also possible to borrow books for 5 Groszy, or even have them delivered for 20 Groszy. This service was very popular.¹⁰⁰ Therefore, in 1941, a special lending library opened that was run by the German bookshop opposite the German House. The ethnic German Peter Paul Kostrzewa made available there a collection of six thousand books that could be borrowed and taken home. At the same time, he also greatly expanded the selection in his bookshop that had existed before the war; in response to the strong demand, he moved onto busy Krakauer Vorstadt.¹⁰¹ Another German lending library opened in 1943 on Krakauer Vorstadt; more than a thousand customers visited it every month, primarily because two-thirds of the inventory consisted of entertaining literature.¹⁰²

The bookshop had many visitors because the occupiers were always looking for new reading material. Sometimes units stationed outside the city even came into Warsaw to stock up on reading material just before their scheduled transfer; this was the case, for example, for the German air force doctor Wolfgang Lieschke.¹⁰³ The German owners received strong support from the *Distrikt* administration, which wanted to comply with its cultural obligations. Nonetheless, there were constant complaints that the available selection was too small and, above all, that intellectual works were missing. Especially the latter were easier to find in Polish than in German bookshops. Wilm Hosenfeld, for example, bought a copy of *Deutsche Aussenpolitik 1933–1940* (German Foreign Policy 1933–1940) by Axel Freiherr von Freytagh-Loringhofen, a book with academic credentials, in a Polish shop.¹⁰⁴ However, such visits to local businesses were absolutely undesirable for the German leadership.¹⁰⁵

In Minsk the supply of books was more disparate. In contrast to Poland, there were no local bookshops or libraries that stocked works in German, whose plundering could have provided an initial stock to meet the needs of the occupiers. Thus Reichskommissariat Ostland was forced to include in its budget money for the establishment of libraries run by the authorities. The number of books remained very limited: only three hundred volumes were planned for each *Generalkommissariat*, one hundred to one hundred fifty for the subordinated offices of the city and regional *commissariats* (Stadtkommissariate and Gebietskommissariate). They were to purchase general-political texts of the Nazi Party and reference works on the East. These included mainly the "Bolshevism" series of the Eher Publisher, and the "Library of the Eastern Realm" series by the Stollberg Publishing House, as well as German classics and contemporary Nazi authors.

Overall, regarding books, cinema, and radio, one can confirm that entertainment clearly predominated over ideological indoctrination or even political content. This reflected the need of the occupiers for distraction from the realities of daily life in a foreign environment that was so different from what they were used to at home. This desire was clearly recognized by both the civilian and the military leadership, which did their best to satisfy their subordinates' needs. By offering a wide variety of individualistic ways to spend their free time, people could distract, or even withdraw, themselves, without necessarily leaving the German community. This expression of self-will was accepted because it remained within the bounds of those prescribed norms that the Nazi Party and the state used to try to control all aspects of daily life. Entertainment also served as a means to maintain the distance between the occupiers and the occupied. Ideological content played only a subsidiary role; the fact that it was less attractive than an entertaining film or musical performance was recognized and taken into account. Therefore, the comment of the keen reader Wilm Hosenfeld can be viewed as typical, when he wrote to his wife at the start of 1941, "War books, political commentaries, newspapers, everything in this direction, I can't stand to see it anymore."[106] Such publications were of only secondary importance for the actual functioning of the society of occupiers.

4. Community Events: Theater, Opera, Sports

Support programs were aimed primarily at anchoring the individual within the community. The regime wanted the occupiers to remain within prescribed channels and spend their free time together.[107] This intention was clear from how the residential hostels, rooms, and canteens were organized and also from the numerous activities arranged to keep people occupied when not at work. Books, newspapers, and radio programs, all of which could all be consumed alone, were in this sense an equally normed way out for all those who did not want to spend all their time in the company of their colleagues and comrades. Since the community existed as a major goal for the society of occupiers, the rulers offered numerous activities that were experienced primarily as a group. Alongside many different kinds of sports, these other activities were mainly theater, concerts, and opera. These cultural events brought people together since they were not experienced alone, but always collectively. At the same time, these programs also provided an opportunity for disseminating ideological influence. In addition, the aim was to demonstrate that the Germans were a cultural nation and—especially—to differentiate themselves from the local inhabitants, who were permitted to put on such performances themselves only on a very modest scale.[108] Whilst for the occupiers a common identity and solidarity should be formed, it should be prevented among the occupied. In spite of their specific ideological goals, it must be admitted that but for the vanity of the local Nazi leaders—that is, Governor Ludwig Fischer of Warsaw, and General Commissar Wilhelm Kube in Minsk, German cultural life in the two cities would have been considerably poorer.

Shortly after the occupation of Warsaw, the planned opening of a German theater was announced.[109] Even before this, a number of evenings of chamber music took place in the Palais Brühl, always in the presence of their initiator, Ludwig Fischer.[110] The somewhat unenthusiastic reports in the *Warschauer Zeitung* probably imply that the artistic quality was not very high; the Festsaal (Hall of Celebration) in the former Polish Foreign Ministry was nonetheless full: in light of the many carefully directed invitations, it was much more a gathering of the powerful than it was an artistic performance.

This changed only in October 1940, when the long-awaited theater was finally opened. Located centrally at the cross section between Krakauer Vorstadt and Neue Welt, it came to symbolize the center of German cultural life in the city. Accordingly, Ludwig Leist, Ludwig Fischer, and Hans Frank, celebrated its inauguration together to the festive tones of Beethoven's Coriolan Overture. At the first performance, staged by the General Government's State Theater troupe led by Friedrichfranz Stampe, brought in from Krakow, the audience saw a production of Friedrich Hebbel's *Agnes Bernauer*. The critic confirmed the apparently enthusiastic reception of the play as the "grippingly achieved victory of the needs of State over the fate of individuals," and wrote that the play stood programmatically for the efforts of the Nazis to subordinate the people to their own will.[111] Much more important for the daily life of the occupiers, however, was that performances could be seen for prices ranging from 1.60 to a maximum 10 Złoty, making them affordable. In order to propagate the idea of community linked to the theater, the theater further reduced or eliminated ticket costs for group visits by military units or civilian offices.

Under Franz Nelkel's direction, a schedule was developed that envisaged a new production every three weeks. The theater had hired twenty-four people as a permanent company; their performances were augmented by many guest productions, so that the theater could present two shows every day.[112] Accordingly, the standard of plays remained rather provincial because there was neither sufficient time nor personnel to prepare for complicated stage productions. For this reason, the occupation press characterized the theater programs as dominated by a "cheerful muse."[113] The dramas and farces of writers such as Max Dauthendey, Hans Schweikart, Heinrich Zerkaulen, or Otto Ernst Groh were scarcely of any permanent historical significance or were branded by a certain proximity to Nazi ideology.

In truth, the programs did match the needs of the public because they mostly distracted or entertained people. Comedies with and without music, and later operettas, mixed in with occasional ballet performances were put on most frequently. The operetta company consisting of nine people successfully staged, for example, Eduard Künneke's *Der Vetter aus Dingsda* (*The Cousin from Nowhere*), but also *Maske in Blau* (*Mask in Blue*) and *Der Vogelhändler* (*The Bird Dealer*) were popular with thirty and twenty-one evenings, respectively.[114] At the end of 1942, Nelkel expanded the repertoire by adding operas; these additions were successful with *Susannes Geheimnis* (*Susanne's Secret*) and *Tiefland* (*Lowland*), two pieces that are rarely staged today. Only Puccini's *Madame Butterfly* at least nominally met the demand for quality that the house had asserted for itself.[115] Even esteemed classical guest companies, such as that from the Deutsches Opernhaus Berlin (Berlin Opera House), put only lightweight fare on stage.[116]

Success with the public confirmed this theater policy; more than a thousand evenings that were almost sold out in three years spoke for themselves. Yet it should be noted, however, that the Wehrmacht declared its group visits to be part of their military service, thereby making it one's duty to attend.[117] The civil administration also tried to fill up seats at cultural performances. There was a special season ticket for winter concerts given by the Orchester der Stadt Warschau (Warsaw City Orchestra), subsidized by the *Distrikt* administration. All members of state offices received a 20 percent reduction, the tickets had to be paid for 50 percent in advance at the German bookstore, acting as a central box office, with the remainder deducted by the cashiers in three monthly instalments from the purchaser's paycheck. In the event of an official transfer a corresponding refund could be made.[118] So it is not surprising that in the 1941–1942 season around 115,000 German patrons saw 182 performances by the Theater der Stadt alone, that is, not including guest performances by other ensembles; the numbers include, however, six evenings only for ethnic Germans and also 19 for the Wehrmacht.[119] In particular, soldiers in transit were very pleased to catch a performance.[120] The variety of the performances was also welcomed by Germans spending a longer period of time in the city.[121]

The classical canon of works was used in rare cases. Only in February 1942 was the Warschauer Kulturring (Warsaw Cultural Society) established under the patronage of Ludwig Fischer, who had committed himself to supporting the city's cultural life. Through its membership contributions and donations, it supported the theater and organized readings, chamber music concerts, and exhibitions.[122] The Society was supposed to serve as a model of intellectual life in the East, which, however, in this form was more a façade than a reality. The production of Goethe's *Egmont* attended by Captain Max Rohrweder in the Theater der Stadt in 1941,[123] remained an exception on the program and was merely meant to showcase the supposedly superior German high culture. Correspondingly, such performances were celebrated in extensive previews and reviews in the press and radio.

At least these offerings of sophisticated entertainment were not confined to guest performances. The absence of a local symphony orchestra made concerts by visiting ensembles unavoidable. The Krakauer Philharmoniker (Krakow Philharmonic Orchestra) of the General Government, a state-run institution made up of Polish musicians,[124] therefore frequently came to perform in Warsaw and enabled works by Beethoven, Bach, Haydn, Mozart, and other German composers to be heard, in which the format of a concert evening, with at least two completely played symphonic works, was preserved.[125]

The *Festspiele* (festival performances) were an advertisement for German culture in Warsaw; they were organized as a theater festival on their inauguration in 1940. They were held in the Łazienki Park, which had a suitable open-air theater dating from the period of the Polish monarchy. Under the patronage of Governor Fischer, Goethe's *Iphigenie* was staged (see figure 2.4), which also became the subject of the *Warschauer Kulturblätter's* (Warsaw Cultural Pages') specially dedicated first edition.[126] In addition, guests from various theaters in the Reich played Calderon's *Loud Secret* and de Molina's *Don Gil of the Green Trousers*. With a colorful evening under the title *Ein Sommernachtsspuk* (A Summer-Night's Spook) that included, for example, the musical *Zwischen Sonne und Mond* (Between the Sun and the Moon), the occupiers of Warsaw commemorated Erich Claudius; Claudius had served as the regional officer for theater and music and died on July 13, 1940.[127] Next to this summertime entertainment, which took place only in 1940, there was in the late fall the annual Days of German Culture, for which well-known ensembles travelled from Germany.[128]

The individualist Wilm Hosenfeld, who was otherwise orientated toward classical topics, was not very enthusiastic about the program because

Figure 2.4. Scene from *Iphigenie auf Tauris* in the Łazienki Park
Source: Gollert, *Warschau*, p. 284.

it seemed too overtly propagandistic for his taste; all the same he attended one concert and even saw the *Rothschilds*. His conclusion: "A tendentious film, but it is not as common as the new Jew-film, 'Jud Süss.'"[129] The instrumentalization of culture, which Hosenfeld had already criticized, continued in the following years. Under the sign of the Days of German Culture in 1941, there were medical lectures, readings, a colorful evening, and a book exhibit, with martial titles and contents such as "Buch und Schwert" (Book and Sword), the euthanasia film *Ich klage an*, as well as music to be played at home and theater. In propagandistic support of this series of events, the Nazi Party conducted a mass rally and during the entire five-day duration of the Days, the houses occupied by Germans were decorated with swastika flags.[130]

The ideological instrumentalization of high-brow cultural entertainment can be observed throughout the entire period of the occupation. *Distrikt* head Ludwig Fischer was only too keen to see Warsaw as the new German cultural center in the East.[131] However, reality remained far behind this wishful thinking. Despite large-scale media support, the demanding events could never develop a mass following because the light muse was much too popular. In addition, its popularity largely succeeded in keeping the occupiers at a distance from the locals, and created a solidarity that could not replace the homeland, but at least through the performances sought to bring it as close as possible. This cultural policy served to subject daily life to norms in such a way that a strong sense of community was developed, which in turn was important for the smooth functioning of the society of occupiers. On the other hand, the almost complete absence of classic works had the undesired effect that the Polish cultural offerings were seen as more or less equal, for example, when the opera *Hansel and Gretel* was played by qualified local musicians, who frequently no longer had regular employment. A comparable German performance for German children could not be seen in Warsaw. In addition, the former Capital City Orchestra was considerably better than the Philharmonic Orchestra of the General Government.[132] Members of the former, therefore, entertained locals and occupiers in the many cafés in Warsaw, despite the ban in force on Germans visiting Polish restaurants and bars. Udo von Alvensleben very movingly describes the "fantastic voices" in pubs, which the German soldiers rewarded with "thunderous applause."[133]

In the numerous German variety clubs and cabarets, mainly musicals and comedies were presented; these were popular as closed performances for the troops, and were called the front theater. In 1940, for example, Gerhards Marionettenbühne (Gerhard's Puppet Stage) showed *Die Zaubergeige* (*The Magic Violin*) twice a day; at each show, ninety places were reserved for members of the police.[134] Front theaters with programmatic names like *Vom Rhein bis an die Donau* (*From the Rhine to the Danube*)[135] also came for guest performances, as did the Varieté Truppe Berry (Variety Troop Berry), whose liberal dance offerings were much appreciated.[136] The most popular stage was the former cinema, which became the theater Hollywood in Hozastraße with 1,250 almost always sold-out seats[137]—in part, because soldiers received free tickets.

The organization of the constantly changing program in Hollywood and other theaters used predominantly by the Wehrmacht lay in the hands of those responsible for the troops. They arranged theater ensembles for their units and organized concerts; most of these events were open to members of the army, air force, police, and Arbeitsdienst (Labor Service). The Reichspropagandaministerium (Reich Propaganda Ministry) provided the artists sent to perform at these guest shows in Warsaw.[138] So, for example, the Frontbühne Oberland (Front Theater Highland) visited the former Polish capital for a week and played "Kajetan Minderlein" by Anderl Kern twice a day to a full house. The author was also the leader of the eleven actors and played a role himself. The *Warschauer Zeitung* concluded in its review, "The simple story did not raise any problems."[139]

The most successful performances in Warsaw were the request concerts that were held during the numerous fundraisers, for example those held on the Tag der Polizei (Day of the Police) or for the Winterhilfswerk des

Deutschen Volkes (Winter Relief of the German People). A preprinted request form was drafted on which fifty songs were listed—mainly folk songs, hits like "Lilli Marleen" and some marches, as well as a few classics, such as the "Victory March" from *Aida* or "When the Stars Were Shining Brightly" from *Tosca*. The individual offices took collections that they handed to the concert organizer with a song request. Thus, for example, the Transferstelle für den jüdischen Wohnbezirk (Transfer Office for the Ghetto) wrote that they had collected 2,400 Złoty among the Firmengemeinschaft (German Companies' Association): "In view of the size of this contribution, I ask that in selecting the music, the request of the Companies' Association for 'Heinzelmännchens Wachparade' by Curt Noak, be included."[140]

The cultural and entertainment program in Minsk and the related application of norms to daily life there scarcely differed from the situation in Warsaw. However, on account of its smaller size, there was less on offer in the city and therefore fewer opportunities to visit a performance at all. Few suitable buildings were available, such that many performances were not open to the public, but were accessible to only a limited number of people from specific offices. For example, the Reichsverkehrsdirektion offered its officials and employees films every Saturday and Sunday, and concerts or variety performances on weekdays at irregular intervals[141]; on one occasion they even visited an operetta that had been successful in the Reich and in Warsaw, *Der Vetter aus Dingsda*.[142] For people open to culture, there was also the possibility of seeing plays in the Belorussian theater and, like Wolfgang Lieschke, attending the opera *Eugen Onegin* in Russian.[143]

The distance from the homeland ensured that the quality of guest performances was lower than in Poland because good ensembles rarely travelled so far east. Nonetheless, the Theater der Stadt Minsk was fortunate to enjoy the special devotion of General Commissar Kube because in August 1942 it had staged his play *Totila*. Actors from the Theater der Stadt Landsberg, who stayed in Minsk for three months putting on guest performances, staged the Gothic drama as their parting presentation, earning the theater additional attention. The critic writing for the *Minsker Zeitung*, however, was hardly enthusiastic; it seems clear that but for the censor and the official status of the newspaper, he would have written a devastating review. Thus he found it necessary to explain apologetically to the reader that the play was above all the work of "a politician and a propagandist," whose difficulties "could not be mastered completely by the director." The public was also not very enthusiastic, since "open sympathy" as a reaction—especially in view of the character of the *Minsker Zeitung*—is clearly to be understood as actual boredom.[144]

In sports, normed daily life embraced another popular pastime. Here, too, the authorities were careful to ensure strict racial segregation; under no circumstances were Germans to train together with locals. Competitions between them were also not tolerated, because a victory over the occupiers could have put their superiority in doubt. But since this kind of physical activity was popular with the occupiers and was valued by the official ideology of the regime as a means for toughening people up, or even as preparation for war, it had to be promoted; this was an archetypal group activity.[145] For the same reasons, organized sports were forbidden for the Poles.[146] Initially, it was mainly the Wehrmacht that made various sporting opportunities available to its soldiers. Then, in April 1940, the Distrikt Warschau administration established a first club (see figure 2.5). The Sportgemeinschaft Palais Brühl (Sports Club Palais Brühl) united numerous different sports under one roof. It especially focused on water sports because the nearby River Vistula provided a suitable facility.[147] It stood under the patronage of Governor Ludwig Fischer, who used it to present himself as a sports' enthusiast. Other German offices followed suit and organized opportunities to play sports—as in other spheres of activity—strictly separated by institution. Only two weeks after the civil administration, five additional German sports clubs had been established by various offices: the Post Office, Ostbahn, Order Police, Sipo/SD, as well as the air force in the suburb and present-day city precinct of Okęcie.[148]

By the end of 1940 the organization of sport in Warsaw was fully established, and it did not experience major changes or important developments

Figure 2.5. The Home of the Sports Club Palais Brühl, Warsaw
Source: Gollert, *Warschau*, p. 267.

thereafter. In December of that year, the Nazi Party assumed supreme authority over it in the General Government. This was justified mainly by the special place that this leisure activity held with respect to physically strengthening the population. In addition, the Nazi Party did not want to lose its claim to complete control over support services.[149] In practice this meant that the Nazi Party organized all the tournaments and championships, and, for example, replaced the Reichssportabzeichen (Reich Sport Medal).[150] In Distrikt Warschau, it had already started with soccer and handball championships in June 1940, and soon it also ran competitions for track and field athletics, tennis, swimming, and rowing.[151] These developments met with general consent. In fact, the competitive element increased interest among occupiers who were not active participants in sport. Many of them regularly visited the stadiums in Warsaw to watch the competitions. The radio and newspapers met the Germans' needs by reporting regularly on sporting events, usually split into two roughly equal sections on the Reich and the General Government. In the *Warschauer Zeitung* and later the *Krakauer Zeitung*, sports reports covered at least one page every day.

Soccer fans were given quite a display on match days; several games were played every Saturday in the Wehrmacht-Stadion (Wehrmacht Stadium).[152] Free entrance to this largest arena in Warsaw promoted interest among spectators and ensured good support. Especially popular were soccer games between cities, in which a select team of the best players from all the teams played: for the match against Danzig—that was staged as part of the Days of German Culture—four thousand people attended;[153] against Posen more than five thousand spectators attended.[154] The absolute high point, however, was the match against the greater German champions, Schalke 04, in November 1942. In the sold-out Wehrmacht-Stadion, 20,000 Warsaw soccer fans experienced a sensational 2-to-1 win by their team,[155] after they had lost in the previous year 8 to 1.[156] Such attendance figures could be expected only rarely because most regional confrontations were not very attractive for viewers. The leading local team from the modern-day city precinct of Okęcie—champions of the General Government—nonetheless attracted up to 2,500 spectators to their games.[157]

Yet soccer was by no means the only sport to enjoy great popularity. Above all track and field could certainly compete with it: at the large Wehrmachtssportfest (Wehrmacht Sports Festival) in the summer of 1940, all 20,000 seats in the stadium were full. Almost 1,500 participants met there from the military units stationed in Warsaw and the surrounding area and competed in such martial disciplines as throwing hand grenades.[158] Generally, however, competitions against sportsmen and teams from outside attracted more interest than the local competitions. Especially the matches against other districts received enthusiastic attention, mainly because the Warsaw teams were usually hard to beat.[159] This was mainly due to their sheer numerical superiority that increased the quality of those available; nowhere else in Poland were so many Germans deployed and stationed as in the former capital. In 1940, alongside track and field, the occupiers could compete for the title of General Government champion in the following sports: canoeing, tennis, swimming, rowing, and handball.[160] Later skiing was added that took place in the winter resort of Zakopane; some Warsaw railwaymen participated, but they were largely unsuccessful due to a lack of training.[161]

All these disciplines enjoyed special support from the German offices; a sporting success was always linked with an increase in prestige for the respective supervisor, as is demonstrated, for example, by announcement of those successes in the Wehrmacht's daily orders.[162] The offices and institutions therefore set aside time and training support for their athletic employees. The Ostbahnsportgemeinschaft (Eastern Railway Sports Association Warsaw), for example, offered regular swimming in the pool at the former YMCA facility[163] on Drei-Kreuz-Platz. It reserved the pool on Mondays from 8:00 P.M. to 8:30 P.M. For training it provided its own bus and afterward there was also the possibility to eat in the canteen after official closing hours.[164] The civil administration also supported its sports association with plenty of money; in 1941 it improved the training ground in Agricola Park at a cost of 67,000 Złoty; that money was used for refurbishing the changing rooms and showers.[165] These measures were intended to further increase the attraction of normed leisure time, which in the form of sport already enjoyed great popularity. The policeman Heinrich H., deployed in the village of Małkinia, reports, for example, that he requested a transfer to Warsaw, so that he "could better pursue his sports and take part in competitions."[166]

The Nazi Party tried to satisfy as many needs as possible in order to give the Germans little opportunity—and little free time—to develop their own self-will. The promotion of sport, therefore, was not limited just to the prestigious championship disciplines. In Warsaw the Germans could learn to fence[167] or play chess, for example.[168] Even a sportsman's residence was established at the YMCA. At certain times individuals could visit this facility to practice sports on their own.[169] Under the direction of Wilm Hosenfeld, the Wehrmacht prepared course participants for their future tasks as trainers at its own sports school. During the two-week courses, some men were instructed in jujitsu and ice hockey.[170] The claim to comprehensive care went so far that for entertainment purposes professional boxers were brought to Warsaw, accompanied by the star attraction Max Schmeling, even though at this time there was nowhere you could learn how to box in the city.¹⁷¹ The participation level in all these activities was high. Hardly any of the occupiers were not actively, or at least passively, involved. Similar to the cultural offerings, it was possible to spend all of your free time, in the evenings and on weekends, at one of the many sporting events.

When Governor Fischer went sailing in his spare time, he was not only satisfying his personal interests, but also engaging in a field of activity normally reserved for the leadership class. He had a boathouse built for the Sports Club Palais Brühl¹⁷² and even took part in races himself. At a regatta on the Vistula in July 1940, he was captaining the fastest boat, but was disqualified when it capsized and had to hand victory to a sailor from the SS, who like the railway men, also had their own boats.¹⁷³ This elitist hobby was reserved for just a few privileged individuals. Certainly the Vistula was a popular destination for outings because in the summer it was good for swimming, but as water sports' enthusiast Ernst Hermann Krause noted from his own experience, most occupiers had to be satisfied with renting a canoe.¹⁷⁴

Similar limitations also applied to fox hunting. Having a horse was a prerequisite, as was having a permit that was usually issued only to senior officials and employees, or officers. Even at horse trials, Wilm Hosenfeld observed that "the masters on their high horses" excluded the "lower ranks" and there was "no trace ... of a shared community."¹⁷⁵ This exclusion was not good for comradeship, but at the same time it met the elitist needs of the high and mighty, whose satisfaction with their deployment to the East was increased by such distancing. For them, participation in a hunt was part of setting the right tone and an important status symbol that made invitations to take part highly sought after; the celebrations afterward also promoted solidarity. The officer Max Rohrweder noted that one and a half hours of hunting were followed by six hours of eating and drinking.¹⁷⁶ In the East, the upper class showed the same status symbols they had in Germany—an arrogance that was promoted with state support. In this way agreement with occupational rule was bought because some senior civil servants or military officers were able to climb rapidly in society, in a manner that would not have been possible in the Reich. In Warsaw and Minsk the elite of the society of occupiers was drawn not only from those circles that already held outstanding social positions in the homeland, but also from lower classes.

Excursions and riding jaunts, regardless of whether they were conducted alone, in a hunting club, or in a riding association,¹⁷⁷ were a pleasure in Warsaw, but not in Minsk and its vicinity because there partisan attacks were an almost daily occurrence. Yet even in Poland, from 1943 the Germans encountered a security problem such that hunting became subject to stringent regulations.[178] In Belorussia sports generally took place under considerably more restricted conditions than in the General Government. The partisans made it impossible to stage activities outside of Minsk at all, and from the end of 1942, even journeys to compete in places beyond the immediate neighborhood took place only rarely, and were confined mostly to soccer teams. As in the cultural field, the city remained well behind Warsaw due to its lower population, even though the forms of organization were very similar. Thus the sporting activities on offer in Weißruthenien were widely used. Owing to the lack of facilities, the possibility to use swimming pools or athletic training grounds remained exceptions because too many people had to share the few suitable places.[179] Team sports were even more predominant than in Warsaw, and even small offices had teams in various disciplines. Office members were obliged to participate to a much greater extent than in Warsaw,[180] and also to take on service tasks such as being a pool attendant.[181] In Minsk one needed greater independence to escape from the pull of normed sporting activities.

5. Political Life: Celebrations, Training Courses, and Nazi Party Work

On May 6, 1940, Hans Frank ordered the establishment of the Arbeitsbereich Generalgouvernement Polen der NSDAP (Section of the Nazi Party in the General Government of Poland), of which he personally became the head. The Party organization was divided into *Distrikt* offices and below them local offices that corresponded to the administrative units of the *Distrikte* and *Kreise*. Government and party posts were held in personal union. The General Governor saw the main tasks of the Party as enforcing Nazi principles among the Reich German officials. In addition, the Party was responsible for looking after all of the 70,000 Reich Germans stationed permanently in the General Government—and not only Party members. In October 1941 this jurisdiction was expanded to include the roughly 200,000 ethnic Germans as well.[182]

The efficiency of the official Nazi Party apparatus must, however, be viewed as rather poor, since due to lack of personnel it was not able even to register all of the Reich Germans in the customary card index, needed for collecting membership fees.[183] A solution to this problem was not even considered, because Frank—as well as Kube in Weißruthenien[184]—was not interested in establishing a competitor to the civil administration that he headed, and therefore tried to keep Nazi Party influence strictly limited. The Nazi Party's claim on the individual and the regulation of all aspects of his life, which implied that the complete control of the population, nevertheless, remained in effect,[185] and was explicitly politically motivated.[186] The supervision of the population this implied differed from that in the cultural and sporting programs: there politics were not explicitly in the foreground.

From the end of 1940, the Nazi Party was divided into six *Standorte* (sections) in Warsaw alone, which Werner Seifert from the Amt des Stellvertreters des Führers (Nazi Party Chancellery) in Munich organized for the *Distriktstandortführer* (district leader), Ludwig Fischer.[187] Just one year later Hans Frank reorganized these structures, in order to better supervise the numerous Germans who were not Nazi Party members. The number of sections was thereby greatly increased: in June 1941, there were now thirty-five instead of sixteen sections, of which nine were in Warsaw.[188] The Germans were organized roughly according to the location of the numerous German offices, but not according to apartments, most of which by 1941 were already inside the German quarter. This demonstrates once again the importance of the institutional fragmentation within the society of occupiers.

The Nazi Party administration was based in the newly constructed Haus der Nationalsozialisten (House of the National Socialists), where most of their activities also took place. There the Party held, for example, weekly comradeship evenings or mothers' training. The ethnic Germans in particular often found themselves to be the focus of such political activity because they were viewed as lacking indoctrination. At the same time, they were made up mostly of families; the authorities, for example, offered to send away ethnic German mothers with children to resort hotels for recreation.[189] In return, the Party obliged the women to perform home chores for the benefit of the German community. In concrete terms this meant that the women sewed or repaired pieces of clothing, shoes, or pillow cases, mainly to assist the wounded, and that they paid visits to the sick. In addition, the women took training courses in home health and care for the sick.[190] Accompanying these practical programs, Nazi *Frauenarbeit* also encompassed speeches for ideological purposes, which explained the role of women in National Socialism.[191]

Such training programs were closely regulated by detailed instructions. Thus the Nazi Party sections were supposed to organize an open evening at least once a month, in which mainly members of the German community were to take part. On these occasions the sections were expected to propagate Nazi ideology themselves because only in exceptional cases could they request a speaker from the *Distrikt* office. The list of topics to be covered included in March, for example, "Our great aim in the East is essentially just the final result of the program, with which we started." In April the "Biography of the Führer" was to be discussed. Since religious and foreign policy questions were not to be raised, the above two topics were seen as "especially suited to familiarize the [ethnic German] compatriots with

National-Socialist ways of thinking.... It has to be pointed out again and again that it was always the same forces that the movement and later the Reich have had to fight against: the Jews, Marxism, and Plutocracy." After nine years of National Socialism, these arguments were nothing special any more for the Reich Germans. For the ethnic Germans, however, these were still concepts that had to be drilled into them.[192]

The Volksbildungsstätte (People's Hall of Education), which the Nazi Party established at the end of 1940, was not very popular. In the following year, official figures indicate that 2,500 people attended its evening lectures, which was exceedingly low in comparison with the numbers for theater and cinema attendance.[193] Since the poor German language abilities of the ethnic Germans were well known, the speakers had to lay particular emphasis on simplicity and presentation.[194] Yet the German language courses organized for them also met with little response, attracting only 1,100 participants.[195] Clearly they did not consider learning the language a decisive priority. Much more important were the numerous social benefits that came with the ethnic German identity card. The Nazi Party strongly contributed to this response. There were not only the HJ and BDM for children and youths with 2,500 and 2,900 members, respectively, in Distrikt Warschau, but also full-time caregivers and social workers, who cared for infants and ran recuperation homes for children. The three kindergartens in the city operated for the entire day free of charge and made it possible for both parents to go out to work—in stark contrast to the official ideology of the woman's place being home and kitchen. In addition, the Winter Aid Drive helped the many financially weak ethnic German families to get through the hardships of frost and snow in chilly Warsaw.[196]

The social welfare for ethnic Germans was more comprehensive and offered more benefits than in the Reich. The recipients were pleased to get these because they provided many advantages. The occupiers from the Reich were scarcely interested in most of these social benefits, and even the weekly consultation hours of Distrikt-Governor Fischer—Thursdays from 11:00 A.M. to 1:00 P.M.—apparently signaling his closeness to the citizens, were no exception.[197] Due to their ideological tendencies, many of the things the Nazi Party organized in Warsaw were scarcely able to compete with the other possibilities for spending leisure time. Since the continuous propagation of such ideas remained, however, a main goal of Nazi policy, German institutions often declared attendance at training events to be an integral part of work obligations. In the spring of 1942 the civil administration held a series of lectures in the Palais Brühl that included numerous topics, including "Volkssüchte, Volksschäden" ("People's Addictions, Damaging the People"), "Die Bedeutung der SA im Lebenskampf unseres Volkes" ("The Significance of the SA in the Life Struggle of our

People"), and "Sachsen und Polen in der napoleonischen Zeit" ("Saxony and Poland in the Napoleonic Period"). The invitation pointed out that precisely because many members of the *Distrikt* administration were giving presentations, it would be unacceptable for others to be distinguished only by their absence.[198]

Exhibitions such as that with the title "Deutsche Leistung im Weichselraum" ("German Achievements in the Region of the Vistula") which was shown within the framework of the Days of German Culture in Warsaw, also conveyed mostly ideological content. The aim of the show was primarily to bring to the attention of Germans working in the General Government the supposed inheritance that they were administering and should also leave behind. The basis of all order in Poland was designated as being of German origin, and this was the solid base on which the new rulers were now building. In addition, the German inheritance represented undeniable evidence of the German claim to leadership in the East. In this sense the Propagandaabteilung (Propaganda Section) of the *Distrikt* administration saw the exhibition as a "building block of the great new mission in the East [which] Adolf Hitler has assigned [to us]."[199] Similar things apply to the show put on in the following year with the title "Book and Sword," in which German roots for the city were also claimed: the accompanying materials pointed to the history of the countryside in the *Distrikt*, the shared history of Dresden and Warsaw, an intellectual pamphlet published in Warsaw in 1799, a celebration of Schiller in the city in 1859, as well as the German school system both before and after 1939.[200]

Exhibitions such as "German Achievements" and "Book and Sword" can be viewed as exemplary for the specific propaganda topics that were important in the East. Next to the racist blood and soil rhetoric that was customary in the Reich and that was mainly referred to in the lectures, the exhibitions sought to promote the legitimation of occupational rule. They especially aimed to stress the importance of the construction work that the Germans supposedly had been undertaking for centuries in Poland, and that now they wanted to continue. The superiority of the new rulers was also to be demonstrated in the cultural realm[201]; an example of this was the show entitled "Deutsches Gold" (German Gold). The Daily Order of the Office of the Wehrmacht commandant read, "The exhibition … conveys the best in German culture. A visit is therefore recommended for all Germans."[202]

The surviving ego documents, however, reveal that visits to exhibitions of this kind were not very popular and only rarely took place voluntarily, especially in comparison with the other possibilities within the framework of daily life shaped by norms. At the same time, the routine and constantly repeated manner in which the Nazi world view was spread should not be underestimated. Although it is not possible to conduct an explicit analysis of its effectiveness, nonetheless ideology should be granted a higher place in the way that daily life was experienced. Precisely the combination of rather abstract content with concrete experiences proved to be effective. An exhibition with the title "Typhus Exhibit"[203] in connection with the ghetto that was ever-present in the image of the city and had been declared off-limits due to disease, painted a picture of the Jews as degraded and dirty, making them thereby also responsible for their own misery in the Jewish residential quarter. How much higher did the Germans stand, on account of their significant cultural roots; this constantly repeated formula was correspondingly applied also with regard to Polish intellectual life, which was confined to a minimum by the German rulers and consequently was perceived to be on a much lower level than that of the Germans.

The occupiers in the East were the living confirmation of the concept of *Lebensraum* (living space), which was repeatedly reinforced by lectures such as "German Living Space in the Course of History." Even when Hermann Aubin, historian, eastern researcher, and professor at the University of Breslau, was brought in specially, and the audience was required to have basic historical, cultural, and economic knowledge,[204] it did not necessarily mean that hundreds of people turned up. The public announcement and the multiplication-effect of the participants ensured, however—as on other occasions—a much greater reception of the contents. It was not always necessary for 2,500 people to attend as at the first Racial-Political Rally in Warsaw in June 1940. This rally was widely publicized and many offices sent their employees to attend.[205] Political events achieved mass participation only when they did not take the form of lectures and exhibitions. For mass rallies, all of the offices sent their staff; in addition there were also many voluntary participants who wanted to see the spectacle. The local propaganda offices exploited the numerous visits by senior officials to the General Government—or subsequently farther to the East—for these events, which almost always included a tour of Warsaw because the Nazi leaders were also curious about the (former) Polish capital and especially its enormous ghetto. The guest list of Distrikt-Governor Fischer reads like a catalog of the most important functionaries of the Third Reich. The most prominent of them was Adolf Hitler, who reviewed the victory parade of the Wehrmacht on October 5, 1939 along the Aleje Ujazdowskie—for this reason the street was later named *Siegesallee* (Victory Alley)—and afterward he was shown the city.[206]

More common than the visits of prominent people from the Reich were those of the powerful in the General Government, coming from Krakow. They took the stage in carefully planned mass rallies before thousands of occupiers, who were often sent to events from their offices.[207] If the speeches could not be held in the open due to the weather, the Nazi Party usually filled the Roma Theater, whose hall held just three thousand people. In the—as almost always—sold out auditorium, for example, in March 1940, Willi Decker, the *Generalarbeitsführer des Generalgouvernements* (General Leader for Work in the Generalgouvernement) spoke to the ethnic Germans on the Tag der Wehrmacht (Day of the Wehrmacht). He blessed the sacrifices that the soldiers had made for the lives of Germans in Poland and called on the latter to be ready to make similar sacrifices.[208] In this he spelled out the central propaganda trope aimed at the ethnic Germans: their liberation from supposed suffering under the Poles was always combined by the General Government administration with the demand for sacrifices for the German people's community, to which they now belonged; the latter was warmly praised by them in thanks for their newly won freedom.[209] This tenor was used also by Hans Frank when he spoke to the ethnic Germans on his many visits to Warsaw.[210]

In addition, the Nazi calendar of holidays was introduced in the East and adhered to just as in the Reich.[211] There were also additional events that the occupiers commemorated with great pathos: alongside the founding of the Nazi Party in the General Government on August 31, there was above all the Polish capitulation on October 5, 1939; March 16 as the Day of the Wehrmacht had the same importance as in the Reich on account of the many troops stationed in the city. On the last two dates, the troops celebrated themselves with parades through the entire city and a "grand hoisting of the flag" on Adolf Hitler Platz. The accompanying program intensified the communal experience with a shared meal and musical entertainment, as well as lectures and celebratory presentations in cinemas and theaters—not forgetting, of course, the central speeches by representatives of the Wehrmacht, as well as the civil administration and the Party.[212]

The organization was scarcely different for the other state holidays, except that there was no parade and one made do with a military concert.[213] In return the organizers, however, often used the ceremonial occasion for recruits to take their oaths,[214] and here they drew on their experience with mass rallies and Reich Party events. In the East, an awakening experience was also supposed to take place.[215] The occasions used by institutions for celebrations, such as the "Day of the Wehrmacht" mentioned above, provided them with an opportunity to demonstrate their power. Therefore, there was a "Celebration of the German Police" on February 15 and 16,[216] and also a "Day of the German Railwayman" on December 8,[217] which was celebrated in the General Government with receptions and rallies. Decorated with swastika flags, Warsaw became a projection screen for the Nazi policy of conquest: through decorations, parades, and roll-calls, the holders of power wanted to demonstrate that the city was now thoroughly in their hands and completely German. This façade reinforced the occupiers' sense of community, and in the mass of participants any divergent opinions were suppressed by the orchestrated scene.[218] Within normed daily life, even celebrations were used as instruments of social discipline, and transmitted the ideals of the system and reduced nonconformity. In contrast to the Reich, it was scarcely possible for occupiers to stay away from these events. The offices ensured this because they made it one's duty to participate; this sense of duty was reinforced by peer pressure in the shape of comradeship, which also involved aspects of compulsion and was strongly promoted.

The celebrations were accompanied by collections, mainly for the Winter Aid Drive. The "Day of the Wehrmacht" in 1941 produced 51,666.51 Złoty in the Warsaw area, against only 17,252 Złoty in the previous year; this sum went completely to support the Winter Aid Drive.[219] This demonstrated on the one hand the generosity of the occupiers, which was considerably greater than in the Reich. On the other hand, the collection had something of the character of a tax payment because civil servants, for example, had to give up half a month of their daily subvention that they received for being deployed to the East, and all other Germans paid 10 percent of their income tax for the same period.[220] In order to increase the returns, the Nazi Party and Distrikt Warschau also organized benefit concerts at which the individual pieces of music could be purchased through donations. In January 1940 two marching bands and a choir from the Wehrmacht earned in this manner 20,366 Złoty for the Winter Aid Drive. Indicative for the way the attendees perceived themselves was the fact that 11,540 Złoty was taken just to play the "March of the Germans into Poland."[221] This nationalistic song symbolized more than any other the claims of the Germans to land in the East.

Other official social events had a different character, such as when the ethnic Germans got together on Mother's Day,[222] or the Reich Germans on Christmas. Regarding the latter, in contrast to other comradeship evenings that were designed to reinforce solidarity, it was a matter of getting together with comrades to forget the longing for home and family that was especially strong at this time. The organizational framework was provided by the Nazi Party and was distinguished by considerable formality. In addition to a public concert, there also had to be Christmas trees, ringing bells, and a visit by Santa Claus. In order to demonstrate the common bonds among the occupiers, alongside the celebrations by the individual units and organizations there was also a communal German Christmas to which the ethnic Germans were also invited.[223] Participation in the event was carefully regulated; as on other occasions, the Wehrmacht specifically ordered soldiers to attend.[224]

Normed daily life in Minsk also did not differ much from that in Warsaw with regard to political indoctrination. In Weißruthenien there was a Nazi Party organization that regularly held training evenings[225] and ideological lectures,[226] there were exhibitions[227] and visits by prominent Nazis from the Reich.[228] The regional leadership of the Party put on morning festivals every two weeks for the Reich Germans with the proceeds going to the benefit of the Winter Aid Drive; for the ethnic Germans there were the singing of folk songs and trips for members of the Hitler Youth to the Reich. Often, however, the strength of the partisans made organization of such events more difficult; it was impossible, for example, to gather together the ethnic Germans from various locations and bring them to Minsk by bus "for a theater performance or cinema visit and thereby to introduce them to German culture."[229] The Nazi Party in the General Government did not have to overcome these kinds of obstacles and the scale of activities was much smaller in Minsk because there were not so many potential participants there and the available venues were fewer and smaller.

Nonetheless, there were even political programs for the women in Weißruthenien, which is to be attributed mainly to the very active women's group leader, Elisabeth Morsbach. For example, she organized a mass rally of all women from the Reich in the Theater der Stadt of Minsk, at which General Commissar Kube spoke on the topic "The German Task in the East." Of the 850 German women in the city, around 500 were present. Morsbach wanted particularly to promote their integration within the community of women, as most people identified primarily with their offices and institutions rather than with the entire group of female occupiers.[230] However, this problem was not limited to women: many men also restricted their comradeship mainly to their colleagues and thereby consolidated the institutional fragmentation of the society of occupiers. Morsbach wanted to counter this with targeted indoctrination, but the security conditions in Minsk did not permit evening gatherings or homeland evenings because after dark the women were not supposed to be out on the streets. Therefore, events had to be held during the day, like those that promoted what were seen as typically female skills, such as a sewing course. It was necessary, according to the women's leader in Minsk, "so that our girls don't always have to run to the Jews, in order to get something sewn." Within the Party the women's leaders could nonetheless be "educated about the question of unmarried mothers," but this remained a topic, that, despite its ideological charge, was not intended for the general public.[231]

In Warsaw and Minsk the Germans were given an explicit framework within which they were to spend as much time as possible. Behind this framework lay the claim to subject all aspects of daily life to given norms. At least in theory this was successful because the regimentation and programs took up the entire course of the day. The civilian and military organs of occupation wanted to dissolve the boundaries between public and private space. Their totalitarian claim on people did not stop at their private sphere, but attempted instead to occupy this as far as possible.[232] These extensive programs were necessary in order to combat opportunities and attractions that might encourage people to act outside the norms. Especially any contacts with the local population were undesired, which is why the comradeship evenings were emphasized.[233] They were intended to strengthen group loyalty and separate the Germans from the Poles and Belorussians. In this respect, the sense of community served more successfully as a means of social discipline than threatened punishments or prohibitions. Also, within the society of occupiers the double face of fascist rule was visible with its alternation between attractions and compulsion, between offers of integration and pressure to conform.[234] In the organization of leisure time, there was also the thought of at least partially compensating for the longings for home and family; thus diversions from the hardships of deployment to the East were offered. Indeed, most of the efforts in this direction were thankfully accepted, despite the limited ability to exert one's own influence. Those programs without any political content were the most popular, even though two decisive political messages were still linked with them: first that the people's community was supposed also to exist in the East; and second that the occupiers distinguished themselves from the occupied especially because for the latter organized leisure was not available—as it was largely prohibited.

Normed daily life was directed at all sections of the society of occupiers with the same intentions, even when the programs differed. Those for women were behind those for men both in quantitative and qualitative terms. They were granted less access to amusement and entertainment than the male occupiers; even though they made an essential contribution to the functioning of the society of occupiers, their role was not supposed to distance itself too far from the official home-and-kitchen ideology. The ethnic Germans also had a special position because it was unnecessary to compensate them for feelings of homesickness. On the one hand, they were recipients of state welfare; on the other, though, they were the targets of strong political indoctrination. Both the welfare and the indoctrination consolidated their bonds to the new holders of power and reinforced their self-perception as being the advanced guard of the Germans in the East.

Notes

1. Welzer, *Täter*, p. 43.
2. Ibid., p. 89.

3. Hillebrandt and Ebrecht, *Einleitung*, p. 8.
4. Welzer, *Täter*, p. 44.
5. Lüdtke, *Alltagsgeschichte*, p. 12.
6. *Warschauer Zeitung*, Nr. 238 vom 8.10.1940: "Der problematische *Distrikt*—Warschau."
7. Vossler, *Propaganda*, pp. 195–196.
8. *Minsker Zeitung*, no. 187, 10.8.1943: "Betriebsappell der RVD Minsk. Gauleiter Wilhelm Kube und Präsident Grimm zum zweijährigen Einsatz der deutschen Eisenbahner."
9. Römer, *Kameraden*, pp. 138–141.
10. Carl von Andrian diary/Peter Lieb transcript, 21.10.1941.
11. BAB, R 19/137, pp. 93–94, "Vermerk über die Dienstreise des Amtsrats Reimers nach Mogilew und Minsk Anfang April 1943", 22.4.1943.
12. Hosenfeld, "Retten."
13. DTA, 280/I, diary Franz Jonas, 5.–8.8.1941.
14. Ibid., 8.8.1941.
15. APW, 482/13, "Verwaltungsanordnung des Gouverneurs des *Distrikts* Warschau", 27.4.1942.
16. IfZA, MA 1790/2; 378-1-388, "Rundschreiben der RVD Minsk", 28.10.43.
17. *Amtsblatt der Ostbahndirektion*, no. 11, 15.10.1943, p. 90.
18. IfZA, MA 1790/22; 370-6-4, "Hauserlass Nr. 9 des GK Minsk", 7.9.1942.
19. StAM, Polizeipräsidien, Slg. Primavesi/270, "Kriegserinnerungen des Oberwachtmeisters der Schutzpolizei Otto Nahlmann", pp. 14–15.
20. BAL, B 162/AR 179/71, Bd. 8, pp. 1502ff., interrogation of Heinz M., 23.2.1972.
21. IPN, 101/18, Wiesmanns to *Distrikt* Warschau, 1.2.1941, and response, 18.2.1941.
22. Ibid., "Internes Schreiben des *Distrikts* Warschau", 22.2.1941 and "Versetzungsgesuch Wiesmanns", 31.5.1941. His application was approved immediately and on 5.6.1941 he was transferred to Lublin, although Wiesmann had asked to be sent back into the Reich.
23. BAL, B 162/AR 179/71, Bd. 8, pp. 1561ff., interrogation of Dr. Friedrich K., 22.3.1972.
24. APW, 49/13, KdO Warschau to BdO, 30.12.1942.
25. Leist, *Bericht*, p. 286.
26. APW, 49/13, KdO Warschau to BdO, 30.12.1942.
27. *Warschauer Zeitung*, no. 84, 11.4.1940: "Ein deutsches Postheim in Warschau."
28. APW, 482/141, Amtschefs des *Distrikt*gouverneurs Warschau to Abteilung Finanzen, 28.9.1943.
29. RGVA, 1323-1-60, pp. 77–78, "Vermerk der Sipo-Kommandantur Warschau", 30.5.1940.
30. *Warschauer Zeitung*, no. 84, 11.4.1940: "Ein deutsches Postheim in Warschau."
31. Jaworski and Peters, *Alltagsperspektiven*, pp. 30–31.
32. *Minsker Zeitung*, no. 131, 15.9.1942: "Ein deutsches Richtfest. Neues Unterkunftsgebäude für Eisenbahner entsteht."
33. BAB, R 19/137, pp. 93–94, "Vermerk über die Dienstreise des Amtsrats Reimers nach Mogilew und Minsk Anfang April 1943", 22.4.1943.
34. IfZA, MA 1790/11; 370-1-53, "Lagebericht des Generalkommissars Minsk", 6.4.1943.
35. Carl von Andrian diary/Peter Lieb transcript, 23.8.1941.
36. APW, 486/63, "Rundschreiben des Distriktchefs Warschau", 7.7.1941. See also chapter 3 section 2, this volume.
37. *Krakauer Zeitung*, no. 247, 15.10.1943: "Ostbahngehilfinnen wohnen behaglich."
38. BAB, R 90/229, GK Weißruthenien (Morsbach) to RKO, 10.8.1942.
39. BAB, R 90/229, Hauptabteilung II of RKO to Abteilung I Frauen of GK Weißruthenien, 5.12.1942. The same assessment can be found also in IfZA, MA 1790/11; 370-1-53, "Lagebericht des Generalkommissars Minsk", 9.8.1942.

40. Kleßmann, *Selbstbehauptung*, pp. 78–79. On the closure of the high schools, see ibid., pp. 54ff.
41. *Krakauer Zeitung*, no. 182, 6.8.1941: "Eine gastliche Heimstatt für die Soldaten."
42. DTA, 280/I, diary Franz Jonas, 7.8.1941.
43. *Warschauer Zeitung*, no. 13, 26.–27.11.1939: "Ein Soldatenheim in Warschau"; *Warschauer Zeitung*, no. 96, 25.4.1940: "Deutsches Soldatenheim in Warschau erweitert."
44. *Minsker Zeitung*, no. 3, 5.1.1943: "'Schön wie zu Hause'"; *Minsker Zeitung*, no. 64, 17.3.1943: "Alles für unsere Soldaten."
45. *Minsker Zeitung*, no. 101, 11.8.1942: "'Haus der Roten Armee'—Soldatenheim."
46. On this see, e.g., the report of General Gotthard Heinrici on the Deutsche Haus in Siedlce, about fifty kilometers (33 miles) east of Warsaw. Hürter, *General*, pp. 57, and 60–61, Heinrici to his family, 30.4.1941, and 17.5.1941.
47. *Warschauer Zeitung*, no. 48, 27.2.1940: "Deutsches Haus—ein Stück Heimat"; *Warschauer Zeitung*, no. 98, 27.4.1940: "Warschaus Deutsches Haus im Werden."
48. *Krakauer Zeitung*, no. 15, 21.1.1941: "Generalgouverneur Dr. Frank weihte Warschaus Deutsches Haus."
49. *Krakauer Zeitung*, no. 11, 16.1.1941: "Repräsentativer Mittelpunkt deutschen Lebens."
50. *Minsker Zeitung*, no. 123, 5.9.1942: "Heute wird das 'Deutsche Haus' eröffnet."
51. *Minsker Zeitung*, no. 33, 23.5.1942: "Fröhlichkeit nach hartem Dienst."
52. Private collection of Gerhard Lieschke, Wolfgang Lieschke to his wife, 18.8.1941.
53. *Amtsblatt der Ostbahndirektion*, no. 7, 18.9.1943, p. 41, Erlass, 3.9.1943.
54. Carl von Andrian diary/Peter Lieb transcript, 24.12.1941.
55. Kühne, *Kameradschaft*, pp. 131–132.
56. Hosenfeld, *Retten*, p. 413, diary, 29./30.11.1940, and p. 424, diary, 10.2.1941.
57. *Warschauer Zeitung*, no. 67, 20.3.1940: "Hauptwachtmeister als Kinodirektor."
58. In the *Warschauer Zeitung* it was not discussed that Sierck/Sirk had in the meantime emigrated. In addition, instead of Lil Dagover, Zarah Leander was promoted to the lead actress in the article.
59. *Warschauer Zeitung*, no. 218, 14.9.1940: "Das Lichtspielhaus der Deutschen in Warschau."
60. AAN, T 501–228/1235ff., Kommandanturbefehl Warschau no. 55, 12.3.1940.
61. IfZA, Fb 63/50, "Monatsbericht des *Distrikt*gouverneurs Warschau für Februar 1942", 17.3.1942.
62. IfZA, MA 142/276, "GK Weißruthenien an die nachgeordneten Stellen", 21.10.1943.
63. IfZA, MA 1790/2; 378-1-388, internal memo of RVD Minsk, 14.10.1943.
64. IfZA, MA 679—3/1155ff., "Monatsbericht der Kommandantur Warschau für 16.10.–15.11.1941", 20.11.1941.
65. IfZA, MA 679—3/645ff., "Monatsbericht der Kommandantur Warschau für 16.7.–15.8.1941", 21.8.1941.
66. IfZA, MA 679—3/1348ff., "Monatsbericht der Kommandantur Warschau für 16.9.–15.10.1941", 21.10.1941; IfZA, Fb 63/32, "Monatsbericht des *Distrikt*gouverneurs Warschau für Januar 1942", 10.2.1942.
67. VtH, Depositum 239a, diary Ernst Hermann Krause, 2.-18.7.1941. Krause saw films in Warsaw on 3, 10, 14.7.1941. Max Rohrweder also used his time in Warsaw to go to the cinema: DTA, 141/4-7, diary Max Rohrweder.
68. IfZA, MA 679—3/263ff., "Monatsbericht der Kommandantur Warschau für 16.4.–15.5.1941", 20.5.1941. On the content of the film, see Moeller, *Filmminister*, pp. 249ff.
69. *Minsker Zeitung*, no. 168, 20.7.1943: "'Münchhausen' geht zur Front." On the film, see Moeller, *Filmminister*, p. 128.
70. IfZA, MA 679—3/999ff., "Monatsbericht der Kommandantur Warschau für 16.11.–15.12.1941", 20.12.1941. On the content of the film, see Moeller, *Filmminister*, pp. 245ff.

71. Vossler, *Propaganda*, pp. 264–265.
72. IfZA, Fb 63/71, "Monatsbericht des *Distrikt*gouverneurs Warschau für März 1942", 13.4.1942.
73. *Minsker Zeitung*, no. 125, 26.5.1944: "Standard-Holzbau-Kino in Minsk."
74. IfZA, MA 1790/11; 370-1-468, "Anordnung des GK Weißruthenien", 23.6.1942.
75. *Warschauer Zeitung*, no. 25, 31.1.1940: "Warschau hörte Gemeinschaftsempfang."
76. *Minsker Zeitung*, no. 147, 21.6.1944: "'Hier ist der Landessender Minsk ...'"
77. *Minsker Zeitung*, no. 9, 13.1.1944: "Wechsel in der Leitung des Landessenders Minsk"; *Minsker Zeitung*, no. 12, 16.–17.1.1944: "Grosser Betriebsappell beim Landessender Minsk."
78. *Warschauer Zeitung*, no. 256, 29.10.1940: "Grosseinsatz des Rundfunks in Warschau."
79. *Minsker Zeitung*, no. 6, 8.1.1943: "Vom Soldatenfunk zum Landessender."
80. IfZA, MA 679-3/263ff., "Monatsbericht der Kommandantur Warschau für 16.4.–15.5.1941", 20.5.1941.
81. Carl von Andrian diary/Peter Lieb transcript, passim.
82. E.g., *Minsker Zeitung*, no. 62, 14.-15.3.1943: "Tageskalender für Sonntag und Montag."
83. *Minsker Zeitung*, no. 252, 26.10.1943: "Musik im Landessender."
84. *Minsker Zeitung*, no. 62, 14.–15.3.1943. "Kunst auf Ätherwellen."
85. *Minsker Zeitung*, no. 38, 14.–15.2.1943: "Neue Sendereihe 'Land im Aufbau.'"
86. *Minsker Zeitung*, no. 218, 16.9.1943: "Lebensraum Weißruthenien."
87. Boberach, *Meldungen*, pp. 1966–1967. Meldung Nr. 159 vom 3.2.1941.
88. Jockheck, *Propaganda*, p. 164.
89. Ibid., p. 169.
90. Ibid., pp. 110–111.
91. See, e.g., *Warschauer Kulturblätter*, no. 2, October 1940, which accompanied the exhibition "Deutsche Leistung im Weichselraum." no. 3 from November 1941 was on the topic "Buch und Schwert." On "Das Generalgouvernement," see Jockheck, *Propaganda*, p. 96.
92. Kleßmann, *Selbstbehauptung*, pp. 94ff.
93. Jockheck, *Propaganda*, p. 162.
94. Ibid., p. 139.
95. Radziszewski and Riecke, *Germanisierung*, p. 120.
96. *Minsker Zeitung*, no. 36/37, 12.–13.2.1944: "'Bitte—eine *Minsker Zeitung*'"; *Minsker Zeitung*, no. 91, 17.4.1943: "Die '*Minsker Zeitung*' feierte Jubiläum."
97. Jockheck, *Propaganda*, pp. 111–112.
98. BALAA, Ost-Dok. 8/830, pp. 2ff., report by Dr. Paul Gruschinske, Regierungsdirektor and Leiter der Abteilung Wissenschaft und Unterricht im Distrikt Warschau, n.d.
99. *Warschauer Zeitung*, no. 61, 13.3.1940: "30.000 Bücher—zwei grosse Lesesäle."
100. *Warschauer Zeitung*, no. 97, 26.4.1940: "Spende für deutsche Bibliothek Warschau."
101. *Krakauer Zeitung*, no 164, 16.7.1941: "6.000 Leihbände für Warschaus Deutsche"; *Warschauer Zeitung*, no. 229, 27.9.1940: "Das deutsche Buch sehr begehrt."
102. The number of readers seemed to have increased: *Krakauer Zeitung*, no. 257, 27.10.1943: "Born des Wissens und der Erholung," counts some 1,700; in APW, 482/1185, "Bericht über den Stand des Büchereiwesens im Distrikt Warschau", 26.2.1943, mention is made of only around 700 visitors.
103. Private collection of Gerhard Lieschke, Wolfgang Lieschke to his wife, 6.7.1941.
104. Hosenfeld, *Retten*, p. 419, diary, 26.11.1940.
105. Boberach, *Meldungen*, pp. 1966–1967, Meldung no. 159, 3.2.1941; and p. 3156, Meldung no. 250, 12.1.1942.
106. Hosenfeld, *Retten*, pp. 440–441, letter to his wife, 4.2.1941.
107. On the Wehrmacht, see Vossler, *Propaganda*, p. 46.

108. Regarding Poland, see Kleßmann, *Selbstbehauptung*, pp. 103ff.
109. *Warschauer Zeitung*, no. 36, 22.12.1939: "Ein deutsches Theater für Warschau."
110. *Warschauer Zeitung*, no. 33, 9.2.1940: "Deutsche Kammermusik im Palais Brühl"; *Warschauer Zeitung*, no. 59, 10.–11.3.1940: "Kammermusik im Palais Brühl"; *Warschauer Zeitung*, no. 97, 26.4.1940: "Kammermusikabend im Palais Brühl."
111. *Warschauer Zeitung*, no. 238, 8.10.1940: "Festliche Eröffnung des deutschen Theaters."
112. *Warschauer Zeitung*, no. 232, 1.10.1940: "Warschau erhält Theater."
113. *Krakauer Zeitung*, no. 168, 18.7.1942: "Warschauer Theaterbilanz."
114. *Warschauer Zeitung*, no. 289, 7.12.1940: "Warschau wird Pflegestätte der deutschen Operette."
115. *Krakauer Zeitung*, no. 150, 25.6.1943: "Wo der Krieg wütete, hob sich der Vorhang."
116. *Warschauer Zeitung*, no. 282, 29.11.1940: "Opernhaus Berlin gastierte in Warschau."
117. AAN, T 501–228, Kommandanturbefehl Warschau no. 216, 26.11.1940.
118. APW, 482/13, "Rundschreiben des Gouverneurs des *Distrikts* Warschau", 2.9.1943.
119. *Krakauer Zeitung*, no. 168, 18.7.1942: "Warschauer Theaterbilanz."
120. BfZg, Slg. Sterz, letter by Wilhelm Hornung, 2.10.1943.
121. DTA, 141/4, diary Dr. Max Rohrweder, 30.9.–5.10.1941. Many visits are reported also in Hagen, *Auftrag*, pp. 183ff.
122. *Krakauer Zeitung*, no. 16, 20.1.1943: "Warschauer Kulturleben wurde gefördert."
123. DTA, 141/4, diary Max Rohrweder, 1.10.1941.
124. Kleßmann, *Selbstbehauptung*, p. 106.
125. For a review, see, e.g., *Warschauer Zeitung*, no. 259, 1.-2.11.1940: "Der Warschauer Erfolg der Philharmoniker."
126. *Warschauer Kulturblätter*, no. 1, 1940.
127. *Das Generalgouvernement* 1 (1940), pp. 32–33: "Deutsches Theater."
128. *Warschauer Zeitung*, no. 253, 25.10.1940: "Der Beginn der Warschauer Kulturtage."
129. Hosenfeld, *Retten*, p. 406, letter to his wife, 28.10.1940, and diary, 29./30.10.1940; the quote is found here, also.
130. *Krakauer Zeitung*, no. 277, 23.11.1941: "Programm der Warschauer Kulturtage"; see also *Warschauer Kulturblätter*, no. 3, November 1941, which was published as an accompanying program to the exhibition "Buch und Schwert."
131. *Krakauer Zeitung*, no. 249, 17.10.1943: "Neuer Kulturmittelpunkt im Osten."
132. Boberach, *Meldungen*, pp. 3268ff., Meldung no. 257, 5.2.1942.
133. Alvensleben, "Abschiede," pp. 141ff., diary, 27.9.1940 and 12.10.1940 (quote).
134. IfZA, MA 708-3/205ff., Befehl no. 22, KdS Warschau, 24.5.1940.
135. IfZA, MA 708-3/255ff., Befehl no. 38, KdS Warschau, 13.9.1940.
136. IfZA, MA 708-3/273ff., Befehl no. 41, KdS Warschau, 4.10.1940.
137. AAN, T 501-228/1281f., Kommandanturbefehl Warschau no. 41, 23.2.1940.
138. BAL, B 162/AR 179/71, vol. 8, pp. 1525ff., interrogation of Theo L., 6.3.1972.
139. *Warschauer Zeitung*, no. 35, 11.–12.2.1940: "Bayerischer Humor in Warschau."
140. APW, 48/4, circular, Amtschefs des *Distrikt*gouverneurs Warschau, 9.2.1942; ibid., Transferstelle für den jüdischen Wohnbezirk to Kommissar für den jüdischen Wohnbezirk, 23.2.1942.
141. IfZA, MA 1790/2; 378-1-388, internal memo, RVD Minsk, 14.10.1943.
142. *Amtsblatt der Ostbahndirektion*, no. 18, 13.12.1943, p. 140.
143. Private collection of Gerhard Lieschke, Wolfgang Lieschke to his wife, 13.11.1941.
144. *Minsker Zeitung*, no. 107, 18.8.1942: "Am Leben liegt uns nichts, an der Ehre alles! Wilhelm Kubes 'Totila' im Minsker Stadttheater."
145. Reichel, *Schein*, pp. 257-258.
146. Szarota, *Warschau*, p. 254.
147. *Warschauer Zeitung*, no. 120, 3.5.1940: "Warschau hat eine Deutsche Sportgemeinschaft."

148. *Warschauer Zeitung*, no. 107, 9.5.1940: "Zehn aktive Sportgemeinschaften in Warschau." The number ten given in the headline is for the entire *Distrikt*.
149. *Warschauer Zeitung*, no. 291, 10.12.1940: "Generalgouvernementssport unter Führung der Partei."
150. IfZA, MA 708-3/273ff., Befehl no. 41, KdS Warschau, 4.10.1940.
151. *Warschauer Zeitung*, no. 140, 15.6.1940: "Auch Warschau führt jetzt Fußballmeisterschaften durch."
152. *Warschauer Zeitung*, no. 152, 26.6.1940: "Gramlich-Mannen gegen die stärkste Warschauer Elf."
153. *Warschauer Zeitung*, no. 256, 29.10.1940: "Glanzvolles Städtespiel Warschau-Danzig endete unentschieden."
154. *Warschauer Zeitung*, no. 279, 26.11.1940: "Posen erlag zum zweiten Mal dem Ansturm der Warschauer Elf."
155. IfZA, Fb 63/188, "Zweimonatsbericht des Distriktgouverneurs Warschau für Oktober and November 1942", 10.12.1942.
156. Hosenfeld, *Retten*, p. 543, diary, 5.11.1941.
157. *Warschauer Zeitung*, no. 154, 2.7.1940: "Nur SV Okecie im Generalgouvernement unbesiegt."
158. AAN, T 501-228/921ff., Kommandanturbefehl Warschau no. 161, 20.8.1940; *Warschauer Zeitung*, no. 202, 27.8.1940: "Okecie triumphiert vor 20.000 in Warschau."
159. *Warschauer Zeitung*, no. 196, 20.8.1940: "Warschaus Leichtathleten gewannen den Wettkampf der 4 *Distrikte*."
160. *Warschauer Zeitung*, no. 149, 26.6.1940: "Schwimmeisterschaften finden in Warschau statt."
161. *Amtsblatt der Ostbahndirektion*, no. 9, 28.4.1944, p. 88.
162. RGVA, 1323-2-302a, Bl. 15, Kommandanturbefehl Warschau no. 132, 10.6.1943.
163. The English abbreviation for the Young Men's Christian Association (YMCA) was also used at that time in Poland.
164. BAB, R 5 Anhang I/127, S. 510f., memo of Reichsverkehrsministerium, Zweigstelle Osten, 2.3.1942.
165. *Haushaltsplan des Generalgouvernements* 1941, p. 65.
166. BAL, B 162/3660, S. 130ff., interrogation of Heinrich H., 15.8.1960.
167. *Warschauer Zeitung*, no. 225, 22.–23.9.1940: "In Warschau wird elektrisch gefochten."
168. *Warschauer Zeitung*, no. 276, 22.4.1940: "Die Sieger des Schachmeisterturniers bei Dr. Fischer."
169. *Warschauer Zeitung*, no. 84, 11.4.1940: "Grosses Heim der deutschen Sportler in Warschau."
170. Hosenfeld, *Retten*, pp. 65ff.; *Krakauer Zeitung*, no. 289n 7.12.1941: "Eine Sportschule im Warschauer Wehrmachtstadion."
171. IfZA, Fb 63/27, "Monatsbericht des *Distrikt*gouverneurs Warschau für Januar 1942", 10.2.1942.
172. *Warschauer Zeitung*, no. 135, 9.–10.6.1940: "Flaggenhissung auf Warschauer Bootshäusern."
173. *Warschauer Zeitung*, no. 178, 30.7.1940: "Gouverneur Fischer steuerte die schnellste Jacht."
174. VtH, Depositum 239a, diary Ernst Hermann Krause, 12. and 13.7.1941.
175. Hosenfeld, *Retten*, pp. 535–536, diary, 29.9.1941.
176. DTA, 141/4, diary Dr. Max Rohrweder, 11.10.1941.
177. APW, 482/12, "Satzung des Reitervereins Warschau", n.d.
178. APW, 482/102, Amtschefs des *Distrikts* Warschau to Leiter der Abteilung Forsten, 11.1.1943.
179. IfZA, MA 1790/3; 379-2-45, Kommandanturbefehl Minsk no. 12, 4.11.1941.

Chapter 2

180. IfZA, MA 792-2/402, Verlagsleitung der *Minsker Zeitung* to ERR, 31.8.1943.
181. IfZA, MA 1790/3; 379-2-14, Befehl no. 167 of OT Minsk, 22.4.1944.
182. Nolzen, "Arbeitsbereiche," pp. 254ff. On the start of the registration of Nazi Party members in June 1940, see *Warschauer Zeitung*, no. 136, 11.6.1940: "Die Erfassung der Parteigenossen eingeleitet."
183. This can be seen in Warsaw from the gaps in the card indexes. AAN, 116/40-47; see also Nolzen, "Arbeitsbereiche," p. 260.
184. Nolzen, "Arbeitsbereiche," pp. 272–273.
185. Ibid., p. 257.
186. *Warschauer Zeitung*, no. 284, 1.–2.12.1940: "Rege Parteiarbeit im *Distrikt* Warschau."
187. *Warschauer Zeitung*, no. 277, 23.11.1940: "Aufbau der Partei im *Distrikt* Warschau."
188. *Krakauer Zeitung*, no. 145, 25.6.1941: "Partei-Organisation wird ausgebaut."
189. *Krakauer Zeitung*, no. 39, 12.2.1941: "Warschaus Haus der Nationalsozialisten."
190. *Krakauer Zeitung*, no. 287, 5.12.1941: "Deutsches Leben von der NSDAP geformt."
191. *Warschauer Zeitung*, no. 146, 22.6.1940: "Deutsche Frauenarbeit im *Distrikt* Warschau."
192. AAN, 116/38, Rundschreiben no. 13/42, NSDAP-*Distrikt*standortführung Warschau, 6.3.1942.
193. *Krakauer Zeitung*, no. 287, 5.12.1941: "Deutsches Leben von der NSDAP geformt."
194. AAN, 116/38, Rundschreiben no. 13/42, NSDAP-*Distrikt*standortführung Warschau, 6.3.1942.
195. *Krakauer Zeitung*, no. 287, 5.12.1941: "Deutsches Leben von der NSDAP geformt."
196. Ibid.
197. *Krakauer Zeitung*, no. 233, 4.10.1941: "Auch dafür ist die Partei im Generalgouvernement da …"
198. APW, 486/48, "Einladung zu Vorträgen", 7.2.1942.
199. *Warschauer Kulturblätter*, no. 2, October 1940, p. 3.
200. *Warschauer Kulturblätter*, no. 3, November 1941.
201. Jockheck, *Propaganda*, pp. 139ff.
202. AAN, T 501-228, Kommandanturbefehl Warschau no. 234, 23.12.1940.
203. IfZA, MA 679-6/273ff., "Monatsbericht der Oberfeldkommandantur Warschau für die Zeit vom 16.2.–15.3.1943", 21.3.1943.
204. AAN, T 501-228, Kommandanturbefehl Warschau no. 48, 2.3.1940.
205. AAN, T 501-228/1022f., Kommandanturbefehl Warschau no. 118, 13.6.1940; see also *Warschauer Zeitung*, no. 142, 18.6.1940: "Zum ersten Male rassepolitische Kundgebung in Warschau."
206. Szarota, *Warschau*, pp. 14–15, and the photos after p. 176.
207. E.g., RGVA, 1323-2-302a, Bl. 34, Kommandanturbefehl Warschau no. 116, 21.5.1943. The Wehrmacht sent 170 men to a mass rally of the Nazi Party in the Roma Theater.
208. *Warschauer Zeitung*, no. 66, 19.3.1940: "Generalarbeitsführer Dr. Decker in Warschau."
209. E.g., *Warschauer Zeitung*, no. 232, 1.10.1940: "Volksdeutsche danken der Wehrmacht"; *Warschauer Zeitung*, no. 197, 21.8.1940: "Volksdeutsche Grosskundgebung in Warschau"; *Warschauer Zeitung*, no. 24, 30.1.1940: "Warschaus Kundgebung der 3000."
210. *Warschauer Zeitung*, no. 238, 8.10.1940: "Dr. Frank im Albert-Breyer-Haus" and "Begeisterte Kundgebung des Deutschtums." Regarding the many visits by Frank to Warsaw, see Präg and Jacobmeyer, *Diensttagebuch*, and on the ethnic Germans esp. pp. 285–286.
211. *Verordnungsblatt für das Generalgouvernement*, part 1, no. 21, 20.3.1940, p. 108.
212. AAN, T 501-228/1235ff., Kommandanturbefehl Warschau no. 55, 12.3.1940; *Warschauer Zeitung*, no. 236, 5.10.1940: "Warschau flaggt zum historischen Festtag"; *Warschauer Zeitung*, no. 238, 8.10.1940: "Die grosse Siegesparade in Warschau."

213. AAN, T 501-228/911f., "Kommandanturbefehl Warschau zur Feier der NSDAP am 31.8./1.9.", 28.8.1940; *Warschauer Zeitung*, no. 207. 1.-2.9.1940: "Auch Warschaus Adolf-Hitler-Platz deutschen Ursprungs"; *Warschauer Zeitung*, no. 73, 21.-22.4.1940: "Der Geburtstag des Führers im Generalgouvernement."

214. *Warschauer Zeitung*, no. 92, 20.4.1940: "So begeht Warschau den Führer-Geburtstag."

215. Vossler, *Propaganda*, p. 50.

216. *Krakauer Zeitung*, no. 35, 14.2.1941: "Warschau feiert das 'Fest der Deutschen Polizei.'"

217. *Amtsblatt der Ostbahndirektion*, no. 1, 1.1.1944, p. 12.

218. Ibid., pp. 343–344.

219. RGVA, 1323-2-302w, Bl. 16, Kommandanturbefehl Warschau no. 55, 29.3.1941.

220. *Warschauer Zeitung*, no. 262, 6.11.1940: "Warschaus Deutsche opfern für das WHW."

221. *Warschauer Zeitung*, no. 18, 23.1.1940: "Warschaus Grusskonzert: über 20.000 Zl." The text of the march by Heinrich Gutberlet (music by Eugen Naumann): "[1] Was dich auch bedrohe,/Eine heilige Lohe/Gibt dir Sonnenkraft./Lass dich nimmer knechten;/Lass dich nie entrechten./Gott gibt den Gerechten/Wahre Heldenschaft. [2] Was auch daraus werde,/Steht zur Heimat Erde;/Bleibe wurzelstark!/Kämpfe, blute, werbe/Für dein höchstes Erbe;/Siege oder sterbe,/Deutsch sei bis ins Mark!"

222. *Warschauer Zeitung*, no. 118, 22.5.1940: "Feierstunde zum Muttertag in Warschau."

223. *Warschauer Zeitung*, no. 36, 23.12.1939: "Frohe Gemeinschaft unter dem Tannenbaum"; *Warschauer Zeitung*, no. 38, 28.12.1939: "Deutsche Weihnacht in Warschau."

224. AAN, T 501-228, Kommandanturbefehl Warschau no. 233, 20.12.1940.

225. See, e.g., IfZA, MA 792-2/415, "Einladung der NSDAP-Bezirksleitung Weißruthenien zu Gemeinschaftsabenden im Juni 1944", 5.6.1944.

226. See, e.g., IfZA, MA 792-2/461, "Einladung der NSDAP-Bezirksleitung zu einer Rede von Generalkommissar Kube mit dem Thema 'Unser Kampf um den Sieg'", 28.7.1943.

227. See, e.g., IfZA, MA 142/277, Generalkommissar Weißruthenien to nachgeordnete Stellen, 19.10.1943: "Im Sitzungssaal der RVD stellen am 20. and 21. d.M. Kriegsmaler etwa 60 für eine Reichsausstellung bestimmte Gemälde aus dem Arbeitsbereich der Eisenbahn in den besetzten Ostgebieten aus." See also IfZA, MA 792-2/430, "Einladung der Reichsverkehrsdirektion Minsk zu einer Lichtbildschau", 31.3.1944.

228. See, e.g., IfZ MA 1790/22; 370-6-4, "Programm anlässlich des Besuches von Gauleiter Sauckel in Minsk", 6.8.1942.

229. BAB, R 93/3, pp. 4–5, "Lagebericht zu Volkstums- und Siedlungsfragen in Weißruthenien", 15.10.1942.

230. BAB, R 90/229, "Bericht über die Frauengrosskundgebung in Minsk am 15.2.1943", 20.2.1943.

231. IfZA, MA 256/417ff., "Protokoll über die Sitzung der Arbeitsgemeinschaft der Führerinnen deutscher Frauengruppen in Minsk", 11.4.1943.

232. Reichel, *Schein*, p. 170.

233. *Krakauer Zeitung*, no. 76, 3.4.1941: "Das Ziel: eine grosse Kameradschaft." See also Vossler, *Propaganda*, p. 46.

234. Nolzen, "Arbeitsbereiche," p. 275.

Chapter 3

Transgression of Norms

The occupiers' acceptance of the organized programs and rules of prescribed daily life could largely be taken for granted, especially when these had little ideological content; even explicitly political events remained well attended. In reality it was difficult to remain absent from the numerous obligations because the authorities' instructions, and especially peer pressure, made this very difficult. Therefore, the lives of the occupiers were largely conducted within the prescribed limits. Those few freedoms that were still left to them, however, as well as those activities that were not specifically regulated, became even more tempting. Here they could display their individuality and, at least in part, organize their daily lives according to their own wishes—and not simply those of their superiors and those in power.

This room for maneuver arose from incoherence in the system of norms and institutions. Not everything that was not desired was explicitly forbidden; not everything that was forbidden was actually punished. Therefore, the reality of daily life for the occupiers consisted of adapting to given situations and rules. Adaptation means interpreting instructions and the nuanced reading of official expectations, in short. Applying one's own personal interpretation of those norms required more than just strict obedience to laws and regulations.[1] Alf Lüdtke has established that during World War II members of the Wehrmacht developed the capacity "to find and discover possibilities for their own freedom of action and to exploit them with skillful determination, but without attracting attention."[2] The Germans in Warsaw and Minsk also sought and found these kinds of opportunities.

1. The Unloved East?

The concept of living space in the East held a key place in National Socialist ideology. Germans were to be settled on the territory of Poland and the Soviet Union and most of the local population was to be driven out or killed, so that the "master race" could develop itself undisturbed. These comprehensively conceived dystopias, which during the war were scarcely implemented in terms of more concrete plans[3] and even in the area of Zamość were only partly realized, were known from 1941 under the name Generalplan Ost (Master Plan East). These ideas, which ultimately tended toward genocide against the Slavs, were linked with idyllic and romanticized conceptions of the East. The Nazis believed they would be performing a civilizing mission in a wild and undeveloped country. With the help of spacial planners, demographers, engineers, and economic experts, the conquerors wanted to bring about a targeted reordering and modernization of the country.[4]

Due to this attitude that ultimately viewed the East as a kind of promised land, the work to be conducted there was described using the most positive images. Precisely because of the confirmed backwardness and expansiveness of the territory, this was viewed as a difficult task,[5] but also as a task that would be very beneficial for the future of the German people. Poland and Belorussia represented a challenge that, in the words of Hans Frank, Germany's "best people" should thankfully accept.[6] For him the East was the "country of the future," in which in 1940 the occupiers already "[had] achieved great things, but [would] still create even greater ones."[7] In Weißruthenien the path to this noble goal would demand sacrifices, but ultimately the effort was an honorable task that had to be fulfilled "with all possible strength and dedication." Reich Minister Alfred Rosenberg even declared in Minsk that "all the men and women" had come to the East "voluntarily and happily" in order to establish there "a strong and flourishing bastion of the German Reich."[8]

The leading exponents of Nazism, therefore, expected of the occupiers that they loved their deployment to the East and took pride in the importance of their assigned mission. Naturally their perceptions were quite different from these ideological aims. There were, of course, a few convinced idealists who reported on their service full of confidence and joy, but they remained rare exceptions.[9] Most of the occupiers wrote letters home that contained little euphoria; they rarely confided pleasant things to the pages of their diaries, either. Even in memoirs or witness testimonies given twenty years later this picture scarcely changes—despite the human habit of generally mythologizing the past. It is indicative of the general validity of this perception that there is only a difference in terms of degree between Minsk and Warsaw, such that Poland is generally described as being slightly more acceptable than Weißruthenien. This is especially notable because in reality a distinctly more pleasant life was possible in the General Government than in Belorussia. Yet in its totality, the East—in stark contrast to the West—had a much more terrifying effect on the Germans and was rarely differentiated. France offered far more pleasant experiences and compensations for the time spent away from home than Poland or the occupied Soviet territories. In the East, obtaining food supplies was more difficult, the population more hostile, and in general less compensation was offered for leaving behind one's job and family, compared to the West.[10] When a unit was informed that they were being sent to the East, among the men there was a general lament, "the East was and remained a deterrent."[11]

The reasons for criticism that the Germans brought up were extremely varied. Most of them stressed resentments that were based mainly on negative expectations. Thus, for example, the climate was viewed as especially harsh and cold, although typically in this respect Warsaw did not differ significantly from Munich. (See figure 3.1 for a view of the ruined city in winter.) Nonetheless, Private Rudolf Fausthammer wrote about Warsaw in 1940: "It is stupid that the winter there never seems to end."[12] Minsk, however, actually does have lower average temperatures than German cities.

Figure 3.1. Warsaw in the Winter of 1939–1940
Source: Du Prel, *Generalgouvernement*, photograph section after p. 320.

There the occupiers often encountered unreliable or inadequate heating equipment,[13] such that, in the words of Carl von Andrian, the winter was also "harsh in the living quarters."[14] In combination with the rather unbalanced diet and not always sufficient rations in Weißruthenien, this resulted in generally poor health conditions. Generalkommissar Kube had to send some of his staff back home again because their "health was deemed unsuited for the East."[15] In view of the constant shortages of staff, which rarely allowed people to be on leave, this was a clear indication of the harshness of service conditions in the East that the occupiers experienced and criticized.

Prejudice also produced the trope of the cultureless East.[16] In view of the impoverished and partly destroyed suburbs of both cities, the Germans concluded that the standard of the accommodations also reflected the racial quality of their inhabitants; this took on especially crass forms in the case of the ghettos. There repugnance was mixed with claims to superiority. The occupiers clearly felt uncomfortable in an unaccustomed environment. The ghettos appeared to them as dirty: from a typical letter from Warsaw in 1941: "Dirt, smells, and noise are the main characteristics of the ghetto."[17] With this perception there was—in contrast to World War I—a shift in meaning of the central criteria for evaluation of cleanliness. The Germans converted external appearances into human, social, or even biological attributes, thereby reproducing one of the decisive elements of modern racism.[18] The consequence was that scarcely any sympathy was expressed because in the eyes of the new masters the Jews or Slavs did not deserve sympathy: they were not capable of living in conditions worthy of a human. Middle-class values, such as domestic order and cleanliness, which were viewed as normal, the occupiers could not find in the East and especially did not want to find.[19] Much more they saw only "dirt and a scary overall condition."[20]

After their arrival in the East the Germans experienced a certain loss of orientation,[21] because Poland and the Soviet Union were foreign countries, which very few of them had visited before the war. As official tourism statistics for Warsaw demonstrate, in the years before 1939 only a few visitors from their western neighbor came to the Polish capital (see table 3.1), and even those, such as the subsequent Luftwaffe doctor in Warsaw, Wolfgang Lieschke, who visited the Polish metropolis in 1930 together with his wife, did not necessarily view the population with any less prejudice as a result.[22] The trips organized by the Nazi organization Strength through Joy also did not take tourists to Eastern Europe, quite apart from the fact that despite these beginnings of mass tourism, many Germans had never left their own country at all. Poland became one of the first travel destinations of the Wehrmacht and the civilian occupiers that followed them (see table 3.1).[23]

Table 3.1. German Tourists in Warsaw, 1933–1937

Year	1933	1934	1935	1936	1937
Number	2,786	5,074	5,090	6,083	5,302

Source: Zarząd Miejski, p. 12.

The alienation connected with the new environment remained one of the elemental experiences that the occupiers made repeatedly during the war; the landscape, culture, language, and way of life in Eastern Europe were all unaccustomed. Precisely the supposed culture gap was exploited as a concept in Nazi propaganda that reinforced this image and constantly repeated it.[24] Yet the stereotypes presented could also strike a chord with collective mentalities to establish structures that helped people accept their new daily routine more easily.[25] So the Germans had formed numerous prejudices long before their deployment to the East, which now sought confirmation and of course found it.

However, it was not the intention of the Nazi leadership that the occupiers should resent having to work in this reputedly desolate environment. Here it worked against them that Poland and the Soviet Union had been described almost only as the primitive old enemies of the Reich.[26] This problem was especially virulent in Belorussia because the propaganda had almost never differentiated between the individual Soviet republics. That the area around Minsk now was supposed to be the home of its own distinctive people who were different from the Russians was difficult to communicate. The policy of divide and rule pursued by the Reich Ministry for the Occupied Eastern Territories planned to treat the region differently, and above all to treat it better that those regions farther to the east, in order to split it off from Russia. Along with that went a limited racial and cultural upgrading of the country and its inhabitants; this, however, scarcely had any effective impact on the occupiers in practice.[27]

The considerable physical destruction that could not be ignored in Minsk and Warsaw also contributed to the appreciation of deployment to the East as an unpleasant task.[28] In the case of the Polish (former) capital, Joseph Goebbels considered the war damage in the fall of 1939 so bad that he did not want to use any pictures of it for his propaganda in order to avoid creating negative impressions abroad.[29] Great disappointment among the arriving Germans was also observed, however, particularly in Belorussia. General Commissar Wilhelm Kube wrote at the end of 1942 about the women who came to the city: "Experience shows that the girls, quite apart from the fact that they cry their hearts out to the offices of the Reich Commissar for the 'Ostland,' through the impression that they have gained in Riga, look forward to the expectations and conditions in Minsk in the most pessimistic way imaginable. It is not possible to keep it a secret that Minsk [is] a pile of rubble."[30]

Not having experienced the subsequent devastation of the homeland, the extent of this initial damage was often overestimated. Wolfgang Lieschke, for example, reported that in Minsk 90 percent of the buildings were destroyed and described the still-standing grandiose communist structures as "a picture of cruel monumentality."[31] On top of the destruction came the sparseness and lack of comfort in the accommodations, which especially in Minsk were characteristic for the deployments there. For example, there was no drinking water in the pipes. Even in the Belorussian capital water had to be boiled because water from the facilities inherited from the Soviets was clear, but not free of bacteria.[32] Some soldiers, like Wolfgang Lieschke, were also annoyed because they did not even receive proper quarters there, but rather had to sleep in tents.[33]

A further shortcoming was the unfulfilled promises that had often been made to those in the civilian administration in order to attract them to the East. This might have come in the form of an announced promotion that was declared as a reward, combined with the assurance that requests for transfers were possible if the new position did not appeal to the person.[34] Especially for service in the conquered territories of the Soviet Union, in the words of the *Generalkommissar* in Minsk, Kube, "The most generous financial promises were made for deployments to the East."[35] Since these promises were not kept, the anger was great. In some cases the officials or employees complained that they even missed out on a promotion or desired position within their home authority on account of their absence. They believed that their Eastern deployment, hailed by propaganda as a heroic deed, was instead punishment that caused irreparable disadvantage.[36]

Most of these criticisms by the occupiers of their Eastern deployment were all too familiar in the administrative offices in Weißruthenien and the General Government. In part this was because their superiors suffered from the same problems themselves, but in part also on account of openly or indirectly expressed opinions. Not uncommonly, official documents reported that the mood was "not especially favorable." In Minsk, Generalkommissar Kube even wrote that above all he needed people for Weißruthenien who were "strong" and "used to making sacrifices,"[37] because conditions there were so bad.

On the other hand, the occupiers continued to misrepresent their own activities. The Post Office described service in the General Government as an experience that was "diverse, educational, entertaining, and at times humorous." For this reason, it wanted to publish a book that portrayed "the difficulties encountered by the Postal Service in its dealings with Poles and Jews."[38] Here a strategy was pursued that tried to turn weaknesses into strengths by calling the hardships entertaining and ultimately laying blame for the annoyances—that had been overcome—on the locals, thereby reducing them to just a small part of everyday life. In Belorussia similar calculations can be observed, for example, at the German Railway. Its Minsk office was looking for photographs that illustrated the climatic problems and praised the achievements of the railway men.[39] The intention was the same as at the Post Office: again, overcoming obstacles in the East was to be celebrated.

The greatest problem that the various office directors had to confront was the homesickness of the occupiers. This was expressed especially in the longing for one's family. Most of the men were at an age at which they had a wife or a girlfriend, and frequently had just had their first children. The separation for them was much tougher than for the many younger women who had volunteered, precisely because they were not tied to home by these sorts of responsibilities. The letters sent home by the Germans draw a clear picture. Even those who kept diaries stressed in their entries repeatedly how much they missed their families. The daily life of Wilm Hosenfeld in Warsaw was dominated by thoughts about the fate of his family and longings for his wife and child; scarcely a day went by on which he did not express this in letters or on a page of his diary.[40]

The strongly felt alienation in Poland and Belorussia due to the separation from family was very difficult to compensate. The most significant response by the authorities and institutions to calm the disquiet was generous leave practices,[41] the aim of which—to some extent in its most elemental form—was still clearly recalled by the occupiers years later: "As we were told, we received leave so frequently, because … in the General Government at that time contact or relations with Polish and Jewish women was strictly forbidden."[42] The German Post Office, for example, allowed special leave every three months. In 1941 this release from work, in addition to the regular vacation of three weeks, was for seven days on the high holidays and otherwise for five days.[43] The supervisors considered it important that these breaks were taken at regular intervals; this, they believed, was the best way to combat homesickness and the longing for one's family. Especially at Christmas this seemed appropriate, and those working for the General Government and its offices received an additional vacation of seven days—including Sundays and public holidays. The journey home could be combined with rest and recuperation leave, but in total it could not exceed twenty-one days plus the journey. In addition, the travel costs were also paid.[44] Fathers of families with children under age sixteen were given special priority, otherwise leave was given to those who had been in Poland the longest because ultimately it was not possible for the entire office to go home at the same time.[45]

In light of the strategy pursued in Poland and Weißruthenien of compensating for the discomforts through generous leave policies, leave of six to eight weeks' home leave per year was not a rarity,[46] although soldiers and officers received considerably less time off because the Wehrmacht was not so generous. While the authorities allowed the occupiers to return home, visits to the East by family members were not desired. This was handled differently, however, by the military than by the civilian authorities. Soldiers and civilian employees of the Wehrmacht were not permitted to receive any visits by family members or fiancées. In the General Government relatives were only allowed under a special exception regulation and only if permission was granted for vacation at a third location. The Oberkommando der Wehrmacht (High Command of the Wehrmacht) was especially concerned about the sexual deprivation of the men; it decreed, "For reasons of discretion, comradeship and the image of the Wehrmacht, extreme restraint is expected in connection with visits of this kind."[47]

Nonetheless, creative soldiers still managed to arrange trysts with their loved ones in the East without being caught. For example, Wilm Hosenfeld's obstinacy was so strong that, despite a specific threat of arrest, he managed to bring his wife into the General Government in April 1942 and met with her during an official trip to the winter sport location of Zakopane. After this they travelled back to Warsaw together, where she stayed an additional week in the Sportheim (Sports Home)—that was under Hosenfeld's authority—without his superiors noticing it. In the city they even managed to meet their son of military age, Helmut, at the railway station on his way to the Eastern Front.[48] These kinds of meetings were of course not forbidden.

The situation in Weißruthenien was clearly less favorable for the occupiers. Not only were visits there completely forbidden starting in May 1942,[49] but also, because of the dangerous security situation, family members were permitted to come out and join their men in service only with special permission from the Reich Commissar for the Ostland or Reichsminister Rosenberg. Exceptions, however, might be granted on grounds of public interest, as was maintained, for example, in the case of General Commissar Kube's wife; mainly for representational reasons, her presence was deemed to be of importance,[50] which some members of the Wehrmacht viewed as completely unfair. Wolfgang Lieschke wrote to his wife from Minsk, "By the way, it's a pity that you didn't marry a government official; Gau Leader Kube and his married colleagues have brought their wives out here, as I heard today."[51] The requirements needed for family members to come out East were made more difficult because it was only then permissible throughout the Reich Commissariat for Ostland. Therefore, only those who were committed to the East as the central point of their lives, and who had postponed their returns for the foreseeable future, could receive an approval.[52] Yet very few people wanted to do that.

The Germans gladly took the chances to go home offered to them. Apart from the soldiers, very few of them spent more than ten months of the year in Poland or Belorussia, and exploited their vacation time as much as possible. They also took advantage of the other leisure time activities offered within the framework of prescribed daily life; nonetheless the basically negative image of the East remained predominant. All the same, most of the occupiers managed, with time, to overcome the initial problems or worries about their own situation. Particularly among the volunteers, who often experienced their deployment as a great disappointment because their ideological dreams and practical career plans were not realized, there was no reduction of cognitive dissonance available.[53] This dissonance resulted from the subjective perception—also promoted by the regime—of fulfilling an important, valuable task in the East that would further their careers. This conflicted starkly with the clearly negative experienced reality, in which such perspectives were not visible.

A reduction of dissonance occurred because those influences that reduce dissonance had much greater influence than those that increased it.[54] Unconsciously, the longer their tour of duty in the East lasted, the more the occupiers stressed the positive aspects of their daily lives and gave the negative points a lower ranking. At the same time they interpreted information that might strengthen the dissonance subconsciously as false or believed it only selectively. An example for this is given by the doctor Wolfgang Lieschke, who initially had expected that in Warsaw he would be "comfortably accommodated in a small villa."[55] Just one day after his arrival, he reported full of disappointment, that he "lived here in a wasteland … a region as flat as a table, without trees, steppe, constant wind with dust or baking heat," in addition the "dreary big city" was more than half an hour distant.[56] Only one month later, his description sounded clearly more positive; all of a sudden he saw "countryside that is attractive," and reported on his quarters: "Warsaw is not a pretty sight, but nearby in the countryside it is better."[57]

For many occupiers these kinds of new and reinterpretations of their environment made it possible for them to come to an arrangement with their daily lives so they could put up with their harsh fate without constant complaints.[58] This was the case, for example, with Carl von Andrian, who was not very impressed by his deployment to the East and frequently complained about the poor conditions. At the same time he repeatedly stressed positive aspects, such as a concert, on which "a dear 20-year-old girl … played fantastically,"[59] occasional celebratory meals,[60] but also his frequent riding forays and hunting expeditions, which he enjoyed.[61] For the convinced Eastern colonists, this kind of stress on the positive side of things was especially important. Only very reluctantly did they want to inwardly concede, or openly admit, that the reality did not correspond with their preconceptions at all. Thus was born within sections of the bureaucracy, and partly also only after the war, the image of an administrative idyll.[62]

Nonetheless, there was a relatively small group that could not cope with the given circumstances and tried everything to escape them. For these people, confrontations with unrestrained violence that they were unable to cope with frequently played a decisive role.[63] Yet their attempts to be transferred elsewhere remained mostly without success. Efforts to help these Germans have not been documented; visits to the official health sanatoria, for example, were mainly issued to people as rewards.[64] Those who really did not fit in with the society of occupiers were isolated in their service environment and left alone. The number of Germans who as the final consequence chose suicide is not known. For Warsaw the suicide of at least one member of the police is recorded. This man became desperate due to the environment in his battalion (no. 61) and especially because of the murders committed by its members.[65]

On the other hand, there were occupiers who viewed the East as pleasant from the start—although in this respect Warsaw was clearly seen more positively than Minsk. In their reports the advantageous aspects strongly outweighed the negative ones. In the former Polish capital, for example, local transport was seen as a model; one soldier even described the streetcar as "more beautiful than in Vienna."[66] The main railway station, built in the 1930s with its underground platforms and its several multistory buildings, was very modern and is also frequently mentioned positively.[67] On top of that there was the impressiveness of the palaces, the "wonderful buildings and wide streets"[68] that reminded Wolfgang Lieschke "to some extent" of Paris,[69] and the numerous parks that were especially pleasant in summer; in some cases the Germans also praised Polish culture.[70] General Gotthard Heinrici even discovered that the Polish nobility "built more and more beautifully" in the seventeenth and eighteenth centuries than, for example, the kings in Berlin.[71]

Although these kind of positive connotations in Minsk were rather the exception, it still remains to be said that the East was not only perceived negatively, as also its pleasant sides were noted; its negative image therefore did not correspond with reality and could in no way claim general validity or a primacy of interpretation. If the first impressions were often bad, most Germans came to terms fairly quickly with the daily life of occupation in Poland and Weißruthenien. The mentality of a superior cultured man who experienced the conditions in Warsaw or Minsk as an insult, influenced the behavior and actions of the occupiers, but did not by any means dictate them entirely.[72] The professional supervision and, above all, the possibility to go home on leave frequently, created a climate that can scarcely be characterized as the unloved East. Naturally, many of the occupiers would rather have pursued a profession at home, but in Minsk and especially in Warsaw they could certainly have satisfying lives. Although they did not love it, as was prescribed by the norm, they managed to accept and get on with daily life in Warsaw and Minsk.

2. Supplying the Occupiers: Theft, Bribery, and the Black Market

The occupiers were comprehensively supplied to meet all their material needs. This included not only their salary or wages, but also food and clothing. Local transport was also subsidized, such that those in uniform could ride for free and other Germans for half the price charged the local population.[73] With their wages they could satisfy almost all other wishes beyond this; for example, in Warsaw they could buy even things from such luxury shops as the retail outlet of the SS Porzellan-Manufaktur (SS Porcelain-Manufacturer) in Munich-Allach.[74] However, for some occupiers—as shown above—the payment was not enough, but in reality the rates of pay, outside of the Wehrmacht at least, were considerably higher than at home, both in Minsk and in Warsaw. In addition to their regular pay, which was calculated according to the official Reich rates for officials or employees, there was compensation for the maintenance of two households in the form of an allowance for deployment away from home, which increased in steps according to rank.[75]

Naturally, the salaries varied considerably, as they did in the Reich. While General Commissar Kube in Minsk received a basic salary of 24,000 Reichsmark per year, midlevel officials had a salary of only 4,000 Reichsmark.[76] In Warsaw the gap between the governor and the ordinary employees was similar; on average, members of the *Distrikt* administration in 1942 had 5,400 Reichsmark per year at their disposal. How great the disparities were is illustrated by the fact that Governor Fischer for the same period received an allowance of 5,000 Reichsmark, which was further increased by a general expense allowance of an additional 12,000 Reichsmark.[77] Financial support for the occupiers was also improved by additional benefits: those working in Warsaw received a special location allowance equivalent to 3 percent of their pay, due to the high inflation rate in the city.[78] In addition, the authorities granted their workers generous tax breaks; in the Reich Commissariat for Ostland, for example, there was a tax-free allowance of 3,000 Reichsmark with an additional 300 Reichsmark permitted per child, as well as exemption from the war surcharge to the income tax.[79]

On top of this assistance came additional benefits that had financial value, such as meals in the canteen. The Distrikt Warschau administration included the sum of 201,000 Złoty as a subsidy for the canteens in its proposed budget for 1941. This did include money for small construction projects, but the communal meals were heavily subsidized.[80] The same applies to the uniforms that almost every German in Poland and Weißruthenien wore. The occupiers, who were obliged to wear this kind of clothing, received, for example, in Minsk from January 1943, a subsidy of between 300 und 750 Reichsmark for their initial uniform depending on their rank, with additional subsidies for necessary repairs. The service clothing already issued at this time became the property of those wearing it. The monthly payments for maintaining the uniform consisted of 30 Reichsmark for men and 20 Reichsmark for women. Of this, 10 Reichsmark (7 for women) was paid in cash; the rest was put on a clothing account that was transferred to the official on completion of their service. These sums were quite considerable, especially if one considers that a coat at subsidized prices cost only 70 Reichsmark and a jacket just 50.[81]

Apartments for the Germans also received subsidies. They only had to pay the landlord some kind of compensation for expenses incurred, which was well below the normal rent price. In Warsaw the sum was not permitted to be more than it had been in August 1939; for accommodations that were rented by the authorities or members of their staff, the guideline was no more than 50 percent of the prewar rent. The occupiers exploited this benefit as much as possible, such that in May 1940 the *Distrikt* authorities issued an order that the rents must at least cover all taxes, public costs, and other running expenses of the property.[82]

Combined with these kinds of ruinous practices for the local population was the targeted expropriation of the Jewish population. The civilian occupation authorities officially confiscated their property[83] and stole from apartments not only furniture, valuables, and money, but also items of clothing such as furs.[84] In addition, they confiscated Jewish businesses, such that many Reich and ethnic Germans in Warsaw could either buy or take over as a trustee one of the 1,700 food shops or 2,500 other businesses outside the ghetto.[85] The occupiers profited to a great extent from the de facto loss of any legal protection by the ghetto inhabitants, from whom large amounts of furniture and interior decorations were stolen so that they could be used to outfit German apartments. Even lowly employees could acquire the following items from the stores of the euphemistically named Treuhandstelle (Trustee Office), which operated a furniture distribution center in Distrikt Warschau: sleep-sofas, beds, cupboards, tables, chairs, armchairs, bedcovers, leather cushions, bed-linens, tablecloths, pillow covers, towels, woolen blankets, and curtain material.[86] Since these kinds of items had been confiscated arbitrarily by the civilian administration since July 1940,[87] the Germans exploited these opportunities extensively; many applications literally used the expression "acquisition of furniture from the ghetto." From the end of 1942 the service even included disinfection—that is, pest destruction, for the confiscated items, for which the NSV had agreed a special price with the firm of Dr. Karl Witte & Co.[88]

The expropriation of the Jews demonstrated—also in Minsk[89]—that the ordinary occupiers were beneficiaries of the Nazi criminal state. Almost all the Germans in Warsaw and Minsk profited from this practice, which was organized by various offices in a division of labor. The applications for distribution of furniture did not cease until mid-1944, and the authorities could scarcely keep up with processing them all. As the man responsible for the suppression of the Warsaw Ghetto Uprising, SS and police leader Jürgen Stroop informed the NSV in May 1943, when the ghetto was burned down and destroyed, a shortage of supplies was to be expected: "The reason lies therein that probably a large part of the property remaining in the ghetto will be destroyed together with [everything else] during the current operation."[90]

The Germans also liked clothing from former Jewish property, especially valuable furs, which were very useful in the winter months. The special conditions in the East made it possible for such luxury goods to be distributed even without, or at least in exchange for far fewer, ration cards than in the Reich. The sense of entitlement of some occupiers went so far that they complained personally to Governor Fischer when no more of these coats—in one case even for the daughter living in Germany—could be distributed, because first officials and employees of the public service had to be outfitted.[91] Similar things could also be observed in Minsk.[92]

In order to fill up their own stores, the Distrikt Warschau authorities also confiscated the packages arriving for the Jews; in September 1941 alone they confiscated 15,000 parcels with a value of several million Złoty. These came mainly from abroad and many contained items such as leather, flour, or fat.[93] In Minsk the occupiers even stole the remaining food items the Jews had with them in the arriving deportation trains. In the kitchen of the Security Police these supplies, known as the Jewish sausage were distributed among the staff.[94] Here all other confiscated items could be purchased using ration coupons and the prices of the things stored in the opera house remained well below their actual value.[95] For dental purposes, on presentation of a doctor's certificate, it was possible even to obtain gold at no cost. A female typist at the office of the Minsk SS and police authority reports that for a dental filling her office issued her three wedding rings.[96]

The application of violence and the daily plundering of the Jews were usually organized by the institutions. The prescribed norms, at least officially, did not permit individual Germans to rob or plunder the local population, not even the Jews. Yet most of the occupiers soon came to recognize that a great disparity existed between the official line and the infractions of it that were actually sanctioned. Since the Nazi authorities still needed the cooperation of the non-Jewish local population, if only to a limited extent, robbery and theft against this group was not tolerated but instead punished. The unofficial framework, however, permitted taking property from the Jews as long as no physical injury was inflicted in the process. If one succeeded in enriching oneself without injuring the person robbed—for example, by threatening the application of violence—such crimes generally went unpunished. In the rare case that they were investigated the word of the occupiers carried much more weight than that of the occupied, who were also afraid to file a complaint with the police.

Especially the Jewish population was subjected to a complete loss of any legal rights, which left them almost defenseless and at the mercy of the arbitrariness of individuals. As long as the Germans proceeded with a modicum of caution, they had little to fear while robbing the locals. In the form of "organizing," theft was quite widespread and accepted, such that it was honored, for example, with its own article in the *Minsker Zeitung*.[97] In addition, it was customary to set the prices oneself in the shops in order to shop cheaply.[98] A further common practice for enrichment consisted in accusing a Jew of having stolen money. The supposedly lost sum was then blackmailed out of him with the threat of summoning the occupational authorities. To avoid this, even institutions such as the Jewish Council were prepared to pay "compensation" for the alleged theft.[99] Also the method of demanding the surrender of a certain expensive object as a form of protection money against the threatened intervention of the authorities was widespread.[100] This manner of proceeding was expanded to apparent controls conducted by armed Germans, in order to confiscate any money they found and keep it for themselves. These kinds of operations, even though they were very common and were rarely reported, were nonetheless strictly punished if they were uncovered because they took place in public and therefore undermined the image of the occupying power.[101]

If the thefts took place without attracting much attention the authorities were willing to ignore them; the exercise of violence, however, seldom remained unnoticed. The way the occupiers handled self-enrichment was similar. As long as nobody spoke about it, nobody had anything against it. Anyone who boasted openly about his thefts or showed off his ill-gotten gains was instructed not to do this for all to see and that it would be better to desist.[102] Comradeship was interpreted such that reporting someone would be seen as denunciation and betrayal. Such things were to be avoided under any circumstances[103] and this attitude facilitated the widespread acceptance of robbing the locals as an everyday occurrence within the society of occupiers. The number of crimes committed by the Germans was therefore very high, as the Abteilung Justiz (Justice Department) in Distrikt Warschau established in 1943. According to the analysis of these lawyers, the ethnic Germans were scarcely behind the Poles, who clearly on account of their extreme need—in contrast to the former—so to speak, were often forced to commit crimes.[104]

If the tolerance threshold was quite high with regard to enrichment at the expense of the locals, this by no means applied to thefts committed against state or Nazi Party organizations. Theft of official property was subjected to the stiffest penalties as in the Reich, and could certainly result in the death penalty.[105] Someone such as the ethnic German Karl Chwastek, who embezzled tax revenue while working for Distrikt Warschau, could not hope for leniency from the judge or sympathy among his comrades. Under application of the so-called Volksschädlingsverordnung (Decree against Damage to the People), Chwastek received a prison sentence of four years.[106] The Reich German Georg Witte was also sentenced under this law. He was employed as a book-keeper by the NSV, embezzled money there and issued false receipts. In total he cheated the NSV of more than 22,000 Złoty and for this he was sent to prison for three years.[107]

Robbing the locals was often combined with black-market activities. When, for example, the Reich German Heinz Unruh, together with a companion, bought six pigs from a farmer at a very heavily reduced price outside of Warsaw, he did not need them for himself. Therefore, he sold the animals on to a third party for a considerable profit. Both of the occupiers were caught red-handed and sentenced to three months by the Special Court for crimes in contravention of the war economy regulations.[108] This unspectacular case makes clear that under the occupation most goods and almost all food items were rationed and could only be bought or traded using the corresponding ration cards.[109] On the other hand, it was very profitable to participate in illegal trade. Especially in Warsaw, where the official prices scarcely exceeded the prewar levels, the glaring disparity between supply and demand determined the actual cost of a specific item, which could only be bought on the black market. Immense price increases were the result (see table 3.2).

In view of the constant shortage of foodstuffs and undernourishment among the locals,[110] they were forced to earn money by selling their valuable items. In this way, they mainly met the considerable demand for luxury items among the occupiers, whose unofficial prices were perceived as very favorable.[111] A large profit could be made, for example, by bringing farm products from the countryside into the city.[112] In Warsaw these black-market activities were on a much larger scale than in Minsk.[113] The oc-

Table 3.2. Black-Market Prices in Warsaw as a Percentage of the Official Price

Item	Amount	Base price in Złoty 1941	January 1941 (in %)	July 1941 (in %)	July 1942 (in %)	July 1943 (in %)
Flour	1 kg	0.50	867	2,830	3,285	6,108
Potatoes	1 kg	0.15	483	2,420	2,547	3,333
Fat	1 kg	3.55	387	916	2,592	6,197
Butter	1 kg	6.00	359	636	1,417	4,500
Eggs	1	0.06	1,623	–	4,067	9,017
Men's suit	1	250.00	210	440	452	1,864
Women's stockings	1 pair	6.70	229	796	850	2,503
Men's shoes	1 pair	45.00	368	609	709	1,739

Note: kg = kilograms.
Source: RGVA, 1457k-3-77, Reichskommissars für die Preisbildung to Vierjahresplanbehörde, 23.9.1943. See also the calculations in Szarota, *Warschau*, p. 125.

cupiers saw traders selling all kinds of wares on almost every unoccupied square.[114] Only rarely did people pay in cash; barter dominated all trade, and cigarettes and vodka served as a substitute currency. In addition, the Germans offered blankets taken from their quarters, toothpaste, and above all basic foodstuffs. Here the Jews also found themselves at the bottom of the food chain because they were forced to sell everything that was not absolutely necessary in order simply to survive. Especially luxury goods came mainly from packages they received from relatives and American aid organizations.[115] The Germans took advantage extensively from this source, partly with the aid of a forced price reduction, such as that for exotic goods such as oranges. In 1943 the usual price on the black market for an orange was between 20 and 30 Złoty, that is, about 10 to 15 Reichsmark according to the official exchange rate.[116] Illegally the occupiers received much more Polish currency for their own. In 1942 on the black market an exchange rate of 10 Złoty for one Reichsmark had established itself—that is, five times the official rate. This meant a considerable increase in the purchasing power of the Germans, who frequently received money in Reichsmark sent to them by relatives at home.[117]

Black-market trading remained illegal. But only the locals were strictly punished[118]—with the exception of a short period in the spring of 1941, when trains in the General Government were no longer being checked for smuggled food items, in order to counter the intensified food shortage resulting from the concentration of the Wehrmacht in preparation for the invasion of the Soviet Union.[119] Efforts at punishment were directed against the Poles, whereas purchases by the occupiers to meet their own needs were tolerated, as long as they did not operate as middlemen trying to make a profit. The Germans exploited the permitted leniency as much as they could; a report for the Partei-Kanzlei (Party Chancellery) summed up this reality in August 1942 with the fitting words, "Everything that can be traded illegally is being traded illegally."[120] The black market offered the possibility to buy supplies in excess of the official rations, which only met the most basic needs. An additional important motive for illegal trade was to send supplies home to family members and give them special gifts.[121] The goods were not only to please the occupiers themselves, but also the families left at home. The many packages, however, did not have—as Götz Aly has maintained—the central function of improving the food supplies inside the Reich.[122] For that the amount was insufficient and the contents consisted mainly of luxury items. Much more, the shipments contributed to a certain extent—as also the black market did—to encourage the acceptance of life in the East by the occupiers; despite all the hardships connected with it, there were also certain privileges and benefits,[123] from which the Germans in Minsk and especially in Warsaw could profit.

Among Germans who were responsible for state goods depots or food stores, there were certainly cases where they sold some of the contents, since the profits to be made were of course enormous. When these kinds of practices were suspected, the authorities intervened and ensured that those responsible were sentenced, although the punishments issued were relatively mild. For example, the ethnic German Hugo Scheiermann, head of the Abteilung Finanzen (Finance Department) at the Gaswerke Warschau (Warsaw Gas Company), was sentenced to eighteen months in prison for embezzlement. In 1942 he illegally sold seven hundred tons of coke and made an estimated profit for himself of between 50,000 and 75,000 Złoty. A fine of this latter amount was imposed on him as an additional punishment.[124] The two restaurant owners Johann O. and Paul E. conducted business in the opposite direction. They received food, household equipment, and gasoline coupons from soldiers and policemen and exchanged them for money; the Special Court sentenced them to fifteen and twenty months in prison, respectively, while another person involved in the trade was not traced.[125]

If the thefts for sale on the black market involved Wehrmacht property, however, the judges were merciless. The previously convicted ethnic German farm worker and factory guard for the Transawia Waffen (Transawia Arms) weapons company, Eduard B., was sentenced to a total of four years in prison for theft and subversion of national defense: his crime was that on the transfer of his company out of the ghetto into the Warsaw suburb of Wilanów, he sold two motors to a Pole for 400 Złoty.[126] Even the theft of just one and a half kilograms of wolfram steel was still punished by the judges with one year in jail.[127] The sanctions were tougher if the accused did illegal trading with inhabitants of the ghetto. For this, the ethnic German Eduard K. and the Reich German SS-Rottenführer Ludwig S. were sentenced to two years and one year in prison, respectively. They had smuggled various goods to Warsaw into the ghetto using their service truck.[128]

The ghetto was supposed to be a forbidden zone for the occupiers, yet this regulation could not be enforced at all effectively (see figure 3.2). As a result of the misery of its inhabitants, extremely favorable business could be done there: the Jewish population in its extreme need was forced to sell almost everything they owned for food. Alongside all kinds of valuables, also on sale were almost worthless items, such as broken dentures, used shoelaces, old corsets, and battered cooking pans or bicycle parts.[129] For the occupiers it was mainly the very low prices that were decisive. In 1941 the Reich German Kurt S. was able to obtain down pillows, a leather jacket, and a fur in exchange for 50 kilograms of flour and 1,150 Złoty. In light of the unofficial exchange rate of one Reichsmark to 10 Złoty, this was a laughably small sum, which demonstrates vividly how the distress of the ghetto inhabitants was exploited. Since S., who worked in a training workshop of the Reichsluftfahrtministerium (Air Ministry), had not harmed anybody in the view of the court, he was sentenced for illegal trading and currency offenses to only a 4,500 Złoty fine, which could also be absolved by forty-five days in prison. In this the Special Court had gone beyond the demands of the state prosecutor, who had considered a fine of 2,500 Złoty as appropriate.[130]

Figure 3.2. An Entrance to the Ghetto in Warsaw
Source: Gollert, *Warschau*, p. 136.

In stark contrast to this mild sentence is the case of the ethnic German baker Heinrich W. He not only obtained goods from the ghetto on a smaller scale for his own use, but also systematically supplied food to the ghetto. This stepped over the line that the Nazis had established because he was thereby explicitly helping the main racial enemy to survive.[131] W. was a Warsaw businessman with two bakeries and he also delivered to the famous Julius Meinl AG (Meinl Company), among others. For their food shops he was supposed to bake 136 kilos of bread from every hundred kilos of flour. Over more than a year, he diverted at least 14,200 kilograms from the flour he received, and he together with six Jewish codefendants sold it for a large profit. The Special Court thereby saw the essential needs of the remainder of the population threatened and viewed this "smuggling into the ghetto [as] especially reprehensible." W. was sentenced to ten years in jail for conduct damaging to the war; one of his intermediaries was even sentenced to death.[132]

On the Warsaw black market even such strange items as clothes lice were on sale, and were also gladly purchased by soldiers passing through because the ensuing lice infestation meant a two-week quarantine period and therefore also a corresponding extension of their leave.[133] In addition, the enormous ghetto in the city with millions of people, as well as the small rations applied to the non-Jewish population, produced a huge demand for food and at the same time a great quantity of luxury items for sale. If Wilhelm Kube concluded, "Many people see the entire deployment to the East as a great opportunity to enrich themselves,"[134] then this surely applies at least as much for Warsaw as for Minsk. The occupiers exploited in this respect every inch of free space outside of the official norms that they could find.

This is demonstrated also by the bribes that, alongside theft and the black market, represented a third possibility to improve one's income. Admittedly bribery was available to only a small section of the society of occupiers because only someone who could offer something in return for the money or goods received was going to be bribed. In addition, this faced the most stringent penalties. For example, the ethnic German Hugo G. was punished with three years in prison because he had permitted two Poles to steal coal from the German Railway. G. was responsible for guarding a warehouse in Warsaw-Praga and received 600 Złoty from the two men for allowing them to help themselves.[135] In view of the constant shortage of heating materials, this crime was by no means an exception; especially from the railway stations fuel was constantly being stolen. The guards either received payment or some of the stolen coals.[136] Other goods in the wagons of the Reich Railway also tempted people to steal. The severity of the punishment for the corrupt guards who turned a blind eye was also influenced by the amount of public attention the case attracted. If no real damage done to the reputation of the Germans could be established, the sentences were much less severe.[137]

3. Churches and Bars: Undesired Activities

At first glance it may appear strange to examine churches and bars together in the same section. Yet for all the differences, there were significant overlaps in their function and status within the Nazi state. Seeking out either pastoral care or alcohol might be an attempt by the occupier to overcome the negative aspects of deployment to the East—regardless of the respective chances of success. Religion can be understood as dealing with contingencies, while alcohol is a means to suppress problems: the Germans in Warsaw and Minsk were interested in both of these responses. At the same time, both of these contrasting aspects of the society of occupiers were viewed as undesirable on principle by those in power: alcohol, because it rendered the men incapable of performing their duty and led to addiction; religion, because it ran contrary to Nazi ideology. However, the leadership had also recognized that the relieving aspects of belief and bars played a decisive role for the Germans. Therefore, at the start of the war, Hitler had already put an end to most activities targeted against the church.[138]

The counseling function of the church found its most important expression in church services. Every Sunday there were always well-attended prayers for the Wehrmacht, which were also open for other occupiers, in Minsk[139] and in Warsaw[140] for both Protestant and Catholic churchgoers. Due to the different respective meanings of the mass, despite the numerical superiority of Protestants in the Reich—whose share in 1939 was around 54 percent against 40 percent Catholics[141]—more Catholic masses were held, and additionally the local Commandant's Offices offered the possibility of saying confession. Soldiers that wanted to participate in the prayers were released from their service obligations. For members of the Wehrmacht, in the ranks of the German army, navy, and air force throughout Europe in May 1943, 17,353 Catholic priests, trainee priests, and members of religious orders, as well as 9,692 Protestant theologians, stood at their disposal.[142] Of these, however—taking both confessions together—only a few more than 1,000 were serving officially as religious advisers.[143]

In any case the military provided the clerics itself because under no circumstances did the Wehrmacht want to use Polish priests for the high mass. This might have led to brotherly relations and mutual understanding of occupiers and occupied on the basis of shared Christian beliefs. Since in the East the authorities always sought to separate the Germans from the local population, any thought of this was scarcely conceivable. In addition, the Catholic church in Poland, which traditionally was closely aligned with Polish nationalism, was severely persecuted by the occupational authorities. It was always suspected of fostering resistance and stirring up hatred against the Germans.[144] Therefore, immediately after the invasion, the new holders of power unleashed terror against the local priests and church institutions. Many clerics in pastoral service and orders were arrested throughout Poland and murdered or sent to concentration camps.

For these reasons the troops were forbidden from participating in any events organized by the local churches.[145] The only exception was the evangelical Augsburg church in Warsaw. The administration, above all Distrikt-Governor Ludwig Fischer, hoped initially to find allies among the 25,000 members of their community, of which at least 21,000 lived in the city itself.[146] On the basis of this German-tinged religious affiliation, it appeared only obvious that the believers assembled here would identify as ethnic Germans and would join the occupiers. But only a few were prepared to take this path. Most of them viewed themselves simply as Protestant Poles; only 2,000 said that German was their mother tongue.[147] The evangelisch-augsburgische Konsistorium (Evangelical Augsburger Consistorium) in the General Government was therefore dissolved, forty-six of the more than one hundred pastors were arrested, and thirty of them deported to concentration camps. The entire church split itself into a collaborating German section under the leadership of Waldemar Krusche and a Polish evangelical church under Juliusz Bursche, who died in a Berlin prison in 1942. The occupiers were permitted to observe their faith only in the former.[148]

The regulation prohibiting visits to local masses therefore applied mainly to the Catholic and the Russian Orthodox church services. Yet, by no means did all occupiers observe this decree. In the only Catholic church in Minsk, for example, several Germans attended regularly in order to lead the mass. However, this was not unproblematic, for on the one hand, they had to expect there would be spies present and that they would be denounced; on the other hand, the terror of the Communists and the Nazis had not spared a single priest in the city. The masses were therefore celebrated without a priest.[149] The Dominican father Gordian Landwehr, who was serving as a nursing NCO in Minsk, took a great risk in celebrating mass in a church for locals and Germans together. He spoke the prayers in Latin, but preached his sermon using Russian words he had learned during his deployment. In this way he tried to conceal his identity from his countrymen since his act might have resulted in severe sanctions. Yet the soldiers who listened to him were also illegal visitors to the church service and confessing believers. They showed great respect for Landwehr's courage, even when subsequently he held prayers for Belorussian Catholics in private houses and in the open air.[150]

The obstinacy of the occupiers made itself very clear here: they consciously flouted numerous decrees. A few, like Landwehr, even risked life and limb in order to serve his religion. On the other hand, it was exactly the clerics that played an important role in exonerating the occupiers. Since they shared all of the experiences with their men—including also the crimes—these acquired an aura of normality and moral legitimacy.[151] Under the given circumstances any public condemnation of the crimes would have provoked reprisals. But the silence of those providing pastoral care with regard to the murders in the East did not signify neutrality: it ultimately gave support to the Nazi policy of domination. Furthermore, in terms of its contents, pastoral care was always directed toward "Führer, People, and Fatherland" in support of the state. Admittedly this was not a recent development, but belonged to a tradition reaching back hundreds of years, when religion was made into an instrument of the state.[152] In this way the clerics helped the Germans to cope with their existence in Poland and Belorussia, and thereby carry out the occupation. Wilm Hosenfeld, for example, at the time of the deportation of the Jews from Warsaw to Treblinka, found comfort in his belief in God, regularly went to mass, and had close contacts with a Polish priest.[153] Max Rohrweder also went to confession, received communion and repeatedly had discussions with the priest assigned to his military post, who "had his heart in the right place" and supported him with good advice.[154]

If church activities in the East in particular were viewed with great suspicion by the state, then this was mainly because religion did not just address itself to specific nationalities or ethnic groups, but rather was open to all people. The concern that closer contact to the local population could awaken among the occupiers sympathy and compassion for the fate of Poles and Belorussians was widespread. Alongside the church services, the supervisors feared similar things might also occur in bars and other places of amusement, which the occupiers visited in Warsaw and Minsk. In order to promote the segregation of the Germans, there were not only bars and restaurants reserved exclusively for Germans, but in addition, also strict regulations not to drink together and celebrate with the locals, or even to sit with them at the same table.[155] It also included a general ban on dancing.[156] Alongside the SS and police, especially, the Wehrmacht was careful to ensure that its soldiers obeyed these orders. So that they would not become too comfortable and possibly even let down their guard, they were not permitted to take off their waistbelt and put down their weapon.[157] Furthermore, for the troops there was a curfew that ranged according to the time of year between 8:00 P.M. and 10:00 P.M.[158] In any case, even those occupiers that were not members of the Wehrmacht were officially not permitted to enter any restaurants that were run by Poles or Belorussians. Exceptions to this were permitted only for high-ranking officials and employees, as well as officers of the Police and the Wehrmacht.[159]

In Warsaw the possibilities for contact with the locals were limited to just a very small number of restaurants that the Germans were allowed to visit and were not forbidden for Poles. The cafés that were so popular among the occupiers, however, were reserved just for them alone. On the other hand, the best restaurant in Warsaw, the Adria, had very high prices.[160] If the occupiers nonetheless did visit pubs that were off limits to them, which generally happened quite frequently, they did so not because they wanted to get to know the locals, but mainly because they could drink cheaply there. In any case, getting drunk promised at least a temporary diversion from the hardships of everyday life in the East. This is confirmed also by the frequent drinking bouts that took place in Warsaw and Minsk. If locals participated, then it was mainly the ethnic Germans who could also communicate with their drinking companions.[161]

Alcoholism represented a large problem for the occupiers. Getting drunk was to some extent socially acceptable and was also promoted by the authorities. Not only did the Germans consume beer and wine, but they also liberally imbibed spirits. When the general commissar in Minsk organized the office outing, it was by no means remarkable that the invitation requested people bring along their schnapps glasses.[162] Almost all Germans like alcohol, and most of them liked it in large quantities. Wilm Hosenfeld reports on evenings in the officers' mess, in which he was the only one that abstained, and for which he was not directly attacked, but nonetheless was smiled at and made fun of.[163] In all of the offices alcohol was drunk, not only after hours, but also at work.[164] The official distribution of spirits was supposed to distract the occupiers from serious crimes in which they were required to participate as part of their duty. The drunken parties organized by the SS and police units, after mass shootings and anti-partisan operations, were already infamous at the time.[165] At the Security Police in Minsk the drinking binges in the office building were always a sign for those not directly involved that another execution had just taken place.[166] In this context the alcohol mainly had a desensitizing effect and was intended to help people forget their own terrible deeds.[167] The drinking culture frequently led to mass alcoholism, and beer or schnapps were seen as a legitimate means for dealing with one's personal crisis, whereby internal tensions or the need to assimilate were compensated.

At the Security Police in Minsk boozing went on not only during and after work hours, but also deep into the night. A number of witnesses described independently from each other that on various occasions members of the detachment were woken up and pulled from their beds in order to drink with their comrades. Especially in demand on such occasions were the female typists, who were brought from their rooms on the pretext that they were needed to type something up. They were to be made sexually receptive by the collective state of intoxication.[168] Those men who refused the schnapps bottle were subjected to very strong peer pressure[169] and were quickly seen as unmanly and scorned as weak and womanly. Among groups of comrades a cult of manliness was instituted that forced everyone to drink along because those who refused were threatened with exclusion from the community.[170]

In the East the commanders and office heads were often heavy drinkers themselves and did not set good examples of abstinence for their employees, but rather on the contrary demonstrated that for them alcohol had important significance. The Governor of Distrikt Warschau, Ludwig Fischer, for example, visited a riding competition in the Belvedere Park, which was to be concluded with a well-attended banquet. Yet this degenerated into a "wild drinking bout, at the beginning of which the Governor was already in a drunken stupor."[171] On the other hand, he turned down the application of an acquaintance who sought a position in Warsaw because this man had the reputation of being an alcoholic. Fischer wrote to him, "As it is forbidden to drink water, due to the fear of spreading disease, one is forced only to drink alcohol; the climate is favorable for one's thirst."[172] Regarding General Commissar Kube it was also said that he and his colleagues would consume far too much schnapps.[173] Eduard Strauch, the KdS in Minsk was given a catastrophic service report. One assessment of him concluded, "The personal conduct of the head of the office in Minsk, especially on account of his alcoholic excesses, has not remained without influence on his subordinates."[174]

Such comments generally resulted at most only in exhortations to show better self-control in future. Only in the case of Strauch was his transfer unavoidable—still as an SS commander—to Belgium (Wallonien). The authorities attributed his alcoholism exclusively to the conditions in Minsk and thereby showed the same understanding that was generally granted to the occupiers in the East: due to the very harsh conditions and sacrifices, it appeared to some extent natural that alcohol consumption was greater there than anywhere else. Thus Hans Frank wrote in a letter to Heinrich Himmler about the "naturally strong danger of alcohol abuse in the General Government."[175] In Weißruthenien and Poland it was usual for almost all of the male Germans to go on drinking binges several times a month, and also to drink a lot of schnapps every day. In contrast to the normal policy of not reporting either on the church or on alcohol, therefore, the

Minsker Zeitung even celebrated the existence of a vodka distillery. The model factory was under the supervision of the Wehrmacht and produced half-liter bottles that were used to give the soldiers "more strength."[176] Wolfgang Lieschke wrote once to his wife that with only "meager" alcohol supplies the mood among his comrades did not attain its "otherwise usual heights."[177]

Military training was viewed as the panacea against alcohol abuse, such that the General Governor wanted to prescribe it for all the men within his jurisdiction; with a perverse logic he thought that they would be protected from alcohol abuse if they could only learn to use their handguns and rifles in a disciplined manner.[178] With this measure, Frank also wanted to counteract the poor reputation that his subordinates had outside of Poland. Next to the widely known tendency for venality, it was mainly the numerous alcoholic excesses that made it difficult for him to represent his work as successful and the service of his men as a war deployment. The office heads should remind their officials and employees "forcefully, at every available opportunity, [of the] commandment to perform their duty and behave decently."[179]

The prescribed norms were formulated clearly, but those in charge set quite a different example themselves. Despite the prohibitions, and because the punishments were rather mild, drunkenness remained a mass phenomenon in the society of occupiers. Transfers, disciplinary measures, and drinking bans were the most common consequences that Germans faced for their drunken behavior. For example, the auxiliary policeman (*Hilfspolizist*) and translator, Arthur Förster, was punished with only two weeks of arrest for multiple bouts of alcohol abuse, although after one drinking binge he even fired his weapon in the air; frequently he failed to show up for duty after a night of drinking. The Security Police, which conducted the investigation and punishment of its own employees, granted in his favor that at least there had been an improvement recently. The investigating officer had recommended more than two weeks of arrest, but on account of his improved behavior this recommendation was ignored by his immediate superiors.[180] The Criminal Police officer Walter Ohle received only three days of arrest for allegedly entering a Polish inn unwittingly in a drunken state and behaving in an unruly fashion. Ohle punched a Pole and disobeyed orders given by two Wehrmacht officers to leave the inn.[181] On the one hand, the incident demonstrates that violence against the locals was not viewed as a serious crime. On the other hand, it makes clear that the prohibition on visiting Polish inns applied only to NCOs and other ranks. Officers of the Wehrmacht were granted considerably more self-responsibility and freedom, which even made contacts with the local population permissible. This only affected a small section of the occupiers, but especially these commanders were more likely to serve as role models for acceptance of norms and observing the regulations.

The understanding shown for alcoholic excesses was so great that even brutal fights under the influence of alcohol—as in the following case—did not result in serious punishment. The investigation report begins euphemistically with the words, "On March 16, 1941, things got quite lively in the office canteen." On this day, SS-Oberscharführer Karl P., who was on emergency duty, got so drunk in the police mess that later he could not remember a thing. In this state, he tripped up one of his colleagues and, once he was lying on the floor, kicked out one of his teeth. After the intervention of two other people present, he hit a policeman over the head twice with a chair. Although he had already been sentenced to fourteen days of arrest for a similar incident, the disciplinary measures imposed remained mild. The responsible officer of the Criminal Police was of the opinion that P.'s behavior "[had] to be viewed as so rough and unworthy of an SS member that the most stringent punishment was called for." Yet this amounted to only three weeks of close arrest and a ban on drinking alcohol for several months. The SS and Police Court in Krakow overturned this verdict and doubled the period of arrest.[182] One cannot speak of genuine atonement in view of the extent of the physical damage done.

If these kinds of incidents had happened inside the Reich, the bar for correct behavior would have been set higher and the resulting punishments more severe. For example, the Criminal Police employee Otto B. from the same SS office was punished with one week of arrest just for entering a jewelry store in Brandenburg in a slightly tipsy state during his leave and becoming rather loud there. In addition, he was subjected to an alcohol ban for three months.[183] Thus the sanctions applied to alcoholic occupiers were numerous, but also comparatively light. The Senior Field Commandant's Office in Warsaw alone announced in its daily orders on average at least two punishments per day for drunkenness off duty throughout 1943.[184] This public shaming was intended to have a deterrent effect on the troops, but in reality there were no practical consequences.

If an occupier was given more than just a few weeks of jail time, this was usually because in addition to his drunkenness he committed other crimes. In particular, it was not tolerated that occupiers spent time with members of the local population. The trainee Criminal Police assistant Gerhard S. was dismissed from the police service because after a pub crawl with an ethnic German and a Polish man he had not met before, they went back to his apartment to continue drinking. Several pieces of the police uniforms belonging to him and his roommate were then stolen from the room. Since during his tour of duty at the office of the KdS in Warsaw, S. had not displayed any great merit, but only become known for his regular and heavy alcohol abuse, his conduct was not judged leniently.[185] Alongside transfers,[186] dismissal from the service was a customary punishment for alcoholics that were repeat offenders; the latter punishment was also applied if they broke the drinking bans that had been imposed. This was applied, for example, to the employee of the Criminal Police Hans K., who got drunk in public then insulted two members of the Wehrmacht, and finally had sex with a Polish woman. In addition, he had already got into trouble before when he had shot at a lamp in a drunken state with his service pistol. By July 1940 his accumulated punishments added up to seven weeks in jail, as well as his dismissal from service with a severe reprimand. The verdict of his commander was quite clear: "[K.] is completely unsuited for deployment in Poland and it is impossible for us to employ him here any longer." Since his dismissal from service could not take place in Poland because he belonged to the office of the State Police in Dresden, he was sent back there with the request for a replacement. His police colleagues in Dresden were to dismiss K. from the police service.[187]

4. Conflicts: Insults, Aggression, and Uncomradely Behavior

The Nazis wanted to achieve an ideal within the society of occupiers, and did not envisage any internal conflicts. On the one hand, the use of violence against the excluded locals was tolerated within certain limits or was even organized by the state itself. On the other, the supervision of the regime with its comprehensive claim to set norms was not supposed to allow any disputes to occur. Everyday life in the East, which especially with regard to the ethnic Germans was supposed to represent an idealized picture of the glorified German people's community, was conceived to be without arguments and confrontations. The comradeship among the Germans and their subordination to National Socialism were viewed as the most precious values—values that could not be questioned by individuals. The discipline and solidarity linked to this were deemed to be German values that had universal validity in Poland, in Weißruthenien, but also in the Reich itself. Only if these closed ranks were preserved would the local population be given the impression of a monolithic block of all the occupiers united together.

The Germans in Warsaw and Minsk largely accepted this conception of how the society of occupiers should operate. Nonconformism was not desired; especially in the hostile environment of the East solidarity had to be maintained under all circumstances. Nonetheless, numerous, mostly smaller, individual conflicts with comrades or with other offices occurred. Only in very few cases, however, were the disputes an expression of resistance to National Socialism or of diversity within a uniform society. Most commonly, problems arose with regard to how the rituals of the community were observed, such as the form of negligence when saluting higher ranks. Against this, quarrels between colleagues were certainly quite common, and they could be set off for a wide variety of reasons. These disputes often ended up in a fist fight.

The judicial authorities issued harsh sentences in the so-called *Heimtücke* (insidious) cases. This category covered critical remarks about the state and its leaders such as those made, for example, by the Reich German Oskar S. in Warsaw. He was sentenced by the Special Court to five years in prison for public defamation and cursing of the Reich, although the state prosecutor had requested only four years. S. had already been punished ten times before, including for criticism of the political leadership. In March 1944 he completed a two-year prison sentence in Warsaw for fraud and sat in a cell with more than fifteen other prisoners, including also some that were still under investigation. Here he made disparaging remarks about Hitler and the Nazi Party on several occasions and was urged by a fellow prisoner to desist. When he continued his critical remarks—saying, for example, "The German leaders are gangsters" or "Germany alone is responsible for starting the war. It attacked Poland and Russia"—the prisoner denounced him to the prison administration. The judge in Warsaw found S.'s remarks designed "to undermine the trust of the People in the political leadership"[188] and therefore increased the length of his jail sentence. As in the Reich, it was also not permitted in the East for Germans to express openly their disagreement with the regime. Even a soldier who complained in a drunken state about the military police who were checking his papers might have to face criminal charges. Comparatively harmless statements made on patrol, such as, "Due to these kinds of things we have already lost one war," or "In this way we also lost the war in 1918 … and it will also be the same again in 1943," were in the eyes of those in power highly dangerous.[189]

Insubordination to a higher authority almost inevitably resulted in sanctions. This is shown by the case of Herbert Hornig. He was an employee in the office of the county administrator (*Kreishauptmann*) of Garwolin in Distrikt Warschau and complained about the *Kreishauptmann*, Dr. Freudenthal, in a letter addressed to the *Distrikt* administration; for this he was transferred back to the Reich. In the eyes of the regime, in view of the difficult conditions in the East it was an impermissible insolence to accuse your superior "within an office of neglecting his duties without good reason." However, Hornig's case before the Special Court was closed after he had paid 100 Złoty to the Winter Aid Drive and made a declaration of honor in favor of Freudenthal saying, "I did not want to accuse the *Kreishauptmann*

... of having committed any punishable crimes or dishonorable acts." The latter said that he agreed to this, so that no further unpleasantness resulted for Hornig.[190] His accusations were not investigated—the façade of closed ranks within the society of occupiers remained intact.

To complain about one's boss was a useless exercise. If he had not actually committed any crimes, then the subordinate could expect sanctions for his complaint. Such an action was quickly perceived as a denunciation, and although this was very much desired by the state, among the circle of comrades it was viewed as a serious sin. It appears not to be an exaggeration to speak of a culture of covering-up (*Deckungsgesellschaft*[191]) with regard to Warsaw and Minsk. This culture refers to a social system that lived on the basis of remaining silent and keeping secrets, in which every German was aware of the moral weaknesses and norm transgressions of his colleagues but kept silent, because he also had so many similar things on his own conscience. The solidarity that resulted from this was an indispensable prerequisite for the men's comradeship, and therefore it was something that simply had to be promoted. Even the slightest attempt to undermine it was punished, while at the same time the authorities were prepared to tolerate many smaller and larger breaches of the norms. For example, a fifteen-page letter by the lawyer Dr. Hans H. regarding the director of the Abteilung Wirtschaft (Economics Section) in Distrikt Warschau, Heinrich Schlosser, remained without consequences for the accused. Schlosser had treated H. badly because the latter had written disrespectful and insulting comments in the margin of his file. H. added also that in the Hotel Bristol at the end of 1941, Schlosser had described him as a rogue in public and on February 28, 1942, he had even claimed that he "had been dismissed from public service." Since the allegations regarding his service made by Schlosser could not be verified, H. was fully rehabilitated. The department head, however, did not suffer any adverse consequences.[192]

In another case SS-Scharführer Willy K. complained in a pub about the order of the police official P., according to which the female Polish serving women had to be taken home in a German automobile. In K.'s view, this was beneath his dignity and this instruction by his superior was an unreasonable demand. His office only gave him a mild reprimand, in part because his concerns were well grounded. Nonetheless, he received three days of severe arrest for "insulting and defaming his superior in public." He completed one day in jail and was then released with a warning. Other crimes, however, that K. was accused of, were deemed not to be worthy of punishment: he beat a fifteen-year-old Polish boy in the motor pool repair shop of his office and publicly whipped some Jews—asking them whether they "had enjoyed a good breakfast"—such that his room had a sign outside saying Torture Chamber.[193] His superiors tended rather to be well disposed to this kind of behavior. The failure to punish K. shows, on the one hand, the complete loss of rights suffered by the Jewish population, and on the other hand, the importance given to obedience and discipline.

As Omer Bartov has established, discipline and order were assigned a decisive role for the fighting strength and efficiency of the Wehrmacht on the one hand and for the brutalization of the war on the other.[194] This applies equally also for the nonmilitary members of the society of occupiers. Every means had to be used to achieve the solidarity of the Germans because in the eyes of the occupation officials rule in the East could only be maintained in this manner. Even more so than in the Reich, the illusion of uniformity had to be maintained because in the occupied territories the local population was viewed as a constant threat. Since in Minsk and Warsaw most Germans were performing an official duty even small examples of negligence in everyday service life were interpreted as intentional bad behavior. This manner of proceeding that can be observed especially in the way individual offices and institutions dealt with each other resulted in frequent disputes.

Not uncommonly differences of opinion built up into arguments, followed by physical fights. Thus in 1941 a brawl developed inside and in front of the Hotel Savoy in Warsaw between two SS NCOs of the Pawiak Prison and a lieutenant of the Wehrmacht. The cause was some insulting remarks made by the SS men to the officer, who replied with the comment that all SS members were "soldiers in ties." In the disciplinary hearing conducted by the Security Police the behavior of the lieutenant was met with disapproval, but it mainly concluded that the two SS men had damaged the reputation of the SS. In fact, however, the investigating policeman had shown understanding for the behavior of his men and therefore recommended that they only be given a warning. The conflict itself was not desired, but ultimately, in the honor of the SS a higher value was at stake, such that the divergence from the norm in this case was tolerated.[195]

Conflicts constantly arose between groups within the society of occupiers. Often an improper salute became the cause for a dispute. Above all it was remarkable how brutal the response was, even with regard to trivialities. For example, a fight started because a sergeant of the Wehrmacht wanted to resolve a dispute between locals, whereas a member of the SS thought that this intervention was unnecessary. Instead of ending the dispute, the two occupiers started going at each other and produced a further conflict.[196] This demonstrates the perversion of discipline; in the East the application of violence against those outside the group was generally welcomed, but condemned within one's own community. Ultimately the Wehrmacht had to concede that a certain barbarization of their own men had taken place when increasingly brutality was seen as the means for solving all problems.[197] As a result conflicts became taken over so quickly by emotional responses that they could not be resolved with words. Therefore, even very unimportant matters, such as the question whether a junior detective was permitted to travel second class by train, could lead to a confrontation. Since for the Wehrmacht second-class travel was permitted only for officers, they were of the opinion that the policeman did not belong in their compartment—although his office had issued him with such a ticket for the journey.[198]

Although the various institutions in Warsaw and Minsk showed considerable understanding for the conduct of their men, conflicts were not desired and resulted in punishment. Therefore, the office heads tried to calm down the mood even when "a certain amount of diplomatic skill" was required—or at least this was the comment of a Wehrmacht officer with regard to the relationship between the troops and the civil administration in Warsaw.[199] In order to smooth over the tensions, care was often taken to avoid exacerbating existing animosity between specific authorities. The Warsaw police, for example, abandoned an investigation against the official of the Distrikt Warschau administration, Dr. Reinhold K. because its pursuit might have led to frictions. Dr. K. had got into a fight in the Hotel Bristol with the comedian Werner G. after he had had more than a few drinks with several colleagues, and decided to interrupt the performance. In spite of K.'s imprisonment, the investigating detective closed the case after the death of one of the witnesses and the departure of G. in order to avoid any further complications with the *Distrikt* administration.[200]

Although brawls between the various groups were undesirable, they were tolerated to a degree in the form of negligible punishment. That there were punishments at all was mainly in order to avoid problems with other institutions; in addition, there was the need to maintain the façade of closed ranks within the society of occupiers. Within an office the reactions were different: there comradeship was directly threatened. These decisive and positively based codes in the lives of the occupiers were appreciated and taken seriously by them, despite the negative aspects such as peer pressure and the threat of exclusion.[201] Someone who stole from his comrades had deserved a stiff punishment; for such a crime, a warning or a few days in jail was not sufficient because the deed carried with it a high potential for conflict and was a breach of the honor code that was always stressed. If this kind of thing had received a certain tolerance, then on the one hand the value of comradeship would have been undermined, and on the other, the thief would face harsh reprisals from those around him. Therefore, judicial sanctions were rigorous. The German Court in Minsk condemned a trainee locksmith to a two-year prison sentence for stealing a total of 370 Reichsmark from two German colleagues.[202] An ethnic German SA man was also sentenced to two years in Warsaw for an armed robbery he conducted together with a railway man against another ethnic German from his unit. Although the state prosecutor had asked for a sentence of five years in prison, the lawyers of the Special Court showed themselves to be lenient and limited his sentence to two years.²⁰³

Physical conflicts within the group were treated quite differently. In contrast to the solution of conflicts with other offices, the authorities accepted violent disputes if they occurred behind closed doors. Beating someone up was an accepted form of conflict resolution if comradeship was not thereby damaged at all. This did not represent an autonomous form of expression, but a broadly accepted norm that permitted confrontations to be resolved not only with words, but also with fists: being involved in a fight, was also an everyday experience for comrades.²⁰⁴ In the officers' mess of the Warsaw police there was a confrontation between Untersturmführer Zank and Hauptsturmführer Jakob, when the latter realized that Zank had come to work drunk. Jakob hit Zank several times in his drunken state—and so brutally that Zank broke a bone. The two, who otherwise had been on friendly terms for five years, forgave each other the next day. Since the incident took place in the officers' mess and therefore "not in front of the Warsaw public," the investigating official recommended closing the case, because continuing the investigation would again create a hostile mood between the two participants, who had already reconciled.²⁰⁵ Only when Zank had to be thrown out of the officers' mess again one month later, due to loutish behavior under the influence of alcohol, did the KdS choose to seek a decision from the SS Court in Krakow.²⁰⁶ Yet the BdS there refused to open a legal case and ordered only that disciplinary measures be taken against him.²⁰⁷

Conflicts between the various groups were not accepted, but despite the brutality with which they were frequently pursued, they were still at least silently tolerated. Among the comrades of one's own institution, however, there were not supposed to be any confrontations because this might endanger group solidarity. Fights were not affected by this norm because they were seen as daily occurrences between comrades. Fights also served as safety valve for the aggressiveness that resulted from the stress the Germans were under, which was clearly higher in the East than in the Reich. Therefore, a specific characteristic of the disputes here was that violence was much more of an everyday event and also punished considerably less severely than at home. At the same time the punishments were severe if the occupiers did something that could endanger the solidarity of their own social system.

If the occupiers only very rarely clashed with the ideals of National Socialism and the values of the society of occupiers in their conflicts, the reason was that despite all the complaints, conditions in Warsaw and Minsk remained relatively good. For example, Hermine Neuhauser, who was deployed to Warsaw, wrote about the city in August 1944, "I heard from the Germans that previously one could live very well there. I believe that one likes it anywhere, where life is good."[208] This shows exemplarily that ultimately the Germans came to terms with their lives in Poland and Weißruthenien because quite a few possibilities existed to make life there more pleasant. Diversions were provided by alcohol and the church, which assisted in their own way, in the short or the long term, in overcoming problems, or at least in pushing them away. Neither religion nor drunkenness was welcomed, but ultimately they were accepted. This applied also to the efforts of the occupiers to organize their own supplies in addition to the official rations. Theft, and especially black-market trading at the expense of the starving locals, represented a legitimate means of enrichment that was used by everybody. This not only made daily life in the East better, but also made it possible for the occupiers to send presents to family members in the Reich.

The norms that were actually supposed to uphold discipline were not strictly implemented. State institutions had no interest in prosecuting the occupiers every time they strayed from the path. This would only have increased dissatisfaction with their service in Poland or Belorussia. As long as the occupiers did not contravene certain essential rules that served to maintain German control, they were permitted to go some distance along those paths, which made their lives in Warsaw and Minsk much easier. This was definitely desirable: many regulations were interpreted less stringently in the East than in the Reich. The daily life of the occupiers was to a large extent controlled by prescribed norms. At the same time, however, the occupiers were granted many opportunities for self-determination, which they gratefully exploited for their own benefit.

Notes

1. Füssel, "Kunst," pp. 17–18.
2. Lüdtke, "Fehlgreifen," p. 67.
3. Gerlach, Morde, p. 112.
4. Zimmerer, "Geburt," pp. 21–22.
5. Gerlach, Morde, pp. 101–102.
6. Interview of Hans Frank by the Völkischer Beobachter on 6.2.1940, published in the issue on 12.2.1940. As cited by Präg/Jacobmeyer, Diensttagebuch, p. 106.
7. Warschauer Zeitung, no. 238, 8.10.1940: "Begeisterte Kundgebung des Deutschtums."
8. Minsker Zeitung, no. 40, 31.5./1.6.1942: "Appell im Generalkommissariat."
9. Chiari, Alltag, pp. 72–73.
10. Latzel, Soldaten, pp. 135ff. and 140ff.

11. StAM, Polizeipräsidien, Slg. Primavesi/270, pp. 9ff. The quote is on p. 11 of the war memoirs of Oberwachtmeister der Schutzpolizei der Reserve Otto Nahlmann regarding his time with Police Battalion 61 in Warsaw.
12. BfZg, Slg. Sterz, Letter sent by Private Rudolf Faustenhammer from Warsaw, 8.3.1940.
13. IfZA, MA 1790/3; 379-2-45, Kommandanturbefehl Minsk no. 32, 2.9.1942.
14. Carl von Andrian diary/Peter Lieb transcript, entry for 29.1.1942. A similar predictive assessment can be found in Private collection of Gerhard Lieschke, Wolfgang Lieschke to his wife, 8.8.1941.
15. IfZA, MA 1790/11; 370-1-53, "Lagebericht des GK Weißruthenien", 9.8.1942.
16. Böhler, *Auftakt*, pp. 43ff.
17. BfZg, Slg. Sterz, Letter from Major Christian Bein in Warsaw, 21.8.1941.
18. Latzel, *Soldaten*, pp. 179ff.
19. Ibid., pp. 171–172.
20. BfZg, Slg. Sterz, Letter from Captain Hermann Göbel in Minsk, 13.8.1941.
21. Chiari, *Alltag*, p. 72.
22. Private collection of Gerhard Lieschke, Wolfgang Lieschke to his wife, 7.6.1941.
23. Böhler, *Auftakt*, p. 42.
24. Jockheck, *Propaganda*, pp. 136–137.
25. Jureit, "Motive," pp. 167–168.
26. For the Soviet Union, see Wette, *Wehrmacht*, pp. 14ff.; for Poland, see Jockheck, *Propaganda*, pp. 41ff.
27. Gerlach, *Morde*, pp. 94ff.
28. See chapter 1 section 5.
29. Szarota, *Luftangriffe*, p. 128.
30. IfZA, MA 1790/11; 370-1-53, "Lagebericht des GK Weißruthenien", 12.12.1942.
31. Private collection of Gerhard Lieschke, Wolfgang Lieschke to his wife, 19.7.1941.
32. IfZA, MA 1790/3; 379-2-45, Kommandanturbefehl Minsk no. 12, 4.11.1941.
33. Private collection of Gerhard Lieschke, Wolfgang Lieschke to his wife, 6.7.1941.
34. Mallmann, *Mißgeburten*, p. 76.
35. IfZA, MA 1790/11; 370-1-53, "Lagebericht des GK Weißruthenien", 9.8.1942.
36. MBliV no. 31, 31.7.1940, p. 1533, "Runderlass des RMdI", 23.7.1940.
37. IfZA, MA 1790/11; 370-1-53, "Lagebericht des GK Weißruthenien", 12.12.1942.
38. *Anordnungsblatt des Leiters der Deutschen Post Osten*, no. 35, 12.2.1941.
39. *Amtsblatt der Haupteisenbahndirektion Minsk*, no. 9, 16.3.1942.
40. Hosenfeld, "Retten."
41. See chapter 2 section 1, this volume.
42. BStU, MfS—HA XX/3110, pp. 180ff., statement of Josef B. on 22.5.1968.
43. *Anordnungsblatt des Leiters der Deutschen Post Osten*, no. 28, 6.2.1941.
44. See, e.g., IPN, 101/18, "Personalakte Dr. Franz Wiesmann", Deutsches Gericht Warschau.
45. APW, 486/68, "Runderlass der Regierung des GG", 25.11.1941.
46. Such as, Franz Wiesmann, who was employed at the German Court in Warsaw as an Amtsgerichtsrat in 1940: IPN, 101/18, "Personalakte Dr. Franz Wiesmann", Deutsches Gericht Warschau.
47. BAB, R 48/35, "Erlass des OKW", 5.12.1941. The regulations for exceptions were issued by the Ober Ost: AAN, T 501-228/1140f., Kommandanturbefehl Warschau no. 83, 17.4.1940.
48. Hosenfeld, *Retten*, pp. 69–70 and 609–610, diary, 22.4.1942, and letters of 24.4.1942 and 2.5.1942.
49. *Mitteilungsblatt des Reichskommissars für das Ostland*, no. 21, 30.6.1942, pp. 85–86.
50. BAB, R 48/35, Reichskanzlei to Oberste Reichsbehörden, 5.12.1942.

51. Private collection of Gerhard Lieschke, Wolfgang Lieschke to his wife, 13.11.1941.
52. *Amtsblatt der Reichsverkehrsdirektion Minsk*, no. 4, 18.1.1943.
53. On this concept, see Festinger, *Theorie*, pp. 15ff.
54. Ibid., p. 266.
55. Private collection of Gerhard Lieschke, Wolfgang Lieschke to his wife, 5.6.1941.
56. Ibid., Wolfgang Lieschke to his wife, 6.6.1941.
57. Ibid., Wolfgang Lieschke to his wife, 6.7.1941.
58. Festinger, *Theorie*, pp. 257 and 264.
59. Carl von Andrian diary/Peter Lieb transcript, 14.9.1941.
60. Ibid., 26.9.1941.
61. Ibid., 30.9.1941.
62. Danker, "Zivilverwaltung," p. 75.
63. Wilm Hosenfeld, e.g., was very desperate in the summer of 1942 when he observed the deportations of the Jews to the Treblinka extermination camp. Hosenfeld, *Retten*, pp. 71ff.
64. IfZA, MA 1790/2; 378-1-388, RVD Minsk to its subordinate offices, 22.10.1943.
65. Klemp, *Ermittelt*, pp. 58–59.
66. BfZg, Slg. Sterz, Letter sent by Private Rudolf Faustenhammer from Warsaw, 8.3.1940.
67. E.g., in StAM, Polizeipräsidien, Slg. Primavesi/270, "Kriegserinnerungen des Oberwachtmeisters der Schupo der Reserve Otto Nahlmann", pp. 18–19.
68. BfZg, Slg. Sterz, Letter sent by Private Rudolf Faustenhammer from Warsaw, 4.3.1940.
69. Private collection of Gerhard Lieschke, Wolfgang Lieschke to his wife, 6.7.1941.
70. E.g., Alvensleben, "Abschiede," pp. 141ff., entries on 24.9.–20.10.1940.
71. BAMA, N 265/16, p. 29, Gotthard Heinrici to his family, 17.5.1941. I wish to thank Johannes Hürter for a copy of this document.
72. Jureit, "Motive," p. 168.
73. *Mitteilungsblatt der Stadt Warschau*, no. 12, 16.4.1940, p. 1, Bekanntmachung, 10.4.1940; ibid., no. 31, 26.8.1940, p. 3, Bekanntmachung, 26.8.1940.
74. *Krakauer Zeitung*, no. 45, 26.2.1941: "Verkaufsstelle der Münchener SS-Porzellanmanufaktur in Warschau eröffnet."
75. MBliV, Nr. 2, 10.1.1940, pp. 35ff., "Runderlass des Reichsinnenministeriums", 2.1.1940, as well as *Verordnungsblatt für das Generalgouvernement*, no. 68, 28.8.1942, pp. 442ff. For the Ostland, see *Minsker Zeitung*, no. 88, 14.4.1942: "Arbeitseinsatz im Ostland neu geordnet."
76. BAB, R 48/38, "Durchführungsverordnung zur Verordnung zur Bildung und Abfindung des Verwaltungsführerkorps in den besetzten Ostgebieten", 16.1.1942.
77. *Haushaltsplan des Generalgouvernements für 1943*, pp. 50ff.
78. *Verordnungsblatt für das Generalgouvernement*, no. 40, 26.5.1942, pp. 258–259, and Nr. 68, 28.8.1942, p. 445.
79. *Mitteilungsblatt des Reichskommissars für das Ostland*, no. 9, 2.3.1943, pp. 47ff., "Runderlass des Reichsministeriums für die besetzten Ostgebiete", 12.1.1943. Also *Minsker Zeitung*, no. 166 vom 18.10.1942: "3000 Mark Osteinsatz-Freibetrag."
80. AAN, 111/428/12, "Voranschlag zu Einzelplan III, Kapitel I, des Entwurfs des Haushaltsplans des Generalgouvernements 1941".
81. *Mitteilungsblatt des Reichskommissars für das Ostland*, no. 6, 10.2.1943, pp. 21–22, "Runderlass des Reichskommissars für das Ostland", 29.1.1943, as well as ibid., no. 12, 25.3.1943, pp. 71–72, "Runderlass des Reichskommissars für das Ostland", 17.3.1943.
82. IPN, 700/6, "Anordnung des *Distrikts* Warschau", 10.5.1940.
83. Regarding state robbery and the differences in the respective occupied regions, see Banken, "Plundering," pp. 11ff. At this point, however, it is not possible to examine the or-

ganizational state structures involved. For a comparative overview for Eastern Europe, see Pohl, *Raub*, pp. 62ff. On the "exploitation" of Polish and Jewish property in the *Generalgouvernement* with the aid of the German banks, see Loose, *Kredite*, pp. 322–373; on Warsaw in particular, see pp. 350–360.

84. Dean, *Robbing*, p. 179.
85. Ibid., p. 188.
86. IPN, 101/19, "Quittung über Wohnungsgegenstände des Leopold Winkler", 25.11.1941.
87. APW, 486/63, "Anordnung des *Distrikt*chefs Warschau", 26.7.1940.
88. APW, 1357/88, Mitteilung no. 16, NSDAP-*Distrikt*führung Warschau, Hauptabteilung Volkswohlfahrt, 11.12.1942.
89. BAB, R 93/3, p. 6, "Lagebericht zum Beschaffungswesen im GK Weißruthenien", 15.10.1942; see also *Mitteilungsblatt des Reichskommissars für das Ostland*, no. 1, 30.9.1941, pp. 1ff., "Ausführungsanweisung zur Anordnung", 17.9.1941.
90. APW, 1357/88, Rundschreiben no. 13, NSDAP-*Distrikt*führung Warschau, Hauptabteilung Volkswohlfahrt, 4.5.1943.
91. APW, 482/111, letter to Gouverneur des *Distrikt*s Warschau, 17.1.1943.
92. YV, M 41/289 (=Belorusskiy Gosudarstvenny Archiv, Minsk, 370-1-634), Ostland Öl to Stadtkommissar Minsk, 11.12.1942.
93. Fuks, *Getto*, pp. 192–193, diary, 8.10.1941.
94. BAL, B 162/1673, pp. 347ff. Statement of Sabine H. on 27.–29.4.1960.
95. BAL, B 162/1681, pp. 1548ff. Statement of Karl-Heinz G. on 24.5.1961, as well as ibid., pp. 1517ff., statement of Wilhelm C. on 16.5.1961.
96. BAL, B 162/1673, pp. 347ff., statement of Sabine H. on 27.–29.4.1960.
97. *Minsker Zeitung*, no. 8, 10.–11.1.1943: "'Papyrossi' aus Leerwagenzetteln."
98. US-NARA, RG 242, T 312, Reel 42/2471–2472, Warschauer Stadtkommandant to commanders of 18. and 19. ID, 6.10.1939. For making a copy available to me I thank Mathias Irlinger. See also IPN, 106/63, interrogation of SS-Oberscharführer Kriminalassistent Wilhelm Jansen, 4.6.1941.
99. Fuks, *Getto*, p. 111, diary, 7.9.1940.
100. BStU, MfS—HA XX/3109, pp. 1ff., statement of Josef B. on 16.1.1967. See also Trunk, *Judenrat*, pp. 394ff.
101. AAN, T 501-228, Kommandanturbefehl Warschau no. 29, 7.2.1940. See also APW, 643/577 (new: 300), "Strafbefehl der Staatsanwaltschaft bei dem Sondergericht Warschau gegen den Reichsdeutschen Horst G.", 23.10.1941; ibid., 643/44 (new: 7), "Urteil des Sondergerichts Warschau gegen die Reichsdeutschen Theodor-August B., Franz H. und Hubert G.", 18.5.1942.
102. BAL, B 162/3696, pp. 65ff., statement of Rolf H. on 17.5.1963.
103. Kühne, *Kameradschaft*, pp. 117ff.
104. APW, 482/35, Abteilung Justiz im Amt des Gouverneurs des *Distrikt*s Warschau to *Distrikt*gouverneur, 29.9.1943.
105. APW, 643/540 (new: 768), "Urteil des Sondergerichts Warschau", 7.11.1942. The ethnic German defendants had robbed a number of Wehrmacht trains together; one of them was sentenced to death for this, the others received a number of years in jail. A similar case can be found in APW, 643/864 (new: 850), "Urteil des Sondergerichts Warschau", 1.9.1942.
106. APW, 643/304 (new: 280), "Urteil des Sondergerichts Warschau gegen den *Volksdeutschen* Karl Chwastek", 18.11.1941.
107. APW, 643/1124 (new:1124), "Urteil des Sondergerichts Warschau gegen den Reichsdeutschen Georg Witte", 3.8.1943.
108. APW, 643/550 (new: 1202), "Urteil des Sondergerichts Warschau gegen den Reichsdeutschen Heinz Unruh", 11.1.1944.

109. *Amtsblatt des GK Weißruthenien*, no. 12, 4.11.1942, p.188; RGVA, 1457k-3-77, Reichskommissar für die Preisbildung to Vierjahresplanbehörde, 23.9.1943.
110. Szarota, *Warschau*, pp. 113ff; for Weißruthenien, see Gerlach, *Morde*, pp. 289ff.
111. Private collection of Gerhard Lieschke, Wolfgang Lieschke to his wife, 6.7.1941.
112. For the black market in Warsaw, see the excellent overview in Szarota, *Warschau*, pp. 118ff.
113. Gerlach, *Morde*, pp. 210f.
114. BfZg, Slg. Sterz, letter by Major C.H. Bein, 21.8.1941.
115. BALAA, Ost-Dok. 8/842, pp. 1ff., report by Raimund Warth, 5.3.1956.
116. IPN, NTN 257, "Bericht über Warschau (eingereicht durch SS-Standartenführer von Korzowski)", n.d. [mid 1943].
117. IfZA, Fa 91/4, pp. 983ff., "Bericht Nr. 1 des Beauftragten des Reichsleiters Bormann im OKW, Albert Hoffmann, über Warschau", 9.8.1942.
118. *Minsker Zeitung*, no. 165 vom 16.7.1942: "Die Bekämpfung des Schleichhandels."
119. IfZA, Fb 105/13, p. 3039, Diensttagebuch Hans Frank, 2.5.1941.
120. IfZA, Fa 91/4, pp. 983ff., "Bericht Nr. 1 des Beauftragten des Reichsleiters Bormann im OKW, Albert Hoffmann, über Warschau", 9.8.1942.
121. VtH, Depositum 40, letters by Dr. Paul Golder, Stabsarzt of Polizeiregiment Warschau. Golder reports several times to his wife about his purchases on the black market that will be sent on to her.
122. Aly, *Volksstaat*, pp. 199ff.
123. Ibid., pp. 131–132.
124. APW, 643/731 (new: 804), "Urteil des Sondergerichts Warschau gegen den *Volksdeutschen* Hugo S.". 28.1.1944.
125. APW, 643/985 (new: 1149), "Urteil des Sondergerichts Warschau gegen die Reichsdeutschen Johann O. und Paul E.", 1.7.1942.
126. APW, 643/967 (new: 1127), "Urteil des Sondergerichts Warschau gegen den *Volksdeutschen* Eduard B. und den Polen Jozef W.", 17.8.1943.
127. APW, 1646/1650 (new: 1601), "Urteil des Sondergerichts Warschau gegen den *Volksdeutschen* Heinrich H. und die Polen Romuald Z. und Henryk C.", 9.5.1944.
128. IPN, 106/65, "Feld-Urteil des SS- und Polizeigerichts VI in Krakau", 7.10.1942.
129. Blättler, *Warschau*, p. 115.
130. APW, 643/877 (new: 926), "Urteil des Sondergerichts Warschau gegen den Reichsdeutschen Kurt S.", 3.11.1942.
131. Gerlach, *Krieg*, p. 160.
132. APW, 643/365 (new: 281), "Urteil des Sondergerichts Warschau gegen den *Volksdeutschen* Heinrich W. und gegen sechs Juden", 17.2.1942.
133. Szarota, *Warschau*, p. 249.
134. IfZA, Fb 85-I, pp. 22ff., "Protokoll über die Tagung der Gebietskommissare, Hauptabteilungsleiter und Abteilungsleiter des Generalkommissars Minsk", 8.4. bis 10.4.1943.
135. APW, 643/822 (new: 637), "Urteil des Sondergerichts Warschau gegen den *Volksdeutschen* Hugo G. und die Polen Stefan J. und Jan M.", 6.7.1942.
136. APW, 643/219 (new: 249), "Urteil des Sondergerichts Warschau gegen vier Reichsdeutsche und zwei Polen", 10.10.1941.
137. APW, 643/416 (new: 221), "Urteil des Sondergerichts Warschau gegen fünf Reichsdeutsche", 10.2.1942.
138. Meier, *Kreuz*, pp. 175–176.
139. IfZA, MA 1790/3; 379-2-45, Befehl des Stadtkommandanten Minsk no. 11.25.2.1942.
140. RGVA, 1323-2-302w, p. 13, Kommandanturbefehl Warschau no. 58, 2.4.1941.
141. Brandt, *Priester*, p. 11.
142. Ibid., p. 11.

143. Bergen, "God," p. 123.
144. Sziling, "Kirchen," pp. 279–280; and Böhler, *Auftakt*, pp. 50–51.
145. IfZA, MA 1790/3; 379-2-45, Befehl der Ortskommandantur Minsk no. 16, 17.10.1941.
146. Gauweiler, *Berichte*, p. 119.
147. Szarota, *Warschau*, pp. 254–255.
148. Madajczyk, *Okkupationspolitik*, p. 364.
149. Landwehr, "Sterben," pp. 345–346.
150. Ibid., pp. 346–347.
151. Bergen, "God," pp. 133–134.
152. Missalla, *Gott*, pp. 47–48 and 185.
153. Hosenfeld, *Retten*, pp. 72–73 and 81ff. See also the letter to his son on 18.8.1942, pp. 641ff.
154. DTA, 141/4-7, diary Max Rohrweder, 5.10.1941, and the entry on 21.10.1941, in which Rohrweder reports on his farewell from the pastor.
155. AAN, T 501-228/1140f., Kommandanturbefehl Warschau no. 83, 17.4.1940. The ban on sitting together with Poles at a table also applied to all waiting rooms and other rooms, in which people passed the time.
156. *Amtlicher Anzeiger für das Generalgouvernement*, no. 17, 11.4.1941, p. 417, Anordnung, 9.4.1941.
157. AAN, T 501-228/1000f., Kommandanturbefehl Warschau no. 126, 25.6.1940.
158. AAN, T 501-228/1265f., Kommandanturbefehl Warschau no. 42, 24.2.1940; ibid., 1166. Kommandanturbefehl Warschau no. 73, 4.4.1940; ibid., 1000f., Kommandanturbefehl Warschau no. 126, 25.6.1940.
159. IfZA, MA 1790/22; 370-6-4, "Hauserlass des GK Weißruthenien" no. 10, 18.9.1942.
160. BAL, B 162/AR 179/71, Bd. 7, pp. 1291ff., statement of Siegfried N. on 7.12.1971.
161. IfZA, MA 1790/11; 370-1-468, "Anordnung des GK Weißruthenien", 18.6.1943.
162. IfZA, MA 1790/11; 370-1-57, "GK Weißruthenien an die Dienststellenangehörigen", 24.8.1943.
163. Hosenfeld, *Retten*, p. 424, diary, 10.2.1941.
164. BAL, B 162/1672, pp. 21ff., statement of Friedrich G. on 9.11.1960.
165. BAL, B 162/1681, pp. 1597ff., statement of Herbert K. on 24.5.1961.
166. BAL, B 162/1689, pp. 3378ff., statements of Theodor O. on 3.3.1961 and on 23.5.1960.
167. Browning, *Männer*, pp. 118–119.
168. BAL, B 162/1682, pp. 1778ff., statement of Erna L. on 14.12.1960
169. BAL, B 162/1672, pp. 92ff., statement of Karl G. on 18.10.1960.
170. Kühne, *Kameradschaft*, pp. 132–134.
171. Hosenfeld, *Retten*, pp. 535–536, diary, 29.9.1941.
172. APW, 482/7, Fischer to Ernst Dürrfeld, 10.4.1940.
173. Klee et al., "Zeiten," pp. 171ff.
174. StAM, Polizeipräsidien, Slg. Primavesi/208, "Beurteilung des SS-Obersturmbannführers Eduard Strauch, KdS Weißruthenien, durch den BdS Ostland", 1.4.1943.
175. BAB, NS 19/2648, pp. 7ff., Frank to Himmler, 13.6.1941.
176. *Minsker Zeitung*, no. 126, 9.9.1942: "Wo der Wodka gebraut wird."
177. Private collection of Gerhard Lieschke, Wolfgang Lieschke to his wife, 13.11.1941.
178. BAB, NS 19/2648, pp. 7ff., Frank to Himmler, 13.6.1941.
179. APW, 482/148, "Erlass der Regierung des Generalgouvernements", 30.1.1942.
180. IPN, 106/25, "Vermerk des KdS Warschau betreffend den *Volksdeutschen* Arthur Förster", 19.11.1940.
181. APW, 49/101, "Vermerk des KdS Warschau", 19.6.1941.

182. IPN, 106/99, "Ermittlungsbericht des KdS Warschau", 19.3.1941 and Aktenvermerk, 12.9.1941.
183. APW, 49/ 68, "Vernehmung des Warschauer Kriminalangestellten Otto B.", 16.12.1940, and "Aktenvermerk des KdS", 16.11.1940.
184. RGVA, 1323-2-302a and b, "Kommandanturbefehle der Oberfeldkommandantur Warschau für 1943".
185. IPN, 106/43, KdS Warschau to RSHA, 1.3.1941.
186. BAL, B 162/AR 179/71, Bd. 3, pp. 653ff., statement of Walter K. on 7.6.1971.
187. IPN, 106/10, "Verfügung des KdS Warschau betreffend den Kriminalangestellten Hans K.", 29.7.1940 and letter to Stapoleitstelle Dresden, 16.10.1940.
188. APW, 643/1723 (new: 1672), "Urteil des Sondergerichts Warschau gegen den Reichsdeutschen Oskar S.", 17.3.1944.
189. APW, 643/1412 (new: 1347), "Anklageschrift der Staatsanwaltschaft bei dem Sondergericht Warschau gegen den Reichsdeutschen Edmund R.", 2.6.1943.
190. APW, 643/724 (new: 761), "Urteil des Sondergerichts Warschau gegen den Reichsdeutschen Herbert Hornig", 26.3.1943.
191. Kühne, *Kameradschaft*, p. 117. Kühne uses here the term "Deckungskameradschaft" (covering-up comradeship).
192. IPN, 101/30, "Beschwerde des Dr. Hans H. an den *Distrikt* Warschau", 7.4.1942.
193. APW, 482/96, "Ermittlungsbericht des KdS Warschau", 10.6.1940.
194. Bartov, *Wehrmacht*, pp. 93–94.
195. APW, 49/106, "Ermittlungsbericht des KdS Warschau", 1.4.1941.
196. APW, 49/84, "Ermittlungsbericht des KdS Warschau", 19.3.1941.
197. Bartov, *Wehrmacht*, pp. 112–113.
198. IPN, 106/15, "Vernehmung des Kriminalassistenten Werner Münkwitz", 8.7.1940.
199. BALAA, Ost-Dok. 8/829, p. 5, letter by Erich Kossans, offizier of Rüstungsbereichskommando Warschau, 6.11.1955.
200. APW, 49/131, "Einstellungsverfügung des KdS Warschau", 15.9.1940.
201. Kühne, *Kameradschaft*, pp. 113–114; Römer, *Kameraden*, pp. 165–167.
202. *Amtsblatt der Haupteisenbahndirektion Mitte* (Minsk), no. 48, 9.11.1942.
203. APW, 643/1639 (new: 1604), "Urteil des Sondergerichts Warschau gegen den *Volksdeutschen* Wiktor C.", 29.6.1944.
204. Kühne, *Kameradschaft*, pp. 124–125.
205. APW, 49/126, "Aktenvermerk des KdS Warschau", 14.12.1940.
206. APW, 49/125, "Aktenvermerk des KdS Warschau", 13.2.1941.
207. IPN, 106/93, BdS Krakau to KdS Warschau, 21.2.1941.
208. BfZg, Slg. Sterz, letter by Hermine Neuhauser, 31.8.1944.

Chapter 4

THE ATTITUDE OF THE OVERLORDS

On the one hand, the daily lives of the occupiers were strongly subjected to norms; on the other hand they had access to numerous freedoms because not all rules and decrees were implemented, nor was their disregard always subject to punishment. The Germans seized the opportunities offered by the state and exploited the room permitted for freedom of action. Many of the ways of acting that were typical for the East would have been unthinkable in the Reich. This, however, does not tell us anything about what these actions meant for the occupiers personally. In this chapter we will ask what special conduct characterized the self-definition of the Germans in Warsaw and Minsk during World War II. What actions defined their social position in dealings with the local population? And, as occupiers, how did they conduct themselves toward and differentiate themselves from the others?

Pierre Bourdieu has used the term "habitus" to describe those human forms of expression that serve to indicate an actor's social position in a situation that is not adequately defined by given contextual relations, such as social interactions at work or relationships between friends. In such uncertain situations, chance and anonymity give individuals considerable scope to adapt their own behavior. Habitus thereby helps them to act in accordance with their social standing in new situations where they have no experience to guide them. First, by identifying the habitus it becomes possible to analyze the meaning of situations and their resolution in order to assign them their place on the scale of meaning.[1]

The environment to which the habitus concept can be applied has been called the "field" by Bourdieu. The field determines those structures that remain largely independent of the will and consciousness of the actors, or the "autonomous spheres, in which 'play' takes place according to different special rules in each case."[2] These rules do not need to be explicitly formulated, but above all they need to be followed in practice.³ In this sense, German occupational rule in Warsaw and Minsk represents a field, and an occupier's habitus can come into existence only under these special conditions. This field of the society of occupiers came into existence by differentiating itself from the field of society in the Reich and especially from the fields of the local societies of the occupied.

The interpretation and meaning of situations in daily life are linked to the process of categorizing and clearly signalizing social inequalities. The habitus provides the capacity to interpret situations correctly in terms of the meaning understood by the actors, and at the same time to conduct one's own actions correctly. Therefore, the occupiers' habitus in Warsaw and Minsk was initially a guide for interactions with Germans who did not belong to one's own office, but especially for how to act toward the locals. Particularly in the East all actions were relevant for determining one's position toward the occupied because the legitimation and the security of one's own rule, which was closely tied up with the Germans' alleged racial superiority, constantly had to be reaffirmed. The code of conduct of the habitus therefore granted security—and at the same time limited one's own horizon, which at least in part explains the small amount of contact with the locals.

In concrete terms, habitus means the linking of these three aspects: first, patterns of perception that interpret the observations drawn from daily life; second, patterns of thought—that is, theories of daily life and patterns of classification, as well as aesthetical measures for evaluating cultural objects and practices, combining to mean taste in general. As the third and most important point, there are patterns of behavior that are produced by the actors' individual and collective practices. In contrast to the norm, which commands or forbids something, the habitus determines the conduct of an action implicitly and individually, and becomes something "natural" and expected—the adopted structures become "second nature."[4]

1. The Reputation of the Germans: Expected Conduct in Public

The core element of the occupiers' habitus—both in Warsaw and in Minsk—was maintaining German prestige. The occupiers always tried to behave in such a way that the reputation of their office was not endangered or even—as the customary grounds for punishment stated—that the "reputation of the Germans was damaged" in any form.[5] In this way the occupied were to be given the impression of a superior "master race" without any blemishes or cause for reproach,[6] such that any thought of rebellion was neither necessary, nor appeared to have any chance of success.[7] For those

Germans not within the society of occupiers the aim was to propagate the idea of an élite in the East that was clearly differentiated from the locals and that raised itself above them. This image was also intended for dissemination at home because both the failure to participate in frontline combat, as well as the—supposedly naturally granted—rule over the subordinated Polish and Belorussian populations were thereby legitimated.

The central category in which reputation had to be maintained was that of moral perception. As chapter 3 shows, this was not about actual obedience to the norms. Of greatest importance was rather the resonance of an action in the public sphere: if it could be conducted without attracting much attention, then it did not necessarily have to follow all the rules and regulations, but might actually transgress them. The legitimacy of an action was only apparently defined by its moral quality. Through this attitude, the state and the Nazi Party promoted a culture of silence and secrecy in which discretion played an important role. From this perspective even massacres of the Jews could be criticized if they attracted too much attention. In Weißruthenien the *Gebietskommissar* (district commissioner) in Sluzk complained about the massacre committed by Police Battalion 11 to General Commissioner Kube, who then opened a criminal investigation. The head of the civil administration was not opposing the genocide: he was concerned with the occupiers' reputation, which he saw as endangered by the brutality of the slaughter. Kube thereby illustrates a stereotype of how the Germans dealt with the killings, which were not condemned on principle, but only with reference to the manner in which they were carried out.[8] However, the transgressions of norms, regardless of whether they were done officially or by private individuals, were never announced publicly in the newspapers or on the radio because then they would have become known by a much broader public, possibly even in the Reich. Announcements regarding punishments and sanctions that were necessary, therefore, took place mainly orally in the form of daily orders, or at most as an internal memorandum within an office. The denunciation of wrongdoing was not abolished completely, but it was restricted to a small circle within the local society of occupiers.

With regard to moral questions, which individuals have to consider under all circumstances, the Nazis in the East explained various aspects that, however, could not clearly be distinguished from each other and often merged into one another.[9] They can be summarized in five main points: First, the sense of honor that was innate to every German and differentiated him from the locals, and was worth defending under all circumstances. Second, order and discipline, which were seen as ancient German virtues and that did not apply to the Poles and the Belorussians, not to mention the Jews. Then third there was the awareness of race, which was meant to make any contact with the local population more difficult. Fourth was comradeship, whose norming effect has already been discussed in chapter 3. Fifth, the occupiers were to be guided by a sense of duty that mainly served to exclude crimes related to service, such as corruption.

The moral charge of these ideals served also to reinforce to the maximum extent the corresponding commandments. The occupiers adapted these values as their own, which meant, above all, that transgressions should not take place publicly. However, this did not mean the normal secrecy of a crime, which can only be prosecuted once the deed and the criminals are known. In Warsaw and Minsk it was much less the deeds themselves, but rather the attention they attracted, that was subjected to punishment. Chapter 3 has already hinted at this tendency, although more-concrete norms than just the degree of secrecy were the focus there. At the same time, the Germans' reputation could be damaged not only by obvious criminality, but also through carelessness, such as undisciplined behavior or by meetings with locals. A large part of the habitus, which the occupiers adopted very quickly on their arrival in the East, encompassed the ability to calculate intuitively how a negative public impression of their own actions could best be avoided. In a social system that lived on secrecy and silence, these kinds of skills were indispensable.[10]

The occupiers' habitus not only helped them to remain undetected, but above all helped them limit the degree of punishment. Once the Germans had internalized this habitus, which in the East usually only required a short period of acclimatization, they knew very well in what manner they should behave when they were acting outside the prescribed norms. In dealings with one another, and above all with the locals, a proud, but especially an irreproachable attitude was most important. At the same time, the habitus also demanded a strong degree of conformism; deviations from the official guidelines were not desired.

So as not to put the honor of the occupiers in a bad light, they were not permitted, for example, to be seen and certainly not caught when conducting their plundering raids or those thefts that were euphemistically described by the term "organizing." Members of the Wehrmacht in particular were instructed not to stop any horses and carts or other vehicles that were driving into the city in order to confiscate food they were carrying. The justification for the ban aimed less at the breach of the law involved, which was pardonable, but rather because "the illegal acquisition of food endangers the good reputation and image of the troops."[11] The language of the occupiers reveals very clearly the efforts to keep these things secret. In the initial days after the occupation of Warsaw, the instances of "forbidden requisitions"—that is, plundering—increased in such a manner that it was seen as "a disgrace for the Army." At that time "there were cases where plunderers started shooting at each other in the wine cellars." Even "excessively" drunken officers were commonplace.[12] All of this was damaging to the image of the Germans because it was not concealed from the local population precisely because the occupiers were under constant observation by the resistance and so-called enemy propaganda.[13]

In Minsk the railway worker Otto F. was sentenced to eight months by the German Court in 1943. He had dug up some potatoes for his own use from the fields, but was caught in the act by a group of Belorussians and still tried to take the stolen potatoes with him.[14] This conduct might undermine the Germans' superiority toward the local population because the occupiers were clearly not able to feed themselves properly without resorting to theft. Eight months in prison therefore appeared to be a suitable punishment.

In extreme cases these kinds of crimes could even result in the death penalty. In 1944 the Special Court in Minsk condemned to death the two railway workers Herbert K. and Johannes Arthur W. for "conduct damaging to the [German] people" because they had stolen property belonging to the Wehrmacht. However, since their crime had attracted scarcely any attention, no other Germans or Belorussians were involved, and the stolen items had not been sold but instead retained for their own use, the president of the Reich Transport Authority in Minsk appealed for clemency. The Special Court resisted this because the conduct of the two Germans demonstrated "clear signs of a well-advanced demoralization, which, while taking into account all appeals for clemency presented, just on its own, but also with regard to the advanced decline of the moral attitude of the condemned and the severity of their transgressions ... demands their destruction." Despite this very clear statement, Reich Minister Rosenberg followed the recommendation of the accuseds' superior and converted the verdict to eight years in prison for each.[15] Certainly it is not possible to say that the defendants got away lightly, but at least they had preserved secrecy and thereby protected the German reputation, which was why their office had approved the appeal for clemency.[16] For the same reason, three railwaymen from Lida were each punished with only fourteen days' arrest, although they had stolen boots and coats from a Wehrmacht railcar; they kept the items for themselves, however, and did not tell anyone about it.[17] In another significant case the railway employee Hermann S. received a punishment of only six months in jail for helping himself from wagons full of confiscated property in the Warsaw suburb of Grodzisk. The Special Court came to the conclusion that this was not a severe case of embezzlement that damaged the welfare of the people because the "illegal transactions were only known to those who had participated in Grodzisk. More widespread damage to the reputation of the [German] people had not occurred." The Reichsbahn then applied for the postponement of the punishment.[18]

Also those who, like the two soldiers Stefan K. and Franz K. together with a German policeman, robbed the apartment of a local watchmaker in Warsaw and then offered the items to various buyers, could still expect to be treated leniently. The two soldiers were given sentences of six months and one and a half years in jail, respectively.[19] The military engineer Willi B. received two years and five months in prison because he had seized everyday items from local inhabitants on three occasions—a cow, a coat, and 20 Złoty. This took place in broad daylight before the eyes of other Germans and Poles. Aggravating the punishment was the fact that B. sold the cow on to a Jew and thereby made common cause with the declared main racial enemy of the Third Reich.[20]

The Reich German Artur R. was sentenced to four months in prison and a fine of 5,000 Złoty by the Warsaw Special Court for breaches of the foreign currency regulations. He was a soldier attached to the army motor pool as a senior truck driver. He brought 6,000 Reichsmark with him into the General Government and exchanged it there on the black market at a favorable rate such that he received more than 30,000 Złoty instead of 12,000 according to the official exchange rate. R. finally transferred the money back to his wife at home using a postal money order and thereby made a considerable profit. In doing this he used the names of his comrades and the postal stamp of his unit, which already earned him a prison sentence of twenty-five months from the Warsaw Field Court in March 1942. The Special Court judged him now for the foreign currency crime and found R.'s conduct to be "unworthy of a German." In this it was not so much his enrichment as rather the fact that on account of his boasting many members of the unit came to know about it and the matter even made waves inside the Reich due to the involvement of his wife. Thereby R. had "broken his obligations as a German in a reckless manner."[21]

The need to set a good example, which was demanded of the occupiers, was not restricted just to the avoidance of criminal actions. The Germans were always supposed to be models of order and discipline. This started with saluting in accordance with regulations, although saluting was often skipped or conducted in a negligent manner. In the view of the superior officers, this "failed to promote comradeship and solidarity," and in addition "such conduct also diminished the reputation … of the Greater German Reich in the eyes of the non-German population."[22] A tidy uniform as well as a belt in conformity with the regulations also belonged to the proper image, even when off duty. Although the Germans were instructed always to take good care of their equipment, losses nonetheless remained frequent. It was repeatedly discovered that those concerned had acted carelessly or even in a grossly negligent manner. It was not uncommon that service weapons had been sold.[23]

Furthermore the occupiers were not supposed to fire their weapons unnecessarily. In view of the pervasive alcoholism, shots were often fired as expressions of joy or to impress others, although this was more common in Minsk than in Warsaw.[24] This careless behavior resulted in a number of deaths. The punishments for the deaths remained comparatively mild if it actually was an accident and took place within the privacy of one's quarters and not on the street. The Minsk Special Court, for example, sentenced a telegraph operator to a monetary fine of 450 Reichsmark in the case of an unintentional killing due to negligence: he had killed a local inhabitant due to careless handling of his service pistol. If Germans were killed in such incidents, the sentences were harsher, such that a worker who shot one of his colleagues received a one-year sentence.[25] In contrast to these lenient sentences, the use of one's weapon without harming anyone, if it occurred outside the workplace or the living space, could result in the comparatively stiff fine of 50 Reichsmark.[26]

A ban on drinking alcohol also belonged to order and discipline. As described in chapter 3, excessive drinking was an everyday occurrence among the occupiers in the East,[27] but it was not desired in public. Two members of the SS from Warsaw were given two weeks in jail in 1941, for instance, because they were picked up dead drunk after one and a half hours of boozing in Café Bulgaria. This verdict was to set an example, as was pointed out very clearly in the investigation report prepared by the Security Police: "In view of the increasing lack of discipline and the endangered reputation of the SS in Warsaw, the [punishment] must not be viewed as too high, especially as when the two reported for duty they both smelled of alcohol."[28] The drinking had endangered the reputation of the occupiers and their institutions. This sort of thing could not be tolerated. For this reason, the ethnic German truck driver Ludwig M. was even dismissed from his job. He was "in a condition ... that defied description ... and behaved in a manner, which was completely unworthy of a member of the Security Police!" M. shot at Polish civilians late in the afternoon in a drunken state and had to be disarmed; in addition, he insulted the investigating officers.[29]

Such behavior was absolutely not suited to demonstrate the superiority of the occupiers to the allegedly inferior locals. Significantly, the ethnic Germans were given considerably more slack when they infringed the regulations than the Reich Germans. Thirteen *volksdeutsche* members of the SA Standarte Feldherrnhalle were found guilty by the Special Court for abuse of office. Their duties included guarding the Palais Brühl, for which they were rewarded with money, accommodation, and food. Yet those found guilty exploited their uniforms in order to "confiscate" goods and impose arbitrary "fines" on many occasions, in part during their guard duty. In addition, on several occasions they had sex with women in the guard rooms. The lawyers granted the young men mitigating circumstances because they were ethnic Germans, "who have a divergent understanding of our legal terms and conception of honor, and over a period of time have to get used to our ways of thinking."[30] It was not expected that they could immediately match the moral standards that were demanded of Reich Germans. They were able to exploit their newly acquired membership of the ruling, allegedly superior, race—and they did this gladly. By contrast the Reich Germans were supposed to have adopted the code of honor and strongly internalized it such that a certain demeanor also came with it. The ethnic Germans were shown a great deal of understanding which was why, for example, Viktoria P. received only one month in prison for an attempted abortion. Her conduct appeared forgivable to the judges because she "had grown up in the middle of a foreign people," for whom the racial criteria of National Socialism were alien.[31] However, if the extent of their transgressions crossed a certain line, the ethnic Germans could expect to be excluded from the society of occupiers. The general mistrust that the Reich German occupiers displayed toward their new national comrades, led to the conclusion that those concerned had not joined them from conviction, but only out of opportunism,[32] which was an assessment that applied in many more cases than the occupiers thought.

In order to protect the Germans' reputation, exclusion from the community could serve as an ultimate sanction. Long prison sentences and the death penalty should also be seen from this perspective: in order to restore their reputation, they were used to send a clear signal against the crime. Draconian punishments were always necessary in cases of abuse of office. In the eyes of the authorities this crime damaged the reputation of the Germans the most; in addition, it ran quite contrary to the propagated sense of honor, according to which an occupier was not supposed to assume a false identity. Nonetheless, the occupiers' uniform created numerous opportunities to enrich oneself at the expense of the Polish or Belorussian population or to extort other benefits. This clothing was a certain symbol that one belonged to the rulers and therefore commanded unconditional obedience from the subordinate locals, who in the event of resistance to official acts—regardless of whether they were actual or pretended—always had to fear for life and limb. Apart from acts of partisan resistance, an occupier in uniform did not have to expect any opposition from the local population. On account of this, two Dutch SS men were able to steal various items of food during a number of house searches in Minsk: they had pretended to be members of the police and were put on trial for impersonating an official.[33] Crimes were facilitated by the confusing variety of German uniforms, which for the uninitiated were difficult to tell apart. A seventeen-year-old ethnic German girl went into a shop wearing a swastika armband and ordered that goods be handed to her without paying for them; this would have been unthinkable in the Reich. But in Warsaw the Poles were afraid that she might really be a member of the SS who could return with reinforcements. Nonetheless, the young woman was observed, reported to the police, and received just a four-month prison sentence due to her age.[34]

Adult occupiers, who did not realize that certain misconduct in public could quickly lead to a police report, had to fear much more severe penalties. For example, those who like the ethnic German Roman F., assumed they could extort money from a Jewish woman in hiding, acted at the very least incautiously. F. was denounced and sentenced to one and a half years. The court found it especially reprehensible that "he committed the crime in the uniform of a factory guard [of the telegraph station] and thereby disgraced this uniform."[35] This demonstrates the comprehensive claims of the Germans' reputation that also covered subordinate offices and even extended to those in civilian office clothes. However, it was hardly of any significance that the victim was a Jewish woman because the damage to German prestige was not related to this. Although other verdicts also confirm that Jews were not worthy of "any special protection," independent of that the misuse of uniforms always represented a "danger to German interests."[36]

In a case like the one above, the court confirmed the absence of a sense of honor on the part of the defendant. It was much worse, however, if in addition there was also an inadequate awareness of race. This covered not only sexual relations with the locals—"racial defilement"[37]—but also friendly relations or even a casual conversation with Poles or Jews. Crimes committed together with locals were given especially draconian punishment. The Warsaw Special Court sentenced the Reich German Georg W. to three years in prison and a monetary fine of 3,500 Złoty for "damaging the [German] people." While working as a bookkeeper for the NSV, and together with a Pole, he had embezzled money and issued false receipts and thereby defrauded the NSV of around 22,000 Złoty. The punishment given to the defendant was to be painful: "He was ordered to the General Government as a Reich German, in order to carry out special duties here, and was expected to behave in a manner that would preserve the Germans' reputation. He had broken his service obligations in a flagrant way by spending his time with Poles."[38]

Equally execrable was corruption, if the occupiers were bribed by the occupied. On these grounds the Special Court condemned the technical secretary of the Reichsbahn Erich G. to nine months in prison. As a *Volks-*

deutscher, he was responsible for purchasing construction materials for the office of the Eastern Railway in Warsaw and therefore constantly received presents from Polish companies including food, a fur coat, a microscope, a camera, schnapps, and wine. One firm even offered him 10 percent of its gross profits, to be paid in Złoty, Reichsmark, and gold dollars. Although no actions in breach of his duties could be proven against G. because it was never clear which official was responsible for which construction project, in the view of the court he had "infringed his duties as a German in the General Government in a reproachable manner and [thereby] severely broken his honor as an official, as he allowed himself to be 'bought' by Poles."[39] Reich Germans had to expect a considerably longer prison sentence than G., not only for larger amounts, but especially if they permitted themselves to be bribed by Jews. The guard Heinrich N. was even condemned to death in Minsk for severe passive corruption: he had accepted presents of money from Jews and did favors in return or stopped harassing them to work harder while supervising them as part of a forced labor column of the Organisation Todt.[40]

In any case, according to the grounds given by the judge, the condemned Germans were not lacking in awareness of their duties, but rather in racial awareness. This was not a rare phenomenon. Thus in November 1939 the Wehrmacht Commandant's Office in Warsaw criticized in almost daily reports the casual attitude of the soldiers in their dealings with Jews and Poles. It was widely known that soldiers in the company of prostitutes—dealings with them were paradoxically not viewed as "racial defilement" because it was not a relationship, but just paid sex—approached Jewish street vendors and bought material for them. Since the prices were set unilaterally by the Germans, arguments often broke out on the street, where there were many observers present. The Commandant's Office criticized the paltry sense of shame among the troops, which had a negative impact on the discipline and reputation of the Germans.[41] Since much more careful behavior with prostitutes could already be observed in 1940 and there were no complaints, this shows that the habitus of the occupiers was now more developed. The soldiers made an effort not to damage the prestige of the occupiers and no longer appeared in public with the women.

Nonetheless, in subsequent years more-discreet infractions of duty did not always remain unnoticed. Two employees of the Distrikt Warschau administration, Hans W. and Karl-Heinz M., were sentenced to two-year prison terms in 1944 for passive corruption. Both worked in the Preisbildungsamt (Office for Price Control) and allowed themselves to receive gifts from German shop owners, including silver cutlery, a coffee machine, a silver plate, a cigarette box, two cigarette cases, watches, and material for a suit, for which in return they ordered certain deliveries and approved excessive prices. After this was documented, the businessmen were brought to justice. The case had attracted attention beyond the immediate circle of people concerned, and therefore stiff punishments were required: both employees had failed to carry out their duties and thereby, as was concluded in the judgement, "[they] have severely damaged the reputation of the German administration in the General Government, ... but also the German reputation in general."[42] But since the events had played out entirely in the General Government, at least no immediate effect on the prestige of the occupiers at home was to be feared. Paul K. received a jail sentence of only two years because his corruption had become known in the Reich. He was also an employee of the Office for Price Control and accepted a golden cigarette case, which was confiscated not in Poland, but rather in Bad Harzburg.[43] This meant that the Warsaw administration was also compromised in Germany, which is why the Special Court imposed the same prison sentence on K. as it had in the much more severe cases of W. and M.

The norms were meant to limit considerably contacts with the locals.[44] Naturally they also prohibited the private use of force. Nonetheless not a few occupiers sought contact with the locals, and the spectrum ranged from occasional conversations to trade, corruption, blackmail, and even murder. Such meetings mostly represented an unaccustomed experience for both parties, although a certain routine set in for the occupiers after a time. In any case, the occupiers' habitus ensured, first, that in dealings with the occupied they demonstrated their own position as overlords. Second, in order to legitimate themselves they used threats and violence, despite the official ban. And third, in spite of the lack of interest in crimes of the Germans against locals, it ensured that they acted carefully without attracting attention. The habitus therefore determined the spectrum within which the occupiers could interact with the population, without coming into conflict with the norms. The methods differed quite a bit according to the position of the occupier: a senior official could often gain favors or payments simply by indicating the extent of his power without having to apply any violence personally.

2. Perceptions of the Locals: Poles and Belorussians as Colleagues, Subhumans, and Bandits

When the Germans initially invaded Poland and later the Soviet Union, the locals were for them the defeated enemy whose countries were to be occupied. They already had an image of the population beforehand that was based on propagandistic indoctrination, word of mouth, and things they had read. Very few occupiers had had contact with Eastern Europe before the war or even undertaken a journey there, such that the conception of the people living there was almost never based on personal experience.[45] Yet the perception of the Poles and Belorussians played a key role in how the occupiers interacted with them. Whether the new rulers viewed someone as a collaborator or as a potential assassin determined their conduct to a large extent. The way in which the locals were classified therefore became an important element in the occupiers' habitus.

All the same, one cannot speak of a uniform or normed prejudice among the occupiers. The images of the Germans varied, depending on their level of education, place of deployment, type of job, and social experiences. The spectrum stretched from colleagues or collaborators, to racially determined subhumans, to resistance fighters and partisans. In addition, the timing of the deployment to the East made a difference; during the course of the war the fear of assassinations and attacks increased, while the trust in possible cooperation with the occupied diminished. The pattern of perception among the majority of the Germans can be reconstructed on the basis of diaries, letters from the front, statements in court, as well as from actions and orders that have been preserved on a large scale. Minority opinions, which were mostly a sign of better knowledge and greater empathy, can be found only sparsely. Nonetheless, they existed because the society of occupiers was not a completely uniform block of coordinated Nazis.

Due to supervision and peer pressure within the group, the significance of divergent views for the way people acted remained limited. Transgressing the prescribed norms was particularly undesired with regard to interactions with Poles and Jews and was punished. The opinions of the majority within the society of occupiers were important for this reason, although they did not always correspond entirely with the picture spread by Nazi propaganda. The image created by propaganda was tied like a carved wooden figure to the idea of the primitive Slavs,[46] against which, for example, Warsaw Governor Fischer wanted to act with all possible brutality and without reservation because "the Pole only works, if you beat him with a whip." Fischer did not want to show leniency or any sympathy: "For us this is shameful and a completely wrong and stupid position. We cannot show ourselves to be weak, and if now a Pole doesn't greet you, then you have to beat him up."[47]

The official press spread the image that in the General Government a German "master race" dominated the racially inferior indigenous population.[48] The Belorussians were viewed as a mixture of Eastern Baltic and Eastern European races. This was not necessarily seen as advantageous, but on account of their slight North European influences they at least were ranked above the Poles,[49] although their intellectual capabilities were estimated to be less than those of other Slavs.[50] On purely practical grounds, the Reich Ministry for the Occupied Eastern Territories softened up its otherwise very strict criteria and established everywhere in occupied Europe a collaborating local administration, although many occupiers unofficially counted the Weißruthenen as subhumans.

For the first occupiers who entered Poland in 1939 and Belorussia in 1941, such categories were of great significance. They encountered the locals with great mistrust because they did not know how they would behave. The occupiers' overwhelming first impression was one of strangeness and difference, which agreed with the propaganda narrative on the level of primitiveness, dirt, or poverty. Thus Private Kurt Seel wrote to his family on his arrival in the General Government, "Well, I can tell you, I thought that France was dirty, but Warsaw or Poland is simply a pigsty from start to finish. ... A perfidious people."[51] In an uncritical way, the occupiers transferred their visual observations onto the mentality of the inhabitants, thereby often equating material needs with an inferior character.[52] Thus from superficial impressions an initial assessment of the population was created that was perceived to be above all alien and inferior. In Minsk the Luftwaffe doctor, Wolfgang Lieschke, described his first impressions, which reflected his scorn: "rabble" and "the worst sorts," "scarcely clothed, faces like wild animals."[53]

Already just a few days after their arrival in the East most of the occupiers had adapted to the unaccustomed situation. Now they no longer behaved uncertainly in their interactions with Poles or Belorussians, but allowed themselves to express their civilizing arrogance unashamedly.[54] They found the Nazi racist propaganda confirmed by their own perceptions and therefore conducted themselves as the official guidelines demanded: they were the overlords, everyone else the subhumans; accordingly, the others were required always to show obedience and submissiveness. It can be established, for example, that the attitudes of Wehrmacht soldiers toward the occupied and victims rarely diverged from the ideological models.[55] Colonel Carl von Andrian, who was deployed in Minsk, expressed this in October 1941 in the dry words, "The Jewish agitation quickly bore fruit among us because nobody has the feeling that the yid [sic.] is also a person."[56]

From their sense of superiority, for example, the soldiers in Warsaw acted aggressively toward the local policemen if they did not have the chinstraps of their helmets properly tied. This actually was in accordance with the dress code, but the Germans felt themselves obliged to teach the Poles discipline.[57] The overlords were not afraid of obstructing members of the Polish police in the exercise of their duty and even to arrest them. The local commandant's office had to expend great effort to teach numerous soldiers that Poles were not Germans, but nonetheless they were not permitted to treat them as they pleased because ultimately the Polish guardians of order were in the service of the German police.[58] If there was such an undifferentiating perception even of those locals that were working for them, it cannot be a surprise that no account was taken of local customs and that local specialties or even the way of life was not viewed as worth preserving. The civilian administration, for example, banned the Polish custom of announcing deaths through the use of placards on the sides of houses, and obliged house owners to ensure that this ban was observed. In the eyes of the occupiers these sorts of announcements were viewed as a sign of a lack of civilization, which was incompatible with German order.[59] Although the perception patterns of the occupiers were derived not only from the ideology of the regime, in the end, the result still corresponded with state prescriptions. The cause should be found less in the constant everyday indoctrination, much more in the widely shared concepts of German nationalism, but especially in a number of mostly reflex judgments, prejudices, and resentments.[60]

Thus the SS Court in Krakow decided that an incident in which a translator had a tram conductor arrested and beaten because the latter had found him riding without a ticket was not worthy of punishment, despite the clear abuse of office.[61] Some ethnic Germans enjoyed being able to show their Polish acquaintances that they belonged to the new rulers.[62] It fits this picture that soldiers were permitted to break the resistance of Poles who "didn't show the necessary respect and care … in an active manner appropriate to the respect of the German Army for any sign of disrespect and resistance—if necessary with armed force."[63] This order opened the door to arbitrary harassment and abuse of the locals. In Weißruthenien, nonetheless, the official line still stated that in order to promote the desired willingness to collaborate the population "is to be won over by friendliness and good-naturedness."[64]

Orders in which consideration was decreed cause one to conclude that such orders probably did not achieve very much. This can be seen both for Minsk and for Warsaw.[65] Nonetheless there were occupiers in the East who developed some understanding for the locals and did not treat them as subhumans. This could be observed especially in places where Germans and locals worked together, such as within an office. It was mostly auxiliary support roles that fell to the occupied, but sometimes collegial feelings nevertheless developed. These feelings of solidarity developed especially in extreme situations. The railway policeman Hans S. reports that during his time in Warsaw he commanded a squad comprising German and Polish subordinates. The Polish officials continued the same tasks that they had conducted before 1939, and for this they were even armed with rifles or carbines. Nevertheless, times had become rougher because necessity forced many locals to resort to robbery at the railway stations. On account of this, exchanges of gunfire in which colleagues of both nationalities suffered fatal losses were not uncommon.[66] Such experiences welded even Poles and Germans together and created a perception of the others as colleagues because prejudices were being disproven in practice. On the other hand, the Order Police thought that it was important for ethnic Germans who worked for them to have their Polish-sounding names Germanized[67] so that nothing served as a reminder of their background and shared past with the subhumans.

As described in chapter 1, the language barrier was the main obstacle to contact with the locals, which ultimately could have led to an understanding of their situation and a less prejudiced perception of them. All the same, in some specialized offices, such as the Warsaw Hydrographical Institute, where Poles and Germans cooperated, a partially collegial relationship could develop. The hierarchies between superiors and subordinates were clear, but since the occupied sooner or later had to learn the language of the occupiers in order not to lose their jobs, unrestricted communication was soon possible. In addition, the institutions had translators at their disposal.[68] Germans who got to know the locals at their workplaces also showed a certain ability to understand their situation after the war.[69] Their judgment was not characterized by superiority or mistrust.

On the higher levels, understanding for the occupied was expressed mainly in a concern for the employees of one's own office—for example, in terms of their food supply or living quarters. The local workers received portions in some canteens that exceeded the prescribed rations.[70] It was customary also to protect them from the Arbeitsamt (Labor Office) that frequently deported Poles or Belorussians into the Reich for forced labor without checking their current status of employment. Some office heads preempted this by generously supplying them with identity cards.[71] Nonetheless, all of this was done less out of neighborly love than from purely utilitarian calculation: ultimately the locals were needed to run the offices smoothly. When the Reichsverkehrsdirektion (Reich Transport Office) in Minsk checked up on the locals working there, it established that the thirty-five cleaning women, kitchen helpers, and other auxiliary workers might appear high, but in the end it was seen as justified. Even the "Jewish column" made up of thirty-four women who did cleaning up work and cleaned the toilets was to remain.[72]

In these cases one can no longer speak only of the overlords looking down on the subhumans, but still the locals did not get beyond the status of useful service workers. As long as the supply of forcibly recruited support workers did not dry up, there was scarcely any need to be concerned about their individual fates. The foreman of the Organisation Todt Alois

H. spoke openly in an interrogation in 1971 about the construction work he directed in Minsk. Herzog had more than 150 Jews working under him, who in his words were "exchanged every two weeks." The recruitment of new men was done by the mayors of the surrounding towns. That the workers were all killed after their "exchange" was of no interest to H., neither during the war nor more than twenty-five years later.[73] Only the completion of the construction work on time was important.

Despite the widespread resentments and group prejudices, in Warsaw and Minsk there were also occupiers for whom the Nazi racial criteria were unimportant and who saw in the local population simply fellow humans. Udo von Alvensleben was not only enthusiastic about Polish daily life in the streets and cafés, but also visited a Polish countess he had known since before the war in the Warsaw suburb of Wilanów. Just in front of Alvensleben, a group of SS-men arrived in the building and plundered the castle of all its art works and valuables in accordance with their orders. The two nobles found this scandalous, but could not see any way of preventing the theft; for several hours they walked together in the palace grounds and complained about the occupying masters' lack of culture.[74] Certainly this was not a typical case of sympathy for the occupied because the locals were predominantly perceived as primitive Slavs who culturally were on a lower level. Thus for Wolfgang Lieschke in Warsaw it was "no pleasure to see the pure culture of the Jewish masses, if one also dare not think about their individual fates."[75]

In the monthly report of the *Ortskommandanturen* in Warsaw from May 1941 it stated, "The numerous welfare organizations established by the Jewish Council are not in the least bit capable of directing the terrible poverty. The ghetto is growing into a cultural scandal, a hotbed for disease and a breeding ground for the worst subhumans. The treatment of the Jews in the labor camps, where they are just guarded by Poles, can only be described as bestial."[76] The author of the document was certainly not free of prejudices against Jews and Poles, but he was convinced that the Germans as a cultural people had a kind of missionary task that included the "improvement" of the Jews, and not their destruction. In official pronouncements, however, such expressions remained exceptional, even if there were supervisors who agreed with this tenor. Private writings, however, frequently expressed sympathy for the living conditions that the Germans forced the locals to tolerate. Despite the empathy that can be detected in these expressions, they did not view the local population as being of equal value; rather the naturally occurring inferiority of the weak, to some extent, was appreciated also as a duty to care for their welfare and education.[77] The impoverishment did not necessarily lead automatically to the desired image of dehumanizing the locals, but not infrequently had the opposite result. Thus for the soldier Josef Schützeicher, in October 1939 Warsaw was the "saddest city in Europe," in which "the suffering of women and children grabs at your heart. The entire city is without food. ... That is the horror, the terror of the city."[78]

Other Germans found that especially the catastrophic situation of the Jews made them feel sympathy: "The ghetto is a terrible hell. Dire needs. Suffering. Disease."[79] However, only a few of them were prepared to follow up such words with deeds. If just talking to the locals was forbidden, those helping had to fear severe punishment for genuine support. In Warsaw an ethnic German and two Poles were sentenced to long prison sentences because together they helped a Soviet POW escape. The ethnic German, Richard T., was saved from the death penalty and punished comparatively leniently with three years in prison only because the escapee returned voluntarily to the camp a few days later. The sentence was perfectly clear: the defendant "damaged German concerns in favor of the Russian in a dangerous manner. ... On the other hand [he] was an ethnic German and for this reason was obliged to be especially loyal to German interests. ... He knew very well, what kind of danger the release of the Russian meant for German concerns and nonetheless took action in his favor. Thereby he betrayed the German people in a reprehensible manner."[80]

Much better known than this episode is the help Wilm Hosenfeld gave to the pianist Władysław Szpilman. Hosenfeld met him in November 1944 in Warsaw, where the musician had hidden in a completely destroyed house to avoid being caught by the Germans. Hosenfeld supplied him with food for several weeks and also helped him move into the attic of the Wehrmacht Fortress Commandant's Office. Szpilman was to survive here for two months until the arrival of the Red Army.[81] With his conduct, Hosenfeld had drawn the logical conclusion from his growing rejection of Nazi policy and its ideology that despised other humans. For this officer Poles and Jews were not subhumans; on the basis of his deep-seated religious beliefs he considered all life forms to be equal before God. Aid for the oppressed and persecuted was for him a commandment of neighborly love. Hosenfeld applied this belief not only to Szpilman, but also since the beginning of 1943 toward others in need of help. For example, he employed the priest Antoni Cieciora, who was wanted by the Gestapo, as a typist for the Wehrmacht using a false name. The excellent relationship between the two soon led the German to describe the Pole as his "dear friend" and "good comrade."[82] The way Hosenfeld helped other Poles and Jews without even thinking about it[83] reflects a perception of the locals that viewed them as equals and did not assess their value according to the categories of racism or prejudice.

Hosenfeld's view of the Poles went so far as to express understanding that they offered resistance against German occupational rule. He made the connection between terror and "reprisals for the mass murders"[84] that most other Germans blocked out. For them the locals were unscrupulous assassins who defended themselves with unfair weapons against the new holders of power. Above all in Minsk the Jews were identified "as carriers of the Bolshevik idea and leaders of the partisan movement" who could be countered best by "liquidation."[85] Even after they had been locked into ghettos, in the eyes of the Wehrmacht, the SS, and the civilian administration they were "without any exception, identical with the term partisan."[86] The distorted equation of Jews and communists led to a complete misunderstanding of the resistance in the countryside; although there were some Jews among the partisans, the vast majority of them were organized along party political lines, and not as a specific Jewish resistance movement.[87]

Outside the towns and the narrow corridor leading to the front, the between 100,000 and 300,000 partisans were a real threat to the Germans. They conducted numerous attacks and sabotaged the transport connections so successfully that the supplies for the combat forces were seriously affected.[88] On just one night—the night of October 15–16, 1943—for example, they conducted twenty-four attacks on trains or railway lines.[89] In addition, in 1942 they attacked quite openly the collaborationist Belorussian administration in the Minsk-Land district: in 126 communities fifty-three offices were completely wiped out, files and property were destroyed, and communal funds and service stamps were removed.[90] The influence of the partisans reached as far as Minsk, where fear was a constant companion for the Germans.[91] Wherever they went—after dark, for reasons of security this was permitted only in smaller groups[92]—they always had to expect an attack.

The occupiers could approach even the local employees in German offices only with great suspicion. For example, the HSSPF for central Russia and Weißruthenien issued the following instruction in July 1943: "During a house search 10 bags, each with 2 grams of arsenic, were found. This case shows again how urgent constant observation of the Russian cooking staff is. People are reminded again about the decree that locals employed in kitchens should be made to taste a portion of the food themselves under observation before it is served."[93] The inspector of the Reich Railway, Kurt Schmid, characterized the Germans' situation as follows: "Even here in Minsk and the surrounding area, hundreds of kilometers behind the front, one is not safe, especially at night."[94] The locals were seen as a threat that the authorities had to take seriously and that the individual occupiers had to fear. Even in 1941 a climate of mistrust established itself in which the Germans no longer placed any trust in the locals.[95] The most prominent victim of the numerous assassinations was General Commissioner Kube, who was blown up while sleeping by a bomb detonated by an employee.

The memorial services that took place locally and in Berlin on a grand scale, made only too clear the threat posed by the partisans.[96] Especially in the *Minsker Zeitung*—in contrast to the newspapers in the General Government—dangerous "gangs" were mentioned repeatedly.[97] There were far more funerals for murdered officials in Minsk than in Warsaw. One example is Fritz Schild, the political leader of the NSDAP Bezirksleitung (Nazi District Office) in the city of Minsk.[98] This drew the attention of the Germans to the threat from the locals and thereby increased their fear.

In Weißruthenien the problem of resistance was considerably more virulent than it was in Poland, even though in Warsaw in 1943 and again in 1944 there were the two largest uprisings in Europe, where the population rose up collectively against the occupiers. In the Polish capital, however, only from 1943 is it possible to speak of an actual escalation of the level of resistance.[99] Occupiers still recalled years later that it was possible there "during the first years, until around the start of 1943, ... to move around undisturbed."[100] Since the Germans initially tended to underestimate the strength of the resistance movement,[101] only from around this time did fear of the locals start to grow. Their attacks attracted considerable attention spread through numerous rumors.[102] The fear of the barbaric and brutal Poles that had characterized the first weeks of the 1939 campaign,[103] but had subsequently abated, now returned, and the ever-present fear in Minsk now began to spread also in the General Government. Max Bischof, the director of the Transfer Office for the Ghetto, is a good example of this. On his first visit to Warsaw at the end of 1939, he had especially observed the passivity of the Poles, from whom he did not expect any resistance.[104] In mid-1943 his reports to his superiors are full of complaints about the aggressiveness of the occupied; he even speaks of their "murderous terror" and the numerous losses among the civilian Reich and ethnic German employees.[105] Also, those occupiers who were in Warsaw only in 1943 or 1944 reported later that "Germans there were shot at from behind or even shot dead." Such experiences were especially dramatic if acquaintances, or even comrades, were victims of these attacks. A member of the Upper Bavarian SS-Polizeiregiment 23 (SS Police Regiment 23), which served in the city before and during the uprising in 1944, made the following statement during an interrogation in 1962 about his neighbor and colleague at that time: "One day in Warsaw, following a shot, which hit him in the lung, he collapsed in a heap in the street; then the Poles took his pistol from him; then they left him lying in the street, where he was found by some Germans."[106] For this man, it was a formative experience that left a lasting impression on his relations with the occupied. Henceforth he viewed them as underhanded and not trustworthy, such that for the remainder of his tour of duty in the East he remained extremely watchful.

Assassinations by the resistance movement were a daily occurrence during last two years of German rule in Warsaw. Alongside bomb attacks at the main railway station and in some cinemas,[107] there were mainly targeted attacks against individual occupiers. On March 14, 1943, between 5:30 and 6:00 P.M., Captain Richard Schenk, a member of the Wehrmacht-Transportkommandantur (Wehrmacht Transport Headquarters), was shot on the street; since allegedly nobody heard the shots, no perpetrator could be found. Still on the same day, toward 7:00 P.M., bottles were thrown at the car repair shop on Kowelskastraße, which was working for the Wehrmacht, but in this instance there was no damage.[108] One day later, additional shots were fired at a moving tram reserved for Germans; during that attack a soldier was severely wounded. In addition, the authorities recovered the body of a member of the Organisation Todt from the River Vistula who had been shot several days before.[109] In the months of April and May 1944, the Stadthauptmann (Senior Official) in Warsaw reported 186 attacks on Germans that claimed 52 lives. In addition, there were 310 attacks on Poles who worked for the occupiers, with 66 victims.[110]

The clear security problem of the Germans developed into an important topic of conversation and was even reported on at home.[111] Thus Wilm Hosenfeld wrote to his wife in April 1943, "Germans are being murdered almost every day."[112] Reports about the atrocities, like the butchering of a soldier in the Mokotów district of the city or explosive attacks, were making the rounds.[113] The Germans' fear soon came to have a large influence on their view of the locals. Through the mounting number of attacks,[114] the occupiers felt themselves to be threatened; this was especially true of the ethnic Germans not living in the German residential district, since the police had officially declared that they were unable to protect Germans outside the district.[115] A female occupier reported on her stay in the city in February 1944: "In the evenings one could not leave the apartment at all, and also during the day one did not feel comfortable."[116]

On account of the precarious security situation, in March 1944 even the visit of Robert Ley was cancelled because the relevant security plans had been stolen, such that it was no longer possible to guarantee his safety.[117] Since just one month before the SS and police leader Franz Kutschera had been killed, this response could scarcely be viewed as unfounded (see figure 4.1). At Kutschera's funeral on February 4, 1944, the local police authorities undertook a massive effort to protect the senior officials of the city and the General Government that were in attendance: out of concern for possible attacks, the route of the memorial procession, which went through half of Warsaw, was closed off in advance and cordoned off by guards. All residents along the route had to clear their houses between 10:00 A.M. and 5:00 P.M.; the keys were to be left with an authorized rep-

Figure 4.1. Funeral of Franz Kutschera, February 4, 1944
Source: Muzeum Niepodległości Warsaw, F-6716.

resentative (see figure 4.1).[118] In 1944, even before the Warsaw Uprising, resistance actions already demonstrated a clear increase in violence. In Kreis Warschau-Land, for example, there were attacks on the local administration offices[119] or on the Labor Offices that organized the deportation of forced laborers into the Reich.[120]

The level of fear and uncertainty among the Germans is reflected also in numerous actions taken and decrees issued by the authorities.[121] Thus the local commandant's office instructed soldiers in June 1943 to always have their weapons at the ready because up until now this had not been observed to a satisfactory extent. In future, even German military vehicles were to be controlled on the bridges across the Vistula because partisans could disguise themselves as members of the Wehrmacht.[122] The leadership of the General Government responded by declaring their own losses to be military losses, and anti-Polish slogans.[123] Hans Frank declared at a mass rally of the Nazi Party in Warsaw in June 1943: "We give way to nobody. … As nothing will stop us, from demanding retribution for every German murdered, which is justified in view of the vileness of such a deed. I have received a general authorization from the Führer to do everything in this country that is necessary in order to restore security and to hold on. Police forces are coming in, and reinforcements are coming to all regions."[124]

Nonetheless, a monthly report by the Abteilung Propaganda (Propaganda Department) expressed correctly what many Germans felt immediately after the assassination of Kutschera: "The unpleasant sense that the Polish resistance organization here can do what they like with us."[125]

Although few previous resistance actions had inflicted fatalities, even before the escalation in 1943 it was not possible to say that the Germans in Warsaw lived without fear.[126] Most occupiers who did not live in barracks or hostels carried a weapon,[127] and some had in addition a guard dog; since such a dog was intended for protection, it therefore was excluded from the otherwise customary dog tax.[128] As an additional defensive measure alongside the ever-present curfews for the local population,[129] in 1941 General Governor Hans Frank had ordered the establishment of a defensive paramilitary force (*Wehrschützenbereitschaften*) that all German men were to join. Its leadership was in the hands of the SA, and membership was obligatory. Next to the power-political interests of the government in Krakow, which were directed mainly against Heinrich Himmler's SS, the aim was to retain and reinforce German "defensive strength," which was to be achieved by various measures including shooting practice.[130] The battalions were also clearly directed against the Poles, who in Frank's eyes always represented a latent danger.[131] Especially outside the towns a threat existed, which is why night journeys by car in the countryside were no longer permitted after October 1942. Only if at least two armed people were sitting in the car was this allowed; otherwise it would be considered to be an infraction of service regulations.[132]

The perception of the locals in Minsk and Warsaw did not differ in the two cities immediately after the German invasion. The new masters assumed that their superiority was secure and treated the population largely as subhumans, or at least, as backward, hardly civilized "children," whom they had to educate into people with culture. This attitude was influenced by numerous prejudices due to a lack of experience with Poles and Belorussians, and it was soon expanded by an assumed underhandedness. This was alleged of the resistance movement in its struggle against German rule, which could be conducted only with unequal weapons. The degree of fear this instilled was greater for the Germans in Minsk than in Warsaw, but increased rapidly due to the uprisings in the General Government in 1943 and 1944. In the subjective and partly irrational perception that was reinforced externally by the resistance actions, their own community was subjected to a continual threat[133] that had to be answered with counter-violence.[134] In view of their personal experiences, which could be easily seen as confirming the content of Nazi propaganda, only a few Germans were prepared to accept the locals as equals and to respect them. At the same time it should be stressed that even for many supporters of the majority view, that view did not imply the destruction of the local inhabitants.

3. Sexuality between Marriage and "Racial Defilement"

Christel S., born in Königsberg in 1914, joined the Security Police in Allenstein in 1934 as a secretary. In 1939 she was assigned to Einsatzgruppe IV, which subsequently formed the Security Police office based in Warsaw. S. worked directly for the commander and got to know her future husband there in 1942, Kurt, who worked as a doctor in the same office. They got married in January 1943, after which she gave up her job and lived as a housewife.[135] At the wedding, her younger sister by six years, Sieglinde, got to know Wilfried J., who was also employed at the Security Police in Warsaw, and whom she married in August of the same year. After this she moved to Poland to join her husband in order to work with the police as a secretary.[136] Although most of the occupiers that went to Warsaw or Minsk did not have a spouse with them, the two sisters were by no means the only married women. The wife of the Security Police commander, Ludwig Hahn, for example, regularly hosted coffee mornings, to which she invited several spouses of her husband's subordinates, including Christel S. and Sieglinde J.[137]

On arriving in the East, most women and men were not married. For this reason many of them sought relations with the opposite sex. This included not only contacts with the locals, but also numerous affairs and marriages between the Germans, as the above examples demonstrate. Therefore, a Standesamt (Registry Office for Germans) was already opened in December 1939, in which the first in line was the official for Volkstumsfragen (Questions of Ethnicity) in Distrikt Warschau, who married his fiancée.[138] In addition to this single case, a collection of some three hundred marriage records has survived in Warsaw for the period between 1941 and 1944, which permits a relatively detailed analysis of the officially certified relationships of the occupiers.[139] From these files, a sample of thirty-one cases is analyzed here, which represents just over 10 percent of the documented Registry Office marriages.[140] The insights gained from this are representative for the society of occupiers, although it should be taken into account that many weddings did not take place in the East, but back home in Germany, if one of the two partners was not serving in Warsaw (see figure 4.2). More Reich German men than Reich German women married in the East. This is easily explained by the numerical superiority of the men, but in addition it is notable that in the selected group, seven Reich Germans married ethnic German women, but none of the ethnic German men found

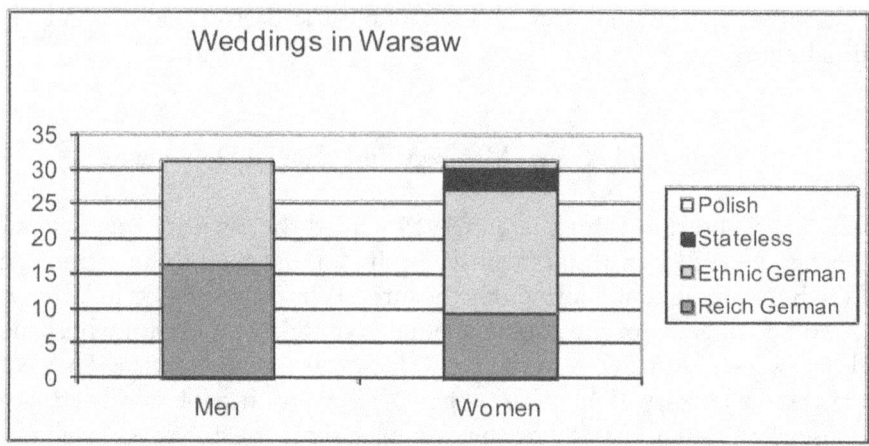

Figure 4.2. German Weddings in Warsaw, 1941–1944

a Reich German wife: that is, the latter preferred to marry other Reich Germans. Nonetheless, marriage to an ethnic German was welcomed because in the ideology of the regime it would ensure that in the new family Aryan, German children would be born, who would also receive a proper German education. The Kommissar für den Jüdischen Wohnbezirk (Warsaw Commissioner for the Jewish Residential District), Heinz Auerswald, was a prominent example of this belief, although his wife was not a Polish German, but instead came from the Baltic region.[141] Hermann Beyerlein, the director of the Telegraphenamt (Warsaw Telegraph Office), married one of his subordinates, the ethnic German Agnieszka or Agnes Tomas.[142]

In the statistics, it is also notable that all the brides lived in Warsaw, while by contrast ten men were not residents of the city and were mostly there for just a short time as soldiers performing military service. In addition, in five cases there were considerable age differences, in which the groom was more than ten years older than his wife; however, this tendency was common everywhere. Whilst for men, it was to a certain extent expected that they would go out with women from outside of their office and circle of comrades—or even together with comrades—women lacked the opportunity to get to know men because a lady was not supposed to meet with men in her free time. In the strictly normed daily life in the East, especially for her it was therefore scarcely possible to get to know an ethnic German, or especially a Pole from outside her office.

Those who flouted these restrictions were quickly seen as morally lapsed, as is demonstrated by the following report on a female employee of the police service. Agathe S., who was employed by the Warsaw police, addressed men in the staff restaurant repeatedly when under the influence of alcohol. This was interpreted as coarse sexual behavior because she "on account of her hereditary racial background [S. was the illegitimate child of a Hungarian woman, as the report established not without some amusement] had a tendency to act in an uncontrolled manner. I have experienced myself, that at a late hour she let people know through her glances, that she is not a child of sadness." On account of this, the investigating officer was of "the opinion that loose women absolutely had to be kept out of our staff canteen." Therefore, Agathe S. was no longer permitted to enter the common room.[143] The female occupiers were not supposed to have any sexual relations before getting married; those who contravened this were not socially acceptable. Therefore it is no surprise if in a court decision the negative comment about a defendant was made that she was "by profession a seamstress, but spent much of her time hanging around with men."[144] On account of this strictly one-sided morality, even publicly known, but not officially engaged, female partners were unwelcome. The above-mentioned wife of the commander of the Security Police, Ludwig Hahn, for example, proved to be very rigid with respect to whom she invited to her coffee mornings: only married women were welcome here, whereas the girlfriends of policemen were avoided and excluded.[145] German society was convinced that women should not live in a relationship without a marriage certificate.[146]

There were even more problems when one of the two partners was already married and the adultery became known. A typist for the Warsaw Security Police, Gretel S., reports that she was working in the personnel section and got to know her future husband, Eugen, there. Because he was already married, there were difficulties with other coworkers and her superiors. For this reason, after about six months Gretel S. was transferred to the section for disciplinary matters. Only once her future husband had got divorced and the ensuing wedding had taken place did the problems with her supervisors come to an end.[147]

In view of the strict racial restrictions imposed on the population by the authorities, there were considerable hurdles to be overcome for relationships between Germans and Polish women—the very few cases the other way around were much more heavily criminalized.[148] Women e.g. had to give up their Polish citizenship in order to have the chance to have an otherwise illegal marriage. Whether the women later made applications for ethnic German identity cards is not known, but their adherence to the Catholic religion probably made things more difficult.[149] A marriage between a stateless Polish women and a "hereditarily sick" ethnic German was approved only on the condition of prior sterilization, and also then only because the pair already had a two-year-old daughter and had been living together for seven years.[150]

Walter I., born 1904 in Riesa and employed at the Post Office since 1929, was transferred in February 1941 to the Main Post Office in Warsaw. In October 1943 he was transferred as a punishment, because—after the suicide of his wife—he had an affair with a married Ukrainian woman. In January 1944 he was even fired for having that affair. Before this, he and his girlfriend had been arrested by the Gestapo and incarcerated for several days in the Pawiak Prison, where she died.[151] Only due to this tragic end to the relationship did I. have no more serious consequences to face than his dismissal.

The ethnic German Anna H., employed as a kitchen help for the Security Police, was also dismissed, because she wanted to marry a divorced Polish man. Thereby she also became Polish, and this demonstrated in the eyes of her superior "that she did not feel herself bound to the German people's community and as a defector, had counted herself as a Pole." The investigating official therefore denied her "the use of the 'Heil Hitler,'" and had her delivered "to the house prison until a further decision was made."[152]

The ethnic German Irene N. and her father Julius also received prison sentences for illegal relationships. The ethnic German woman, who spoke only Polish, wanted to marry a Pole, and with the help of two witnesses deceived the priest, who was to marry them, about her ethnic-racial background. While the bridegroom only acted negligently, because he always heard the bride's family only speaking Polish, it was decided that Julius N. had "seriously failed to meet his obligations as an ethnic German. As a father it was his duty to resist his daughter and to prevent the Polish marriage. Seen from this national-political standpoint, his crime weighs extremely heavily." The Special Court condemned him to one year in prison. His daughter, who at the "time of the crime" was only eighteen years old, was granted mitigating circumstances and went to prison for only eight months.[153]

In order to be lucky in love in Poland or Belorussia and to express it in the form of a marriage, it was necessary to come to terms with the occupiers' way of life in the long term because with the union the central point of family life was also relocated. The marriage in Warsaw or in Minsk was therefore welcomed because with it the Germans were moving into the East. For married couples a considerably smaller range of activities had to be prepared because now much spare time was spent outside the circle of comrades and they would also move out of the official living quarters. These people had chosen the life of occupation, and at least for a time had postponed the desire to return back home to their relatives. For these Germans, Warsaw and Minsk became home, where they sought shared friends, which usually were other couples.[154] The postwar statement of the Warsaw Security Police member Heinz M. can be seen as typical. In 1972 he said, "After I got to know my wife in Warsaw, I was together with her as much as was possible, because then nothing else really interested me any more.... Already before this, before I met my wife, I had an ethnic German girlfriend and spent my free time at her place [and not in the squad's living quarters]."[155]

Marriage had other benefits for the functioning of the society of occupiers because the women, on account of their loyalty and acceptance of the cruelties, served a similar role to the priests in easing the male conscience as perpetrators.[156] Through their presence the occupation acquired a high degree of normality, and at the same time it was natural for many men to protect their home and their family. This protection, with which most wars have been justified, was now exercised by the occupiers right on the spot and especially efficiently, because the emotional connection to Warsaw or Minsk as the new home of their own family increased their willingness to serve. The German wives, who enjoyed a higher status in the East than in the Reich, as shown by the large apartments and servants,[157] indirectly became female perpetrators by their participation in German rule because the ambitions of the occupiers received strong support from the marriage. What Gudrun Schwarz concluded with regard to the wives of SS members is also valid here: marriage provided an effective and modern contribution to the Nazi crimes because thereby a career in Poland or Weißruthenien took on the shape of a normal job.[158]

The psychologically relieving function of marriage was lacking for the many unmarried occupiers as well as those whose partners were far away back at home. Since they, nonetheless, did not want to and could not go without sex, the Nazi authorities had to find ways to satisfy these needs. This was also important because it provided a source of distraction from the ostensible hardships of the East. Only superficially was it a problem that on "racial" grounds no sex was permitted between Germans and the locals. It quickly became clear that this restriction applied only to private and at the same time public relationships, but not for the organized and promoted visit to a state-established brothel[159] or the secret lover whose existence would become known at most within a small circle. Occasional denunciations and sentences for "racial defilement"[160] therefore served as examples for maintaining morality, but they were aimed primarily at maintaining appearances in public and not at the existence of such relationships at all.

In contrast to the numerous raped women, these women at least received a certain amount of compensation: money, food, or protection from destruction. However, one can only rarely, if at all, speak of voluntariness because alongside actual lovers there were many Polish or Belorussian women who shared their bed with German men only out of necessity.[161]

The so-called Eastern marriage—that is, the relationship of a German with a woman from a "racially lower-class" ethnicity—was by no means rare and could be observed in both cities from the start of the occupation.[162] At the end of 1939 in Warsaw, for example, the Jewish actress Johanna Epstein moved into a shared apartment with SS-Untersturmführer Werner, using the name Petzold as an ethnic German.[163] Since the SS was particularly strict in these matters, the frequency of such arrangements confirms even that many of its members left their wives at home only in order not to have any problems with their local girlfriends.[164] According to reports from an SS judges' conference in May 1943, sexual relations with members of the population of other "races" was customary for around half of all members of the SS and police.[165] As long as the reputation of the Germans was protected—that is, the relationship remained concealed from the public—the authorities, which otherwise liked to be seen as morally strict, tolerated these sexual activities. In Warsaw the assistant of the Criminal Police Heinz Brückner slept twice with a Polish woman between Christmas 1939 and New Year 1940. He also admitted this when confronted, but since the liaison was only known to his roommates, the investigating official decided in August 1940 not to press any charges and issued only a verbal warning.[166] Brückner was fortunate that he had not been with a Jewish woman. In these cases the sexual morality of the Nazis was just as uncompromising as the judges were severe,[167] and within the SS even Germans were hanged for this.[168]

The contrast between the ideal and reality with respect to "racial defilement" can be seen also in the fact that the Reich even assumed responsibility for providing financial support for the illegitimate children born to German men in Reichskommissariat Ostland. Many of them were transferred to Germany and put in children's homes, or given to foster parents after an evaluation conducted by the respective district commissioner, which confirmed their racial suitability and thereby also their capacity to be germanized. Initially this decree applied only to the civil administration and the SS, but due to the intervention of Reich Minister Rosenberg, from October 1943 it was valid also for all Germans.[169] In the Baltic states, the Reich Ministry for the Occupied Eastern Territories estimated there were about one thousand to two thousand such children, but was unable to give a more precise estimate.[170] A registration exercise conducted in 1944 by the NSV ultimately found that only around five hundred children from the Reich Commissariat for Ostland were receiving benefits.[171]

The institutions of occupation agreed that their subordinates should be able to meet their sexual needs, and by and large tolerated it. In addition, the negative aspects of the deployment to the East could also be partially overcome, if positive benefits—like the availability of female partners—were strengthened. A striking example of this is given in the postwar statement of the then-deputy to the commander of the Security Police Hermann Friedrichs: "On arriving in Minsk, after making certain observations, I ordered the former SS-Obersturmführer Gerhard Müller, the Head of the Jewish Section, to come and see me, when he was stumbling around the office. In addition, it was known to me that he had an 'Eastern marriage.' When I confronted him regarding his behavior, initially he was recalcitrant, but then he broke down and explained to me: 'Sturmbannführer, if you had experienced what I have been through the last years, then you would also drink and look for someone, who is close to you.'"[172]

Not infrequently those overlords who did not have a lover in the East visited the numerous prostitutes. The institutions of the society of occupiers ensured that there were sufficient brothels in which sex could take place with safeguards and under supervision. Shortly after the start of the war, Heinrich Himmler as the Reichsführer SS and head of the German police issued an order for brothels to be established at all main SS and police deployment sites (*Standorte*). At the beginning of 1941 a house with thirty to forty prostitutes was also to be opened in Warsaw, which according to the decree could only be entered by members of the SS and police, but not by soldiers of the Wehrmacht, who had their own facilities. The intentions behind this were clearly formulated: 1. "To prevent breaches of basic orders and to prevent the emergence of perversity, homosexuality, and masturbation, brothels supervised most carefully by doctors are to be established." 2. "The selection of the prostitutes is to be done according to the following principles: Exclusively young and, as far as possible, good-looking Polish girls are to be used, in order at the same time to prevent them subsequently becoming mothers [sic.] and also to teach the German SS and policemen that the Polish girls, since they are prostitutes, cannot be considered as a possible wife."[173] In Warsaw as in Minsk, the recruitment of these women was largely a form of slavery because by no means all of the prostitutes were there voluntarily. Nonetheless, Jewish women were always excluded from forced prostitution whenever Polish or Belorussian women were available because they were even lower in the racial hierarchy and therefore forbidden even in the brothels.

In order to prevent the spread of sexual disease, the prostitutes were overseen by a female Polish Criminal Police officer under the supervision of the German Security Police. Although the women were supposed to be examined by a doctor every other day, the visit to a legal brothel was subjected to an administrative procedure for the johns, who had to obtain written permission to go there, which also prescribed a medical examination afterward, conducted in sanitation rooms directly in the brothels.[174] Nonetheless, the turnout of the Germans, especially among members of the military, was quite large, which can be ascribed to the low price of 10 Złoty for a visit to a prostitute[175] and the impression of security due to the supervision and guarding of the brothels.[176] The Wehrmacht operated two establishments for the soldiers in Warsaw and considered opening another one several times.[177] Officers were not permitted to visit the brothels because this would have damaged their status as leaders and role models. Since they nonetheless repeatedly tried to go there,[178] unofficially[179] there was the possibility, for example, to have prostitutes go to their room in the Hotel Bristol. This building was very well known among members of the Wehrmacht in Eastern Europe due to this arrangement, which in part stemmed from the fact that already during a raid in the beginning of October 1939, thirty-four prostitutes were found in just forty rooms.[180]

There was no brothel for civilian officials because the demand was thought to be too small for it to be economic. The SS also discovered from its own experience that running a brothel was not profitable. In Warsaw it became clear shortly after the opening that attendance left much to be desired and the costs could not be covered because there were financial burdens and obligations to meet for the property. The planned profits, which the Police had intended to make as pimps working for the state, proved to be unrealizable. Therefore, completely contrary to the original intention, it was agreed "that a small number of Wehrmacht members will also be admitted without advertising this fact."[181]

Those Germans that did not want to visit an official brothel could satisfy their sexual needs with the many illegal and mostly very young prostitutes that could be encountered on the streets of the two cities after dark. These women believed themselves to be severely hindered by the curfew for soldiers because they could do their best business in the anonymity of the night.[182] For half a loaf of bread or 5 to 10 Złoty many women were prepared to take a john back to their apartment.[183] In contrast to regulated prostitution, this kind of thing was forbidden, but nonetheless took place all the time. Wilhelm S., who was a truck driver employed by the police, was arrested in a drunken condition in a Polish apartment where he had already had intercourse several times with the two Polish streetwalkers who lived there; in doing so he had made so much noise that the neighbors had complained. S. was to be punished for his crime that had attracted public notice with a three-month alcohol ban and two weeks close arrest, but this was temporarily postponed because his wife who was pregnant and close to her due date wanted to come and visit for four weeks.[184] The comparatively minor punishment demonstrates that it was not a serious crime that S. had committed. Despite very clear rules and racial restrictions, sexual morality remained ambivalent. A good example of this is the decree issued by the General Commissar's Office in Minsk, which states, "The Wehrmacht

Commandant in Minsk reports in the Commandant's Order No. 18, that for two weeks a serious increase in cases of gonorrhea have been diagnosed among the civilian population, therefore [there needs to be] restraint in interactions with the civilian population."[185]

In particular, General Commissioner Wilhelm Kube did not set a good example for his subordinates, such that his sexual escapades repeatedly became the subject of rumors and investigations. It was said about him that he had repeatedly requested that the Weißruthenische Ballett (Weißruthenian Ballet), which allegedly was made up two-thirds of Belorussian women and one-third of Jewish women, perform for him and his officials, sometimes even in his apartment. Afterward the women were allegedly invited for food and drinks, and Kube even gave them presents of bras and panties so that he could observe them as they tried them on. Although he denied these allegations,[186] the incidents only came to an end—and with them also his bad reputation—on the arrival of his very resolute wife in Minsk.[187] In the city, however, not only was the civil administration caught in a dubious sexual-moral light, but also the SS, which constantly complained about the lack of morals, distinguished itself not by its integrity, but rather by its leniency toward shortcomings. A report on the commander of the Security Police, Eduard Strauch stated apologetically, "[The] irregular life style and sexual deprivation are the causes of [his] sexual excesses."[188]

With regard to prostitution, for the authorities, along with the numerous cases of sexual disease, it was the damage to the German reputation that was a serious problem. The Wehrmacht was not concerned that its members gave themselves up to paid sex, only that they did this publicly. Despite numerous exhortations and punishments, there were almost daily reports in Warsaw from which it can be deduced that soldiers frequently went with prostitutes or slept with Polish women outside the official brothels.[189] As was stated in a report to the Partei-Kanzlei (Party Chancellery), occasionally even "officers, as well as NCOs and other ranks," could be seen publicly on the streets "arm-in-arm with Polish women."[190]

From these pleasures it was not such a big step to sexual violence. The occupiers, as masters of the two cities, were often convinced that the women should submit to them. This way of thinking led to numerous rapes and cases of sexual abuse, even with Jewish women in the ghetto.[191] The German courts imposed severe punishments in these cases that had less to do with protecting or rendering justice to the victims, and more to do with maintaining discipline among the Germans. The preeminent goal of the verdicts was upholding order and discipline within their own ranks; therefore an occupier was not permitted to damage the reputation of the Germans and thereby indirectly the people's community through these kinds of actions.[192] It was only of marginal interest for the authorities that, by prosecuting the criminals, the sense of justice of the local population would also to some extent be satisfied.

It was difficult for the victims to get anyone to listen to them about the injustice they had suffered. In the eyes of the judges, Polish, Belorussian, and especially Jewish women were not seen as credible; if there were not several witnesses who could confirm the crime and thereby make the misdeed public, the rapist had scarcely anything to fear, since in any case his comrades would often cover up for him. In the official instructions for the judges, it stated explicitly that they should get by as far as possible without the help of local witnesses.[193] The admission of a Reich German during an investigation by the Security Police in Warsaw can be seen as typical of this attitude that the occupiers had quickly internalized: "I think that my exculpatory witnesses and myself, as long-term members of the SS, have to be believed rather more than Polish or ethnic German witnesses, who have stated the opposite."[194] This practice, together with the corresponding attitude of the authorities in cases of rape, was augmented by a harsh posture toward local men who tried to resist the German perpetrators. Wilm Hosenfeld records in his diary about an execution squad of the Wehrmacht that shot two Poles who had tried to stop a German soldier from violently abusing a woman. Hosenfeld's commentary could not have been any clearer: "What sort of conception of law is that! If that had happened in G[ermany] with a Frenchman, then they would have been national heroes."[195]

Only rarely did the courts take stern measures against the occupiers because they were all too keen to grant them mitigating circumstances. As has already been established for the judicial authorities of the Wehrmacht, alcohol consumption, which otherwise served to increase the punishment, had an exculpatory function for sexual crimes and led to more lenient verdicts.[196] In other cases the judges trivialized the crime by accepting that the rapists acted out of "sexual deprivation."[197] In order for the maximum punishment actually to be applied, which in especially serious cases meant the death penalty, several criminal acts had to be combined. In March 1941, for example, the ethnic German Edmund B. visited a farmhouse in a suburb of Warsaw, sent away the husband of the victim, and then raped the woman at gunpoint. Three days later, he repeated the crime in another apartment. According to the mayor of his place of residence, B. did not have a job and was active frequently as a highway robber, stopping carts, searching them, and extorting money, which on account of his violent nature gave rise to continual complaints. In view of the large number of his crimes and this negative character reference, the Special Court concluded that the death penalty was appropriate.[198]

Racial criteria played scarcely any role in the evaluation of rape cases because here it was not a matter of sexual relations between partners.[199] Quite on the contrary, the violence exhibited toward the local women expressed an attitude that was in alignment with Nazi ideology: Poles, Belorussians, and especially Jews had no right to the protection of their honor. Victims among the female population were not entitled to protection because they were scarcely ascribed any human qualities. In this respect the male part of the society of occupation needed women only to satisfy their own needs.

Overall, regardless of whether in Minsk or Warsaw, sexuality played an important role in the daily life of the occupiers, although Harald Welzer stresses that its expression was not genuinely specific to violent rule because people were only doing in a different framework things they would in any case like to do.[200] Even for married couples who lived in the East, sexuality had a relieving function that took on a central importance. However, if the men had sexual relations with local women, the element of partnership was pushed completely into the background. Only in very few cases was there really any element of love; for the most part the men were concerned only in the use of sexual relations to divert themselves from the harsh realities of daily life. This escapism was taken to the extreme when the abuse of local women resulted in rape. Frequently the men simply reduced the women to sexual objects that were to be ready to satisfy their own sexual needs at any time.

4. A New Elite as Role Models: Hierarchies and Social Segregation

Nazi ideology gave the Germans in the East a clear image that was intended to determine how they viewed themselves. Wilhelm Kube summarized this succinctly as follows: "Those who go to the East, have to represent the German people and the German Reich authoritatively! He has to be the best guy that there is."[201] General Governor Frank, who tended toward pathos, saw "an ideal type of the politically decisive administrative official" on duty. His men were no "tired, dusty file-mongers, bureaucratically tainted journeymen, [but a] cast of true competence [and] ambitious young men, who were absolutely determined to destroy the Poles."[202] In his eyes the occupiers represented Germany's best people. Among them there were no weaklings, no slowpokes, and also no exam candidates. This alleged selection had only been possible because in the General Government National Socialist principles had been applied to the recruitment of personnel for the first time.[203]

Naturally convinced Nazis in the East were aware that these largely remained imaginary ideals that did not correspond to reality. In Weißruthenien Kube recognized in April 1943, "A mistake was made in the training back in 1941. It was said: 'You are the masters in the East! Yes, masters who had never been riding and who went through the streets with a riding crop and wanted to play at being masters! Those who came to the East with such preconceptions, they were in the wrong place—word has gone around about this in the meantime."[204] Yet precisely because the desired image did not correspond with reality, the rulers in the General Government and in Weißruthenien repeatedly tried to drum into their subordinates their ideals, which ultimately amounted to a "master race." Thus the German Railway explained to its employees, "Behind you is the German Railway, the largest and best transport business in the world! Every one of you is its representative in the occupied eastern territories. Demonstrate every moment through your conduct, that you can correctly call yourself a follower of Adolf Hitler."[205]

Nobody in the East was unaware that the Germans did not match the desired image of Nazi propaganda. Their conduct did not meet the demanding visions of their supervisors and it is significant that a decree issued by the authorities in the General Government named snobbery as the most prominent characteristic of the occupiers. The decree went on to say that this was "not a sign of proper 'overlordship.'"[206] An "imperial attitude,"[207] as Udo von Alvensleben confirmed in 1940 in Warsaw, was not sufficient to do justice to the exclusively racial Nazi sense of superiority. Yet in other ways the appearance and self-image of the occupiers did not always meet the expectations that the leadership demanded of overlords. The self-perception of the occupiers in Minsk differed only in degree from that in Warsaw, and it is likely that this reality applied also to other cities in the East.

Most Germans thought that they were superior to the locals. Alongside German dominance in terms of military strength this was expressed above all in visible things such as the occupiers' cultural life, made up of edifying events of a relatively high standard that took place quite frequently, and to which the local population was largely denied access.[208] Many occupiers believed that their daily life distinguished itself "100 percent in its artistic level from the cultural life of the Poles."[209] As with the other aspects of the occupiers' lives, only a few Germans were able to distinguish clearly between cause and effect. Recognition that their comfortable situation, as well as the denigrating and life-threatening situation of the locals, was only a product of Nazi expansion and the regime's policies was scarcely ever granted. Instead the occupiers simply accepted the living conditions as a given and thereby saw the prejudices and clichés of Nazi propaganda confirmed.[210]

If comparisons with the occupied were drawn, racial arguments became mixed up with observations about the social situation: while the occupier viewed himself as part of a large group of comrades, the locals appeared to be left largely to rely on themselves in their daily struggle to survive. The illegal activities they conducted such as theft, black-market dealings, or prostitution, dominated the German perception of them, precisely because they profited from these kinds of activities themselves, but still considered that they stood far above such things and were not participants themselves. The decreed submissiveness of the Poles and Belorussians contributed quite considerably to this picture. If a decree issued by the Warsaw city administration stated, "Jews have to give way to Germans in uniform in a clearly visible manner on encountering them and if necessary to leave the sidewalk,"[211] this was an order that the inmates of the ghetto could ignore only at risk to their life and limb. At the same time, for the Germans it was easy to see themselves as an important person deserving respect from the crawling locals. This respect had to be paid. The demand of Warsaw governor Fischer—"If a Pole does not greet you, then you have to beat him"[212]—was certainly intended to be taken literally and was also implemented.

The deprivation of the local population was the prerequisite for supplying the occupiers cheaply with all kinds of goods, including the satisfaction of their sexual needs, and thereby contributed indirectly to the acceptance of their existence in the East. Admittedly Warsaw or Minsk was not the so-called promised land of France, but it was certainly much better than deployment to the front because most occupiers enjoyed—especially in Poland during the early war years—"one peaceful day after another."[213] Many of those who were subsequently sent elsewhere found it difficult to leave, even when they were sent to the West. If the average occupier managed to come to terms with his existence in Warsaw, then he lived—compared, for example, with the front soldiers—"very pleasantly, had a nice apartment, and could maintain intimate contact with the ladies' world,"[214] such that the hardships experienced mainly at the start of the deployment could be overcome. In addition to comprehensive support from state and Nazi Party offices that touched almost all aspects of life through their universal claims and met widespread approval, there were also better material conditions than could be found at home. Hans Frank himself legitimized this lifestyle because it made it possible to demonstrate to the Poles German confidence and superiority.[215] The excesses linked to the lifestyle, such as corruption and plunder of the local population, already led at the time to criticism from those who did not belong to the society of occupiers,[216] and indirectly to a self-determined isolation of the occupiers because envy and resentment were to be feared from other Germans.

At the same time it was possible to act as ruler and master over the locals and consequently to enjoy great freedoms in relation to the majority of the population. The ethnic German youths had already internalized their elevated status and behaved accordingly toward Poles of their own age. That this was tolerated is demonstrated, for example, by a verdict of the Warsaw Special Court from the end of 1943. It sentenced two seventeen-year-old ethnic Germans to one month of youth arrest each because they seized the bicycles from two young Poles on the street. In contrast to the judge's verdict, the state prosecutor, however, had requested two-and-a-half and one-and-a-half years because he viewed it not as an everyday crime but rather as one of abuse of office and extortion.[217] Among both the Reich Germans and the ethnic Germans, the custom was widespread to show the Poles, with a "certain megalomania" and intense aggression, what sort of guys they were.[218] The courts reacted mostly with little empathy for the many local victims that the Germans' conduct left in its wake.

The local population responded to the occupation with resistance, which in part took the form of armed struggle. The Germans took the threat from this "devious people" very seriously,[219] yet the widespread fear of assassinations and ambushes especially in the second half of the war did not correspond with the official image of an overlord. The occupiers proved not to be the desired fearless Teutons, revealing rather that they were seriously concerned. This destroyed the impression of strength that the occupiers had in part retained from the rapid military victories of the Wehrmacht. Those who did not approach Minsk along the well-guarded road from Warsaw to the Eastern Front, for example, would have to drive for several hours through partisan territory in which armored protection was a matter of survival.[220] Heroic conduct did not help under these circumstances, and was also rather uncommon among the occupiers. Therefore, the Warsaw city administration, for example, in response to the comparatively harmless Soviet bombing attacks, decreed that the Germans should distinguish themselves in the presence of the locals by "self-control, calmness, and discipline." This was preceded by several panic attacks among the occupiers during a bombardment that had been registered by the local population very precisely as cowardice[221]—while they themselves, as Wolfgang Lieschke admitted, "were not impressed at all by such trivialities," and thereby at least earned a certain respect from the Germans.[222]

It is likely that the occupiers had not experienced most of these self-perceptions before in the Reich. Yet precisely because they had gone through the alienation involved in their transfer from Germany to the completely new situation in the East together, the occupiers now created a new collective realm of experience. The central location for this was the society of occupiers in which all those people came together who were linked by the same or at least similar impressions of their situation in Warsaw or Minsk. The feeling of solidarity—at least within their own office—was strong, because the alien and novel character of their existence as occupiers was common to all of them; it was precisely this shared experience that bound them together. The small group of Germans in the middle of a numerically vastly superior mass of locals was already a focal reference point for their identification; apart from this there were very few familiar things around which the occupiers could orient themselves.

If a minimal consensus existed about what characterized the self-perception of the occupiers, then it was the sense of community of those who shared the same fate in the East. Its central element was the constantly stressed comradeship that secured their solidarity; in addition, it ensured that the numerous breaches of the norms, such as sexual contact with local women, enrichment, or excessive alcohol consumption, remained largely concealed and therefore unpunished. Since almost all comrades benefitted from this solidarity, it represented a positive achievement for nearly everyone involved. Its function in shaping identity was strengthened by the fact that outside the society of occupiers there was hardly any understanding for their situation neither among the locals or the population in the Reich, for whom some of their ideas on morals would have had an alienating effect,[223] nor among the soldiers at the front, who suspected those serving in the rear areas were mainly shirkers and profiteers. The experience of occupation in Warsaw and Minsk, in any case, was shared only with their comrades. The transformation of values in the East, at least part of which was accepted and exploited by everyone, was so radical and in such conflict with the norms at home that to some extent the occupiers had excluded themselves from society as it existed in the Reich, or from "normal" civilization.

A reconstitution of the German war society could be observed in the East. In contrast to what has previously been assumed, however, this did not take place as a reflection of the ideal Nazi racial society.[224] The occupiers matched only in part the propaganda vision of the overlords, for their conduct and self-perception other criteria were much more important. Decisive for the everyday repression of the locals were—in slight contrast to the Nazi people's community[225]—less racial ideas than the absolute and not-to-be-transgressed segregation into them and us,[226] which necessarily united all of the occupiers. By classifying themselves as humans and the locals as subhumans or even inhuman, one of those asymmetrical anticoncepts was created to which Reinhart Koselleck has pointed so trenchantly.[227] The Germans did not have to show consideration for the others at all, and the sympathy expressed in the following letter for their situation remained an exception and was not written by a member of the society of occupiers, but by a soldier of the Wehrmacht who was only passing through: "Emil wrote about the starving children in the Warsaw ghetto, he had seen briefly. In the last war the foreigners had shown pictures of children's hands that had been hacked off. And now this! The truth is worse, more cruel and bestial than anything we can imagine!"[228]

Anyone within the circle of comrades who criticized the lifestyle of the occupiers did not make any friends and frequently had a bad conscience, because he had acted against his own community. A person of such integrity as Captain Wilm Hosenfeld described a discussion among officers, in which the murder of the Jews was criticized. One of the seven expressly welcomed the destruction, five others remained silent and "didn't have an opinion like most others, also in agreement." Hosenfeld, however, chastised the policy sharply, but afterward he felt like he had been "exposed," because he had opposed his comrades and their majority opinion.[229]

From social psychological research it is known that even minor and apparently incidental aspects of social transformation can have considerable consequences for how individuals perceive themselves within the collective structure: each change of position by the others also results in a change in one's own position.[230] But in the East a social milieu was being completely recast in the arena of tension between the locals and the occupiers. The change in position for the Poles, Belorussians, and especially for the Jewish population was extreme. Their exclusion from the community meant for the occupiers, who now belonged to the ruling minority, ennoblement to some extent. The felt and subjectively perceived position of one's membership in the group of occupiers was therefore important and signified prestige, which in turn promoted solidarity.[231]

In the hierarchical structure of the occupation, the Jewish population stood right at the bottom. They were completely defenseless against the occupiers. The Poles were ranked above them because they were at least needed as workers, and therefore were not completely without rights. The Germans were not permitted to murder them, and robbing them was constrained within certain limits that was related, however, primarily to how public the deed was. In Minsk it was the Belorussians who were seen as more valuable than the Jews by Nazi ideology. In the perceptions of the occupiers, their role was scarcely any different from that of the Poles, even though official policy granted them a higher racial rank that, among other things, offered more protection against the individual arbitrariness of the occupiers. Without exception it was true for all these people that they did not belong to the society of occupiers, but to an excluded group that was there to satisfy the needs of the Germans, but otherwise had scarcely anything in common with them.

Within the community of rulers it was the ethnic Germans who were viewed with suspicion by the other occupiers as a kind of second-class

German.[232] Nonetheless, they belonged to the occupiers and viewed themselves as standing above the locals, and were treated accordingly. Similar rules applied to them as to the Reich Germans. The authorities even allowed them somewhat more latitude because they came from a different cultural background and had not yet absorbed all the values and rules of their new state. The Reich German occupiers were also equally skeptical in the way they treated their own countrymen who were passing through. This presented the constant danger of some criticism of their lifestyle. It was these guests, who spread a negative picture of the occupation of the East in Germany and thereby threatened to undermine daily life in Warsaw and Minsk, by confronting it with contrasting moral values.[233]

Among the Reich German occupiers the institutional splintering led to competitive attitudes between the respective groups, whether it was the Wehrmacht, the SS and police, or the civil administration. They viewed themselves as the real bearers of culture and the masters in the East. The respective others, however, were often seen as lazy profiteers from one's own sacrificial service, who constantly caused trouble and provoked conflicts; one institution generally spoke of another in a correspondingly negative manner.[234] Nonetheless the competitors for the unofficial title of the "best occupier" belonged to the community and the common claim to German rule over the East and its inhabitants was not disputed internally. This inclusion applied even to the small, rich, higher class of commanders, who were certainly criticized[235] and envied of their enrichment, but without any doubt also belonged to the society of occupiers. The comradeship that was so important for solidarity in the East, however, applied primarily within the respective group, and was only partially extended to other Germans.

Self-perceptions play a decisive role for the habitus of the Germans. The occupiers were members of the ruling elite that enjoyed privileges that went far beyond what was customary. It appeared natural to them to exploit this status. Only in the East was such delinquent behavior possible, such as that by the already mentioned several young members of the SA Standarte Feldherrnhalle assigned to guard Palais Brühl in Warsaw. Wearing their uniforms they repeatedly confiscated goods and collected arbitrary "fines"—that is, they extorted money. This activity would still not have been especially remarkable under the conditions in Warsaw, but in addition they simulated an attack on the guard in order to kill a Pole in cold blood and rape two women. In addition there were repeated incidents among the guards at Palais Brühl in which they had consensual sex with women while on duty. And although they felt completely comfortable with this and—apart from the murder—had no sense of guilt, their conduct was deemed even by the society of occupiers not to be acceptable: the verdicts of the Special Court ranged from three months in prison up to the death penalty.²³⁶ Certainly this was an extreme example, but it makes clear what it could mean to be an occupier.

The status of the occupiers met with agreement from almost all Germans in the East, which was expressed, for example, in that they donated almost twice as much per head as the population at home to the collections of the Winter Aid Drive.²³⁷ Yet the self-perception and the conduct of the occupiers in Warsaw and Minsk had very little to do with the Nazi ideal of the overlords. In practice, most important was the sense of belonging to that small group that, in contrast to the much more numerous others, had access to wealth, privileges, and above all violence.

The habitus was formed by these perceptions. It was created in the alien space of the East, whose impressions were only partially confirmed by the ideological indoctrination the occupiers had received. In this the sense of superiority of the occupiers was combined with the extreme loss of rights among the locals, such that the norms, which did not envisage contacts with the local population, were largely set aside. Only thanks to covering by one's comrades was it possible to speak without difficulty to Belorussians, Poles, and even Jews, and even to use violence against them with the aim of material enrichment, the fulfilment of sexual needs, or simply to humiliate them. For all these, discretion was of central importance because officially these kinds of things were not permitted. Therefore, the habitus of the occupiers was the decisive basis for dealings with the locals because it stabilized the brutal one-sidedness of these contacts and at the same time enforced their secrecy, at least such that knowledge of them was not permitted to penetrate the public space beyond the small circle of comrades. On duty it was only partly necessary because there the room for maneuvering was clearly defined and more strictly controlled than in the private sphere. In addition, it can be determined that the rank and the service unit of the respective occupiers certainly influenced their treatment of the occupied. The habitus of the female occupiers was different from that of their male counterparts because the women mainly acted as grandes dames and avoided contact as far as possible or at least reduced it to the relationship of a grande dame toward her servants.

The characteristic of the female overlord habitus in some respects had many similarities to that found in colonialism—the term describes the attitude of the colonizers to the colonies—yet a description of the German occupation in the East as colonial or even just inspired by colonialism appears to be inappropriate. A study of the administration of the Warthegau names its main characteristics as the sense of superiority and the cultural mission stemming from an alleged German colonialism that was reinforced further by propaganda.²³⁸ Both aspects were certainly constitutive elements in the consciousness of more than a few occupiers in Warsaw, but above all in the ideology of the regime; complaints about climate, lack of culture, and dirt are typical both for the eastern deployment and for service in the colonies, such as the British in India or Africa. Yet analysis shows that the self-perception and the reception of the occupiers were based much more on other factors.

Colonialism's immanent sense of mission was completely alien to the occupiers in Warsaw or Minsk. Very few of them had the idea that their stay in the East was intended to civilize the locals to some extent, and to bring them culture and economic development. Occasional sympathy expressed for the locals had nothing to do with colonialism, but referred rather to the consequences of an occupation policy that had primarily caused the misery of the population. A colonial lifestyle was also not able to establish itself. With the exception of the main leaders and their wives, very few of the occupiers lived outside of a hostel, an apartment block, or a barrack, and therefore were unable to develop any specific representative lifestyle. Furthermore, the locals were by no means viewed only as inferior.

The decisive counterargument, however, is that neither the regime nor the occupiers viewed themselves as colonists or the occupation as colonization. As the planning and implementation for the various population groups demonstrates, a temporary policy from which the occupied could benefit was not intended. Naturally ideals and reality also differed within British colonial policy,[239] but the Nazis never aimed to "improve" the Eastern Europeans because they were not viewed as worthy of protection, nor in need of help, but first as enemies—of their own race and their own drive for living space. Therefore, the regime did not want the occupational personnel to set the Eastern Europeans an example for them to follow, but intended to set themselves apart from the occupied by order and discipline in their own ranks, although the differences between the races stressed by propaganda were not always so clear for many Germans. For them the colonies were just the former territorial possessions across the sea.[240]

Notes

1. Janning, "Habitus," pp. 100–101.
2. Bourdieu, *Rede*, p. 187.
3. Schwingel, *Bourdieu*, p. 83.
4. Bourdieu, *Rede*, p. 84.
5. The quote is from *Amtsblatt der Reichsverkehrsdirektion Minsk*, no. 17, 27.3.1944. On the frequent and stereotypical use of the term "reputation" in the sphere of military justice, see Beck, *Wehrmacht*, p. 252.
6. Jockheck, *Propaganda*, pp. 199ff.
7. Beck, *Wehrmacht*, p. 259.
8. Danker, "Zivilverwaltung," pp. 57ff.

9. Hans Frank's ideas in this regard can be found in Präg and Jacobmeyer, *Diensttagebuch*, p. 106, "Interview Hans Franks mit dem Völkischen Beobachter", 6.2.1940. The personnel in Warsaw are also characterized in this way in Gauweiler, *Berichte*, pp. 43–44. Important also are the "12 commandments for the German administrative officials in the occupied eastern territories," which have been published in Jacobsen, *1939–1945*, pp. 413ff. Wilhelm Kube stressed the central characteristics of his subordinates; IfZA, MA 795/599–603, Kube to RMbO, 12.9.1942.

10. Kühne, *Kameradschaft*, pp. 117–118.

11. APW, 1705/1, Kommandanturbefehl no. 38, 10.11.1939.

12. US-NARA, RG 242, T 312, Reel 42/2471f., Stadtkommandant Warschau to commanders of IDs 18. and 19., 6.10.1939. [For making a copy of this document available, I thank Mathias Irlinger.]

13. Beck, *Wehrmacht*, p. 257.

14. *Amtsblatt der Reichsverkehrsdirektion Minsk*, no. 16, 5.4.1943.

15. BAB, R 6/397, "Urteil des Sondergerichts Minsk", 19.2.1944 and letter by Alfred Rosenberg, 16.3.1944.

16. Ibid.

17. *Amtsblatt der Haupteisenbahndirektion Mitte* (Minsk), no 7, 27.12.1941.

18. APW, 643/416 (new: 221), "Urteil des Sondergerichts Warschau gegen fünf Reichsdeutsche", 10.2.1942 and Reichsbahn to Sondergericht, 22.7.1943.

19. AAN, T 501-228, Kommandanturbefehl Warschau no. 64, 23.3.1940.

20. Ibid.

21. APW, 643/961 (new: 1070), "Urteil des Sondergerichts Warschau gegen den Reichsdeutschen Artur R.", 10.9.1943.

22. *Amtsblatt der Ostbahndirektion*, no. 6, 15.9.1943, p. 34. Erlass, 23.8.1943.

23. *Amtsblatt der Reichsverkehrsdirektion Minsk*, no. 20, 24.4.1943.

24. IfZA, MA 1790/22; 370-6-4 SSPF to Generalkommissar Weißruthenien, 12.5.1942.

25. *Amtsblatt der Haupteisenbahndirektion Mitte* (Minsk), no. 43, 19.10.1942.

26. *Amtsblatt der Reichsverkehrsdirektion Minsk*, no. 19, 19.4.1943.

27. See chapter 3 section 3, this volume

28. IPN, 106/35, "Ermittlungsbericht des KdS Warschau", 2.1.1941.

29. IPN, 106/47, "Ermittlungsbericht des KdS Warschau", 21.3.1941.

30. APW, 482/79, "Urteil des Sondergerichts Warschau", 21.5.1943.

31. APW, 643/1702 (new: 1601), "Urteil des Sondergerichts Warschau gegen die Volksdeutsche Viktoria P.", 29.6.1944.

32. APW, 49/94, "Verfügung des KdS Warschau", 27.7.1940.

33. BAB, NS 7/1084, p. 16, "Anklageverfügung und Haftbefehl des SS- und Polizeigerichts XVII in Minsk", 16.5.1944.

34. APW, 643/172 (new: 115), "Strafbefehl der Staatsanwaltschaft bei dem Sondergericht Warschau gegen die Volksdeutsche Valentina K.", 4.6.1940.

35. APW, 643/528 (new: 621), "Urteil des Sondergerichts Warschau gegen die Jüdin Amelja B.-B. und den *Volksdeutschen* Roman F.", 29.4.1942.

36. APW, 643/1317 (new: 1080), "Urteil des Sondergerichts Warschau gegen die *Volksdeutschen* Eugen S. und Michael K.", 2.4.1943.

37. See chapter 4 section 4 this volume.

38. APW, 643/1124 (new: 1124), "Urteil des Sondergerichts Warschau gegen den Reichsdeutschen Georg W.", 3.8.1943.

39. APW, 643/1325 (new: 1110), "Urteil des Sondergerichts Warschau gegen den Reichsdeutschen Erich G.", 2.6.1943.

40. IfZA, MA 1790/3; 378-1-149, "Urteil des Sondergerichts Minsk", 13.4.1943.

41. APW, 1705/1, Kommandantur to Polizeiregiment Warschau, 13.11.1939.

42. APW, 482/1101, "Urteil des Sondergerichts Warschau", 5.5.1944.

43. APW, 643/1136 (new: 1029), "Urteil des Sondergerichts Warschau gegen den Reichsdeutschen Paul K.", 4.11.1943.
44. See chapter 1 section 5, this volume.
45. Wolfgang Lieschke, who undertook a big trip to Poland in 1930 with his wife, did not acquire a picture divergent from the official view as a result. Private collection of Gerhard Lieschke, Wolfgang Lieschke to his wife, 7.6.1941.
46. IfZA, MA 823/521ff., "Richtlinien des RMbO für die Propaganda in den besetzten Gebieten", 25.9.1943.
47. IPN, NTN 61, "Betriebsappell im Palais Brühl, Ansprache Fischers", 10.8.1943.
48. Jockheck, *Propaganda*, p. 203.
49. As cited in Gerlach, *Morde*, p. 100.
50. Kay, *Exploitation*, p. 166.
51. BfZg, Slg. Sterz, letter by private Kurt Seel, 10.5.1941.
52. Böhler, *Auftakt*, p. 42.
53. Private collection of Gerhard Lieschke, Wolfgang Lieschke to his wife, 8.8.1941.
54. Latzel, "Feldpostbriefe," pp. 178–179.
55. Ibid., p. 178.
56. Carl von Andrian diary/Peter Lieb transcript, 24.10.1941.
57. AAN, T 501-228, Kommandanturbefehl Warschau no. 219, 29.11.1940.
58. AAN, T 501-228/1287f., Kommandanturbefehl Warschau no. 36, 20.2.1940.
59. *Amtlicher Anzeiger für das Generalgouvernement*, no. 83, 28.11.1941, pp. 1757–1758, Anordnung, 20.11.1941.
60. Latzel, *Soldaten*, pp. 370ff.
61. APW, 49/118, "Ermittlungsbericht des KdS Warschau", 20.12.1940.
62. IPN, 106/52, "Ermittlungsbericht des KdS Warschau", 4.9.1941.
63. APW, 1705/1, Kommandanturbefehl Warschau no. 44, 17.11.1939.
64. BAMA, RH 26-707/15, Lagebericht, 707. ID, 20.2.1942.
65. Gerlach, *Morde*, pp. 104–105.
66. BAL, B 162/5845, pp. 13ff., statement of Hans S. on 13.2.1962.
67. Mallmann, *Mißgeburten*, p. 76.
68. BALAA, Ost-Dok. 13/275, pp. 4ff., report by Walter Sperling, Hydrographisches Institut Warschau, 26.6.1958.
69. BAL, B 162/5845, pp. 13ff., statement of Hans S. on 13.2.1962.
70. IfZA, MA 1790/3; 379-2-45, Kommandanturbefehl Minsk no. 39, 3.10.1942.
71. BALAA, Ost-Dok. 13/529, pp. 1ff., "Bericht von Hans Rudolf Jahn, Leiter des landwirtschaftlichen statistischen Amts des Generalgouvernements in Warschau", 2.3.1962.
72. IfZA, MA 1790/2; 378-1-530, internal latter by RVD Minsk, 1.9.1943.
73. BAL, B 162/AR 1495/69, S. 165ff., statement of Alois H. on 28.7.1971.
74. Alvensleben, "Abschiede," pp. 141ff.
75. Private collection of Gerhard Lieschke, Wolfgang Lieschke to his wife, 10.6.1941.
76. IfZA, MA 679—3/263ff., "Monatsbericht der Kommandantur Warschau für den 16.4.-15.5.1941", 20.5.1941.
77. For Minsk, e.g., see DTA, 884, diary Michael Ritter.
78. BfZg, Slg. Sterz, letter by Josef Schützeicher, 2.10.1939.
79. DTA, 280/I. diary Franz Jonas, 3.8.1941.
80. APW, 643/712 (new: 878), "Urteil des Sondergerichts Warschau gegen den *Volksdeutschen* Richard T. und die Polen Stanisław M. und Czesław S.", 19.12.1942.
81. Hosenfeld, *Retten*, pp. 108–109.
82. Ibid., p. 750, letter to his wife, 15.9.1943, and pp. 799ff., letter to his wife, 25.3.1944.
83. Ibid., pp. 81–82.
84. Ibid., pp. 711–712, diary, 23.6.1943.
85. BAMA, RH 26-707/2, "Monatsbericht der 707. ID", 8.12.1941.

86. BAMA, RH 26-707/15, "Lagebericht der 707. ID", 20.2.1942.
87. Gerlach, Morde, pp. 859–1036.
88. Ibid., pp. 860ff.
89. IfZA, MA 1790/2378-1-871, "Schadensmeldung der RVD Minsk", 15./16.10.1943.
90. BAB, R 93/3, pp. 8–9, "Lagebericht zum Kommunalwesen im GK Minsk", 15.10.1942.
91. Chiari, Alltag, pp. 74ff.
92. IfZA, MA 1790/2; 378-1-698, Tagesbefehl no. 24, Wehrmachtkommandant Weißruthenien, 27.10.1941.
93. BAB, R 70 SU/21, pp. 97ff., Tagesbefehl no. 9, HSSPF Russland-Mitte und Weißruthenien, 22.7.1943.
94. BfZg, Slg. Sterz, letter by Reichsbahn-Inspektor Kurt Schmid, 8.10.1941.
95. Carl von Andrian diary/Peter Lieb transcript, 23.9.1941.
96. Minsker Zeitung, no. 224, 23.9.1943: "Ein Kämpfer fiel—sein Geist lebt weiter."
97. Minsker Zeitung, no. 89, 14.4.1943: "Das Bandenunwesen"; ibid., Nr. 281 vom 1.12.1943: "Die Maske der sowjetischen Banditen."
98. Minsker Zeitung, no. 81, 6.4.1943: "Wir ehren Fritz Schild."
99. Borodziej, Aufstand, p. 64. A complete overview of the individual resistance actions in Warsaw can be found in Strzembosz, Akcje.
100. BAL, B 162/3663, pp. 149–151, statement of Hans A. on 5.12.1960.
101. An essential source is Borodziej, Terror, pp. 210ff. In general, see also Jacobmeyer, "Widerstandsbewegung."
102. IPN, NTN 61, "Betriebsappell im Palais Brühl, Ansprache Fischers", 10.8.1943.
103. Szarota, Poland, pp. 230ff., and Böhler, Auftakt, pp. 54ff.
104. ÖGZA, NL 93, report by Max Bischof on the situation in Warsaw, 18.10.1939.
105. See, e.g., ÖGZA, NL 93, report by Max Bischof on the situation in Warsaw, 28.7.1943.
106. BAL, B 162/3693, pp. 18ff., statement of Wilhelm E. on 1.8.1962.
107. BaySta, Staatsanwaltschaften 34865/18, "Anlage 4a zum Zweimonatsbericht des Gouverneurs des Distrikts Warschau für Dezember 1942/Januar 1943", 10.2.1943.
108. BAB, R 102 I/36, p. 1, "Aktenvermerk des I c der OFK Warschau", 15.3.1943.
109. BAB, R 102 I/36, pp. 3–4, "Aktenvermerk des SSPF Warschau", 16.3.1943.
110. APW, 485/398, "Zweimonatsbericht des Stadthauptmanns Warschau für April und Mai 1944", 5.6.1944.
111. BfZg, Slg. Sterz, letter by private Erwin Müller, 21.5.1944.
112. Hosenfeld, Retten, pp. 711ff., letter to his wife, 11.4.1943.
113. APW, 482/2, "Zweimonatsbericht des Gouverneurs des Distrikts Warschau für Dezember 1942 und Januar 1943", 11.2.1943.
114. In the monthly reports of the Senior Field Commandant's Office in Warsaw for 1944, every one includes several so-called gang attacks: IfZA, MA 679.
115. BaySta, Staatsanwaltschaften 34865/18, "Wochenbericht der Abteilung Propaganda des Distrikts Warschau, Anlage 5a", 16.1.1943.
116. BfZg, Slg. Sterz, letter by Hermine Neuhauser, 31.8.1944.
117. BAB, R 102 I/40, "Aktenvermerk des KdS Warschau", n.d.
118. Stawarz, Pawiak, p. 68.
119. APW, 482/70, "Lagebericht des Kreishauptmanns Warschau-Land für April/Mai 1944", 6.6.1944.
120. APW, 482/70, "Lagebericht des Kreishauptmanns Warschau-Land für Februar/März 1944", 6.4.1944.
121. IPN, NTN 257, "Bericht über Warschau (eingereicht durch SS-Standartenführer von Korzowski)", n.d. [mid 1943].
122. RGVA, 1323-2-302a, p. 3, Kommandanturbefehl Warschau no. 144, 24.6.1943.

123. IPN, NTN 61, "Betriebsappell im Palais Brühl, Ansprache Fischers", 10.8.1943.
124. IfZA, Fb 105—30/7452ff., "Ansprache Franks auf einer Großkundgebung der NSDAP", 19.6.1943.
125. APW, 482/74, "Zweimonatsbericht der Abteilung Volksaufklärung und Propaganda Warschau für Februar und März 1944".
126. IfZA, Fb 63/51f., "Monatsbericht des Distrikts Warschau für März 1942", 13.4.1942. On the measures of the resistance that were to instill fear in the occupiers without the direct use of violence, see Szarota, *Warschau*, pp. 264–265. In Belorussia Poles were also seen as dangerous: BAMA, RH 26—707/2, "Monatsbericht des Wehrmachtbefehlshabers Ostland vom 11.10. bis 10.11.1941"; ibid., "Monatsbericht des Wehrmachtbefehlshabers Ostland vom 1.11.-30.11.1941".
127. BAB, R 102 I/21, pp. 1–2, "Rundschreiben des *Distrikt*gouverneurs Warschau", 8.6.1944.
128. *Amtlicher Anzeiger für das Generalgouvernement*, no. 44, 15.7.1941, pp. 1079–1080, "Hundesteuerordnung für Warschau", 24.6.1941.
129. APW, 482/1552, "Monatsbericht des Distrikts Warschau für März 1941", 10.4.1941. In the report the moving up of the curfew to 8:00 P.M. is described explicitly as a reaction to the attacks against the Germans.
130. BAB, NS 19/2648, pp. 7ff., Frank to Himmler, 13.6.1941.
131. *Verordnungsblatt für das Generalgouvernement*, no. 1, 2.1.1942, p. 1, Erlass, 17.12.1941.
132. BAB, R 102 I/18, pp. 1–2, Amtschef *Distrikt* Warschau to Leiter Abteilung Propaganda, 14.10.1942.
133. Welzer, *Täter*, p. 245.
134. See chapter 5 section 1 and section 3, this volume.
135. BAL, B 162/AR 179/71, Bd. 2, pp. 272ff., statement of Christel S. on 21.1.1971.
136. BAL, B 162/3709, pp. 219ff., statement of Sieglinde J. on 23.8.1965.
137. Ibid.
138. *Warschauer Zeitung*, no. 1, 3.1.1940: "Erste deutsche Trauung in Warschau."
139. This collection probably documents almost all German marriages in Warsaw, although the total number cannot be given with any certainty. On estimating the total number, see the comments in APW, 482/62, "Zweimonatsbericht des Stadthauptmanns Warschau für Februar und März 1944", 4.4.1944. See also Leist, *Bericht*, p. 54, in which for 1940, 32 marriages and for 1941, 85 are given. On the Registry Office files, see APW, 485/296-326. In the documents there are included, e.g., details about job, age, place of origin or residence, citizenship, and the religion of the bride and groom.
140. The files are organized alphabetically according to the names of the husbands. For the sample, the following files were evaluated: APW, 485/296-326.
141. Fuks, *Getto*, pp. 155–156, diary, 28.5.1941.
142. Jaworski and Peters, *Alltagsperspektiven*, pp. 28–29.
143. IPN, 106/95, statement of Agathe S. on 21.2.1941.
144. APW, 643/973 (new: 979), "Urteil des Sondergerichts Warschau gegen die Reichsdeutsche Angela P. und den Polen Edward M.", 10.3.1943.
145. BAL, B 162/AR 179/71, Bd. 2, pp. 386ff., statement of Gerhard S. on 15.3.1971.
146. Heineman, *Difference*, pp. 18–19.
147. BAL, B 162/AR 179/71, Bd. 7, pp. 1164ff., statement of Gretel S. on 26.8.1971.
148. Heinemann, *Difference*, pp. 56ff.
149. APW, 485/310, 314 and 323.
150. APW, 485/310, "Ehestandsunterlagen", 21.4.1941.
151. BAL, B 162/3697, pp. 256ff., statement of Walter I. on 23.9.1963.
152. APW, 49/85, "Ermittlungsbericht des KdS Warschau", 18.7.1940.
153. APW, 643/971 (new: 969), "Urteil des Sondergerichts Warschau gegen die *Volksdeutschen* Julius N. und Irene R., geborene N.", 21.4.1943.

154. BAL, B 162/AR 179/71, Bd. 7, pp. 1164ff., statement of Gretel S. on 26.8.1971.
155. Ibid., Bd. 8, pp. 1502ff., statement of Heinz M. on 23.2.1972.
156. See chapter 3 section 3, this volume.
157. The wife of a Warsaw police doctor reports, e.g., of frequent participation in riding competitions and receptions: BAL, B 162/3709, pp. 215ff., statement of Thekla B. on 25.7.1965. Large apartments and servants are mentioned in BAL, B 162/3662, pp. 53ff., statement of Gertrud W. on 28.9.1960; BAL, B 162/3661, pp. 89ff., statement of Christel S. on 14.9.1960. See also Schwarz, *Frau*, pp. 130ff.
158. Schwarz, *Frau*, p. 103.
159. Mallmann, *Mißgeburten*, p. 76.
160. *Amtsblatt der Reichsverkehrsdirektion Minsk*, no. 5, 17.1.1944, n.p.; ibid., Nr. 6 vom 24.1.1944, n.p.
161. Blättler, *Warschau*, p. 44. See also Röger, "Sexual Contact."
162. For Minsk see BAMA, RH 26-707/15, "Lagebericht der 707. ID", 8.1.1942: "On various sides it has also been reported confidentially that primarily in the city of Minsk, the common interaction of members of the Wehrmacht and of the civil administration with the civil population in their apartments has established itself."
163. BAMA, RH 53—23/23, "Bericht der Wehrmacht über Vorkommnisse in Polen", 20.4.1940.
164. Schwarz, *Frau*, p. 187.
165. Jäger, *Verbrechen*, p. 153.
166. APW, 49/73, "Vernehmungsprotokoll des Kriminalassistenten Heinz Brückner", 9.8.1940.
167. Heineman, *Sexuality*, p. 61.
168. BAL, B 162/3661, pp. 72ff., statement of Heinz K. on 5.9.1960.
169. BAB, R 6/383, p. 32, "Erlass des Führers", 11.10.1943.
170. BAB, R 6/383, p. 41, RMbO to Reichskanzlei, 17.11.1943.
171. BAB, R 6/383, p. 125, RKFDV to RMbO, 31.7.1944.
172. BAL, B 162/1691, pp. 4153ff., statement of Hermann Friedrichs on 14.2.1963.
173. APW, 49/159, SSPF to KdS Warschau, 21.2.1941.
174. Seidler, *Prostitution*, pp. 186–187.
175. APW, 49/156, "Bericht des Sittenkommissariats des KdS Warschau an die Gesundheitsabteilung des *Distrikts*", 3.11.1940.
176. BAL, B 162/3661, pp. 75–76, statement of Günter F. on 5.9.1960.
177. APW, 49/159, KdS Warschau to BdS GG, 29.9.1942.
178. IfZA, MA 708-3/332ff., KdS Warschau, Befehl no. 52 des KdS Warschau, 13.12.1940; RGVA, 1323-2-302b, p. 13, Kommandanturbefehl Warschau no. 206, 16.9.1943.
179. APW, 1705/1, Kommandanturbefehl Warschau no. 13, 14.10.1939.
180. Seidler, *Prostitution*, pp. 181ff.
181. APW, 49/156, "Bericht des Sittenkommissariats des KdS Warschau an die Gesundheitsabteilung des *Distrikts*", 18.1.1943.
182. StAM, Polizeipräsidien, Slg. Primavesi/270, p. 21, "Kriegserinnerungen des Oberwachtmeisters der Schutzpolizei Otto Nahlmann".
183. Blättler, *Warschau*, pp. 43–44.
184. APW, 49/114, "Ermittlungsbericht des KdS Warschau", 13.12.1940.
185. IfZA, MA 1790/22; 370-6-4, Hauserlass no. 1, GK Minsk, 25.7.1942.
186. IfZA, Fa 91/4, pp. 866ff., "Bericht Nr. 4 des Beauftragten des Reichsleiters Bormann im OKW, Albert Hoffmann, über Weißruthenien und die Stadt Minsk, 26.5.1942.
187. Klee et al., "Zeiten," pp. 171ff.
188. StAM, Polizeipräsidien, Slg. Primavesi/208, "Beurteilung des SS-Obersturmbannführers Eduard Strauch, KdS Weißruthenien, durch den BdS Ostland", 1.4.1943.

189. APW, 1705/1, Kommandantur to Polizeiregiment Warschau, 13.11.1939.
190. IfZA, Fa 91/4, pp. 983ff., "Bericht Nr. 1 des Beauftragten des Reichsleiters Bormann im OKW, Albert Hoffmann, über Warschau", 9.8.1942.
191. IPN, 106/46, "Ermittlungsbericht des KdS Warschau", 20.3.1941.
192. Beck, *Wehrmacht*, pp. 129–130 and 154ff.
193. Ibid., pp. 186ff.
194. IPN, 106/8, interrogation of Wilhelm W., 2.2.1940.
195. Hosenfeld, *Retten*, p. 423, diary, 4.12.1940. The addition is as found in the published edition.
196. Beck, *Wehrmacht*, pp. 266ff.
197. Ibid., pp. 272–273. Sexual crimes during the war were only sporadically prosecuted and without any enthusiasm, even by the Allies after the war. Mühlhäuser, "Gewalt," pp. 36–37.
198. APW, 643/525 (new: 503), "Urteil des Sondergerichts Warschau gegen den *Volksdeutschen* Edmund Braun", 2.11.1942.
199. Beck, *Wehrmacht*, pp. 277ff.
200. Welzer, *Täter*, p. 202.
201. IfZA, Fb 85-I/pp. 22ff., "Protokoll über die Tagung der Gebietskommissare, Hauptabteilungsleiter und Abteilungsleiter des Generalkommissariats Minsk vom 8.4. bis 10.4.1943".
202. As cited in Präg and Jacobmeyer, *Diensttagebuch*, p. 18, "Ansprache Franks beim Besuch von Robert Ley", 7.11.1940.
203. As cited in Präg and Jacobmeyer, *Diensttagebuch*, pp. 106–107, "Interview Franks vom 6.2.1940, erschienen im *Völkischen Beobachter*", 12.2.1940.
204. IfZA, Fb 85-I/pp. 22ff., "Protokoll über die Tagung der Gebietskommissare, Hauptabteilungsleiter und Abteilungsleiter des Generalkommissariats Minsk vom 8.4. bis 10.4.1943".
205. IfZA, MA 1790/1; 378-1-36, "Merkblatt der RVD Minsk über das Verhalten in den besetzten Ostgebieten", n.d.
206. APW, 482/148, "Erlass der Regierung des Generalgouvernements", 30.1.1942.
207. Alvensleben, "Abschiede," p. 145, diary, 12.10.1940.
208. On this attitude, see Kleßmann, *Selbstbehauptung*, pp. 48ff.
209. APW, 482/5, "Grundsätzliche Bemerkungen über die Gestaltung Warschaus während des Krieges und nach dem Kriege, von Gouverneur Fischer", n.d. [1944].
210. Latzel, "Feldpostbriefe," pp. 177–178.
211. *Mitteilungsblatt der Stadt Warschau*, no. 37, 10.10.1940, pp. 1–2, Bekanntmachung, 8.10.1940.
212. IPN, NTN 61, "Betriebsappell im Palais Brühl, Ansprache Fischers", 10.8.1943.
213. Hosenfeld, *Retten*, pp. 606–607, diary, 17.4.1942.
214. Ibid., p. 446, letter to his wife, 15.2.1941.
215. IfZA, Fb 105—6/545ff., "Ansprache Franks bei einem für ihn ausgerichteten Empfang im Palais Brühl", 28.5.1940.
216. APW, 482/148, "Erlass der Regierung des Generalgouvernements", 30.1.1942. For individual criticism, see, e.g., BfZG, Slg. Sterz, letter by Unterfeldwebel Hermann Schilling, 6.8.1944, or BAB, NS 19/2648, pp. 45ff., Hans Peter Kraemer to Reichskanzlei, 7.4.1942.
217. APW, 643/1202 (new: 949), "Urteil des Sondergerichts Warschau gegen die *Volksdeutschen* Raimund-Ernst L. und Alfred G.", 9.11.1943.
218. IPN, 106/52, "Ermittlungsbericht des KdS Warschau", 4.9.1941.
219. BfZg, Slg. Sterz, letter by private Kurt Seel, 10.5.1941.
220. BfZg, Slg. Sterz, letter by private Wilhelm Hornung, 2.10.1943.
221. Szarota, "Luftangriffe," p. 131.

222. Private Collection of Gerhard Lieschke, Wolfgang Lieschke to his wife, 24.6.1941.

223. IPN, NTN 257, "Bericht über Warschau (eingereicht durch SS-Standartenführer von Korzowski)", n.d. [mid 1943].

224. Jersak, "Entscheidungen," p. 321, describes an ideal racial society in the East.

225. See, e.g., Wildt, "Ordnung," esp. pp. 58–59.

226. Welzer, *Täter*, p. 245.

227. Koselleck, "Semantik," pp. 212–213 and 257–258.

228. BfZg, Slg. Sterz, letter by Unteroffizier Gottard Eiermann, 24.6.1941.

229. Hosenfeld, *Retten*, pp. 659–660, diary, 1.10.1942.

230. Welzer, *Täter*, p. 251.

231. Ibid., p. 73.

232. The question of first- and second-class members of the people's community is briefly discussed with regard to the Sudeten Germans in Zimmermann, "Volksgenossen," pp. 269ff.

233. APW, 486/8, "Lagebericht des Gendarmeriezugs Warschau Land an den KdG Warschau", 31.12.1941.

234. The statements and documents on this topic are innumerable. See, e.g., BayStA, Staatsanwaltschaften 21695, "Ermittlungen gegen Gustav von Mauchenheim, Kommandant der 707. ID"; BALAA, Ost-Dok. 8/829, p. 5, letter by Erich Kossan, Adjutant of Rüstungsbereichskommandeur Warschau, 6.11.1955; BAB, R 19/137, pp. 123ff., "Erfahrungsbericht über den Einsatz der Verwaltungspolizei in Russland-Mitte und Weißruthenien von Willy Dahlgrün, Polizeihauptmann und SS-Sturmbannführer", 16.6.1943; IfZA, MA 1467/541f., GK Minsk to RMbO, 5.11.1943.

235. E.g., Hosenfeld, *Retten*, p. 722, diary, 23.6.1943.

236. APW, 482/79, "Urteil des Sondergerichts Warschau", 21.5.1943.

237. APW, 1357/1, "NSDAP-Lagebericht des Standorts Warschau-Land für Mai 1941", 27.5.1941.

238. Furber, *East*, pp. 49ff.

239. Ibid., p. 67.

240. Ibid., pp. 57ff.

Chapter 5

VIOLENCE IN EVERYDAY LIFE
The German Occupiers and the Local Population

A central element of German occupational rule was the violence against the local population. Its constant presence claimed the lives of close to 1 million victims in Warsaw and Minsk together. Of those, around 600,000 were murdered Jews. Some had not lived in the two cities before the war and some had been transported into the ghettos shortly before their murder. An investigation of the perpetrators and their motivation cannot be complete without examining their crimes. Therefore, this chapter will take a look at the various forms of violence.

In a groundbreaking study in 1967, Herbert Jäger developed a typology for participation in Nazi crimes that differentiated excess crimes, crimes of initiative, and crimes committed under orders. The murders in Warsaw and Minsk can also be divided into these three categories, which are further differentiated in detail by Jäger. Building on his pioneering study, this chapter will show how the "individual crimes and contributions to crimes were interwoven with the collective criminal network."[1] Special attention will be given to how the perpetrators justified their crimes. For if their conduct seemed legal to the occupiers, this was not the case for the occupied, nor was it legal from the perspective of present-day human rights' conventions, which provide protection of life and limb from attacks by others and by the state. Next to the immediate physical and psychological effects of violence, in the East there were also repressive structures. In Poland and Weißruthenien they showed themselves in the daily persecution of the locals. Their most important forms of expression toward the Jews were the ghettoization, the inadequate supply of food, and the practical loss of rights in their interactions with the Germans.

The primary focus of this study is the legitimation of the various forms of violence. It is concerned less with the Nazis' plans for killing the Jews and Slavs, which was an elementary part of their ideology,[2] but rather with the "ordinary men" who implemented the mass murders personally or indirectly and so made them possible by their organization of occupational rule. Without thousands of Germans who secured the implementation of the occupation, the destruction would not have been possible. Their legitimations, however contrived they might seem by modern standards, were essential for the murders because without an actual or imagined necessity hardly anyone takes another life or is prepared to support it. Those who were willing to take responsibility for killing a person also created a justifying pretext.[3] On the other hand structural violence, like starvation, can scarcely be attributed to specific individuals. Therefore, it is necessary to investigate the legitimation of the values, norms, and institutions, which made it possible; that is also the legitimation of their own existence as occupiers.

There were numerous legitimations for the killing of the locals that varied according to the population group affected. Therefore, the specific forms of violence to which the inhabitants of Warsaw and Minsk were subjected will be examined individually. Crucial to this is the public nature of the crimes: combined with the obvious fact of the destruction is the question of what role violence played in everyday life and how its meaning for the occupiers' own existence should be assessed, or rather how it was cognitively reduced in order to alleviate any sense of guilt.

If one speaks about the public nature of the murders, first of all one refers to their visibility in the cities. On the second level, however, the communication about the violence both within and outside the society of occupiers is also relevant. The ways of obtaining information, as well as the type and content of its articulation, are important; thereby the meaning of violence for everyday life is revealed. The flow of information back home can only be briefly referred to because there are scarcely sufficient sources on this. Nonetheless the study of Peter Longerich, for example, indicates that within the Reich there was not complete ignorance about the murder of the Jews, but rather numerous details about the public mass murders were known.[4]

1. Suppressing Resistance or Reprisal Crimes? Open Violence against Poles and Belorussians

"The population is collapsing in the street from hunger."[5] In these words, Order Policeman Otto Nahlmann summed up after the war his impression of the food supply situation for the locals in Warsaw. His description shows in an exemplary way that the structural violence, which was expressed mainly in terms of the chronic deprivation of food from the Poles, Belorussians, and Jews, did not go unnoticed among the occupiers. The Germans could not avoid walking the streets of Warsaw and Minsk and seeing how bad the locals' food supply was. The small amount of food was available only for ration cards and the administration tried to reduce consumption by regulating the number of shops where food could be bought at all, and thereby limiting it indirectly. Occasionally observers came to the obvious conclusion that the problem of resistance was linked to these measures.[6] Especially those occupiers in higher positions with local employees subordinate to them were well-informed about the inadequate food supply because it had a direct effect on those employees' work efficiency. Therefore, it was carefully noted that for months there had been no fish for Poles; some office heads responded to the situation with special rations for their employees that were against regulations, but this remained primarily a utilitarian exception that was intended only to retain their own workers.[7] Types of food other than bread, jam, and potatoes could not be obtained regularly in Warsaw's shops and remained a rarity.[8]

The planned systematic undernourishment that calculated that many locals would starve nonetheless could not be implemented through to its ultimate conclusion in the two cities. Completely cutting off the food supply would have led to uprisings, but would in any case have endangered the Germans deployed in Warsaw and Minsk—and their work—as riots and disease had to be feared.[9] The level of calories per head distributed remained well below that necessary to sustain life; in Belorussia the official rations ranged between 420 and 1,200 calories per day, according both to racial background as well as employment, and thereby were clearly less than the necessary minimum of at least 2,400.[10] The residents of Warsaw received even less because the daily ration for Jews in the middle of the years 1940 and 1941 varied between 413 and 253 calories. Table 5.1 shows the situation for the non-Jewish population, in percent of daily needs.

The rations for the Polish population were improved in the first six months of 1944, but even then they did not exceed 900 calories for adults and 550 for children.[11] For the many POWs in Minsk there are no precise

Table 5.1. Official Daily Rations of Required Forms of Nutrition in Warsaw (in percent)

Year	Protein	Fats	Carbohydrates	Calories
1940	20.9	4.3	35.8	27.9
1941	25.6	8.0	37.7	29.7
1942	22.2	3.2	32.9	25.8
1943	23.1	2.4	37.2	28.6
1944	27.8	2.5	43.3	38.5

Source: Szarota, *Warschau*, p. 114.

figures, yet their rations were probably even lower.[12] The conflicts between POWs in the camps were repeatedly the subject of dramatic descriptions, such as three men fighting each other over a loaf of bread who had to be separated with armed force.[13] Carl von Andrian reports on a POW camp in Weißruthenien in which "on several occasions prisoners literally tore apart deceased fellow prisoners a[nd] ate the flesh of the dead."[14] These kinds of things appear not to be exaggerated, if one considers that initially in Minsk around 100,000 prisoners were crammed together in a very small area and were cut off from any food supplies whatsoever. Their murder had already been decided.[15]

Shortly after the capture of the Belorussian capital in July 1941, the POW camp there was severely overpopulated,[16] and it was especially difficult to feed the inmates: hardly any food was captured in Minsk and the Wehrmacht did not want to spare any of its own supplies. As the Luftwaffe doctor Wolfgang Lieschke in Minsk correctly concluded, the food available to the locals was dependent on "the good will of the German troops."[17] Even two months after the start of the occupation, there was still a strained, if no longer catastrophic, situation. The policy of starvation cost the lives of thousands of people. Some nine thousand victims are known by name.[18] One year later there was no longer a POW camp in the city, nonetheless "columns of tattered prisoners that could not be overlooked" were visible almost daily marching into the Reich on foot along the road that passed through the center of the city heading west. The occupiers could not avoid seeing and hearing how the Red Army soldiers pleaded with their compatriots for a piece of bread and occasionally simply collapsed from starvation and died.[19]

The number of deaths from starvation among the non-Jewish population was less than in the ghetto because they were able to obtain additional food in the countryside from relatives, on the black market, or from their own small plots of land and could therefore survive; diseases of malnutrition were nonetheless present.[20] The serious shortages suffered by the city population were made worse by the effects of inflation, such that black-market goods remained beyond the means of many people. This fact was carefully monitored by the occupational authorities.[21] All the same, Wilhelm Kube was of the opinion that, according to the official quotas, the Belorussians should have died long ago, but quite to the contrary they were in a "very well-fed condition."[22] Outside the cities the situation was really better because despite the draconian requisition regulations of the German authorities, the population that was predominantly occupied in agriculture was able to feed itself to a large extent. In the ghettos the situation was considerably more critical, such that there were many cases of death and disease from malnutrition, and the death rate in the Warsaw ghetto even well before the deportations was several hundred people per day.[23] Despite the illegal sources of food, only very few inmates of the Jewish residential district were able to consume even 1,300 calories per day.[24]

The hunger of the locals was even worse in Warsaw than in Minsk, and it did not remain concealed from the occupiers. Yet nonetheless starvation demanded a certain degree of attention and interest from the occupiers in order for them to clearly recognize the situation of the locals and to realize the consequences arising from the inadequate food supply. However, that the supplies were insufficient and unvaried was seen by most Germans who spent more than just a few days in either of the two capitals. Careful observer Wilm Hosenfeld noted in his diary in April 1942, "With every day food becomes scarcer, gradually in W[arsaw] a famine is developing."[25] The consequences were the spread of numerous diseases, such as tuberculosis or typhus, but the connection between inadequate nourishment and disease was not recognized by most Germans. Doctors like Wilhelm Hagen[26] or Wolfgang Lieschke did make a correct diagnosis, but Lieschke linked it to the cynical conclusion that only a few occupiers may have agreed with: "In my medical opinion, the Polish people is experiencing a very big selection right now; anyone that is weakened ... , will succumb."[27] This shows how far racial ideology had penetrated the thinking of leading officials. Against this background it was easy to accept the deaths in the ghetto or even to be in favor of them and as a supervisor to pass this acceptance on to your men.

Another form of violence against the population was forced labor, which so many locals had to perform.[28] More even than hunger, this was always visible; on the one hand there were the local auxiliary workers, and on the other the deportations to Germany. For the Germans it was completely clear that without a great number of laborers—who worked in part voluntarily, in part by being coerced, but mainly out of necessity—the occupation could not have been conducted. In the East it was mainly the Jews who were compelled to perform forced labor,[29] while the non-Jewish population there mostly continued with their former jobs. At least at the start the new rulers hoped that, in view of the unemployment, their measures would at least be welcomed by the locals and that they would work for them voluntarily. Accordingly a newspaper article from December 1939 exclaimed, "Doing nothing in Warsaw is a thing of the past!" Especially the Jews were accused of collective laziness.[30] Under the supervision of the ethnic Germans, who were supposed to set a good example, the task was to educate the Poles to work. This exploited a widespread prejudice, which by and large assumed that the locals would by no means be capable of the same work performance as Germans. But especially in view of the effort required for the war, the defeated were now to work for the victors to provide a certain degree of restitution for those killed, for the difficulties involved in exercising authority, as well as for the economic losses due to the war. Under these conditions there was considerable support for forced labor within the society of occupiers that relied to a considerable extent on the local work force; every German office employed them somewhere.[31]

Police raids were daily occurrences in Warsaw and Minsk, in which men were grabbed from the streets at random and were sent to Germany for forced labor. From the territory of Weißruthenien, for example, around 116,000 were grabbed and sent to Germany.[32] Only at the start did the massive propaganda campaign for the voluntary recruitment experience a certain degree of success, yet word soon spread that the generous promises made by the Germans regarding the work conditions and pay in their homeland should not be believed.[33] The occupational press also still reported positively about the Polish laborers at the start and praised their willingness to work.[34] However, the image of a healthy world full of cooperating volunteers survived only a short time since the reality experienced by the occupiers clearly spoke a different language; the German authorities soon resorted to compulsory recruiting and forced deportations.

There was a great need for workers in the Reich. In 1944, for example, the city of Warsaw had to meet a quota of 6,100 people to be deported for forced labor, for the *Distrikt* altogether it was 27,000. Therefore the civil administration discussed with representatives of the police how "the recruitment of workers can be augmented during the Police actions, without these actions coming to be regarded simply as man hunts." The negative image of an unscrupulous occupational power was to be avoided among the occupiers as well as among the locals. Because between six hundred and eight hundred people were having their papers checked daily, in future the police were to arrest around five hundred men and women per month for deportation to Germany. "School identity cards for students over the age of 17 should no longer be recognized."[35] The occupiers carefully observed the authorities' approach[36] and were in part surprised by the brutality that was being used; they were clearly aware that this would do nothing to improve motivation of the Poles and Belorussians toward their work.

Even the civil administration sometimes criticized the methods of the SS and police because they proceeded "at times extraordinarily summarily and brusquely." Their concern for practicalities was stronger, however because many Poles who were working for German offices and "were almost irreplaceable on account of their linguistic abilities or their proven experience," were "caught up in these raids as workers and sent into the Reich."[37] The henchmen proceeded with extreme ruthlessness; for example, they would surround Polish cinemas during the performance and subject the moviegoers to a thorough check of their papers. Anyone who did not have with them a document showing that they were employed was immediately deported into the Reich. In addition, the police cordoned off entire streets and forcibly rounded up those living in the houses there, and pulled passengers off the trams. They were all loaded into trucks, taken to a collection camp, and "sorted" there for their deployment in the Reich. As early as September 1940, Max Bischof, the head of the Transfer Office for the Ghetto, for example, reports on these kinds of tactics in a letter to the representative of the Reichsbank's Krakow office, Fritz Paersch.[38]

An even more drastic procedure is described in a postwar statement, in which a former leader of the company air-raid protection force reported, "On a public holiday there was a wedding in a church; the church was completely full. Suddenly the church was surrounded and all those present capable of work, men and women, were loaded onto trucks."[39] The measures in Minsk did not differ from those in Warsaw. In May 1943, for example, a major roundup lasting six days was organized there involving three police battalions and two Wehrmacht battalions, that checked the identification of 130,000 inhabitants, including 40,000 children. And although this resulted in only 39 arrests, the roundup yielded 1,062 new forced laborers.[40]

It is hardly surprising that in view of such tactics, more and more Poles and Belorussians tried to evade compulsory forced labor. Thus the occupiers discovered that the number of workers who had deserted their jobs in the city of Warsaw alone had risen from 9,000 to 12,000 people within one year; that the root cause lay in the laborers' worse treatment was not difficult to recognize.[41] What was being criticized indirectly here, and more openly elsewhere, was less the fact that the locals were being coerced into working for the Germans, but rather the brutality with which they were coerced. Apart from Wilm Hosenfeld, however, almost nobody used the term "manhunt" to call these terror measures what they really were.[42]

The next steps in the escalation of violence were murders of the local population by order of the state; these murders were constantly visible in Warsaw and Minsk. According to Herbert Jäger's typology, these murders should be defined as crimes committed under orders "in which orders clearly laid out how the perpetrators were to behave, leaving nothing to their own judgment."[43] The murderers acted out of obedience, out of conviction, but also from opportunism and actual or perceived peer pressure. According to the understanding of the Nazis, however, the crimes committed on orders were not seen as crimes, but only as a means of combatting resistance. In order to make it clear that it was not a matter of freedom-loving people with a just cause, the Nazis were very keen to avoid using the word "partisan." This word would have "branded the fighters who laid ambushes as heroes and patriots. People, who carry out these attacks, have to be described for what they really are: snipers, franc-tireurs, highwaymen, thieves, and gangs. In official correspondence the terms bandits and bandit suppression, or at most franc-tireurs suppression are to be used."[44] In this way the authorities created an asymmetrical counter-concept to that of the soldier that was to be used only for their own men in this connection and thereby established separation and promoted the delegitimation of resistance.[45]

Especially in the area around Minsk, the concept of *Bandenkampf* was accepted as a legitimate and necessary tool against the threat from the partisans; this was even reflected in the language used in the newspapers. The desired interpretation was prescribed. On the other hand, the relative rarity of the articles—except for large antipartisan operations, not more than one or two per month—was intended to calm down the occupiers. The articles, some with martial titles and most including few facts, were similar to the contemporary army newspapers with their sensational descriptions and did not waste any space on trying to justify the destruction of the civilian population.[46] In addition, no figures for the numbers of victims were published because these stood in crass disproportion to their own losses. The monthly report of the 707th Infantry Division for October 1941, as the attacks of the partisans became more numerous, is characteristic for these crimes.[47] This report mentioned only German losses of two dead and five wounded against 10,940 prisoners captured, of which 10,431 were shot. The figure of less than ninety captured firearms also reveals[48] that here it was not a question of overcoming a threat, but much more a matter of wiping out the Jewish population in the countryside. The disproportionate relationship between their own and enemy losses was noted and criticized by a few contemporaries, but mainly because the rural population was no longer available to bring in the harvest.[49] All the same the massacres remained unchallenged on principle as a suitable means to break resistance. Nonetheless, it is significant that some senior Wehrmacht officers in contrast to the war against the bandits spoke of "proper partisans," meaning those who actually offered resistance.[50]

Although the massacres took place outside the city, they nonetheless attracted considerable public attention, even when the reports and rumors rarely contained precise figures. The local SS and police forces did most of this work: during their stay in Minsk every member of the office of the Commander of the Security Police participated in at least one such execution.[51] For them as for other Germans the legitimacy of the war against the bandits never came into question despite the horror of some "unpleasant things."[52] Precisely because they perceived themselves as being under an extreme threat,[53] not a few occupiers hoped that the local partisans would "suffer massive losses."[54] If there was any skepticism at all it was directed—

as in the case of the forced laborers—at most against the methods used in the "the war against the bandits.... The partisans are victims of the Soviet leadership. They threaten German people and therefore needed to be rendered harmless, but the how [sic] could be more honorable,"[55] von Andrian noted in his diary.

Even occupiers who were scarcely directly exposed themselves to the attacks of the resistance movement explicitly supported the violence against the local population. Thus the railway official Kurt Schmid wrote in a letter sent through the military post, "The partisan activity is making life difficult for us on the railway lines, such that the harshest methods have to be employed. In the event of attacks, in short measure a number of people from among the residents of neighboring villages, especially Jews, are seized and shot on the spot, their houses burned to the ground."[56] In especially emphasizing the Jews, Schmid defamed them as the main force behind the resistance movement, and was thereby following one of the patterns of interpretation prescribed by Nazi propaganda,[57] which contributed considerably to the apparent legality of the murder of the Jews. Furthermore, Schmid was, like most of the occupiers, aware of the Germans' methods of proceeding and he approved. It appeared that only by clearing whole swaths of land was it still possible to establish a deterrent.

It is remarkable that on isolated occasions the violence of the German approach drew criticism even from so unscrupulous a person as Wilhelm Kube. Shortly before his death at the hands of an attack by the resistance in 1943, he spoke of a "ruthless campaign of destruction against the peaceful civilian population [in which] women and children will be shot or burned *en masse.*" Kube saw Weißruthenien "gradually being completely emptied of its population"[58] and preferred the application of less cruel methods. Significantly his successor was Curt von Gottberg, who had made his name as a ruthless butcher in the war against the bandits and was appointed to the position of *Generalkommissar* for his explicit approval of the alleged necessity for proceeding in this manner.[59]

His appointment demonstrated once again that the Nazis had no interest in a restrained approach to the supposed suppression of resistance; that approach might have given them hope for a degree of understanding among the locals. In view of the dimension of the crimes, it is not possible to speak only of reprisals; it is more the case that the Germans bet on massive deterrence through brutal massacres. A key element of this strategy was the public nature of their actions, especially in the cities, such that on the one hand the locals were constantly shown the rulers' power, and on the other the occupiers saw that their state was doing something against this threat. A discussion about the proportionality of their measures did not take place. Instead, Hans Frank's comment applied: "Nothing will prevent us from demanding atonement for every murdered German, which is definitely called for in view of the underhanded nature of such deeds."[60] The customary quota in the East for attacks was initially fifty, later one hundred locals to be shot for each German killed, which clearly shows the supposed value of the occupiers in comparison to the occupied. This approach stood in clear contrast to the less drastic measures in the West, where in general ten hostages had to lose their lives for a fallen German.[61] In addition to reprisals for deaths of Germans, there were also reprisals such as executions of hostages by shooting or hanging[62] in response to acts of sabotage.

The unquestioning manner, in which the occupational authorities quenched their thirst for revenge was expressed by the general commissariat of Weißruthenien in 1942 in an article in the *Minsker Zeitung,* in which the execution of 150 members of sniper gangs was celebrated under the title "A harsh but fair verdict."[63] Although coverage of those massacres cannot be found later on and was replaced by placard announcements[64] that are considerably harder to document, the public nature of the violence, especially with regard to the numerous executions, was a basic element of the Nazi reprisal crimes. Władysław Bartoszewski has prepared a list of the executions in Warsaw and shows that in total more than 27,000 people were killed in this manner.[65] Although many of them were Jews who were murdered mainly in the ghetto and therefore officially out of the occupants' field of sight, these shootings did not remain unnoticed.

In cases where the occupiers were shot at, the reprisal actions usually took place in the center of the city, where the original event had taken place.[66] The occupiers distinguished themselves by a veritable love of sensation, attending and photographing the hangings with great interest,[67] although they were strictly warned not to do this.[68] Only members of the office of the Commander of the Security Police, if they were not themselves part of the firing squad, were occasionally required to participate as observers.[69] The seemingly paradoxical ban on photography reveals once again the conflict between public deterrence on the one hand and strict secrecy on the other, so that the murders did not endanger Germany's reputation. The rulers in the East were well aware that the harsh reprisals would by no means be met with understanding at home and especially not abroad. By contrast, most of the occupiers had a positive view of the executions. These events were so completely accepted as normal that they could be commented on using these succinct words: "Early today three German soldiers [Landser] were shot by bandits, for this 40 Poles were killed. Here it is getting more and more noisy."[70]

Since in the view of the German authorities an effective deterrence could only be achieved if the reprisal was visible to the public, hanged locals were frequently left on the gallows for several weeks (see figure 5.1, photographed from a tramcar). This was the case, for example, for fifty alleged communists close to destroyed railway tracks in Warsaw at the end of 1942,[71] or twelve members of a "partisan-recruiting, document-forgery, and change-of-clothing group" in Minsk.[72] Especially in Weißruthenien it was an everyday occurrence to see locals hanged from telegraph poles with signs around their necks describing them as bandits.[73] The attention these scenes attracted was probably similar to the shootings; although with shootings the corpses were cleared away immediately afterward, still the fire brigade had to come along to remove the blood stains.[74] Knowledge of the public executions was widespread among the occupiers in Warsaw and Minsk and also accepted as an alleged means of suppressing resistance.[75] Although frequently the hostages had been selected previously, they were usually well-known academics, who had held leading positions before the war or had achieved prominence in some other way and were alleged to be, at least in spirit, responsible for the struggle against the Germans.[76] Only rarely did the SS and police succeed in actually uncovering communist ringleaders or resistance cells in the cities.[77]

Many of the executions conducted outside the public view were then announced by the SS and police using placards.[78] These announcements printed in two languages on red paper were distributed throughout the entire city. The fact that they were seen by the occupiers is documented in

Figure 5.1. The Public Hanging of Twenty-Seven Prisoners of the Pawiak Prison in Warsaw on Gerichtstrasse (now Lesznostrasse), February 11, 1944
Source: Muzeum Niepodległości Warsaw, F-909.

many cases, including sometimes even the response of the resistance, who wrote on the placards comments such as "murderers."[79] Between 1942 and 1944 the names of 1,598 victims could be read on twenty-nine placards in Warsaw; the authorities published these so that the population would be especially shocked if they happened to see the name of someone they knew.[80] In the less than four months between November 13 and February 26, 1943, there were 643 publicly announced deaths to mourn.[81] In view of these high numbers, it is hardly surprising that the "police vehicles, which were used for transporting arrested Poles, ... almost became Warsaw's trade-mark."[82] But violence against the locals was also an ever-present part of daily life in Minsk and was seen primarily as a legitimate tool for securing German rule—that is, for suppressing resistance.

In addition there were numerous actions carried out by individuals that had not been ordered by the state. Extorting money from Poles, Belorussians, or Jews at gunpoint, or beating them up were expressions of German rule that were not officially approved, but nonetheless were to be found everywhere and were silently accepted. For the locals, as Wilm Hosenfeld observed, "Real terror ruled everywhere, fear, violence. Arrests, deportations, and shootings were daily occurrences. The life of a human being, not to mention personal freedom, was of absolutely no importance."[83]

2. Invisible behind the Ghetto Wall? Violence against Jews

Those locals the Germans marked as Jews were subjected to even more brutal violence than their compatriots outside the ghettos. Yet in preparation for their elimination, first the foundations had to be laid. The basic steps in the escalation up to systematic mass murder in the extermination centers did not differ very much in the city of Warsaw from those in the other towns of the General Government.[84] In Minsk the murders took place primarily in the form of shootings, to which large parts of the ghetto population repeatedly fell victim.[85] The essential difference between the two cities consisted in the number of people who died during Nazi rule, as well as in the perception of these events, which were closely observed, supported, or even implemented by numerous occupiers. We next examine the perception of the genocide of the Jewish population by the German occupiers up until the beginning of the ghetto clearances, in which the inmates of the residential districts were deported to the extermination camps.

The first step of the Holocaust in Poland was the deprivation of rights and discrimination targeted against the Jewish population. For the Germans this development was easy to follow because it was reflected in proclamations in various official publications and decrees issued by the authorities.

Thus, for example, the official newspaper of the city of Warsaw published bilingual proclamations in which ever more new measures of chicanery were decreed. These included, for example, the already mentioned regulation that on encountering Germans in uniform Jews had to give way in a clearly visible manner and if necessary get off the pavement,[86] the ban on Jews entering public parks and specially designated streets,[87] and the regulation that banned anyone from trading with them outside of the ghettos.[88] This policy, which continued depriving Jews of their rights as had been done already inside the Reich,[89] was nothing remarkable for the occupiers. Especially the obligation for Jews to wear the Star of David on their arms, which was applied within the General Government in December 1939, presented the occupiers with plenty of opportunities to subject the population to chicanery because now it was clear who stood on the bottom rung of the hierarchy, in accordance with Nazi racial ideology. Without having to fear further consequences, an SS *Hauptscharführer,* for example, could beat a Jewish woman because her armband was allegedly not properly visible. He took it away from her and only returned it in exchange for money the next day. After the woman complained to the Security Police, at least she was excused the payment, but the *Hauptscharführer* did not even receive a reprimand because he was one of the "most needed truck drivers."[90]

The introduction of forced labor that was applied to Warsaw's Jews from December 1939 aggravated the situation. In August 1940 forced labor was being performed by around 10,600 people in some 130 offices run by the occupiers, including thirty-one military offices, thirty-nine police offices, twenty-two railway workshops, eight post offices, and around thirty of the civilian administration.[91] By April 1941 the figures had increased to 15,000 ghetto inmates in factories and 25,000 for various improvement works, especially outside the enclosed area.[92] In Minsk 1,400 Jews were employed by the railway, and several hundred worked for the Wehrmacht and the Organisation Todt, of which four hundred were working in a cart factory that made horse-drawn carts for the military.[93] Next to people for simple auxiliary work, above all specialists were needed, such as the craftsmen who worked for the Mechanische Werkstätten Neubrandenburg (Mechanical Workshops of Neubrandenburg) in Warsaw.[94]

At work it was hard to avoid contact between the German supervisors and the workers,[95] even when it was mostly marked by one-sided brutality, and at the least by scorn and low estimation. Until the Fall of 1940 it was natural for Jewish work groups or so-called Jewish columns to be recruited directly from the streets; people were arbitrarily assigned to work without going through official channels via the Labor Office.[96] In addition, in the private homes and accommodations of the Germans in Minsk, Jewish servants were sought after until a decree issued by the civilian administration in mid-1943 banned this employment relationship—allegedly on grounds of security, but mainly because "the harshest punishments had had to be applied against some Reich Germans, because they had not obeyed the Nuremberg Laws," and some occupiers had had illegal sexual relations with their female servants.[97] The catastrophic conditions under which the Jews had to work were widely known among the occupiers and in part were also the subject of conversations,[98] but were generally accepted on account of their apparent necessity. These interpretations are supported by some postwar statements in which occasionally degrading circumstances are described, but the system itself is never questioned.[99] Even the official reports of the authorities came to the conclusion that the treatment of the Jewish labor force can "only be described as bestial."[100]

The Germans observed the developments in the "Jewish question" very closely. Especially the establishment of the ghettos was a spectacular event that they could scarcely overlook, and that clearly differentiated policy in the East from that in Western Europe. After considering the idea initially, already shortly after the capture of Warsaw, in the summer of 1940 the civilian administration started planning the isolated Jewish residential area, and by August already 47 sections of the dividing wall had been erected. On October 2, 1940, Ludwig Fischer signed the decree on the establishment of the Jewish residential area. The resettlement of the Jews,[101] linked also to the confiscation of their former apartments that was carefully registered by the occupiers,[102] started immediately afterward. Wilm Hosenfeld, a curious and always well-informed observer, confirmed, however, that by September 30 all the Jews of Warsaw had been transferred into the ghetto.[103] Although the Wehrmacht did not want to participate in driving the people into the enclosed quarter,[104] support for this measure was nonetheless widespread. In one letter it was written, "Pressed together in one quarter enclosed by a wall. There they can get by as they please!"[105]

In Minsk and Warsaw, the ghettos were located in the center of the city. For organizational reasons it was not possible for the civilian administration to establish Jewish quarters on the edge of the cities as originally intended, because in the short time available insufficient living space could be prepared there. In Warsaw ultimately around 250,000 people were resettled, including 138,000 Jews and 113,000 Poles, who had to move out of their apartments to live elsewhere within the city limits. In January 1941 the ghetto comprised an area of somewhat more than three square kilometers, on which just a short time later already 450,000 Jews were accommodated—which corresponded to a population density of 146,000 people per square kilometer.[106] The region bordered the Neustadt (New Town), the Sächsischen Garten (Saxon Garden), and the adjoining German administrative buildings; it began scarcely two hundred meters from the main railway station. The regional extent and its central location meant that a streetcar route cut right across the quarter and subsequently cut it in half, such that it could only be traversed using an overcrowded wooden bridge linking the two separate halves (see figure 5.2).

The situation in Minsk hardly looked any different: the main difference between Minsk and Warsaw was that in the former, with 100,000 people, there were considerably fewer ghetto inmates. The quarter lay between the Jewish and the Polish fish market and accommodated, in view of the city's total population before the war of 240,000 people, considerably more than one-third of the entire population.[107] Assisted by an initiative of the Wehrmacht, which in Warsaw had been very reluctant, partly even critical, Police Battalion 309 began resettling Jews and Belorussians within the city in the second week of July, directly after the capture of Minsk. The Jews had to move into an area of only two square kilometers, which consisted primarily of one- and two-story wooden houses.[108] In contrast to the ghetto in the Polish capital, this ghetto was not surrounded by a continuous wall but mainly by a barbed-wire fence that was interrupted occasionally by sections of wall.[109]

The Wehrmacht served as the driving force behind the ghettoization of the Jews living in the surrounding area. In the eyes of the military commandant for Weißruthenien, "The Jews had to disappear from the countryside and the Roma [*Zigeuner*] also had to be destroyed."[110] Around Minsk,

Figure 5.2. The Connecting Bridge between the Halves of the Warsaw Ghetto
Source: Gollert, *Warschau*, p. 137.

however, the 707th Infantry Division also murdered thousands of Jews. The military acted based on an irrational need for security that identified the Jews as the carriers of communist resistance, and therefore it imagined that measures such as locking Jews into ghettos or even their murder would promote the pacification of the country.

The Jews were scarcely confined within their so-called residential districts when the occupiers started to prohibit them from leaving the latter and imposed draconian punishments on any infractions because ultimately the ruthless "Jewish regulations [were supposed] to protect the Aryans from the Jews."[111] Many Germans were informed about these kinds of "protective measures" and observed children in Warsaw at the numerous transit points into the ghetto who were mainly engaged in smuggling foodstuffs. Their physical abuse by members of the police battalions, but also by Jewish and Polish policemen—one inside and the other outside the wall—was greeted not only with approval, but also with rejection.[112]

German judicial authorities had no mercy for legal infractions committed by Jews. Yet in view of the restrictions imposed on them, this group was not capable of surviving without breaking the numerous regulations. Due to the overflowing prisons, the state prosecutors of the German court united with the civil administration in February 1942, such that Jews henceforth could only be punished with the death penalty or a monetary fine—without trial of course, since these were reserved for "more important" cases; this demonstrated once again that in their estimation Jews were "less valuable," according to Nazi ideology. Youths under eighteen years old were not to be executed inside the city, but instead were deported to the Zwangsarbeitslager Treblinka I (Treblinka Labor Camp / Treblinka I).[113] At least the local Wehrmacht commandant tried to avoid implementing these reprisals and refused to participate in the shooting of Jews that had escaped from the ghetto.[114] Although it was contravening prohibitions, some soldiers were even prepared to transport fugitives out of the city in their trucks in exchange for money.[115] Most soldiers in Warsaw—in contrast to Minsk—were only passive and at the same time very curious observers and confined themselves to their role as members of the Wehrmacht, which just by their presence facilitated the actions of the other German institutions.

The occupiers not only obtained information with their own eyes, but also could read quite a bit about the persecution of the Jews and their deprivation of rights in the local newspapers.[116] By contrast, reports about Poland in the papers published in Germany were either very limited, or absent completely, in accordance with instructions issued by the Propaganda Ministry. Joseph Goebbels feared that news about German politics there might only encourage the "atrocity propaganda" of the enemy.[117] In contrast to the home newspapers, however, the *Warschauer* or *Krakauer*

Zeitung, which were distributed throughout the General Government and could also be obtained inside the Reich, reported on the establishment of the Jewish residential areas (ghettos) in Poland because the readers were in any case aware of them. In addition these papers also wrote about the situation of the Jews in the rest of Europe in order to explain the European-wide context of anti-Jewish policy.[118] It is significant to note, however, that just two years later in Minsk, the same thing could not be observed. The *Minsker Zeitung* gave very little coverage to the measures against the Jews, but focused instead much more on the question of resistance and partisans, which was not a topic in Warsaw. Quite clearly in this the media was reflecting the needs of its readers; in the occupiers' perception, the topics of Jews or partisans were mainly connected to specific regions, and priorities frequently differed between Poland and Belorussia.

Reporting on the Jewish population had already begun in the *Warschauer Zeitung* at the end of November 1939, when for the first time a district of the city was declared to be a ghetto and was cordoned off, such that German soldiers in future would no longer have access to it.[119] The article claimed that the measure was dear to the hearts of the city's residents because the "parasites' inferior character" had contributed to material shortages by their greed and created a breeding ground for disease on account of their inadequate hygiene. These clichés, which were intended to promote acceptance for the civil administration's policy that was clear for all to see, were reinforced just one month later when a report described a walk through the ghetto and transmitted numerous negative images.[120] After this article in December 1939, there was no more coverage in the paper until October 1940. Instead the paper wrote about the alleged hate of the Jews among the Poles,[121] and in two sensationalist reports defamed the religious customs of the Jews and the supposed typical Jewish economy.[122] This aimed at achieving two goals: to keep the question of the ghetto in the consciousness of the reader, and to remind the readers that they did not have to think about the justification for the anti-Semitic measures because it was deemed to be so obvious that it was not even discussed.

Only in October 1940 did the agitation begin to intensify. At the same time as the establishment of the German residential district, the Jews were now forced into the ghetto. The corresponding article in the *Warschauer Zeitung*, "German Quarter in Warsaw," included significantly a map of the ghetto,[123] whose location was shown on all the maps of the period. The alleged rational grounds for the Jewish residential district were explained in accompanying lectures that were commented on in detail in the newspaper.[124] There it stood that "the Jew is a carrier of dangerous diseases, which harm him less than the rest of the population," pretending once again that not only anti-Semitism, but also alleged protection against disease and health and political reasons justified the compulsory measures. In addition the article reinterpreted the hunger of the Jewish inhabitants of the ghetto, stating that black-market trading and driving up prices were typical Jewish traits, which in the interest of the rest of the population had to be stopped. The policy was given an apparently rational basis so that no doubts could be raised about its necessity, and on this basis the measures could even be celebrated as successful. The ghetto dominated the labor reports of the administration in 1940,[125] as the alleged decline in the number of typhus cases was repeatedly stressed. 92 percent of the registered cases in Warsaw were in the ghetto, which in the eyes of the Nazis was the reason to cordon off the district.[126] This interpretation, however, deliberately reversed the cause and the effect.[127]

The civilian administration in Warsaw was very well aware of the morbid fascination exerted by the city within a city. In order to satisfy the curiosity of the occupiers and to deter Germans from entering the ghetto, the *Warschauer Zeitung* repeatedly published descriptions of the conditions reigning there. The line of interpretation followed the prescribed tendency that tried either to remain silent about the misery or portray it as a deserved fate, which ultimately only corresponded to the unique characteristics of Jews.[128] This policy of guided publicity resulted in a relatively strong flow of information. For example, the large-scale confiscation of real estate and houses that accompanied resettlement into the ghetto was noted in the reporting and was equally positively reinterpreted as the destruction of Jewish craft workshops or the compulsory relocation of factories and production facilities into the already severely overcrowded quarters of the Jewish residential district.[129] The latter together with descriptions of forced labor served well as an accompaniment to the agitation about the allegedly lazy inmates of the ghetto who were not prepared to do hard physical work. Especially the textile workshops producing for the Wehrmacht, such as those of Fritz Schultz or Walter Caspar Toebbens, that were under German direction, profited from the brutal piecework system, which was portrayed as the only means by which the Jews could be motivated to work at all.[130] The civilian administration, however, was very well aware that an economically viable existence for the ghetto was not possible.[131] This manner of representation, which considerably strengthened the anti-Semitic agitation quantitatively and qualitatively in 1942,[132] together with the first reports about the destruction of the Jews in Lublin, can be seen as foreshadowing the start of the deportations to Treblinka in July of the same year, for which the occupiers were gradually being prepared.[133]

The newspapers informed the Germans relatively well about conditions for the Jews in Warsaw. The reports were tendentious and confined mostly to racially charged atmospheric descriptions. Facts about the suffering on the streets of the ghetto, the constant hunger, and the thousands of deaths from starvation and associated illnesses could not be found in the articles. Nonetheless, the occupiers were also well informed about the situation inside the ghetto, although most could only rarely recognize the full extent and the connections involved. It did not demand any great observational skills to establish that the Jews had been "declared to be without rights."[134] The reason for the good level of knowledge lay in the visits to the ghetto that the Germans undertook in spite of the repeatedly announced prohibitions.[135] For this one could pull rank on the gate guards or gain access through persuasion or by simple corruption, while others simply jumped off a tram that was passing through or simulated an official visit.[136] Thus Wilm Hosenfeld, for example, describes more than once the "terrible conditions" that he saw there while conducting various tasks on behalf of the Wehrmacht.[137] Curiosity about a world that was alien to them, the misery, sometimes official tasks, but often also the possibility to "acquire" items very cheaply or for nothing led almost all of the occupiers into the Jewish residential district.

It is not surprising that the first walk by many new arrivals in the city naturally was into the ghetto, about which they had already heard so much.[138] For soldiers of the Wehrmacht also, who were in the city just for a short time, passing through on their way to the front or back home, such visits were part of the program of things to do, and even buses of the Deutsche Arbeitsfront (German Labor Front; DAF) organization Strength through Joy led civilian as well as military occupiers through the residential district.[139] What they experienced was described in detail to family members at home in many letters—together with comments ranging from general rejection to agreement that the Jews were getting what they deserved.[140] It seems to be no exaggeration in this connection to speak of genuine ghetto tourism because the visitors could still recall it years later in their statements during postwar investigation cases, although they only travelled through the district several times with the tram out of mere curiosity.[141]

The Jewish quarter in Warsaw held a special position throughout German-occupied Eastern Europe and a notorious reputation as a hotbed for opportunities and alien things, a visit to which was more or less obligatory. Almost all Wehrmacht soldiers who reported from the city, mention the ghetto as one, if not actually *the* highpoint of their stay. For Minsk the same could be said with reservations because although it was the largest ghetto on the occupied territory of the Soviet Union, its dimensions remained, however, clearly behind Warsaw and Łódź. In addition it did not exist nearly as long as its opposite number in the Polish capital and it did not have a comparable reputation among members of the Wehrmacht. Nonetheless, most Germans that were in the city for a longer period and could be counted among the occupiers visited it.[142]

Encounters with German Jews, who had been deported from the Reich into a ghetto in the East, were deemed by the occupiers to be especially worthy of being reported in letters. While in Warsaw there were only around 4,000 Jews from Germany[143] (see table 5.2), in Minsk there were some 16,000, who had been transported to the city in cattle cars belonging to the German Railway (see table 5.3); an additional 7,500 Jews were sent directly to the extermination camp in Maly Trostenets, located just outside Minsk, who almost always were murdered immediately on arrival there.[144] The occupiers could meet their former compatriots only from 1941 onwards; the first German Jews arrived in Minsk in November 1941, in Warsaw only from April 1942. Mass murder started only a few months later, and on account of the clear numerical superiority of the other ghetto inhabitants, the occupiers in the Polish capital only rarely recognized German Jews. In Minsk by contrast, around 15 percent of the inmates came from the homeland of the occupiers; in order to make room to accommodate the German Jews, around 11,000 Minsk Jews were murdered in November 1941, such that now a specially cordoned-off area existed in which the German Jews had to live.[145]

The arrival of the German Jews did not remain concealed from the occupiers in Minsk for long, because so many different authorities were involved in the ensuing measures. The German Railway had to meet regularly for extensive discussions with the SS and police who were responsible for unloading the trains and overseeing the transfer into the ghetto. In Minsk, for example, it was customary to have arriving trains wait on Friday evening or Saturday morning at the suburban railway station in Kojdanow so as not spoil the free weekend of police officials with work.[146] Because

Table 5.2. Deportations of Jews from the Reich to Warsaw

Departure	Arrival	Number	Places of Origin
March 31, 1942	April 1, 1942	994	Gelsenkirchen, Münster, Hannover
April 2, 1942	April 5, 1942	984/1,025	Berlin
April 14, 1942	April 16, 1942	835/1,000	Magdeburg, Potsdam, Berlin
April 25, 1942	April 27, 1942	1,000	Theresienstadt
July 11, 1942		295	Hamburg, Schwerin
July 11, 1942		210	Bielefeld, Paderborn
July 11, 1942		192	Berlin
	at least	4,000	

Note: For the last three transports the date of arrival and the destination of Warsaw are uncertain.
Source: Gottwaldt and Schulle, *Judendeportationen*, pp. 188ff. and 219ff.

Table 5.3. Deportations of Jews from the Reich to Minsk

Departure	Arrival	Number	Places of Origin
Nov. 8, 1941	Nov. 11, 1941	968/1,004	Hamburg
Nov. 10, 1941	Nov. 15, 1941	993	Düsseldorf
Nov. 11, 1941	Nov. 17, 1941	1,042/1,052	Frankfurt am Main
Nov. 14, 1941	Nov. 18, 1941	956/1,030	Berlin
Nov. 16, 1941	Nov. 20/21, 1941	1,000	Brünn
Nov. 17, 1941	Nov. 21, 1941	1,006	Berlin
Nov. 18, 1941	Nov. 21, 1941	978/1,010	Bremen, Hamburg
Nov. 28, 1941	Dec. 5, 1941	1,001	Wien
May 20, 1942	May 23/26, 1942	986/1,000	Wien
May 27, 1942	June 1, 1942	981	Wien
June 2, 1942	June 5/9, 1942	999	Wien
June 9, 1942	June 13/15, 1942	1,006	Wien
June 24/26, 1942	June 26, 1942	770	Königsberg, Berlin
July 14, 1942	July 17, 1942	1,000	Theresienstadt
July 20, 1942	July 24, 1942	1,164	Cologne
	at least	16,000	

Source: Gottwaldt and Schulle, Judendeportationen, pp. 84ff. and 230ff.

the railway men did not use any secret code words in their internal communications about the deportations,[147] word got out about these events more quickly than usual. Thus the Luftwaffe doctor Wolfgang Lieschke recorded on November 13, 1941—that is just two days after the arrival of the first train from his home town of Hamburg—that a comrade had told him about their arrival.[148] On November 22, 1941, he wrote in a letter that one can hear "Frankfurt, Hamburg and Cologne dialects from the Jews that have moved into" Minsk.[149] The euphemistic reference to the deportation indicates that he did not condemn this fact, but welcomed rather that now back home "quarters had been vacated for those made homeless as a result of the air raids."[150]

Other occupiers showed themselves to have more scruples in this respect. Carl von Andrian noted the arrival of German Jews in Minsk at the end of November 1941; they could be accommodated within the ghetto only because many of the locals had been shot to make room for them. Andrian condemned the deportation of the unsuspecting people, who up until the last moment could not believe that they would suffer such a "terrible thing."[151] It is indicative of the public nature of the destruction of the Jews that it was even possible for a female secretary in Minsk to talk with a female Jew from Frankfurt am Main and discover from this woman that the Germans had already killed some of her relations, who had been deported with her from the Reich to Minsk.[152]

Compared to the awareness of the German Jews in Minsk, their observation by the occupiers in Warsaw was considerably less—or at least no record of such conversations there has survived. Also the transfers from the area around Warsaw, that is from the numerous smaller ghettos in the surrounding towns, were not very spectacular compared with the incarceration of their own compatriots and is only rarely mentioned even in the official reports.[153] The ego documents show that sympathy for German-speaking Jews was more common than for Polish or Belorussian Jews, which led to a clearly increased awareness of their living conditions. By contrast the simple existence of a ghetto for the local Jews provoked criticism on principle or even sympathy only in the eyes of very few occupiers. For this to happen, the latter would have to correctly identify the relationship of cause and effect with regard to hunger, disease, and epidemics, and not simply accept these as the given circumstances of Jewish life, as was suggested in the propaganda. The numbers of deaths in the ghettos were enormous,[154] and the German authorities in Warsaw observed the monthly death rates very closely, often calculating even the daily death tallies, which in the years 1941 and 1942 scarcely sank below a hundred people.[155] The Wehrmacht *Ortskommandanturen* proved to be equally well-informed and critical, complaining frequently in their reports about malnutrition, diseases, and death rates,[156] while the civilian administration was concerned only that no corpses were lying on the street, because this gave a bad impression of German order in the East.[157]

Many occupiers who visited the Jewish residential district in Warsaw described the catastrophic conditions prevailing there in their letters home, including seeing the corpses of starved children lying on the streets.[158] Doctors like Wolfgang Lieschke or Wilhelm Hagen reported—although they had different views—about the diseases that produced the deaths, their causes, and the chances of being cured.[159] The danger of a typhus epidemic, which was constantly exploited by the authorities as a pretext to legitimate the ghettoization, also caused the occupiers to be vaccinated shortly after their arrival in the East.[160] The causes for the diseases were malnutrition and the constant hunger, which was so obviously visible on the streets that individual Germans on their journeys or walks through the Warsaw ghetto would throw bread as they passed by for the children and the beggars.[161] These humanitarian acts had to be done with a certain degree of secrecy because sympathy for the Jews was strictly forbidden. Much more widespread was the silent acceptance of this misery, the observance of which was reported back to the homeland using formulations like "daily a number of this rabble starves to death."[162]

Death in the Jewish residential quarter was a daily occurrence in the eyes of most occupiers, but it scarcely touched their own lives at all. The awareness even of details such as the monthly death figures was so great that the business manager of the ghetto textile company Toebbens, Rudolf Neumann, recalled even in 1962 during a statement to the police that in February 1942 he made estimates of the death rate of the Jews together with a friend. At that time they concluded, "If this death rate continued, the ghetto would have completely died off within six years, without any violent external intervention."[163] Yet this shocking conclusion did not affect him, either in 1942 or twenty years later; although many people died naturally, he thought he had seen many rich people who could live as they wanted. This interpretation was common among many occupiers, and the German authorities believed that the Poles also felt this way.[164] In this manner, the occupiers were unconsciously following the set propaganda line of the Jews being responsible for their own suffering, which existed only because so many Jewish profiteers did not care for their fellow citizens.[165] The Germans claimed that the ghetto was wealthy, based on the incoming rent payments or the extensive amount of smuggling, which in their eyes could only take place because the ghetto was apparently still so rich.[166] Observations of the dirt, suffering, apathy, and even of the corpses lying around openly meant that possible sympathy could quickly turn into revulsion and scorn.[167]

This kind of thing could be seen most spectacularly in the cemetery of the Warsaw ghetto, which to some extent represented the high point of such visits.[168] Occupiers liked taking pictures of the corpses there, which were piled up naked and transported in wheelbarrows to be buried in mass graves. Joe Heydecker, at that time employed in a propaganda company, reports of a comrade whose photos were circulated, upon which an officer confiscated the negatives and gave the soldiers a lecture on the damage they could have done if they had fallen into enemy hands.[169]

The corpses that the Germans saw in the ghetto were not all of people that had died from starvation or disease; in Warsaw and Minsk there were already numerous shootings before the liquidation of the ghettos. Many occupiers in Belorussia had already been witnesses of murders in smaller places before their arrival in Minsk.[170] Carl von Andrian, for example, recorded in his diary several mass killings that the SS and police had committed—often in cooperation with the Wehrmacht—and criticized the lack of discipline among the troops, who sometimes plundered the corpses afterward.[171] Despite occasional objections on principle, in this case he confined himself to the kind of regret that was most common among the occupiers: focusing almost always on the surrounding circumstances and not on the killings themselves.

Although such massacres with several hundred victims clearly made a deep impression on the occupiers, they nonetheless represented something out of the ordinary that most of them did not experience frequently. By contrast, in the cities individual shootings were mostly less spectacular, but on account of their frequent occurrence, were a part of daily life that merged seamlessly with the violence that the Germans constantly witnessed or carried out themselves. Wilm Hosenfeld, for example, reported how a Gestapo man shot indiscriminately into a crowd of people gathered in a doorway.[172] A factory air-raid warden described how the Jewish employees in his factory "were dragged away from the machines while they were still working, herded into a group, and then mown down with machine guns."[173] A soldier passing through on his way to the Eastern Front noted in his diary that every Jew who "was encountered on the street in the evening after a certain time [... was] ruthlessly shot."[174] A civilian working in Warsaw recounted that the police detail that patrolled around the ghetto shot without warning at Jews who they found in the area of the wall: the occupiers themselves called these "kills."[175] Every German who spent some time in the ghetto in Warsaw or Minsk, therefore, had to "notice that there was plenty of shooting in the ghetto,"[176] and identified the SS and police almost always correctly as the perpetrators.[177] In these cases the transition from crimes committed under orders to crimes of initiative was fluid because the occupiers acted within the framework of generally valid guidelines, but still in a very independent manner and in the form of an individual crime. Commission of the crime was strongly influenced by personal motives because only in rare cases was there a specific order to shoot.[178]

The occupational authorities in the Polish capital treated Jews that were captured outside the ghetto with extreme brutality and had them shot by units of the Order Police (gendarmerie and Schutzpolizei).[179] Among members of these forces it was viewed as quite self-evident after the war that they had participated in such *Aktions*.[180] In Warsaw Police Battalion 61 ran its own bar in which they not only got massively drunk, but also where they kept a careful tally of the number of Jews shot by the unit in the form of marks chalked up on the wall: the list encompassed some four thousand to five thousand dead toward the end of the deployment, not including those people shot by the firing squads.[181] For these men—as for all other members of the society of occupiers—it was important not to display any "weakness" toward the Jews, but to be proud of their "work." In Minsk even General Commissioner Kube had to give evidence to an investigation following a shooting—which he had criticized on account of the attention it had attracted—for allegedly "giving sweets to some of the children who had been crying the loudest."[182]

The occupiers also found it very interesting to attend executions, as did their leaders such as Heinrich Himmler, who was present during a massacre by Police Battalion 322 on August 15, 1941, not far from Minsk.[183] Yet this was a mass killing; by contrast there was usually no particular fuss connected with the daily violence in the ghettos, and once one's initial curiosity had been satisfied at the beginning of the deployment by seeing it personally, soon a general indifference and passive acceptance of the destruction of the Jews set in. The murder of the Jewish population in the East was a widely accepted component of daily life for the occupiers. Even before the start of the deportations to the extermination camps, or the two major uprisings in Warsaw in 1943 and 1944, most Germans were at least partially informed about the goals and consequences of Nazi policy, although it was only rarely expressed so clearly as during a conference in Minsk in March 1943: the occupiers in the East must try "to clear the Jews from the area, that is to destroy them without exception, and to completely solve the Polish problem."[184]

3. Excesses of Violence: Ghetto Clearances and Uprisings

The wiping out of the Jews, which had already started with ghettoization, was completed by the German authorities with the deportations to the extermination camps. These complicated *Aktions* represented outbreaks of violence that were unusual even for the occupiers. The deportations thus resembled closely the suppression of the two uprisings: one erupted in 1943 in the Warsaw ghetto and one broke out in 1944 throughout the entire city. The latter uprising entailed a certain degree of threat to occupiers' lives, and so there was a difference in how the two uprisings were perceived by the Germans. The decisive commonality, however, was the brutality with which the Germans implemented their claim to be the rulers: murder, shootings, explosions, and sometimes even the use of heavy military equipment were all characteristic for both the deportations and the suppression of the uprisings. In these eruptions the violence lost its common and everyday appearance and the otherwise customary indifference among the Germans could no longer be observed. Instead, the Germans' responses were dominated by decisive support or equally clear rejection of the crimes. In the course of these outbreaks of violence there were frequent excesses which, like other crimes of initiative, were committed without any orders but differed from them in their form. These excessive acts of violence can be designated as "individual crimes committed within collective states of emergency."[185] Among these crimes can be counted, for example, shooting into a crowd of people during an excessive bout of violence, as well as the massacre of resistance fighters. These crimes were committed in anticipated obedience: the perpetrators expected that brutality was particularly desired.

In comparison with Warsaw, in the Minsk ghetto there were many poorly organized shootings outside the city that claimed tens of thousands of victims into the summer of 1942. Later on, the Security Police murdered around 10,000 Jews in close coordination with the civilian administration in four days from July 28 to July 31, 1942, mainly in Maly Trostenets. At the end of the year around 12,000 ghetto inmates were still alive in Minsk.[186] In September 1943 the Jewish residential district was "liquidated," which was the customary Nazi expression for the murder of the remaining Jews.[187]

For the Germans in the city the murders were not invisible, even though they did not take place directly before their eyes. This was because all of the employees of the SS and police took part in one or more executions during their deployment,[188] and thereby many occupiers were directly engaged in the genocide. The department head at the office of the KdS, Rudolf S., was still prepared to admit in 1960, "that at that time quite a lot [sic.] of Jews were shot."[189] For him there was no question of legitimacy; even in retrospect, when he made that statement in 1960, he was convinced that he had acted correctly. In this he agreed with the majority of his colleagues, who spoke voluntarily to the West German investigating officials in the 1960s about the many shootings in Minsk; more than a few even admitted their own participation therein.[190] Both the executions and the use of gas vans (a vehicle equipped as a mobile gas chamber) were *selbstverständlich* (self-evident) for them.[191] This stands in clear contrast to the events in Warsaw that are almost always disputed by the participants. To justify themselves, they claimed later untruthfully that, in contrast to Belorussia, in Poland there were no deaths during the deportations from the ghetto, and that transports to the Treblinka death camp occurred on a voluntary basis without knowledge of the policy of destruction.[192]

Because in Minsk, in contrast to Warsaw, there was not just one especially noticeable *Aktion* that decisively expedited the genocide of the Jews, and also because proportionally many more occupiers were directly engaged in the murders than in the Polish capital, the destruction in Weißruthenien took on a much more everyday character. The events and the dimension of the individual mass murders were not spectacular enough to evoke a special response from the Germans.[193] Whenever the members of the police departed in large numbers and organized a drinking party on their return, the other occupiers concluded correctly that there had been another massacre of the Jews.[194] They all knew that "freight trains arrived in Minsk at irregular intervals carrying Jews," and that they were then "shot in a nearby wood in pre-dug graves."[195] Although in this way the executions were not directly visible, machine-gun fire could be heard in the city "day and night" and the occupiers soon learned what research later confirmed, that the SS and police units carried out the murders, but that they did this with the approval and/or on the instructions of the civilian administration.[196]

At the highest level the general acceptance of the violence among the occupiers created such a degree of normalcy in dealing with the murders that General Commissioner Kube presented Italian diplomats the suitcases and packages of Jews deported to Minsk as their only remaining traces and even demonstrated with pride a gas van. In Berlin the German Foreign Office had to undertake great efforts in order to calm down the Fascists, who had been shocked by this confrontation with the reality of genocide.[197] At the same time the heads of departments and regional chiefs within the general commissariat spoke quite openly at their secret conferences about the progress of the destruction of the Jews and boasted about how many thousands of people had been "finished off" and that they had conclusively solved the "Jewish question" in their region.[198]

The situation could not have been more different in Warsaw: the purely numerical scale was of another dimension, but also the implementation of the destruction was conducted quite differently from in Weißruthenien, since the murders mainly took place in the extermination camp Treblinka, located some sixty kilometers (37.5 miles) northeast of the city. The deportation of the Jews of Warsaw within the framework of Aktion Reinhardt began on July 22, 1942, and lasted until September 21 of that year. In this short time span, at the beginning of which the SS had assumed authority over the ghetto from the civilian administration, considerably more than 250,000 people were deported to the camp and murdered there, another 5,500 were shot in the city itself, and 11,000 were sent to labor camps.[199] Together with colleagues from Distrikt Lublin, the SS and police units organized with brutal precision the collection of the people, their loading onto cattle cars of the Eastern Railway, and the journey to Treblinka—between five thousand and six thousand people per day[200] (see figure 5.3). At the end of October 1942, there were still around 60,000 people in the ghetto.[201]

The deportations did not remain concealed from the Germans in the city. The civil administration was concerned with maintaining discretion; it stated just three weeks after the start of the operation, on August 15, 1942, that it "was gradually becoming known to the general public," although at this time only one quarter of the Jews had been deported.[202] Members of the civilian administration had been able to read in the budget Plan for the General Government the plans for the dissolution of the ghetto at the end of 1941. This plan stated that the residential district "would be abolished during the course of the 1942 fiscal year" and the Office of the Commissioner for the Jewish Residential District would then be dissolved.[203]

Figure 5.3. Jews from Warsaw Are Forced to Board a Train for Treblinka in the Summer of 1942
Source: United States Holocaust Memorial Museum (USHMM), Photo no. 36170.

That this would actually mean the physical destruction of the Jews was not initially apparent because even at the beginning of the *Aktion* official sources still spoke of a resettlement into the Soviet territories.[204] The insight that one was observing mass murder was confirmed by early August at the latest, as more and more occupiers spoke about Treblinka as an extermination camp and the events there could no longer be concealed,[205] even though, for example, passenger trains no longer stopped at the Treblinka railway station.[206] Significantly, this was also the time at which detailed knowledge about the proceedings in the extermination camp reached the remaining inmates of the ghetto[207] and they started to inform their German exploiters in the factories about it.[208] Next to the offices of the Ghettoverwaltung (Ghetto Administration) and the SS and police, those railwaymen who organized the trains and accompanied them—and prepared the paperwork often without any secrecy stamps—were also precisely informed about it.[209] At least in individual cases, psychological problems experienced by railway officials are documented; the German health system attempted to solve these problems by issuing them immediate home leave,[210] and thereby ensured that a further dissemination of knowledge about the events within the Reich would result.

On the other hand, those not directly involved in the destruction, such as Friedrich Haßler, a major in the Wehrmacht-Rüstungskommando (Wehrmacht Armaments Detachment), received detailed information about the genocide: "It was observed, for example, that the same railway cars always departed and from the frequency with which the trains returned to Warsaw, one could tell that it was impossible for them to have travelled to Russia."[211] Haßler then inquired about the destinations and about the place Treblinka, and in this way learned that the Jews had been murdered there. A German employee from the ghetto textile company Toebbens even travelled to Treblinka in order to get back a Polish employee who had been mistakenly deported there, but was only able to confirm his death; he informed his colleagues in detail about the gassings.[212] The doctor Wilhelm Hagen,[213] for example, used similar channels to obtain information through contacts and confidants, as did Wilm Hosenfeld, who had already reported about gassings in Auschwitz in April 1942.[214] On July 23, 1942—just one day after the start of the deportations—he already spoke of a *Vernichtungsaktion* (destruction operation).[215] The figures he gives are surprisingly precise: he reports that during the first week 30,000 people were deported[216] and entrusted to his diary horrific details about the proceedings in Treblinka, which his confidant had heard from a Jew who had escaped from there.[217]

Hosenfeld's level of knowledge was not necessarily typical for the majority of occupiers: he was interested in the fate of those being oppressed, and was concerned about them and so made efforts to find out about their destruction in as much detail as possible. Exact knowledge about the course of the destruction was in any case not widely spread, although some Germans attempted to understand or grasp the situation in their city. This was not possible via the newspapers: the *Krakauer Zeitung* did not squander a single word on the *Aktion*. Only on December 23, 1942, which was just over three months after the end of the first wave of destruction, the *Zeitung* finally reported in a lecture presentation, "Resettlement of the Jews as the Last Rescue," that the "question of the Eastern Jews" was an "administrative problem." This was not a specific reference to the events of the summer, however.[218]

Nonetheless, the deportations were so spectacular that in the months of August and September 1942 they formed a considerable part of Germans' conversations. The occupiers shared their observations, their own actions, and the widely spread rumors with each other and were capable of recognizing the scale of the destruction of the Warsaw Jews and the method of killing using exhaust fumes in Treblinka's gas chamber,[219] although initially they were rather skeptical and did not want to believe in the genocide.[220] Significantly, in this communication the word "murder" was rarely used and was avoided by using numerous other terms.[221] They ranged from euphemisms to expressions widely used by the SS like "making them into soap."²²² Even within the circle of comrades violence was only rarely a direct topic of conversation, as other standards also applied here, which would not have been viewed as normal outside the society of occupiers. Nonetheless, a German in Warsaw during the second half of 1942 could not avoid personally noticing the events or being informed about them, if only because he became aware of the considerable reduction in the area of the ghetto after the murder of the majority of its inhabitants.²²³ And also after 1942, curious visitors who asked about the ghetto quickly received precise information about the events of the deportation and the destruction, such that basically hundreds of thousands of soldiers who made a stop in the city on their way to the front became aware of the systematic and industrial murder of the Warsaw Jews. Even in the smaller towns around the city, such as Siedlce, the murder of the Jews was common knowledge. In 1942 the German soldier Johannes Hennig photographed a group of Jews here, on the way to the railway station heavily laden with luggage. Significant is the hand-written comment on the back of the photograph, which states: "Driving out the Jews by force into the gas chambers."²²⁴

The events in the ghetto also quickly became the talk of the town among the occupiers. The "heart-wrenching scenes"²²⁵ like the brutal collection of the inmates as well as the mass shootings of them could scarcely be kept secret. Many Germans who visited the ghetto at that time still recalled the "constant shootings" and the "many corpses on the streets" some fifteen years later.²²⁶ A boy that was twelve years old at the time, who had moved to Warsaw with his parents, had heard so much about the events in the ghetto that together with several classmates from school he skipped class and went to a taller apartment building with a direct view of the entrance to the Umschlagplatz, from which the Jews were deported, in order to observe with their own eyes the spectacular and gory *Aktion*.²²⁷

The fact that even children had a certain knowledge of the mass murder refutes the alleged secrecy and the denials of numerous adults who claimed not to have seen or known anything: in the many hundreds of statements that have been collected on this topic at the Central Office for War Crimes Investigations in Ludwigsburg, only around 40 percent of those asked about events in Warsaw or Minsk admitted knowing anything about the murders in the ghetto or the destruction of the Jews. Their statements in their own defense were often given credence by the earlier researchers.²²⁸ The fascination with violence, which even tempted youths to become observers, was characteristic for all of the occupiers. Deployment to the East without knowing about the destruction of the Jews, even when the overall picture remained unclear, is out of the question.

The question whether the Germans approved of or rejected the course of events in Warsaw is not easy to answer. There are no representative samples of public opinion, but the reports of the civilian administration and the military capture the mood of the occupiers until 1942 quite accurately. Thus a document prepared for General Governor Frank by the *Distrikt* administration stated, "The evacuation of the Jews had attracted great attention among the public. But it can be reported that ultimately this evacuation of the Jews has been welcomed also by the Polish population."[229] While the first sentence is indisputable, the assessment in the latter demands an explanation. The attitude of the Poles to the destruction of the Jews is not the topic of this study. If the evaluation may also have contained a grain of truth, in view of the virulent anti-Semitism in parts of the population,[230] it appears, however, mainly to have come from the wishful thinking of the occupational authorities. This applies also for the implicit statement that the Germans naturally had also welcomed the "evacuation"—the word "also" with reference to the Poles indicates as much. The negative perception of the ghetto, however, allows one to conclude that the vast majority of the occupiers were certainly well-disposed toward the dissolution of the ghetto in "their" city, without initially expecting the consequence of the destruction or wishing for it. When they recognized during the course of the *Aktion* that the Jewish population was actually being murdered, they remained silent regarding this aspect of the ghetto clearance. Ultimately for many of them it was the logical consequence of their idea for the solution of the "Jewish question."[231]

The deportations in the summer of 1942 comprised the first large-scale act in the destruction of Warsaw's Jews. The remaining 60,000 people, who lived thereafter in the severely reduced ghetto were originally intended to be sent to Treblinka in January 1943. However, the ghetto offered resistance and between January 18 and January 22, despite the mobilization of considerable manpower, the SS was able to gather only some 5,000 Jews for deportation. The *Aktion* was a failure and was therefore stopped; Jews and Poles assessed the events as a German defeat, but it had consequences for the conduct of the occupational authorities. It was now clear to them that the inmates of the ghetto, in contrast to the summer of 1942, were no longer prepared to submit to the will of the oppressors without offering any serious resistance.[232]

The SS and police therefore now prepared themselves very carefully for the planned destruction of the ghetto, and called in additional men to implement the plan. Nevertheless, the German authorities did not expect the open resistance that broke out on April 19, 1943. What started then was an unequal struggle in which around 750 barely trained, undernourished, and completely inadequately equipped people turned on their heavily armed persecutors with the courage of desperation and resisted until the middle of May.

More than two thousand Waffen-SS men, who had been assembled just in case of a resistance operation within the city, stormed the district supported by tanks and found themselves confronted with serious hostilities. However, they were successful against the ghetto inmates only when they blew up each house one by one, such that Jürgen Stroop in his notorious concluding report of May 15 really meant literally: "The Jewish Residential District [ghetto] in Warsaw no longer exists."[233] Not only were all the Jews—apart from a few that were still in hiding—deported or many more than 12,000 shot on the spot, but in the territory there was not a single house left standing; instead a layer of rubble and stones covered the earth up to two meters deep. According to Stroop's figures in the concluding report, German losses amounted to only sixteen dead and eighty-five wounded, but his own daily reports indicate that actually there were well over two hundred Germans dead.[234]

When the Federal German judiciary investigated crimes connected with the suppression of the uprising, it encountered only a very limited awareness of any wrongdoing among those men who took part. The desensitizing toward their own actions went so far that one policeman expressed to the wife of a colleague back in Germany that in her place he would have simply killed her disabled daughter in Warsaw, without having to fear any rebuke or even punishment for it.[235] Yet just as with the deportations, only a small proportion of the occupiers was directly confronted with the uprising. Most of the Waffen-SS men deployed against the ghetto had been brought into the city only shortly beforehand, and most of the Germans who had been living there before were not involved in the suppression of the uprising. However, nobody could avoid being aware of the operation itself: the pillars of smoke over the ghetto could be seen for miles all around, the explosions and shots could also be heard outside the ghetto, the event, although it was not mentioned in the newspapers, was on everyone's lips. Despite the censorship of letters, Wilm Hosenfeld wrote to his wife about the "black clouds of smoke coming from the ghetto, which had been burning for three weeks" and the "incessant shootings" in the night. In his rejection of the "appalling scenes" he did not mince his words: "A new, indelible mark of shame for those who are responsible, and an enormous blunder to boot."[236]

Once again it was the fascination of violence that was linked to a thirst for sensation: the wife of a policeman revealed that even twenty years after the war these events had left a deep impression on her and she reported to the Federal German investigators "that a number of members of the Security Police Office [KdS], with the women, climbed onto the roof of our accommodation, in order to watch the fire" (see figure 5.4).[237] Clearly, for many occupiers the uprising was a spectacle that drew their attention,

Figure 5.4. The Burning of the Warsaw Ghetto during the Uprising in 1943
Source: USHMM, Photograph no. 51077.

and that they observed enthusiastically, without having to put their own lives in danger. Despite the skirmishes, which were fought between the SS and the resisters, and the initially only tough progress, even employees of the companies in the ghetto viewed the uprising as a "trifle." Under no circumstances did they want to speak about "serious combat, as if in a war." The Germans did not see a planned uprising, but only resistance actions.[238] The war diary of the Wehrmacht Armaments Detachment, for example, recorded numerous attacks in the months of April and May 1943 in which Germans were killed and buildings were blown up, but did not speak of an uprising or coherent actions, but continued to report them in just the same way as before the uprising.[239] In the perceptions of most occupiers the standpoint maintained by propaganda was dominant, that it was a matter of "individual sniping attacks by Jewish partisans, firing from concealed positions in the rear,"[240] which also corresponded with their own understanding because being masters of a city, that apart from a few exceptions, was completely under control.[241] In this sense they could not recognize an uprising, because it was not supposed to exist; in addition, the Jews as an "inferior race" were not capable of putting up any resistance to the Germans.

That the troops proceeded against the resistance with all possible force was taken for granted,[242] as it appeared necessary in the interests of maintaining order. Ultimately it was important not to show any weakness in the face of a small group of resistance fighters. Doubts about whether the massacre was justified were even less common than during the deportations in the summer of 1942. The authorities and offices spoke quite openly now of killing all the inmates of the residential district. A circular issued by the Nazi People's Welfare at the beginning of May 1943 reported that no more additional furniture from Jewish property could be expected in the future because "a large part of the furniture present in the ghetto would be destroyed during the ongoing Aktion."[243] The only problem raised by the "Police measures during the clearance operation" was that the security of the Germans "had deteriorated considerably compared with before, even though after the Aktions in the ghetto and in connection with them, Warsaw was supposed to be free of Jews."[244]

The Warsaw Uprising broke out on August 1, 1944, and lasted sixty-three days, until finally on October 2 representatives of the Armia Krajowa (Polish Home Army; AK) signed a capitulation agreement with the German senior commander, SS Obergruppenführer Erich von dem Bach-Zelewski. Von dem Bach-Zelewski was well-suited for suppressing the Uprising: in the battles against the Soviet partisans, serving as the plenipotentiary of the *Reichsführer* SS (Heinrich Himmler) for combatting banditry, he had distinguished himself in the regime's eyes by his extreme brutality. For this reason, Hitler sent him to Warsaw on August 5 to lead the German troops, and von dem Bach-Zelewski fulfilled the expectations placed in him.[245] After two months of house-to-house fighting, 30 percent of the city's buildings had been destroyed and an estimated 200,000 inhabitants killed, among them some 15,000 armed insurgents. The occupational authorities took care thereafter to ensure that no locals remained in Warsaw: some 350,000 people were driven into other regions of the General Government, around 90,000 deported for forced labor, and another 60,000 sent to concentration camps; 18,000 members of the AK—as stated in the capitulation document—were sent to POW camps. The German losses amounted to some 10,000 dead and 9,000 wounded. Following the removal of the city's population, on instructions from Himmler, von dem Bach-Zelewski started to blow up all the remaining buildings systematically, to erase Warsaw from the memory of the Poles. By January 17, 1945, when the Red Army crossed the Vistula, German troops had destroyed another 30 percent or so of the prewar housing inventory.[246] The period after the Armia Krajowa's capitulation, however, is no longer the subject of this study because scarcely any occupiers still lived in the city and they were just waiting for the advance of the Soviet forces, without pursuing a comparatively "normal" daily life of occupation.

Clearly it is not possible to speak of everyday life during the Warsaw Uprising, since what happened then was in every way exceptional. A massive rebellion by the locals, which did not express itself only in partisan fights in the countryside, but also in major cities, had not previously been experienced by the Germans in Eastern Europe, and the revolts in Paris could not be compared with that in Warsaw. Since the city's authorities responded in August by withdrawing their personnel and in addition by ordering the civilians to leave, not many occupiers remained whose lives were the same before and after August 1944. In contrast to the time before, several tens of thousands of soldiers of the Waffen-SS and the Wehrmacht were now present who had not been stationed in the *Distrikt* prior to this; Berlin—also due to the weakness of the Warsaw garrison—had sent them there specifically to combat the uprising.[247]

These men were made up only to a small extent of average soldiers, but much more of troops who were trusted to suppress the Poles with particular efficiency. Alongside the large formation of the 9th Army, one should name in particular the 1st Parachute-Armored Division Hermann Göring, the Dirlewanger Brigade, and the 29th Grenadier Division of the Waffen-SS Русская Освободительная Народная Армия (Russian People's Liberation Army; RONA), the last two were combined with other units to form Kampfgruppe (Combat Group) Reinefarth.[248] In view of the enormous numbers of casualties on the Polish side, one cannot speak of regular combat in this case; the battles, rather, were directed against the entire population, and the troops were explicitly instructed to conduct massacres—and specially selected for this purpose.[249]

Nonetheless, Germans also participated in the battles that had previously belonged to the society of occupiers. For example, more than 3,000 railway men who tried to maintain the service and resist the Polish attacks at the same time reported 85 dead and 141 missing.[250] Workers of the Post Office likewise counted 102 fallen and 48 missing.[251] Concerning the views and opinions of German civilians regarding the nature of daily life in the city for those who remained, relatively little material is available because hardly any of the authorities were able to continue with their previous work. In any case, the offices were too widely dispersed to be defended efficiently.[252] Service records or private descriptions by the officials were largely not made on account of the hectic nature of the fighting, and subsequent reports were mostly inopportune due to the atrocities because they would have served to improve neither one's own reputation nor one's self-esteem. In contrast to the Polish survivors whose recollections dominate the perception of the uprising's events, very little is known about what happened as seen from the German perspective.

In contrast to Warsaw Ghetto Uprising, during the 1944 uprising there was a very concrete threat of danger for the occupiers. The actions by the resistance had already led to increasing anxiety among the Germans from the end of 1942, and they gradually came to fear the violent responses of the oppressed.[253] The force of the uprising and the initial successes of the

Armia Krajowa surprised the Germans, who initially saw themselves forced onto the defensive and also subjectively felt themselves to be severely under pressure.[254] The events in Warsaw were something that the rulers of the General Government had been expecting for several years,[255] and that finally gave them—if also under different circumstances than originally planned—the longed-for opportunity to wipe out the city, which in their eyes was the heart of Polish national sentiment and especially of the resistance attacks.[256] Similar to in the previous year, the occupiers found it incomprehensible that the Poles rose up against their rule—even the critical Wilm Hosenfeld spoke occasionally of bandits[257]—and brutal countermeasures, which ultimately would lead to the suppression of the resistance movement, were in their eyes the only legitimate answer: "The Poles have been worked over by our Stukas [dive-bombers], tanks, and Cossacks [the SS RONA Division]. Only a few isolated houses remain standing. The Cossacks have done good work there."[258]

The excessive violence that is only hinted at here was a daily occurrence for two months; alongside heavy artillery like the mortar Karl, which delivered shells with a diameter of 60 centimeters, the Germans deployed bombers, tanks, flame-throwers, and even remote-controlled explosive vehicles. The large numbers of civilian casualties resulting from these tactics were further swollen by numerous mass shootings, in some instances with several thousand dead. The commander Heinz Reinefarth complained to the senior commander of the 9th Army, "What should I do with the civilians? I have less ammunition than prisoners."[259] On August 5, von dem Bach-Zelewski of all people was responsible for a deescalation: in spite of the contrary orders of Hitler, he prohibited the shooting of women and children, such that "henceforth only" men could be executed, a restriction that of course was not always obeyed.[260]

The massacres committed against the locals were seen by almost all Germans in the city.[261] A soldier wrote on August 12 to his family: "The picture offered to us in Warsaw, was gruesome.... The next day the city was surrounded and fire was poured into the city from all the barrels at our disposal. Hundreds of airplanes dropped heavy bombs on the city. The dead are lying in heaps on the street. The city itself is a pile of rubble." The conclusion of this letter shows a man, who certainly had some sympathy for the situation of the occupied, who had not grasped the aims and ultimate consequences of Nazi policy: "The saddest thing is, that in the last five years we didn't manage to win these people over to our side."[262] He shared this lack of insight with Hosenfeld, who entrusted notations to his diary conveying the same basic mood.[263] Despite long years of observation, neither was convinced that precisely the destruction of everything Polish was a central goal of occupational rule.

For the troops gathered for the struggle in Warsaw, the uprising was only of secondary significance compared to the advance of the Red Army, which presented a much greater threat to Germany.[264] The men arrived at this relativized assessment of the uprising also because, in contrast to some other occupiers who had already spent several years there, they had no emotional connection to the city. For them the uprising was just another part of their life as soldiers, although the city appeared to be quite western European, impressive, and civilized to them. This assessment also produced—despite the general characterization of those participating in the uprising as bandits—some recognition of the Armia Krajowa's goals, which they certainly admitted to be freedom-loving and anti-Bolshevik.[265]

The public perception of the uprising at home was to a large extent determined by propaganda, which reported on it and even showed scenes of the combat operations five times in the weekly newsreel. Significantly, in its twenty articles and caricatures between August 18 and October 8, the *Völkische Beobachter* portrayed the uprising as an operation organized by the Polish government in exile in London, which was double-crossing those involved and sending them to their deaths out of power-political calculation, because they had in turn been caught in a trap set by the United States, Great Britain, and the Soviet Union. Nonetheless, the reports spoke of bandits and not of victims, when they mentioned the Armia Krajowa because ultimately this organization was committing crimes against its own people, who were only exposed to destruction by the Germans as a result of their own attacks.[266] The press coverage took a new turn after the end of the uprising, when the bandits suddenly became freedom fighters who had been betrayed and cheated by the Soviet Union. The intention behind this, which was to stir up the anti-communist Armia Krajowa against the Red Army, of course did not succeed. In addition, reports by the Security Service show that the occupiers were by no means in agreement with the reinterpretation of the bandits as heroes because it contradicted their own self-image as fighters for a just cause.

4. Topic of Conversation: Mass Murder. On the Legitimation of Violence

It is clear therefore, that the occupiers in Warsaw and Minsk were well informed about the mass murders committed against the local population. Neither the "struggle against the bandits" in Weißruthenien, the violence against the Poles, nor the genocide of the Jews, remained concealed from them. Certainly the overall dimension of the genocide became visible only in 1944 because until then complementary information from elsewhere in

Europe, and even from parts of Eastern Europe, remained missing. Yet already the elimination of the Jewish quarter in the city of Warsaw, which the occupiers could not help but observe, permitted them to draw certain conclusions concerning Nazi policy and its goals. In retrospect, it remains impossible to establish exactly how strong the flow of information available to the occupiers actually was—this commodity in any case is very difficult to measure—but it is possible to make statements about what information was communicated, how it was communicated, and to what extent mass murder was a topic of conversation. In part it is even possible to register the flow of information back home. At the same time these details cannot be quantified; public opinion among the occupiers remains somewhat abstract. Nonetheless, this chapter will attempt to assess communication about the genocide within the society of occupiers, using the available documentation.

First it should be noted that reports about the atrocities committed by the Germans in the East were forbidden as a topic of conversation or in the content of letters. The senior Nazi officials, especially Heinrich Himmler, were not keen that the massacres should become common knowledge. On the one hand, it would damage the reputation of Germany abroad, and on the other it would cause the occupiers themselves to doubt the correctness of their own actions or that of their leadership, whose rule was based on these kinds of murders. Thus a letter written by Himmler on December 12, 1941, to the SS and police offices in the East left no room for doubt about his intentions regarding discussions of the genocide: "Equally I desire that it is seen as unacceptable and indecent to have conversations or speak about [certain] facts and the numbers connected with them."[267] Any mention of the crimes at all, let alone boasting, was not to take place.

The Wehrmacht in Warsaw had received similar instructions about two years earlier. On October 3, 1939, that is, shortly after the conquest of the city, the Commandant's Office ordered, "Reports home by members of the Army about the situation in Warsaw should be as objective as possible and be done without stressing at all the city's completely ruined condition. It is not in the interest of the leadership that news about atrocities should reach other countries via these channels."[268] The contradiction between "objective reporting" and conditions that were characterized as being so bad that they could only be understood as "atrocity news" seems to indicate a precise perception of the situation in the city. In addition, the Wehrmacht knew very well that their soldiers could easily identify that the causes of this situation had been created by the occupiers themselves.

In Himmler's view the ban on speaking about them applied also to the mass murders committed on the orders of the state. The occupiers did take photographs of the crimes, which they carried around with a certain pride as trophies,[269] and they talked to their comrades about them, but comparatively little found its way back to the civilians at home. As Klaus Latzel has discovered, the letters sent home from the front contained only unspecific references to the crimes. This is an important discovery precisely because the censorship in place was of only limited effectiveness and there was no actual checking of the letters. In this respect it is rather more accurate to speak of self-censorship.[270] The concept of self-censorship applies especially because many letters were not sent through the Post Office but passed from hand to hand and delivered personally by people on leave.[271] Wilm Hosenfeld, who was quite critical of the killing Aktions conducted by the regime and disclosed his attitude on many pages of his diary, provides evidence of this: he scarcely mentions murders in his letters to his family.[272] In private documents,[273] like letters home from the front, war crimes are only very rarely described in detail or even mentioned; instead the authors gave atmospheric descriptions like those of the Warsaw ghetto; these did not remain silent about the misery, but remained fairly unspecific. Only in exceptional cases could the recipients read about murders or killing actions.[274]

What could happen if this practice, and the secrecy connected with it, was not observed, can be seen from the case of Wilhelm Hagen, which represents an exception but nonetheless demonstrates that such deviations from the norm were not to be tolerated by any means.[275] This doctor, who was employed in the health administration of Distrikt Warschau, complained several times about the health situation and the deaths of the Jews in the ghetto, including directly to Hitler, to Reich Health Leader Leonardo Conti, and SS and Police Leader Ferdinand von Sammern-Frankenegg.[276] With his letters he broke the silence on the mass murders and institutional violence; this led ultimately to his dismissal, such that Hagen only narrowly avoided being sent to a concentration camp.[277] Hagen's superior in the administration of the General Government, Lothar Weirauch, pointed out in a letter to Higher SS and Police Leader Friedrich Wilhelm Krüger in Krakow, that he could not be blamed for the actions of the doctor in Warsaw: "At every meeting held in the last few months concerning the question of combatting the spread of tuberculosis, I have pointed out the obligation to keep things secret within the very small and unchanging circle of participants. ... As these basic principles [health services only for Germans] should under no circumstances become known to the Poles, in order not to endanger the intended success, I even informed the participants that this discussion was to be treated as a "Secret Reich Matter" [Geheime Reichssache; the highest level of secrecy], as necessarily the ethno-political attitude of the respective offices in the General Government towards the Polish Question had to be mentioned."[278] Therefore, whereas Weirauch had met his official obligation to keep secret the destruction of the Jews, Hagen had broken it.

If soldiers wrote about the "final solution," then that remained an exception: viewed quantitatively, the "Jewish question" played hardly any role in the letters from the front.[279] Exemplary for the coded formulations in the letters and for the way in which people reported on the genocide is a letter by Max Bischof, the head of the Transfer Office for the Ghetto responsible for questions concerning the ghetto economy. In an update for Hans Pilder, a member of the board of directors of the Dresdner Bank in Berlin, being fully informed about the policy of destruction on account of his position, he wrote in August 1942 about the "sudden start of the resettlement of the Jews from the Warsaw ghetto, which had already now encompassed more than 200,000 people and caused various changes" as a result.[280] Thanks to these and other, clearer, indications, the people at home were at least partially informed about the destruction of the Jews. From conversations, rumors, and their own observations, around one-third of the German population had received some knowledge about it already during the war, even if, in terms of concrete details or a complete overview, only a part of the story was accessible.[281] Among the occupiers in the East the proportion was considerably higher. There could have been hardly any Germans in Warsaw or Minsk who did not know about the genocide of the Jews, and who had not observed details with their own eyes, such as the deportations to the extermination camps, or at least heard about them. With certain qualifications, this applies also for the visitors to the two cities who admittedly only in rare cases personally experienced how the crimes took place, but could find out about it without any difficulty.

Within the society of occupiers, the massive destruction of the Jews was an open secret about which one also spoke. Thus Cavalry Captain Max Rohrweder noted in his diary on October 22, 1941, that on the train to Minsk several soldiers told him with pride that they had shot 1,400 Jews; the next day it was the conductor that informed him about a massacre in Borisov that left 7,000 dead.[282] Two things about this are remarkable: first that just three days after the mass killing in Borisov, which took place in the night of October 19–20, information was circulating with a very high degree of accuracy—the stated number of dead corresponds precisely with the figures established by historical research[283]—and second, how widely dispersed this news had become in such a short time. In this case the train was a public space in which men from various units were brought together and spent the journey, which lasted a long time, by engaging in conversations. Quite clearly in this situation the murders represented a topic that they could also discuss even with comrades they had never met before. Rohrweder's conductor, who had received his information from the local commandant in Borisov and now shared it with the cavalry captain, is just as typical in this respect as the soldiers who told him previously about their own deeds.

The bloody events in Borisov were also reported by Carl von Andrian. On November 29, 1941, he was having a conversation over lunch with three officers of the Luftwaffe. In the period of more than a month in which recollections and news about the massacre were widely dispersed, in transmission the number of dead had also more than doubled; the men spoke of 15,000 victims and considered this total to be absolutely credible. Their attitude toward the murder of the Jews was not generally one of opposition, but they found mainly that its implementation had been inappropriate; particularly in Borisov there had been "terrible excesses committed against Jewish women by the Russian policemen [collaborating with Germans] during the shooting." The conclusion of the officers was quite clear: "All of us who discussed this together were of the same opinion: we condemned these shootings, as for a cultured people, which we like to consider ourselves, they were unworthy."[284] This did not mean a basic condemnation of the genocide on principle, as can be seen, for example, when Andrian ordered a subordinate in February 1942 to leave executions of Jews to the Security Service. In this he was making a contribution to the interests of the Wehrmacht, which he wanted to protect from involvement in those kinds of crimes, however, he did not oppose the massacre on principle.[285] In October 1941 Andrian reflected, however, on the reasons for this indifference, which ultimately amounted to a form of implicit acceptance.[286] Nonetheless, the instruction to his subordinates certainly demonstrates that the destruction was certainly a topic of conversation in everyday life—even while on duty, which cannot come as a surprise in view of the role played by the troops in implementing the Holocaust.[287]

Although the genocide was something that was only mentioned in conversations, even these were restricted. Among acquaintances, they were naturally scarcely susceptible to control, and small groups of people, who, although they had never met before, nonetheless recognizably belonged to the society of occupiers, represented a customary forum. Such circles had in common that they always inherently enjoyed a certain degree of confidentiality. The forum chosen by the lawyer Karl M. in Warsaw was completely inappropriate. He inquired of an SS leader in public at the German House whether news about the destruction of the Jews was correct. He was harshly reproached to desist in future from asking such questions, and when M. persisted, the SS man did not even bother to indulge him with an answer.[288]

Further objects of the prevalent curiosity[289] were the hidden or fleeing inmates from the ghetto, who were mercilessly hunted down by the police.

Those, who had gone into hiding and thereby eluded the Germans' immediate grasp were of interest for the occupiers, because their persecution offered opportunities for denunciation and blackmail.[290] A German asked a Polish policeman how one could tell a Jewish woman from a Polish one. The policeman explained, "In such cases you make the woman say the Lord's Prayer; as the Jews don't know it."[291]

Despite the occupiers' fairly exact degree of knowledge, conversations about the genocide were rather the exception. In contrast to the numerous shootings and the misery, apart from a few circles of critical individuals,[292] the systematic destruction of the Jews was scarcely a topic of discussion before the start of the deportations. Even when the ghetto clearance started in the summer of 1942, most Germans still believed the official fiction that it was just a resettlement operation. As events unfolded, however, very few people could avoid reaching the conclusion that the repeatedly heard stories about the Jews being sent to an extermination camp were true.

In order to see this fact clearly, it was not necessary for the Germans to travel to Treblinka personally—although there are instances of this taking place.[293] Instead, it was sufficient to observe that always the same freight cars were shuttling back and forth. From the short time in which the trains returned again to Warsaw the occupiers concluded that it was impossible for them to have travelled as far as Russia.[294] This information, which they acquired in speaking with their own railway workers, soon spread and brought the correct number of 5,000 Jews deported per day into circulation.[295] Other occupiers, such as those working in the factories inside the ghetto, saw the course of the *Aktion* with their own eyes and soon noticed how the residential district progressively became depopulated. That this was not a resettlement could be recognized by the fact that no further news arrived from those "resettled." In addition, there was some contact among the Jewish workers within the companies who quite often carried out, at least unofficially, important supervising tasks. Rudolf B., who worked for Toebbens, therefore heard from people who had escaped from the cattle cars and were now trying to warn their fellow-sufferers. In this way he learned about the gassings, was able to estimate quite accurately the scale of the deportations and to discuss these events with friends and acquaintances.[296]

In the occupiers' public sphere, not only the events in one's own city and the surrounding area were known: Knowledge about the Auschwitz extermination camp was considerable and was also passed on. An official at the Main Post Office in Warsaw reported that in 1941 and 1942 packages of clothing and personal items were arriving from Auschwitz daily that belonged to people that had been murdered there—around 150–200 such packages every day. Awareness about the fate of those murdered was spread not only among the occupiers, but also among the Poles. The Poles had known for some time what was happening in Auschwitz and in some cases had spoken with their German colleagues about it.[297] They were not the only people that correctly interpreted these signs. The typist Christel S. observed that Jews dispatched to the camp, whose effects were mentioned in the service mail, almost always were reported as having died from weakness of their blood circulation—and after numerous discussions with other occupiers she interpreted it correctly as evidence of mass murder.[298]

In April 1942 Wilm Hosenfeld mentioned "Auschwitz, the feared concentration camp in the East" in his diary; he noted that people there were "tortured to death" and killed using gas.[299] Hosenfeld does not say where or from whom he received this information, but the accuracy and detail of his reports were remarkable. In the East the terror that the word "Auschwitz" already inspired at the beginning of 1942 was so great that four ethnic Germans aged between eighteen and twenty-two were able to successfully extort money from a baker just with the threat that he belonged in this camp. The crime, which combined impersonating an official, extortion, and deceit, was punished with three years in prison by the Warsaw Special Court.[300]

In the summer of 1942—according to the testimony of typist Friedel M.—within the society of occupiers the destruction of the Jews was "the talk of the town,"[301] a topic open for public discussion, which was talked about in many pubs without attracting particular attention or even moral outrage, as if it was everyday information.[302] As already before the clearance of the ghetto, foreign businessmen were inquiring about the possibility of buying a house or a factory in the area, which demonstrates clearly the failure of the authorities to keep these things secret.[303] Only the units of the SS and police were held responsible for all of the cruelties in order to exculpate oneself. Not without reason it was said in Warsaw that their members "could not have breakfast until they had shot ten Jews."[304] The motorized patrols that drove around the ghetto perimeter and shot at Jews caught climbing the ghetto walls were also a topic of conversation.[305]

There were quite different forms of communication within the SS and police offices that organized the deportation transports. There the intended murder of the Jews was known from the start[306] and was scornfully commented on accordingly; as already mentioned, references to the deported Jews being made into soap circulated freely.[307] For these men, the shootings, which they had already been conducting as the Jews were being rounded up, were a daily occurrence; after the consumption of alcohol the shootings might, however, give cause for arguments and accusations of alleged cowardice or cruelty.[308] In the police it was "generally known that Jews were being shot arbitrarily in the ghetto."[309] Police Battalion 61, with its bar on Krochmalnastrasse where the number of murdered Jews was recorded by marks on the wall, was notorious far and wide for its acts of excessive violence;[310] and even new recruits arriving from the Reich were afraid of particular company commanders even before starting their service, because word had already got out about the brutal tasks awaiting them.[311]

In contrast to Warsaw, in Minsk it was not the attention-grabbing clearance of the ghetto that provided material for conversation, but rather the many shootings inside and outside the city that the occupiers discussed—such as the shootings in Borisov, for example. Even before their arrival in the city, where the leaders boasted about their successes in destroying the Jews at their conferences[312] or to visitors from foreign allied states,[313] many had already heard about the numerous murders on the spot.[314] Curious Germans were able to visit the sites of mass graves in the General Commissariat without difficulty; even where at first glance those graves were no longer recognizable, locals provided information when asked, but such information was also frequently exchanged among the occupiers.[315] Conversations about the genocide were also quite *selbstverständlich* ("natural") in Minsk.[316] They could, for example, take place in the presence of a moral representative such as the priest Gordian Landwehr, who as a sign of the normality of such events was present even at a demonstration execution.[317]

For those present in the city during the deportations of Jews to the Minsk ghetto, the arriving trains gave people something to talk about because before their murder all their valuables and foodstuffs were confiscated. These items were then distributed to Germans via the respective offices, so there was a good reason for people to share information about this. Merely out of greed the events entered the society of occupiers' public space; not only members of the SS and police were entitled to benefit, but also all officials and employees in public service.[318] Also for occupiers that arrived in Minsk in 1943 or 1944, and therefore mostly did not experience the ghetto personally, it was possible without difficulty to find out from other Germans that all its inhabitants had been killed.[319]

Beyond just the murders, in Minsk the Germans also observed and discussed the attempts to conceal them by Sonderkommando 1005 under the direction of SS Standartenführer Paul Blobel. This detachment, which was established on the occupied territory of the Soviet Union in 1943, exhumed there and elsewhere the corpses of murdered Jews and burned them, to expunge the traces of their crimes. Although this operation had been assigned the highest level of secrecy as a *Geheime Reichssache* the men living in Maly Trostenets attracted some attention with their activities. It did not escape the occupiers stationed in Minsk that the so-called excavation detachment had plenty of work in the surrounding area and burned between 40,000 and 50,000 corpses; this activity provoked a lively discussion.[320] A defendant in the case against the Security Police in Minsk testified after the war that the opening of the mass graves and the burning of the corpses was not a subject for discussion during office hours, but that it still attracted attention, because "the smell of burning flesh was perceptible in Minsk" and "smoke and the glow of fires" could clearly be seen.[321] The spoken exchanges over this kept the occupiers busy for several weeks.

Among the occupiers in Poland the process of acclimatizing themselves to the violent measures began in 1940. Discussions about the crimes began immediately after their commission, yet mostly discretion was maintained and they were not talked about with outsiders—for example, those back at home. Members of the resistance group Weiße Rose provide an example of this: their hospital train stood for several days at the railway station in Warsaw from July 26, 1942, shortly after the start of the deportations. The young men observed starving children who were begging for bread, as well as ruins that had not been cleared since the capture of the city in 1939. Overall they were not able to find out very much and the start of the ghetto clearance action remained concealed from them.[322] Nonetheless, precisely because they were not members of the society of occupation, already these few impressions were sufficient for them to be shocked by the misery and cruelty of the ghetto and to report this in a letter to Professor Kurt Huber in Munich.[323]

Within the society of occupiers the radius of communication was large, and information about the crimes usually passed via persons involved or observers to the many people who were curious, such that a large circle of accessories were reached who also talked about the events. The news was given an astonishingly high degree of credence, and even figures that were much higher than the horrific reality were also circulated. The inclusion of many details that were then passed on even about distant killing *Aktions* increased the probability that they were true. Overall, it must have been difficult in the East not to learn anything about the mass murders.

The public sphere of the occupiers proved to be a relatively open space. However, in talking about the murders, only rarely was a position taken toward them, and only a few Germans in Warsaw or Minsk opposed the crimes on principle. Interest in the violence was considerably greater than sympathy, or certainly any identification with the victims. The genocide was not fundamentally controversial, but rather at most regarding the way it was implemented. In this respect Minsk and Warsaw did not differ; the manner and contents of the discussions about the mass murder varied only on account of the regional differences, but not fundamentally. The regime directed or even controlled the public sphere only regarding its external relations; conversations among the occupiers took place largely without any restrictions. Through the secrecy, as well as the basic consensus about the alleged legitimacy of the crimes, this space, which was both public and closed at the same time, developed a permanency that persisted into the postwar period: in their statements to the investigating policemen and lawyers about their time in the East, the individual occupiers largely resembled each other in their exculpatory content and formulations.

But in 1939, after just a few weeks of German occupation, it was clear that previously binding social norms in Europe were no longer valid for the areas within Germany's tight grasp in the East. The previous order was turned on its head; the locals were deprived of their rights and any protection from the new rulers, while the occupiers represented now the top of the hierarchy, enjoying extensive privileges and defining themselves by their clear distinction from the "others."[324] This reassessment was an essential precondition for the genocide: based on their military successes it became possible now for the Nazis to enforce their own norms of race and living space on a new society they were establishing.[325] Violence became something normal through the distortion of values, and therefore it could also be committed by "normal" people.[326]

The exercise of brutality was directly connected to the rights of the stronger. To the regime this appeared to be the most effective way to demonstrate their superiority over the occupied and to make clear that any resistance was futile. The fear resulting from constant violence was supposed to wear down, demoralize, and paralyze the locals. For precisely this reason, it was essential that the terror took place in public and that the locals saw it. In addition, the population had to be informed about the crimes of violence without them or the individual occupiers knowing the full extent of those crimes. Secrecy and publicity about the violence were thus two sides of the same coin; lack of knowledge also contributed to the efficacy of the terror because uncertainty reinforced the fear it instilled. At the same time they made it possible to transmit externally an image of cleanliness, in which information about large massacres could be denied as excessive atrocity propaganda, which could be swept aside as only rumors.

An additional consequence of the violence needs to be considered: as long as cruelty was being constantly exercised and therefore a counterreaction was possible, the Germans faced a permanent threat and a state of war reigned in the supposedly pacified area behind the front lines. The perception of service as a soldierly activity was promoted, but distorted virtues, such as sacrifice, comradely spirit, and courage, were reinforced, while the danger required that the community stand together against the external opponent. [327]

Anyone who participated in the ordered or "individual" violence in Warsaw or Minsk knew themselves to be united with the broad mass of the occupiers.³²⁸ Reinforcing the actions of the state targeted against the locals was the shared experience with colleagues and comrades who carried out, made possible, or silently tolerated the same crimes—since in the East silence regarding an action could only with difficulty be interpreted as opposition—especially when they were in line with official policy. Wilm Hosenfeld reports, for example, on a conversation, which he had with a comrade regarding a deportation of Jews. "The adjutant there, Senior Lieutenant Hasse, did not agree with our viewpoint, he was in favor of wiping out the Jews and thought it was correct to do it now. The other five officers remained silent during the entire discussion, it seems that they did not want to express their opinion in front of the adjutant, or like most people without making a judgment they were in agreement."³²⁹ Thus being part of the crowd removed the burden of individual responsibility; that burden would have been even heavier if an individual decided to oppose the vast majority. The society of occupiers balanced out the differences in perception and served also to ease people's consciences.³³⁰ Those who agreed with the goals of the majority did not need to justify their opinions, but rather belonged to the community. The alien nature of the East, and the unaccustomed situation, seemed to make it necessary to retain at least this one constant element in life.

Furthermore, there was an awareness of collective causality that also helped people to view the violence as normal and in accordance with the law: especially because all occupiers made their contribution to the mass murder, the individual was not personally responsible as long as he did not commit a crime on his own. All the same most people were also powerless to stop the murders because they could simply be replaced if they refused and ultimately they were just a small cog within the machine of occupational rule. Max Jesuiter may have reflected the attitude of the vast majority when he stated, "As I said, we were all completely convinced that the fate of those people going to Treblinka was sealed."³³¹ The significance of this way of thinking is made clear by the fact that in ego documents the murders are almost exclusively described from the viewpoint of an impartial observer, while much less important events of an interpersonal nature were certainly capable of stirring up excitement; this form of reportage diminished the horror of the memory and thereby also salved one's conscience.

This widely shared interpretation of collective morality served not only to reduce the sense of guilt, but also to overcome the inhibitions toward killing.³³² Directly connected with this were the enormous numbers of victims that the war—and also the actions of the resistance—had so far claimed, whose memory had to be preserved by redoubling efforts to secure and build up German rule, and by continuing down the only possible path of rule: the path that was based solely on the use of force.³³³ A less violent course or even any sympathy for the fate of the locals could have been interpreted by those locals as a sign of weakness and also could have threatened one's self-perception as a strong occupier. Thus for most Germans violence also served as a deterrent[334] to prevent acts of resistance—in which, however, they were scarcely able to admit their own "fear." In October 1941, for example, a soldier's letter home from Minsk reported an attack against a German column of vehicles: "At one point our vehicle was fired upon and unfortunately three of us were wounded. But we managed to grab the brothers and hanged them to set a chilling example."[335]

That occasionally some empathy for the victims emerged had very little to do with understanding their situation and was—as is shown, for example, by many entries in the diary of Hosenfeld—at most expressed only within a small circle, but not revealed to the occupied. The sympathy soothed the conscience and created a certain moral satisfaction; however, positive identification was mainly with the perpetrators because the fascination exercised by violence was linked to the action and not the suffering.[336] Thus it was stressed repeatedly in descriptions of the executions what a "dreadful task" the shooters were obliged to carry out.[337]

Openly expressed regret could easily be criticized as sentimental humanitarianism or a sign of weakness—that is, as inhibitions that were not appropriate in view of the toughness of the East and the intransigence of the population there. From perpetrators with a "normal" conscience were created people, who—in agreement with the prescribed interpretation of how to act issued by the regime and its Führer—felt sorry for themselves and complained about their difficult tasks.[338] In Minsk, for example, members of the SS and police were repeatedly exhorted to become "tough" because "weak Willies" were of no use in the police service.[339] The mass shootings during Jewish Aktions and the Partisan Aktions made considerable psychological demands on those participating.[340] This kind of self-pity quickly caused the occupiers to stop asking, "What am I doing?" but rather to lament, "How I have to torture myself in carrying out my dreadful tasks, how my duty oppresses me." In this way the Germans protected themselves against the suffering of the locals and tried through these transformations of values, both consciously and subconsciously, to stave off damage to their own self-respect.

This way of seeing things had a strong exculpatory function: responsibility for the escalating brutality was assigned to those locals who, as provocateurs and bandits, deserved only to be killed. In this manner even the destruction of the Jews could be justified on seemingly rational grounds that could be reconciled with traditional conceptions.[341] The destruction of the population was only a punitive action against the "guilty," "enemies," or the "Jewish danger." For example, in Minsk this interpretation was made considerably more palatable by the stereotypical equation of Jews with communist partisans.[342] In connection with the perception of Poles, Belorussians, and Jews as being on a lower level in terms of their culture, civilization, and race, which was also reinforced through propaganda, their dehumanization was intensified, thereby also contributing to the lowering of moral inhibitions. Slogans like "filthy Russians"[343] or "Jewish masses," who conducted themselves in an "arrogant and provocative" manner and allowed "their own people to go to the dogs,"[344] were in common use.

In Warsaw and Minsk even in semipublic situations, for example among comrades, generally no criticism of the violence could be heard. The Nazi ideology provided here also a frame of reference that was guaranteed to maintain a consensus. In agreement with the contents of Nazi propaganda, police sergeant Adalbert Balley wrote home in 1939, for example, "In Warsaw and Praga many Jews are living, almost unbelievable. Yet God has punished them!! … For a long time they have had it good. Now they will have to pay for it."[345] Another example for this kind of repetition of ideological tropes can be found in a letter written one year later by the noncommissioned officer Karl Graf: "The Jews are now being crammed together in one district and enclosed behind a wall. There they can mess around all they like."[346]

In view of the everyday violence and the "climate of mass murder"[347] in Warsaw and Minsk, it is not an exaggeration to call violence the habitual mode of expression.[348] It ran its course with almost constant repetition in these cities, and received mostly emotionless acceptance or agreement from the occupiers. In August 1941 Franz Jonas made this comment about the Jews in the Warsaw ghetto: "How many are dying every day? Certainly a considerable number. The ghetto can be dissolved one day, when there is nobody left."[349] After a short time, most Germans got used to constantly observing direct or structural violence in their daily lives that took on a variety of forms, such as deportations for forced labor, the ghetto, hunger, and poverty, but also executions, or at least official announcements that they had taken place. In addition, the fact that the Germans viewed as normal these constant attacks on the lives of the occupied contributed considerably to the conviction that they would never themselves become victims of this same violence. The great distance between occupiers and occupied that arose for numerous reasons was thereby increased more and more because an occupier would have lost his pride, his honor as a German, and his internal strength if he had identified in any way with the victims.[350]

The sense of immunity from punishment that accompanied the crimes rested on the stability of the society of occupiers that guaranteed this immunity.[351] An extreme example of this is the above-mentioned typist Sabine H., who needed a replacement tooth in Minsk: "I asked Mr. Heuser about this, because I knew that ... there were gold items in the office [KdS]." She received "three wedding rings."[352] Thus violence was also present here, and above all as a means to protect one's own privileged existence as an occupier. They stood above everybody else and were justified in using every available means to defend this position. A railway man in Minsk wrote about a number of murdered Soviet POWs: "You have to treat them like this, or otherwise you will never be their master. The Russians have previously been ruled by fear, it can't be done any differently now."[353] Thus violence was ultimately only the logical, and at the same time, most extreme expression of the occupiers' habitus. The self-perception of the Germans and the locals' perception of the enemy lead to one main conclusion: violence was a legitimate—and mostly also appropriate—way of dealing with the locals. Their habitus allowed the occupiers to react and act in accordance with their intentions in unfamiliar situations. In concrete terms this meant that ultimately violence came to represent the only possible way of handling the locals. For the occupiers in Warsaw and Minsk, its exercise was an everyday and completely legitimate component of their lives.

Notes

1. Jäger, *Verbrechen*, p. 21. On the differentiation between excessive crimes, crimes of initiative and crimes committed under orders, see pp. 22–75.
2. See, e.g., Bartov, *Space*, pp. 88ff.
3. Matthäus, *Judenmord*, p. 73.
4. Longerich, *Gewusst*.
5. StAM, Polizeipräsidien, Slg. Primavesi/270, "Kriegserinnerungen des Oberwachtmeisters der Schutzpolizei Otto Nahlmann", p. 21.
6. BaySta, Staatsanwaltschaften 34865/18, "Kriegstagebuch des Rüstungskommandos Warschau, Vierteljahresabschluss für das zweite Quartal 1943".
7. BALAA, Ost-Dok. 8/842, pp. 1ff., "Bericht von Raimund Warth, Werksluftschutzführer in Warschau", 5.3.1956.
8. Szarota, *Warschau*, p. 113.
9. Gerlach, *Morde*, pp. 266–267.
10. Ibid., p. 276.
11. Ibid., pp. 113ff.
12. Pohl, *Herrschaft*, p. 211.
13. BfZg, Slg. Sterz, letter by Reichsbahn-Inspektor Kurt Schmid, 8.10.1941.
14. Carl von Andrian diary/Peter Lieb transcript, 5.10.1941.
15. Gerlach, *Morde*, pp. 788–789, 796ff.
16. Pohl, *Herrschaft*, p. 212. Here can be found a photograph of the POWs in Minsk.
17. Private collection of Gerhard Lieschke, Wolfgang Lieschke to his wife, 8.8.1941.
18. Pohl, *Herrschaft*, p. 229.
19. Hahn, *Eisenbahner*, p. 50. See also private collection of Gerhard Lieschke, Wolfgang Lieschke to his wife, 24.6.1941.
20. For *Weißruthenien*, see Gerlach, *Morde*, pp. 289–290.

21. APW, 482/62, "Zweimonatsbericht des Stadthauptmanns Warschau für Februar und März 1944", 4.4.1944.
22. IfZA, Fb 85/I, p. 36, "Rede Kubes vor den Gebietskommissaren und Abteilungsleitern", 8.4.1943. See also Gerlach, Morde, p. 291.
23. See chapter 1 section 3, table 1.2, this volume.
24. Szarota, Warschau, p. 117.
25. Hosenfeld, Retten, p. 607, diary, 17.4.1942.
26. IfZA, Ed 66-I, Hagen to Reichsgesundheitsführer Leonardo Conti, 20.7.1942; IfZA, Nuremberg Document NO 1415, SSPF Warschau to Himmler, 20.1.1943.
27. Private collection of Gerhard Lieschke, Wolfgang Lieschke to his wife, 21.6.1941.
28. Essential for forced labor in the General Government is Marszałek, Obozy. For Jews in Warsaw, see Berenstein, "Praca."
29. "Verordnung über die Einführung des Arbeitszwangs für die jüdische Bevölkerung des Generalgouvernements", 26.10.1939, Verordnungsblatt für das Generalgouvernement, 1939, p. 6.
30. Warschauer Zeitung, no. 22, 17.12.1939: "Mit dem Nichtstun ist es in Warschau vorbei!"
31. Quinkert, "Terror," p. 702.
32. Gerlach, Morde, pp. 460ff.
33. For Weißruthenien, see Quinkert, "Terror," p. 707.
34. Warschauer Zeitung, no. 36, 13.2.1940: "Zum Arbeitseinsatz nach dem Reich."
35. APW, 482/16, "Vermerk des Distrikts Warschau", 19.1.1944.
36. On the methods used for the recruitment of forced laborers, see Gerlach, Morde, pp. 464ff.
37. BaySta, Staatsanwaltschaften 34865/18, "Wochenbericht der Abteilung Propaganda des Distrikts Warschau, Anlage 5a", 16.1.1943.
38. ÖGZA, NL 93, Max Bischof to Reichsbankdirektor Fritz Paersch, 23.9.1940.
39. BALAA, Ost-Dok. 8/842, pp. 1ff., "Bericht von Raimund Warth, Werksluftschutzführer in Warschau", 5.3.1956.
40. BStU, MfS—HA XX/4842, "Meldungen aus den besetzten Ostgebieten", no. 55, 21.5.1943.
41. BaySta, Staatsanwaltschaften 34865/18, "Kriegstagebuch des Rüstungskommandos Warschau, Vierteljahresabschluss für das zweite Quartal 1943".
42. Hosenfeld, Retten, p. 686, diary, 25.1.1943.
43. Jäger, Verbrechen, p. 62.
44. BStU, MfS—HA XX/3817, "Entwurf eines Schreibens des RFSS an Major Suchanek", n.d. [end 1941].
45. Koselleck, "Semantik," pp. 257–258.
46. E.g., see Minsker Zeitung, no. 54, 5.3.1943: "Banditennester werden ausgeräuchert"; ibid., no. 4, 6.1.1943: "Banditenbrigade 'Aleksej' zerschlagen."
47. Gerlach, Morde, pp. 870ff.
48. BAMA, RH 26-707/2, "Anlage 4 zum Monatsbericht der 707. ID", 10.11.1941. Hilberg, Täter, pp. 77ff., and Lieb, Täter.
49. BStU, MfS—HA XX/3817, GK Weißruthenien to RMbO, 29.6.1943.
50. Carl von Andrian diary/Peter Lieb transcript, 22.12.1941.
51. Matthäus, Heuser, p. 117.
52. BfZg, Slg. Sterz, letter by Unteroffizier Georg Heidenreich, 24.10.1941.
53. See chapter 4 section 2, this volume.
54. BfZg, Slg. Sterz, letter by Unteroffizier Georg Heidenreich, 24.10.1941.
55. Carl von Andrian diary/Peter Lieb transcript, 26.10.1941.
56. BfZg, Slg. Sterz, letter by Reichsbahn-Inspektor Kurt Schmid, 8.10.1941.
57. See, e.g., in BAMA, RH 26-707/2, "Monatsbericht der 707. ID", 8.12.1941.

58. IfZA, MA 249/510ff., RKO to RMbO, 14.10.1043.

59. IfZA, Fb 85-I/S. 22ff., "Protokoll über die Tagung der Gebietskommissare, Hauptabteilungsleiter und Abteilungsleiter des Generalkommissariats Minsk vom 8.4. bis 10.4.1943, Vortrag von Gottbergs über den 'Bandenkampf'."

60. IfZA, Fb 105—30/7452ff., "Ansprache Franks auf einer Großkundgebung der NSDAP", 19.6.1943.

61. For an example of the quota 1:100, see IfZA, MA 708—2/817, Wochenbericht des Distrikts Warschau vom 3.3.1942.

62. *Amtsblatt des Reichsministers für die besetzten Ostgebiete*, no. 9, 16.10.1943, pp. 67–68, "Runderlass des RMbO", 13.10.1943.

63. *Minsker Zeitung*, no. 20, 3.5.1942: "Ein hartes, aber gerechtes Urteil." In Warsaw these kinds of executions were published in the official newspapers, see e.g., *Mitteilungsblatt der Stadt Warschau*, no. 7, 25.10.1939, p. 1, Bekanntmachung, 21. and 22.9.1939.

64. Jockheck, *Banditen*, pp. 448–449.

65. Bartoszewski, *Todesring*, pp. 357ff.

66. BAL, B 162/3693, pp. 18ff., statement of Wilhelm E. on 1.8.1962. On the locations of the executions, see Bartoszewski, *Todesring*, pp. 357ff.

67. A visit to a public execution is described, e.g., in Blättler, *Warschau*, pp. 108–109.

68. See, e.g., *Amtsblatt der Haupteisenbahndirektion Mitte* (Minsk), no. 1, 15.1.1942, n.p. On the ban on photographing executions and other murders, see Hoffmann-Curtius, "Trophäen," pp. 63–64.

69. BAL, B 162/3662, pp. 176ff., statement of Kurt N. on 21.10.1960.

70. BfZg, Slg. Sterz, letter by private Hans Hastreiter, 13.11.1943.

71. IfZA, Fb 63/172f., "Zweimonatsbericht des *Distrikt*gouverneurs Warschau für Oktober und November 1942", 10.12.1942.

72. BAMA, RH 26-707/2, "Monatsbericht der 707. ID", 10.11.1941.

73. Hahn, *Eisenbahner*, p. 50.

74. BAL, B 162/3662, pp. 23ff., statment of Johannes K. on 20.9.1960.

75. BAL, B 162/3688, pp. 183ff., statement of Karl M. on 28.1.1963.

76. For Warsaw, see Szarota, *Warschau*, pp. 48ff.

77. RGVA, 504-1-8, "Zweimonatsbericht des HSSPF Ostland", 14.12.1942.

78. A picture of this can be found, e.g., in Morawski, *1939*, p. 73.

79. For Warsaw, e.g., see BAL, B 162/3664, pp. 40ff., statement of Ehrhard S. on 18.1.1960; BAL, B 162/3663, pp. 149–150, statement of Hans A. on 5.12.1960; BAL, B 162/3662, pp. 61ff., statement of Konrad W. on 28.9.1960. See also Hosenfeld, *Retten*, pp. 772–774, letter to his wife 12.12.1943 and diary, 17.12.1943.

80. Bartoszewski, *Todesring*, p. 347.

81. IfZA, MA 708-5/522ff., various announcements of retaliation acts in Warsaw.

82. BayStA, Staatsanwaltschaften 34865/18, "Kriegstagebuch des Rüstungskommandos Warschau, Vierteljahresabschluss für das dritte Quartal 1943".

83. Hosenfeld, *Retten*, pp. 626–627, diary 23.7.1942.

84. For Lublin, see Musiał, *Zivilverwaltung*; for Eastern Galicia, see Pohl, *Judenverfolgung*; for Radom, see Seidel, *Besatzungspolitik*, as well as Młynarczyk, *Judenmord*. An overview of the General Government is given, e.g., in Longerich, *Politik*, esp. pp. 243–272. The situation in Warsaw is described in Sakowska, *Menschen*, pp. 36–80.

85. On the violence against the Jews in the occupied Soviet Union, see, e.g., Longerich, *Politik*, pp. 293–351, and Gerlach, *Morde*, pp. 503–682, which gives the best overview for Minsk.

86. *Mitteilungsblatt der Stadt Warschau*, no. 37, 10.10.1940, pp. 1–2, Bekanntmachung, 8.10.1940.

87. *Mitteilungsblatt der Stadt Warschau*, no. 27, 1.8.1940, p. 1, Anordnung, 18.7.1940.

88. *Mitteilungsblatt der Stadt Warschau*, no.8, 25.2.1941, pp. 1–2, Anordnung, 13.2.1941.

89. Longerich, *Politik*, pp. 224ff.
90. IPN, 106/26, "Aktenvermerk des KdS Warschau", 18.7.1940.
91. Sakowska, *Menschen*, pp. 53–54. In reality, the Jews of Warsaw had already been deployed into forced labor columns since October 1939.
92. IfZA, Fb 105/12, pp. 2812ff., "Diensttagebuch Hans Franks, Besprechung in Warschau", 3.4.1941.
93. Smolar, *Ghetto*, pp. 50–51.
94. APW, 643/1317 (neu: 1080), "Urteil des Sondergerichts Warschau gegen die Volksdeutschen Eugen S. und Michael K.", 2.4.1943.
95. BAL, B 162/1682, pp. 1778ff., statement of Erna L. on 14.12.1960.
96. AAN, T 501-228/930f., Kommandanturbefehl Warschau no. 156, 23.8.1940.
97. IfZA, MA 1790/11; 370-1-486, "Anordnung des Generalkommissariats Minsk", 9.8.1943.
98. BAL, B 162/1672, S. 92ff., interrogation of Karl G., 18.10.1960.
99. BALAA, Ost-Dok. 8/842, S. 1ff., "Bericht von Raimund Warth, Werksluftschutzführer in Warschau", 5.3.1956.
100. IfZA, MA 679—3/263ff., "Monatsbericht der Kommandantur Warschau für 16.4. bis 15.5.1941", 20.5.1941.
101. Sakowska, *Menschen*, p. 55; the preceding decrees can be found in *Mitteilungsblatt der Stadt Warschau*, no. 28, 9.8.1940, p. 1, Anordnung, 7.8.1940, and ibid., no. 38, 18.10.1940, pp. 1ff., Bekanntmachung, 16.10.1940.
102. BAB, R 102 I/2, pp. 1ff., "Referat des Leiters der Abteilung Umsiedlung im *Distrikt* Warschau", 20.1.1941.
103. Hosenfeld, *Retten*, p. 401, diary 30.9.1940.
104. AAN, T 501-228, Kommandanturbefehl Warschau no. 212, 19.11.1940.
105. BfZg, Slg. Sterz, letter by Unteroffizier Karl Graf, 1.11.1940.
106. Sakowska, *Menschen*, p. 56.
107. Chiari, *Alltag*, pp. 238–239.
108. Gerlach, *Morde*, pp. 523–524.
109. Gartenschläger, *Stadt*, pp. 56–57.
110. IfZA, MA 1790/2; 378-1-698, Befehl no. 24, Wehrmachtkommandant Weißruthenien, 24.11.1941.
111. APW, 643/528 (new: 621), "Urteil des Sondergerichts Warschau gegen die Jüdin Amelja B.-B. und den *Volksdeutschen* Roman F.", 29.4.1942.
112. Hosenfeld, *Retten*, p. 534, diary, 27.9.1941.
113. BaySta, Staatsanwaltschaften 34761/05, "Protokoll des Kommissars für den jüdischen Wohnbezirk", 7.2.1942.
114. IfZA, MA 679—3/1155ff., "Monatsbericht der Kommandantur Warschau für 16.10. bis 15.11.1941", 20.11.1941.
115. RGVA, 1323-2-302w, p. 17, Kommandanturbefehl Warschau no. 54, 28.3.1941.
116. On the topic of "Jews" in the German and Polish language press in the General Government, see Jockheck, *Propaganda*, pp. 315–332.
117. Longerich, *Gewusst*, p. 148.
118. Ibid., p. 210.
119. *Warschauer Zeitung*, no. 7, 19.–20.11.1939: "Warschauer Ghetto wird abgesperrt."
120. *Warschauer Zeitung*, no. 30, 16.12.1939: "Warschauer Ghetto."
121. *Warschauer Zeitung*, no. 77, 3.4.1940: "Polen verprügeln jüdische Wucherer"; ibid., no. 171, 21.–22.7.1940: "Die Polen machten Warschau zur Judenmetropole."
122. *Warschauer Zeitung*, no. 145, 21.6.1940: "So badeten die Juden in Warschau—in schmutzigen Pfützen und finsteren Kellern"; ibid., no. 177, 28.–29.7.1940: "Wie man im Ghetto 'fabrizierte.'"
123. *Warschauer Zeitung*, no. 245, 16.10.1940: "Deutsches Viertel in Warschau."

124. *Warschauer Zeitung*, no. 251, 23.10.1940: "Warum Judenwohnbezirk in Warschau?"
125. *Krakauer Zeitung*, no. 17, 23.1.1941: "Warschaus jüdischer Wohnbezirk bannt die Seuchengefahr." In a subheading it read, "The establishment is a complete success. Typhus rate astonishingly low. Black-market trading and profiteering effectively suppressed."
126. *Krakauer Zeitung*, no. 21, 28.1.1941: "Warschau wieder eine gesunde Stadt"; ibid., no. 29, 7.2.1941: "Der jüdische Wohnbezirk bannte die Seuchengefahr."
127. Caumanns and Esch, "Fleckfieber," pp. 233–234. In general on equating Jews with disease carriers, see Browning, "Ghettoisierungspolitik."
128. *Warschauer Zeitung*, no. 286, 4.12.1940: "Warschaus Juden ganz unter sich"; ibid., no. 280, 27.11.1940: "Der Verkehr mit dem Judenwohnbezirk"; *Krakauer Zeitung*, no. 189, 12.8.1942: "Juden aus dem Handwerk ausgeschaltet."
129. *Warschauer Zeitung*, no. 252, 24.10.1940: "Hausbesitz jüdischer Profitgier entzogen"; ibid., no. 293, 12.12.1940: "Die Umsiedlung Warschauer Betriebe."
130. *Krakauer Zeitung*, no. 96, 24.4.1942: "Großbetriebe in Warschaus Judenviertel"; ibid., no. 165, 15.7.1942: "Isaak Veilchenduft näht Knopflöcher." On the German companies in the ghetto and their forced laborers, see Sakowska, *Menschen*, pp. 255–256.
131. IfZA, Fb 105/12, pp. 2812ff., "Diensttagebuch Hans Franks, Besprechung Franks mit den örtlichen Behörden in Warschau", 3.4.1941.
132. E.g., *Krakauer Zeitung*, no. 29, 4.2.1942: "Die Rindshaut unter dem Judenhemd"; ibid., no. 40, 17.2.1942: "Eine Brücke für die Warschauer Juden."
133. Jockheck, *Propaganda*, p. 325.
134. Alvensleben, "Abschiede," pp. 141ff., diary, 16.–21.9.1940.
135. E.g., in AAN, T 501-228, Kommandanturbefehl Warschau no. 229, 16.12.1940, or in RGVA, 1323-2-302a, Bl. 42, Kommandanturbefehl Warschau no. 107, 10.5.1943. For Minsk see, e.g., IfZA, MA 1790/3; 389-1-1, "Tagesbefehle des KdS Weißruthenien 1942".
136. BAL, B 162/3664, pp. 40ff., statement of Ehrhard S. on 18.1.1960; BStU, ZUV 53/7, pp. 129ff., statement of Walter H. regarding the deployment of Police Battalion 304 in Warsaw, 1940–1941, on 2.1.1975.
137. E.g., Hosenfeld, *Retten*, p. 452, diary, 3.3.1941; other visits, e.g., in DTA, 280/I, diary Franz Jonas; or ibid., 141/4, diary Max Rohrweder. In addition, see Blättler, *Warschau*, pp. 27ff.
138. StAM, Polizeipräsidien, Slg. Primavesi/270, "Kriegserinnerungen des Oberwachtmeisters der Schutzpolizei Otto Nahlmann". Curiosity as the motivation for a visit to the ghetto is mentioned, e.g., in BAL, B 162/AR 179/71, Bd. 6, pp. 938ff., statement of Werner S. on 9.9.1971.
139. Szarota, *Warschau*, p. 46.
140. Neutral descriptions can be found in BfZg, Slg. Sterz, letter by Major C.H. Bein, 21.8.1941; ibid., letter by Rotkreuz-Schwester Anna Weber, 20.5.1941. Agreement with the fate of the Jews is expressed, e.g., in ibid., letter by Unteroffizier Heinrich Zils, 30.6.1941. The misery is rejected in ibid., letter by Unteroffizier Gottard Eiermann, 24.6.1941. In view of the small number of letters, however, it is not possible to give representative quotas for the numbers accepting and rejecting.
141. BAL, B 162/3709, pp. 215ff., statement of Thekla B. on 25.7.1965.
142. Smolar, *Ghetto*, p. 22. Curiosity as the reason for the visit is given, e.g., in BAL, B 162/1682, pp. 1778ff., statement of Erna L. on 14.12.1960.
143. IfZA, Fb 63/77, "Monatsbericht des *Distrikts* Warschau für April 1942", 12.5.1942. Here the arrival of Jews from Germany is noted and their number given as 3,872.
144. Gottwaldt and Schulle, *Judendeportationen*, pp. 230ff. Surviving records of the relevant railway documentation can be found in IfZA, Fb 85-II.
145. Hecker, "Juden," pp. 826–827.
146. Gottwaldt and Schulle, *Judendeportationen*, pp. 234–235.
147. Hilberg, *Quellen*, p. 71.

148. Private collection of Gerhard Lieschke, Wolfgang Lieschke to his wife 13.11.1941.
149. Ibid., Wolfgang Lieschke to his wife, 22.11.1941.
150. Ibid., Wolfgang Lieschke to his wife, 13.11.1941.
151. Carl von Andrian diary/Peter Lieb transcript, 28.11.1941.
152. BAL, B 162/1682, pp. 1778ff., statement of Erna L. on 14.12.1960.
153. Exceptions include, e.g., the transfer of six hundred Jews from Tłuszcz to Warsaw in May 1942, in APW, 486/8, "Lagebericht des Gendarmeriezugs Warschau Land an den KdG Warschau", 1.6.1942, or the delivery of seized Roma into the city, in IfZA, Fb 63/96, "Monatsbericht des Distrikts Warschau für Mai 1942", 15.6.1942.
154. See chapter 1 section 3, table 1.2, this volume.
155. The monthly reports for Distrikt Warschau generally included these numbers. See e.g.: IfZA, Fb 63/8, "Monatsbericht des Distrikts Warschau für Januar 1942", 10.2.1942.
156. IfZA, MA 679—3/263ff., "Monatsberichte der Kommandantur Warschau für das Jahr 1941".
157. Fuks, Getto, p. 151, diary, 21.5.1941.
158. E.g., BfZg, Slg. Sterz, letter by Major C.H. Bein, 21.8.1941; ibid., letter by Unteroffizier Gottard Eiermann, 24.6.1941; ibid., letter by Krankenschwester Anna Weber, 20.5.1941.
159. Private collection of Gerhard Lieschke, Wolfgang Lieschke to his wife, 21.6.1941; IfZA, ED 66-I, Nachlass Wilhelm Hagen.
160. BAL, B 162/6256, pp. 814ff., statement of Karl-Heinz S. on 26.7.1977.
161. Sloan, Notes, p. 204, diary, 30.8.1941.
162. BfZg, Slg. Sterz, letter by Unteroffizier Heinrich Zils, 30.6.1941.
163. BaySta, Staatsanwaltschaften 34865/18, statement of Rudolf Neumann on 20.9.1962. A similar "mathematical" calculation can be found also in DTA, 280/I, diary Franz Jonas, 3.8.1941.
164. APW, 1357/1, "Lagebericht des NSDAP-Standorts Warschau-Land für Dezember 1940", n.d.
165. See esp. Browning, "Ghettoisierungspolitik."
166. IfZA, MA 679—3/645ff., "Monatsbericht der Kommandantur Warschau für den 16.7.–15.8.1941", 21.8.1941; ibid., Fb 105–12, pp. 2812ff., "Besprechung in Warschau", 3.4.1941.
167. Caumanns and Esch, "Fleckfieber," p. 256.
168. Sloan, ed., Notes, p. 294, as noted by Ringelblum in June 1942; Sakowska, Menschen, p. 166; as well as Blättler, Warschau, pp. 81ff.
169. Heydecker, Getto, p. 33. Fundamental is Arani, "Augen." Esp. relevant is the exhibition catalog by Jackiewicz and Król, Objektiv, which not only contains essays on German photographic reporting from Warsaw, but also a collection of 358 (propaganda-) photographs.
170. Longerich, Gewusst, pp. 220ff.
171. Carl von Andrian diary/Peter Lieb transcript. Clear examples, in part with figures, in the entries from 4, 16, 19, 24.10.1941 (the plundering of corpses is mentioned in this last entry).
172. Hosenfeld, Retten, pp. 640–641, diary, 13.8.1942.
173. BALAA, Ost-Dok. 8/842, pp. 1ff., report by Raimund Warth, 5.3.1956.
174. DTA, 280/I, diary Franz Jonas, 3.8.1941.
175. BAL, B 162/1898, pp. 215ff., statement of Martin P. on 2.5.1963.
176. BAL, B 162/3667, pp. 88ff., statement of Rudolf B. on 17.5.1961.
177. E.g., BAL, B 162/3667, pp. 113ff., statement of Curt R. on 16.5.1961.
178. Jäger, Verbrechen, p. 44.
179. On these shootings, see e.g., IfZA, MA 679—4/442ff., "Monatsbericht der Oberfeldkommandantur Warschau für die Zeit vom 16.12. bis 15.1.1942", 21.1.1942; APW, 486/8, "Lagebericht des Gendarmeriezugs Warschau Land an den KdG Warschau" 1.6.1942.

180. BAL, B 162/1679, pp. 1247ff., statement of Alfred M. on 29.9.1960.
181. StAM, Polizeipräsidien, Slg. Primavesi/144, testimonies dating from 1951 concernig the crimes of Bataillon 61; see also Klemp, *Ermittelt*, pp. 129ff.
182. IfZA, Fa 91/4, pp. 866ff., "Bericht Nr. 4 des Beauftragten des Reichsleiters Bormann im OKW, Albert Hoffmann, über Weißruthenien/Minsk", 26.5.1942.
183. Angrick et al., "Tagebuch," p. 340; and Klemp, *Ermittelt*, pp. 289ff.
184. IfZA, MA 265/425, "Bericht über die Arbeitstagung der politischen Leiter der Bezirksleitung Weißruthenien und der Gebiete Minsk Stadt und Land am 19.3.1943", 20.3.1943.
185. Jäger, *Verbrechen*, p. 22.
186. Gerlach, *Morde*, pp. 690 and 704ff.
187. Ibid., p. 738.
188. Matthäus, *Heuser*, p. 117.
189. BAL, B 162/3665, pp. 161ff., statement of Rudolf S. on 4.1.1960.
190. E.g., BAL, B 162/1681, pp. 1548ff., statement of Karl-Heinz G. on 24.5.1961.
191. BAL, B 162/1680, pp. 1336ff., statement of Friedrich S. on 23.3.1960.
192. Numerous statements of this kind can be found, e.g., in the case against the Security Police in Warsaw: BAL, B 162/3658-3727.
193. BAL, B 162/AR 3044/65, pp. 6ff., statement of Erna G. on 13.12.1965.
194. BAL, B 162/1680, pp. 1344ff., statement of Edith S. on 10.1.1961.
195. BAL, B 162/AR 1495/69, pp. 160ff., statement of Josef B. on 9.7.1971.
196. Ibid. On the role of the civilian administration in the genocide in Belorussia, see Gerlach, *Morde*, pp. 1149ff.
197. Adler, *Mensch*, p. 327.
198. IfZA, Fb 85-I/S. 22ff., "Protokoll über die Tagung der Gebietskommissare, Hauptabteilungsleiter und Abteilungsleiter des Generalkommissariats Minsk vom 8.4. bis 10.4. 1943".
199. Sakowska, *Menschen*, p. 244.
200. Gutman, *Jews*, pp. 197ff.; and Sakowska, *Menschen*, pp. 238ff.
201. Sakowska, *Menschen*, pp. 252–253.
202. IfZA, Fb 63/110, "Zweimonatsbericht des *Distrikt*s Warschau für Juni und Juli 1942", 15.8.1942.
203. *Haushaltsplan des Generalgouvernements 1942*, p. 61.
204. Sakowska, *Menschen*, p. 237
205. BaySta, Staatsanwaltschaften 34865/18, statement of Rudolf Neumann on 20.9.1962.
206. IPN, NTN/70, Fahrplananordnung no. 243, 27.8.1942
207. Sakowska, *Menschen*, pp. 246–247.
208. BAL, B 162/3667, pp. 88ff., statement of Rudolf B. on 17.5.1961; ibid., B 162/3720, pp. 100ff., statement of Hans B. on 11.8.1969.
209. Hilberg, *Quellen*, pp. 71–72. Only rarely were train documents marked with the lowest level of secrecy, "only for official use." In general, see Hilberg, *Sonderzüge*. Several timetables can be found in IPN, NTN/70, Fahrplananordnung no. 548, 3.8.1942.
210. BAL, B 162/3696, pp. 65ff., statement of Rolf H. on 17.5.1963.
211. BaySta, Staatsanwaltschaften 34865/18, statment of Friedrich Haßler on 28.7. 1964 (quotation); ibid., Staatsanwaltschaften 34865/13, statement of Friedrich Haßler on 8.6.1962. On this assessment, see also: BAL, B 162/3696, pp. 65ff., statement of Rolf H. on 17.5.1963.
212. BAL, B 162/3694, pp. 77ff., statement of Hans B. on 25.4.1963.
213. Hagen, *Auftrag*, pp. 174–175.
214. Hosenfeld, *Retten*, pp. 606–607, diary, 17.4.1942.
215. Ibid., pp. 626–627, diary, 23.7.1942.

216. Ibid., pp. 630–631, diary, 25.7.1942.
217. Ibid., pp. 653ff., diary, 6.9.1942.
218. *Krakauer Zeitung*, no. 303, 23.12.1942: "Die Aussiedlung der Juden als letzte Rettung."
219. This is mentioned, e.g., in BAL, B 162/3720, pp. 93ff., statement of Wilfried J. on 31.7.1969; ibid., B 162/6268, pp. 1386ff., statement of von Karl K. on 27.6.1978; ibid., B 162/3667, pp. 88ff., statement of Rudolf B. on 17.5.1961.
220. See, e.g., BAL, B 162/3696, pp. 65ff., statement of Rolf H. on 17.5.1963; ibid., B 162/3660, pp. 35ff., statement of Alfred C. on 22.4.1960.
221. Musiał, *Zivilverwaltung*, pp. 324–325.
222. BAL, B 162/3720, S. 100ff., statement of Hans B. on 11.8.1969.
223. APW, 485/333, "Bericht des Wohnungsamtes Warschau", 15.7.1942.
224. APW, 2421/63, Photo by Johannes Hennig, n.d. [1942]. Also from Siedlce are the photos taken by Hubert Pfoch, which were used as evidence in the Düsseldorf trial of Treblinka's commandant, Franz Stangl. See Pfoch, "Dokumentation zur Judendeportation," pp. 62–63.
225. BAL, B 162/3682, pp. 199ff., statement of Wilhelm G. on 12.3.1963.
226. BAL, B 162/3667, pp. 88ff., statement of Rudolf B. on 17.5.1961 (quotation); ibid., pp. 65ff., statement of Rolf H. on 17.5.1963; BaySta, Staatsanwaltschaften 34865/08, statement of Otto H. on 27.2.1962; ibid., statement of Hermann R. on 26.3.1962; ibid., statement of Arthur T. on 14.2.1963.
227. BAL, B 162/3660, pp. 145ff., statement of Wilhelm H. on 22, 23.8.1960.
228. For an overview, see Longerich, *Gewusst*, pp. 10ff.
229. IfZA, Fb 63/144, "Zweimonatsbericht des *Distrikts* Warschau für August und September 1942", 15.10.1942.
230. Friedrich, *Kollaboration und Antisemitismus*.
231. Thus, e.g., Wolfgang Lieschke spoke in November 1941 of the "struggle against everything Jewish," in which for "us there is now no other means" left other than violence: Private collection of Gerhard Lieschke, Wolfgang Lieschke to his wife, 13.11.1941.
232. Gutman, *Jews*, pp. 312ff.
233. This was the title and main statement of Stroop, *Wohnbezirk*.
234. Ibid.
235. Scheffler and Grabitz, *Ghetto-Aufstand*, pp. 328ff.
236. Hosenfeld, *Retten*, pp. 714–715, letter to his wife, 9.5.1943.
237. BAL, B 162/3708, pp. 120ff., statement of Gertrud H. on 3.6.1965. Anneliese K. Made similar observations from her apartment, see BAL, B 162/3708, pp. 79ff., statement of Anneliese K. on 1.6.1965. Hermann Beyerlein also photographed women, who were observing the burning ghetto from the roof of the Telegraph Office: Jaworski and Peters, *Alltagsperspektiven*, p. 54.
238. BAL, B 162/3682, pp. 199ff., statement of Wilhelm G. on 12.3.1963.
239. BaySta, Staatsanwaltschaften 34865/18, "Kriegstagebuch des Rüstungskommandos Warschau für das erste Halbjahr 1943".
240. BAL, B 162/3682, pp. 199ff., statement of Wilhelm G. on 12.3.1963.
241. IPN, NTN 257, Bericht über Warschau (eingereicht durch SS-Standartenführer von Korzowski), n.d. [mid 1943].
242. On this, see also Römer, *Kameraden*, pp. 414–417.
243. APW, 1357/88, "Rundschreiben Nr. 13 der NSDAP-*Distrikt*führung Warschau—Hauptabteilung Volkswohlfahrt", 4.5.1943.
244. BaySta, Staatsanwaltschaften 34865/18, "Kriegstagebuch des Rüstungskommandos Warschau, Quartalsbericht", 30.6.1943.
245. Krausnick and Wilhelm, *Truppe*, pp. 597ff.
246. Borodziej, *Aufstand*, pp. 190–191 and 205ff.

247. Thieme, "Erinnerungen," p. 302.
248. Borodziej, *Aufstand*, pp. 118ff. RONA is the acronym for Русская Освободительная Народная Армия (Russian People's Liberation Army), which was under the leadership of Mieczysław Kaminski and therefore is also known as the Kaminski Brigade.
249. Borodziej, *Aufstand*, pp. 121ff.
250. *Amtsblatt der Ostbahndirektion*, no. 17, 30.11.1944, p. 141.
251. BAB, R 48/33, "Liste der bei den Kämpfen in Warschau Gefallenen", n.d. [end of 1944].
252. BAB, R 6/260, pp. 2–3, Reichskanzlei to RMbO, 15.8.1944.
253. See chapter 4 section 2, this volume.
254. Hosenfeld, *Retten*, pp. 823–824, letter to his family 6.8.1944, and ibid., pp. 824–825, letter to his family, 8.8.1944.
255. Borodziej, *Aufstand*, p. 121.
256. Ibid.
257. Hosenfeld, *Retten*, pp. 840–841, letter to his wife, 8.9.1944.
258. BfZg, Slg. Sterz, letter by Leutnant Zimkeit, 13.8.1944.
259. As cited in Krannhals, *Aufstand*, p. 312.
260. Borodziej, *Aufstand*, pp. 121ff.
261. E.g., Hosenfeld, *Retten*, p. 824, diary, 8.8.1944; Jaworski and Peters, *Alltagsperspektiven*, pp. 55–59.
262. BfZg, Slg. Sterz, letter by Obergefreiter Meier, 12.8.1944.
263. Hosenfeld, *Retten*, pp. 827–828, diary, 11.8.1944; see also Stephan, "Banditen," pp. 481–482.
264. Stephan, "Banditen," p. 480. On the difficulties presented by the small number of sources, such that the ensuing statements cannot be viewed as representative, see ibid., p. 489.
265. Ibid., pp. 482ff.
266. Villinger, "Aufstand," pp. 272ff.
267. Published in Hilberg, *Quellen*, pp. 134–135, Himmler to HSSPFs and SSPFs, 12.12.1941.
268. APW, 1705/1, Kommandanturbefehl Warschau, 3.10.1939.
269. Hoffmann-Curtius, "Trophäen."
270. Latzel, "Feldpostbriefe," p. 173.
271. *Amtsblatt der Haupteisenbahndirektion Mitte (Minsk)*, no. 31, 24.8.1942 and ibid., no. 8, 14.2.1943.
272. Hosenfeld, "Retten."
273. On communication about the mass murder in offical letters, see Hilberg, *Quellen*, pp. 70ff.
274. Latzel, "Feldpostbriefe," p. 178.
275. On Hagen's activity in Warsaw, see Caumanns and Esch, "Fleckfieber." A positive evaluation is given in Pośpieszalski, "Protest." Very critical on the other hand are Wulf, *Reich*, pp. 334–335, and Aly and Heim, *Vordenker*, pp. 216–217. Hagen himself presented the case in the best light in his memoirs: Hagen, *Sozialarzt*, pp. 163ff. On the postwar discussion surrounding Hagen's activities, see Berg, *Holocaust*, pp. 594–615.
276. IfZA, ED 66-I, Hagen to Conti, 20.7.1942 and 8.1.1943; ibid., Hagen to von Sammern-Frankenegg, 17.10.1942, 20.10.1942, 31.10.1942 and 5.12.1942; ibid., Hagen to Hitler, 7.12.1942.
277. Ibid., Himmler to Conti, 29.3.1943 and answer, 31.3.1943.
278. Ibid., Weirauch to HSSPF Krüger, 4.2.1943. Weirauch later became the Federal Party manager of the FDP, undersecretary in the Bundesministerium der Verteidigung (Federal Defense Ministry), undersecretary in the Bundesministerium für gesamtdeutsche Fra-

gen (Federal Ministry for All-German Questions), and at the same time an informant for the Stasi. See Musiał, Zivilverwaltung, p. 397.

279. Longerich, Gewusst, pp. 224–225.
280. ÖGZA, NL 93, Max Bischof to Hans Pilder, 26.8.1942.
281. Longerich, Gewusst, pp. 239–240.
282. DTA, 141/4, diary Dr. Max Rohrweder, 22. and 23.10.1941.
283. Krausnick and Wilhelm, Truppe, pp. 576ff., and Gerlach, Morde, pp. 598–599.
284. Carl von Andrian diary/Peter Lieb transcript, 29.11.1941.
285. Ibid., 4.2.1942.
286. Ibid., 24.10.1941.
287. See, e.g., the overview in Pohl, Wehrmacht.
288. BAL, B 162/3688, pp. 183ff., statement of Karl M. on 28.1.1963.
289. Musiał, Zivilverwaltung, pp. 330–331.
290. Sakowska, Menschen, pp. 293ff.; in general on blackmail, see Grabowski, Żyda, as well as Engelking, Panie.
291. BAL, B 162/6268, pp. 1386ff., statement of Karl K. on 27.6.1978.
292. Hosenfeld, Retten, p. 527, diary, 4.9.1941; ibid., p. 529, diary, 12.9.1941.
293. BAL, B 162/3696, pp. 65ff., statement of Rolf H. on 17.5.1963; ibid., B 162/3694, pp. 77ff., statement of Hans B. on 25.4.1963.
294. BayStA, Staatsanwaltschaften 34865/18, statement of Friedrich Haßler on 28.7.1964. See also chapter 5 section 3, this volume.
295. BAL, B 162/3663, pp. 149–150, statement of Hans A. on 5.12.1960. The same source for his information is given also in ibid., B 162/3696, pp. 65ff., statement of Rolf H. on 17.5.1963.
296. BAL, B 162/3667, pp. 88ff., statement of Rudolf B. on 17.5.1961.
297. BAL, B 162/3697, pp. 256ff., statement of Walter I. on 23.9.1963.
298. BAL, B 162/3661, pp. 89ff., statement of Christel S. on 14.9.1960.
299. Hosenfeld, Retten, pp. 606–607, diary 17.4.1942.
300. APW, 643/859 (new: 831), "Urteil des Sondergerichts Warschau gegen vier Volksdeutsche", 7.8.1942.
301. BAL, B 162/3666, pp. 30–31, statement of Friedel M. on 20.2.1960.
302. BAL, B 162/AR 179/71, Bd. 6, pp. 938ff., statement of Werner S. on 9.9.1971
303. BAL, B 162/AR 179/71, Bd. 7, pp. 1291ff., statement of Siegfried N. on 7.12.1971.
304. BAL, B 162/3667, pp. 113ff., statement of Curt R. on 16.5.1961.
305. BAL, B 162/1898, pp. 215ff., statement of Martin P. on 2.5.1963.
306. BAL, B 162/6268, pp. 1386ff., statement of Karl K. on 27.6.1978.
307. BAL, B 162/3720, pp. 100ff., statement of Hans B. on 11.8.1969.
308. BAL, B 162/3660, pp. 145ff., statements of Wilhelm H. on 22, 23.8.1960.
309. BAL, B 162/3667, pp. 116ff., statement of Ernst K. on 15.5.1961.
310. StAM, Polizeipräsidien, Slg. Primavesi/144, testimonies dating from 1951 concerning investigations against Polizei-Hauptwachtmeister Brunst. Klemp, Ermittelt, pp. 129ff.
311. StAM, Polizeipräsidien, Slg. Primavesi/270, "Kriegserinnerungen des Oberwachtmeisters der Schutzpolizei Otto Nahlmann", p. 12. Nahlmann was assigned to the 2nd Company of the battalion: "There Wannemacher is in charge of the Company. Oh how terrible, Hauptmann Wannemacher! Just the mention of his name back home gave every policeman goose bumps."
312. IfZA, Fb 85-I/S. 22ff., "Protokoll über die Tagung der Gebietskommissare, Hauptabteilungsleiter und Abteilungsleiter des Generalkommissariats vom 8.4. bis 10.4.1943".
313. Adler, Mensch, p. 227.
314. BAL, B 162/1678, pp. 1042ff., statement of Elfriede A. on 20.1.1961; ibid., B 162/1673, pp. 347ff., statement of Sabine H. on 27–29.4.1960.

315. BayStA, Staatsanwaltschaften 22292, statement of Herbert W. on 12.3.1962.
316. The German word translated here to natural is *selbstverständlich*. See BAL, B 162/1679, pp. 1247ff., statement of Alfred M. on 29.9.1960; a similar choice of words can be found in ibid., B 162/1680, pp. 1336ff., statement of Friedrich S. on 23.3.1960.
317. Brandt, *Priester*, pp. 345ff.
318. BAL, B 162/1673, pp. 347ff., statement of Sabine H. on 27–29.4.1960; ibid., B 162/1681, pp. 1517ff., statement of Wilhelm C. on 16.5.1961.
319. BAL, B 162/1672, pp. 21ff., statement of Friedrich G. on 9.11.1960; ibid., B 162/1679, pp. 1159ff., statement of Gisela B. on 22.2.1961.
320. BAL, B 162/1680, pp. 1336ff., statement of Friedrich S. on 23.3.1960; ibid., B 162/1681, pp. 1517ff., statement of Wilhelm C. on 16.5.1961.
321. BAL, B 162/1689, pp. 3378ff., statements of Theodor O. on 3.3.1961 and on 23.5.1960.
322. Zankel, *Mit Flugblättern*, p. 294. In addition, Bald, *Weiße Rose*, pp. 70ff.
323. Zankel, *Mit Flugblättern*, p. 294.
324. Welzer, *Täter*, p. 37.
325. Zimmerer, "Geburt," pp. 18ff.
326. Jersak, "Entscheidungen," p. 322.
327. Sofsky, *Prinzip*, p. 101.
328. Blass, *Perspectives*, pp. 42ff.
329. Hosenfeld, *Retten*, pp. 659–660, diary, 1.10.1942.
330. Sofsky, *Traktat*, pp. 113–114.
331. Scheffler and Grabitz, *Ghetto-Aufstand*, pp. 189–190, statement of Max Jesuiter.
332. Jäger, *Verbrechen*, pp. 313–314 and 321ff.
333. Rossino, *Hitler*, pp. 193ff.
334. Jockheck, *Banditen*, pp. 448–449.
335. BfZg, Slg. Sterz, letter by Unteroffizier Georg Heidenreich, 24.10.1941.
336. Sofsky, *Traktat*, p. 108.
337. BAL, B 162/3663, statement of Alfons Cz. on 9.11.1960.
338. Jäger, *Verbrechen*, pp. 275ff.
339. BAL, B 162/1689, statement of Theodor O. on 3.3.1961.
340. BAL, B 162/1681, statement of Wilhelm C. on 16.5.1961.
341. Jäger, *Verbrechen*, pp. 273–274.
342. See chapter 4 section 2, this volume.
343. BfZg, Slg. Sterz, letter by Unteroffizier Georg H., 24.10.1941.
344. Private collection of Gerhard Lieschke, Wolfgang Lieschke to his wife, 10.6. and 21.6.1941.
345. BfZg, Slg. Sterz, letter by Polizeiwachtmeister Adalbert Ballay, 15.10.1939.
346. BfZg, Slg. Sterz, letter by Unteroffizier Karl Graf, 1.11.1940.
347. Musiał, *Zivilverwaltung*, p. 338.
348. Sofsky, *Traktat*, pp. 54ff.
349. DTA, 280/I. diary Franz Jonas, 3.8.1941.
350. Sofsky, *Traktat*, p. 108.
351. Jäger, *Verbrechen*, p. 284.
352. BAL, B 162/1673, statement of Sabine H. on 27–29.4.1960.
353. BfZg, Slg. Sterz, letter by Reichsbahn-Inspektor Kurt Schmid, 8.10.1941.

Conclusions

The German occupation of Warsaw lasted five years, that of Minsk three years. A maximum of 60,000 and 15,000 Reich and ethnic German soldiers, policemen, members of the civilian administration, as well as private individuals were present in the two cities, respectively. For the entire duration of the war, however, considerably more men were deployed there in total: there were many transfers and replacements. Especially among the members of the Wehrmacht there was constant fluctuation because they rarely stayed for more than a few months. All these Germans contributed in some way to the occupational regime—some more than others—and to the fact that in 1945 Warsaw and Minsk were little more than a heap of ruins, and in each case about half of the prewar population had been plundered, expelled, deported, or murdered.

Yet why did the occupiers apparently make their contribution to the exercise of Nazi rule and violence so willingly? A glance at the occupiers betrays that their self-identification was primarily based on the tasks they performed, which through their membership in the respective offices led to an institutional fragmentation of the society of occupiers. The rivalries between the various groups of Wehrmacht, SS and police, as well as the civilian administration were notable and were not limited just to the leadership. The ordinary soldiers, policemen, and officials also interacted primarily with their colleagues and viewed with suspicion members of the other institutions. Despite the basic solidarity within the society of occupiers, each section believed that it was the main pillar of that society. The individual organizations and their men claimed this status for themselves and were scarcely willing to grant the other occupiers a similar importance.

The Reich and ethnic German private individuals, who did not wear any of the uniforms of the society of occupiers, were subjected to many sweeping suspicions that they had only come to the East from pure opportunism or to make a quick profit. Especially the ethnic Germans, whose commitment to the Nazi holders of power was demonstrated by their voluntary acceptance of an identity card, always had the reputation of profiteering from the German military victories. This assessment was reinforced by the inadequate German language skills among this population group, many of whom were unable to make themselves understood in German without the help of a translator. However, many of the social and ideological events were organized specifically for these people: the rulers viewed them on the one hand as proof that Eastern Europe was an ancient German territory, and on the other that they were the starting point for the future German settlement of the East, which was to begin once the war was won.

Yet although numerous German families were present in the two cities a comparison with the population in Germany with regard to age and sex would be mistaken; there were many more young people in their twenties and thirties than any other age groups, while the proportion of women was far lower at around 15 percent of the population. Older people aged over age fifty and people younger than eighteen were represented only among the ethnic Germans and those Reich German families who had decided in favor of life in Warsaw or Minsk for the long term. In German society in the East it is possible to identify a much broader age spectrum than just the generation that was in its youth during World War I. Although the generation born between 1900 and 1910 formed the top echelon of the administration and the SS, the realities of daily life during the occupation were determined only to a small extent by this political leadership corps.

Overall the society of occupiers presents quite a heterogeneous picture. The Germans in the East came from all classes, backgrounds, and regions in the Reich. Special recruiting criteria were only rarely applied and only for specific units, such as the Security Police, although almost all top leaders and commanders were convinced Nazis. All of the others who became perpetrators or at least accessories in the mass murders in Poland or Belorussia, who prepared the way for or supported the reign of terror and the Holocaust, and those who committed the crimes, did this not thanks to any specific biographical details that might have made them especially well-suited for this role. It should not be overlooked that especially among the broad mass of occupiers, all possible constellations were present with regard to their socialization. In their personalities or biography nothing can be found, which specifically or genuinely qualified them for service in the East or made them become perpetrators. Since the bureaucratic selection process at least indirectly produced an occupation policy along the lines the regime intended, other more-specifically Nazi recruitment demands were not really necessary. This does not, however, answer the question of why the mass murder of the local population was possible. In view of the conclusions regarding the perpetrators' personal biographies, this has to be looked for in the processes and situations that made occupiers from "ordinary men," for whom the murder of a large part of the local population represented a "normal" matter.

The identity of most of the occupiers in Warsaw and Minsk was determined by feelings of superiority toward the occupied. The occupiers belonged to an elite ruling group that enjoyed many privileges. On top of this, due to a lack of personal experience with the occupied prejudices dominated that made one's own existence and culture appear to stand far above that of the locals. If not all occupiers viewed themselves as the overlords, as those who had to appear precisely in accordance with Nazi ideology, yet they considered themselves the legitimate rulers of the East; this position had been hard fought and required constant defense in view of the attacks by the resistance. For this reason, the comradeship that was always stressed and that cemented solidarity within the various groups of occupiers played a significant role. In this respect it was much more effective as a means of social discipline than were threats of punishment or prohibitions, and it dominated self-perception to a considerable degree, thereby contributing to the widespread acceptance of the status of occupier.

Thus the perception of the East was certainly positive. Although the first reactions directly after arriving in Minsk and Warsaw were often negative or at least ambivalent, most Germans soon came to terms very quickly with the daily life of occupation. Even if subsequently they did not value it so highly, as the norm required, they still conformed to it. When the occupiers arrived in the cities, they had to acclimatize to a completely unfamiliar situation because the surroundings, the service duties, and the people with whom they came into contact were not known to them and represented something completely new. The insecurity of the Germans with respect to the new circumstances in the East can therefore be viewed as formative for the society of occupiers. Frames of reference and orientations that had been structured previously by their conduct at home had to be created anew, and daily life was molded through adaptation and adoption. Analysis has shown that their interpretation of the situation at the time was much more important for how the occupiers behaved than was their previous experiences. Therefore the rationality of their actions will also be explained mainly by means of an examination of their daily life.

The daily life of occupation in which the Germans worked in Warsaw and Minsk was shaped by many norms and prescriptions issued by the authorities. Not only their work duties that took up a large part of their day were subjected to regimentation, but also spare time. Because private contacts with the locals were essentially undesired, the occupiers were also supposed to spend as much of their free time as possible within their own circles. Through numerous requirements the entire daily life of the occupiers was to be determined, in order thereby to dissolve the boundary between work and private space. The regime's totalitarian claim therefore extended—even more intrusively than in the Reich—into people's private sphere and thereby revealed a model of how Nazi social policy might have looked after the war. The hostels in which—from the room, via the canteen up to the comradeship evenings—life was completely organized, were a hallmark of this. The collective and individual organization of spare-time activities beyond this through sport, cultural events, reading, radio, or cinema were intended to cover other needs and at least partially compensate for the longings for home and family. On account of the variety and the familiar structures within an alien environment—despite their limited influence upon them—the occupiers took advantage of most of these offerings gladly. Their acceptance was enhanced also because the activities took place together with their German colleagues and thereby created familiar surroundings.

The offerings enjoyed even greater popularity the less their contents were determined by ideology or politics. Propaganda events were not rare; however, the numbers of participants remained clearly below those for the other activities. Since at the former mainly Party officials and those in authority were addressed as multiplying factors, the extent to which the contents were disseminated should not be underestimated, especially if the extensive coverage in the newspapers is also taken into account. The offerings of normed daily life were addressed essentially with the same intentions to all sections of the society of occupiers. Admittedly the support offered to women was less comprehensive and varied than that for the men, but apart from the smaller number of women, this lower support was also because the goals of distraction and entertainment were seen as less necessary for women than for men. The reason for this was Nazi ideology that did not recognize the important role women played in the smooth operation of the society of occupiers; this policy, however, largely corresponded also with the contemporary image of women among non-Nazis. The ethnic Germans also enjoyed a special status because among them it was not necessary to overcome homesickness. For members of this group it was most important to strengthen their sense of belonging to the society of occupiers that the authorities mainly attempted with an extensive package of social measures, but also by entrusting them with important positions in the economy and by placing them above the other locals in terms of their legal status. Due to their different socialization, the judiciary even granted them considerable leniency with respect to numerous crimes because they were considered to have an incompletely developed sense of German honor. In order to develop this sense, among other things their integration within the circle of the other occupiers was the most important political objective, yet this intention could only be realized in small steps: a different way of life, a different social background, and especially language barriers prevented genuine inclusion. Ultimately, for the other occupiers the ethnic Germans remained only second-class Germans, or worse still, just opportunistic Poles.

Even in the East the ideals of the people's community ultimately could not be converted into reality, although it was possible there to get much closer to the intended goal than in the Reich. There was a new social order, the promise of a better future, and a clear separation between national compatriots and those alien to the community; in addition, the people's community served as a legitimation strategy and possessed a clearly behavioral dimension.[1] Especially with regard to the ethnic Germans whose realm of existence was in many respects a clean slate, the Nazis were able to initiate them into almost the purest form of the concept—yet politics failed because they were unable to integrate the "new" Germans with the "old" ones.[2] Nonetheless, research in this direction that until now has scarcely been done could reinvigorate the debate on the people's community, a debate that has recently come to a standstill.[3]

The failure of the visions of the people's community was expressed also in the reality that ethnic and Reich Germans rarely lived together. The Germans who entered the cities in 1939 and 1941 as military victors soon created their own residential districts in which the ethnic Germans only hesitantly found their place. Within the residential districts, the locals were largely excluded, although the walling off of the districts from the world outside was only implemented later. Nonetheless, there the communal idea of the occupiers was given spatial expression, which also offered the advantage of security, since the subjectively perceived threat posed by the local population was thereby at least partially countered. Alongside aspects linked to security and the symbolism of an alleged return of German domination to the East, which the rulers linked to such a city within the city, the deliberate choice of modern buildings with maximum comfort—at the expense of the dispossessed locals—made it possible to increase considerably the occupiers' acceptance of their new lifestyle.

The occupiers' daily lives were to a large extent shaped by prescribed norms. Nonetheless, it should be noted that despite all the rules and regulations there was some space left open in which the Germans could express their individuality and shape their daily lives according to their own wishes. Precisely how people responded to the norms revealed the difference between claims and reality for Nazi rule in the East. Thus there were frequent conflicts between the different groups within the society of occupiers that were silently tolerated by the commanders. This tolerance applied also to the fights between comrades, which were seen more or less as usual events;

the leaders tried to prevent more serious disputes as undesirable and also helped to resolve them. However, it should not be forgotten that the sanctions were especially draconian if the society of occupiers' solidarity was at all threatened. In this it can be seen, that violence—also as a solution to problems—was much more readily accepted in the East than, for example, in the Reich.

The conflicts between Germans only rarely reflected opposition to National Socialism or the values of the society of occupiers. This was because despite all the complaints, things were relatively good for the occupiers in Warsaw and Minsk. Alongside the collective reduction of cognitive dissonance and numerous desired and less desired possibilities for diversion, the reasons for this lay primarily in their social status and the availability of material goods. In contrast to the Reich, the Germans in the East were members of a small, privileged group that ruled over a mass of occupied people and that could allow itself many freedoms. Possible problems regarding their own existence, which nonetheless cropped up, could at least be rendered bearable by escape into belief and religion. The latter was not necessarily welcomed by the regime, but it was at least tolerated. Similar attitudes applied also to the consumption of alcohol. Also here the occupiers exploited as much as possible the available room for maneuver and drank large quantities of spirits.

An additional aspect of the occupiers' daily life that was experienced as positive was the availability of all kinds of goods beyond the official rationed supplies. Through theft or purchase on the black market, the occupiers exploited the extreme shortages facing the locals. The locals could scarcely prevent themselves being taken advantage of in trade or public robbery without fear of reprisals. In this manner the occupiers acquired food, valuables, and other things that made life more pleasant for them and—thanks to the field post packages—also their family members in the Reich.

The authorities showed little interest in restricting these kinds of freedoms because it would only have increased dissatisfaction with service in the East. The same was true in the sphere of sexual activity: prostitution not only was tolerated, but also was organized by the state in order to satisfy the occupiers' needs. With their money and access to food and other goods, it was easy for the Germans to attract local women by exploiting their material needs, although having a Polish or especially a Jewish lover was stigmatized as race defilement and could result in punishment. Yet even rape was at times tolerated, if it was committed without attracting too much attention. Daily life for the occupiers was subjected to a high degree of regulation through norms. At the same time, though, there were also numerous openings for acts of self-will—that is, conscious deviation from the norms—that the occupiers seized, since those bearing most of the consequences were members of the local population, whose fate was indifferent for the German authorities.

Breaches of the norms were mainly punished when the supervisor or judge determined that the "reputation of the Germans" had been compromised. This imprecise slogan was defined primarily as the occupiers' supposed moral superiority over the occupied. In practice this meant mainly that crimes were not permitted if they attracted too much attention. In addition to the locals, the Germans back home in the Reich were also not supposed to become aware of the occupiers' misdeeds. Especially lack of discipline, corruption, but also sexual crimes were punished if they became public; in these spheres the occupiers were supposed to serve as role models. In contrast, self-will was permitted if the rules were not broken, or were broken in complete secrecy. One could expect to be denounced by one's comrades only in exceptional circumstances. As long as the crimes did not attract much attention, the authorities had only a slight interest in investigating cases where the victims were members of the local population. Therefore, the occupiers were permitted a broad spectrum of liberties outside of their official duties; they could go beyond the official program and pursue unhindered a wide variety of activities that were officially undesired by the authorities. The implementation of the norms was primarily enforced if (1) the crime became known to a wider public, (2) it concerned an infraction of discipline or was directed against the circle of comrades, or (3) core elements of Nazi ideology were breached, such as "racial defilement" or criticism of the leadership.

In Warsaw and Minsk many daily experiences were unprecedented, and there were no accustomed modes of behavior available to the occupiers that they could easily draw on. The Germans took advantage of the organized state programs as well as the room for maneuver granted them. This still does not say anything about their significance for the occupiers' habitus, which was shaped by the practical experiences of daily life. It helped them to react in accordance with their own social position in unfamiliar situations. In contrast, the prescribed norms were much more strictly applied during the occupiers' official duties than in their spare time.

The habitus consisted initially of a perceptional framework, according to which the occupiers viewed themselves as the new masters in the East and as superior to the locals, although at the same time the locals represented a serious threat to the occupiers. There were various groups within the society of occupiers whose interests had to be taken into account, and against which one had to maintain one's own reputation. The perception of the various groups of occupiers promoted a pattern of thinking based on rivalries, which in a slightly altered form also applied to those Germans who were not members of the society of occupation: they were not privileged like the occupiers and therefore became potential competitors. Only the occupiers were entitled to all of the pleasant sides of the East, and the locals just stood at their disposal more or less to fulfil their wishes. Converted into a pattern of behavior this meant that the Germans in Warsaw or Minsk could almost do as they pleased if the victims were members of the local population and the crimes did not attract any attention. Acting discretely was directly connected with one's reputation as a master who did not show any weakness. Violence was widely accepted for precisely this reason: it appeared only to demonstrate one's superior position and at the same time confirm the inferiority of the locals.

Thus the shaping of the occupiers' habitus was of central importance for dealings with the locals, as it would be decisive for how they would behave. The newly arriving Germans soon adopted the habitus as their own, as it determined whether many practices were acceptable or not. Although contacts with the occupied outside of service hours were officially prohibited, these contacts constantly took place. Despite norms to the contrary, the occupiers robbed, beat, raped, or murdered even without orders, without constantly having to fear being punished: they shared a common basis of understanding in which such things appeared not only as relatively normal behavior, but also as prevention of denunciation. They committed the crimes in a comparatively discrete space, which minimized attention both among the occupied and the occupiers. In addition, self-will was also limited to the extent that transgressions of norms did not take place publicly, infringe against discipline and the circle of comrades, or challenge the central components of Nazi ideology. This placed hardly any limitations on the violence against the locals, since the regime had largely deprived them of all protection.

On top of the self-perception as a cultured superior being with a sense for order, discipline, cleanliness, and comradeship, as well as pride in German achievements, came also the sense that in the East one was carrying out an important mission, which in part also had to be conducted under pleasant circumstances. From these self-justifications of one's actions influenced by ideological and economic factors, it was just a short step to the legitimation of violence. It is estimated that around 10 percent of the occupiers in Minsk, and a little less in Warsaw, directly participated in the murders of the local population. Apart from a small number of exceptions, however, almost everybody profited from, and thereby promoted, the violence indirectly, for example by participating in the black market.

Self-critical perspectives were not widespread; much more common was an interpretation in which the Germans defended their existence with all available means—apparently completely appropriately—against hostile, uncivilized Slavs or Jews. It was not difficult to justify the mass murders of Poles and Belorussians as "suppressing resistance," or to interpret the destruction of the Jews as a necessary preventive measure against the alleged standard-bearers of resistance.

Despite all of the prohibitions and attempts at secrecy, the everyday violence and the murders and massacres that were conducted with great brutality were common knowledge within the society of occupiers, as well as a clearly visible public fact that, with certain restrictions, could be read about even in the newspapers. This brutality did not, however, represent a constant topic of discussion, but communication among the occupiers ensured that they were quickly and well informed about the respective crimes. In view of the attendance at, and photographs of, the executions and mass graves, it is not an exaggeration to speak of a fascination with violence. This is demonstrated, for example, by the way in which even horrific details about the mass murders became known and were circulated. Detailed knowledge about the deportation of the Jews from Warsaw in 1942, for example, was the talk of the town just one week later, as was the Warsaw Ghetto Uprising in 1943. Communication about it also became possible because the violence was seen as both natural and legitimate, such that there was no reluctance to discuss it; within the society of occupiers scarcely any corresponding restrictions were imposed. Rumors and facts spread quickly, and even back home in Germany significant parts of the story became known.

At the same time, there was a direct relationship between the public nature of the violence and its acceptance; the discussions were only rarely characterized by outrage at the events and thereby contributed also to their normality—and to the overcoming of moral inhibitions. As the number of people aware of the crimes increased, the circle of comrades or even the entire society of occupiers became complicit in the crimes and thereby part of the individual responsibility was transferred to the entire society. The Germans in Warsaw and Minsk took on the role of eyewitnesses, accomplices, and perpetrators at the same time because ultimately state-sponsored violence was in their eyes something that was not unusual or reprehensible. Quite the contrary, it demanded recognition: as part of the "suppression of resistance," it even represented a necessity.

The unquestioned and legitimate nature of the violence during the occupation had its legacy and revealed itself again twenty years later during the interrogations by West German investigators,[4] who were confronted with an astonishing indifference by some perpetrators when confronted with their former crimes. Any awareness of possible guilt was expressed neither during the occupation nor in the postwar period. At least in part this confirms the continued operation of the society of occupiers, which stressed discretion and solidarity against those outside the community; also, of course, in light of the possibility of criminal punishment it was hardly to be expected that the occupiers would willingly admit their crimes.

The comparison of the two cities of Warsaw and Minsk reveals only slight differences, but mainly has revealed many basic commonalities in the occupiers and their daily lives. As the largest city occupied by the Wehrmacht in Eastern Europe, Warsaw distinguished itself from Minsk mainly by its greater dimensions. More occupiers were stationed in the Polish capital, and more people were murdered there than in Minsk. The quantity of occupiers resulted also in a qualitatively better range of support services, yet in the extent to which daily life was penetrated by the state, Weißruthenien was no different from the General Government. Service in Warsaw was viewed as comparatively more pleasant than in Minsk: This depended initially on circumstances such as the weather, the image of the city, or the shorter distance from home, but was consolidated decisively by the range of services and supplies on offer, which in Weißruthenien, due to the comparative poverty and the smaller population, was considerably worse than in Warsaw. The Warsaw ghetto with around half a million inhabitants created possibilities of profiteering from the desperate needs of the locals, possibilities that were not available farther east. In Warsaw the occupiers could plunder more and wealthier Jews than in Minsk. Another decisive factor that made life in Minsk more difficult for the occupiers was the security situation there. A noticeable level of resistance activity, which caused the occupiers to fear for their lives, emerged in Warsaw only at the start of 1943. In the area around Minsk, by contrast, the partisans began responding to Nazi policy with counter-violence at the end of 1941; in the city itself it was mainly the Communist Party that conducted underground activities. Thus while the Germans in the General Government experienced more than three years of relatively peaceful existence, such an existence was not granted to them in certain occupied territories of the Soviet Union.

Numerous other patterns of events described in this study, however, could not only be observed during the German occupation of Minsk and Warsaw: Rivalries between various authorities and institutions also occurred at other times and places. The composition and comradeship of the society of occupiers was similar in almost all German controlled regions of Europe, even when there were no ethnic Germans there. The isolation of the occupiers from the occupied was not so strict in Western Europe, but made an appearance in almost every foreign occupation, as did the attempt to subject the lives of the occupiers as much as possible to norms, or their intention to make material gains. Looking down on the defeated and the more or less strong fear of them also belongs to those things that can be observed elsewhere. Against this the Germans' sense of superiority stemmed from special resentments toward the Eastern Europeans that had already developed to some extent during World War I.

The occupiers' habitus, however, that incorporated the acceptance of violence and also made possible its constant presence, could only come into being under the specific conditions of Nazi rule in Eastern Europe. Its patterns of perception and conduct are not imaginable under other circumstances. Within it were combined universal aspects of every occupation together with conceptions of Eastern Europe and specific local circumstances that achieved their individual character in connection with Nazi ideology and the exercise of power. Only in this manner did the dynamic develop that made the mass murders possible.

The differences between Warsaw and Minsk had little impact on shaping the occupiers' habitus. The conduct of the occupiers, their attitude to the occupied, and especially the role of violence differed only marginally. Nonetheless, it can be established that on account of the concrete threats faced by the occupiers in Minsk, the role of violence was more self-evident there than in Warsaw. On the other hand, due to the enormous ghetto and the two uprisings, the violence attained a spectacular dimension in the Polish capital and additionally was visible for the majority of the soldiers who were on their way to the Eastern Front. It can also be concluded that the solidarity and also the sense of community that lingered even after the war was stronger among the occupiers in Minsk than in Warsaw. The reason for this is the smaller number of occupiers who served in Weißruthenien. The circle of comrades was smaller, and in comparison with Warsaw, a higher proportion was directly involved in the killings, so that the sense of solidarity was even more strongly developed than in the General Government.

It is likely that this tendency would also be confirmed by other case studies. The smaller the place and the fewer the perpetrators, the stronger is the level of inclusion and loyalty within the collective. The converse conclusion, however, is that a society of occupiers with these values and patterns of behavior would not be able to function if too many people participated in it. In this case the discretion and maintenance of secrecy regarding the violence—which, despite its relatively public nature, was limited to a comparatively small circle of those directly involved—could no longer have been guaranteed. Thereby the violence that in the East was so commonplace and also viewed as legitimate would have lost precisely these key attributes.

The specific details of German occupation in Warsaw and Minsk clarify the contrast to German rule in Northern and Western Europe. As opposed to the Slavs and Jews, the French or Dutch, for example, were not viewed as primitive subhumans, and the Nazis also did not count them as enemies on the basis of their race. Racial barriers imposed by the state existed to a much lesser extent, as did language difficulties. Since French culture in many respects was perceived to be at least equal to its German counterpart, isolation from the locals was by no means as strict, and a self-exclusion by the occupiers, as could certainly be observed in Warsaw or Minsk, hardly took place in Paris. The life of Germans in Eastern Europe contrasted starkly with that in the West, as is shown clearly by the significance of violence for the exercise of German authority: the excessive brutality and mass murders visible in Minsk or Warsaw did not occur in the large cities of Northern and Western Europe. The reason that this took place in the East, however, lay on the one hand in the political-ideological aims, and on the other—to a considerable extent—in the self-perception that the occupiers developed on the basis of their experiences on the spot. The experience of daily life there was a necessary and sufficient precondition for violence to become a completely acceptable mode of behavior toward one's fellow man.

Notes

1. The core elements are summarized in this way by Steber and Gotto, *Volksgemeinschaft*.
2. Lehnstaedt, "Volksdeutsche," p. 451.
3. The state of the debate is documented in Steber and Gotto, *Volksgemeinschaft*.
4. On the memory of the occupation from the Polish perspective, see Tucker, *Remembering Occupied Warsaw*.

BIBLIOGRAPHY

Archival Sources

1. Archiwum Akt Nowych, Warschau—AAN

T 501/580	Microfilm copies (T-Series, US-NARA)
111	Regierung des Generalgouvernements
113	Werbestelle des Generalgouvernements in Berlin
116	NSDAP—Arbeitsbereich GG

2. Archiwum Państwowe m.st. Warszawy—APW

48	Amt des Gouverneurs des Distrikts Warschau. Der Kommissar für den jüdischen Wohnbezirk
49	Amt des Gouverneurs des Distrikts Warschau, SSPF
449	Gesundheitskammer Warschau
484	Wehrüberwachungsamt Warschau
482	Amt des Gouverneurs des Distrikts Warschau
485	Stadthauptmannschaft Warschau
486	Kreishauptmannschaft Warschau-Land
496	Hauptgruppe Gewerbliche Wirtschaft und Verkehr in der Distriktkammer für die Gesamtwirtschaft in Warschau
498	Der deutsche Kommissar der Sozialversicherungskasse Warschau
643	Sondergericht Warschau
1040	Polizeipräsident Warschau
1207	Deutsches Gericht Warschau
1357	NSDAP Warschau-Land
1393	Deutsche Handelskammer für Polen
1419	Landwirtschaftliche Zentralstelle, Distriktstelle Warschau
1601	Staatsanwaltschaft bei dem Sondergericht Warschau
1705-II	Stadtkommandantur Warschau 1939
2421	Fotografische Sammlung Johannes Hennig

3. Instytut Pamięci Narodowej, Warschau—IPN

Zbiór fotografi skrzynka	Fotografische Sammlung
PG	Generalstaatsanwaltschaft
Sąd Wojewódzki	Wojewodschaftsgericht Warschau
NTN	Oberster Volksgerichtshof
101	Amt des Distrikts Warschau
106	KdS Warschau
120	NSDAP im Distrikt Warschau
357	Kommandeur der Gendarmerie im Distrikt Warschau
694	Stadthauptmann Warschau
700	Sondergericht Warschau

4. Российский Государственный Военный Архив [Russan State Military Archive], Moskow—RGVA

504	Befehlshaber der Sicherheitspolizei Ostland in Riga
720	Reichsministerium des Innern
1323	Polizei in den besetzten Gebieten
1358	Reichsministerium für die besetzten Ostgebiete
1401	Einsatzstab Reichsleiter Rosenberg
1458	Reichswirtschaftsministerium

5. Bundesarchiv Berlin—BAB

NS 7	SS- und Polizeigerichtsbarkeit
NS 19	Reichsführer SS
NS 30	Einsatzstab Reichsleiter Rosenberg
R 6	Reichsministerium für die besetzten Ostgebiete
R 19	Hauptamt Ordnungspolizei
R 43 II	Neue Reichskanzlei
R 49	Reichskommissar für die Festigung des deutschen Volkstums
R 52	Regierung des Generalgouvernements
R 58	Reichssicherheitshauptamt
R 59	Volksdeutsche Mittelstelle
R 70 Polen	Polizeidienststellen in Polen
R 70 SU	Polizeidienststellen in der Sowjetunion
R 90	Reichskommissar Ostland
R 91	Generalkommissar Weißruthenien
R 93	Gebietskommissare im RKO
R 102 I-IV	Distriktverwaltungen im Generalgouvernement
R 124	Eisenbahnverwaltung in den besetzten Gebieten
R 1501	Reichsinnenministerium
R 3101	Reichswirtschaftsministerium
R 4317	Generalverkehrsdirektion Osten, Warschau

6. Bundesarchiv-Außenstelle Ludwigsburg—BAL

B 162 Nachkriegsermittlungen wegen NS-Verbrechen

7. Bundesarchiv-Lastenausgleichsarchiv, Bayreuth—BALAA

Ost-Dok. 8 Bestand Ost-Dokumentation 8
Ost-Dok. 13 Bestand Ost-Dokumentation 13

8. Bundesarchiv-Militärarchiv, Freiburg—BAMA

RH 26 Infanteriedivisionen
RH 53-23 Wehrkreiskommando Generalgouvernement

9. Bundesarchiv-Zwischenarchiv, Berlin-Hoppegarten—BAZAH

R 5 Reichsverkehrsministerium
R 48 Reichspost

10. Bayerisches Staatsarchiv, München—BayStA

Staatsanwalt-
schaften Bestand Staatsanwaltschaften

11. Bayerisches Kriegsarchiv, München—Kriegsarchiv

Nachlass Carl von Andrian

12. Deutsches Tagebucharchiv, Emmendingen—DTA

141 Tagebuch Max Rohwerder
280 Tagebuch Franz Jonas
884 Tagebuch Michael Ritter
983 Erinnerungen Werner Kleine

13. Bibliothek für Zeitgeschichte, Stuttgart—BfZg

Sammlung
Sterz Verschiedene Feldpostbriefe

14. Der Bundesbeauftragte für die Unterlagen des Staatssicherheitsdienstes der ehemaligen Deutschen Demokratischen Republik, Berlin—BStU

MfS-HA
XX Hauptabteilung XX: Materialsammlung zur NS-Zeit
ZUV Zentrale Untersuchungsvorgänge

15. Archiv des Instituts für Zeitgeschichte, München—IfZA

Fb Drucksachen
G Gerichtsserien
MA Mikrofilm-Sammlung
Nbg. Dokumente der Nürnberger Prozesse

16. Staatsarchiv Münster—StAM

Polizeipräsidien   Sammlung Primavesi zur deutschen Polizei im NS

17. Villa ten Hompel, Münster—VtH

18	Depositum Klaus Strodthoff
40	Depositum Stefan Klemp
230	Depositum Bernd Konrad
239+239a	Depositum Giersiepen

18. Zentralarchiv zur Erforschung der Geschichte der Juden in Deutschland, Heidelberg—ZAH

NL Joseph Wulf   Nachlass Joseph Wulf

19. Archiv der Österreichischen Gesellschaft für Zeitgeschichte, Wien—ÖGZA

NL 93   Nachlass Max Bischof

20. Yad Vashem, Jerusalem—YV

M 41	Copies from Belorussian archives
O 51	Nazi Trials

21. Privatsammlung (Private Collection) Dr. Gerhard Lieschke, Hamburg

Briefe und Tagebucheinträge von Dr. Wolfgang Lieschke

Periodicals

Amtlicher Anzeiger des Reichskommissars für das Ostland
Amtlicher Anzeiger für das Generalgouvernement
Amtliches Mitteilungsblatt des Stadthauptmanns in Warschau
Amtliches Nachrichtenblatt der Generaldirektion der Ostbahn
Amtsblatt der Ostbahndirektion Warschau
Amtsblatt der Reichsverkehrsdirektion Minsk
Amtsblatt des Chefs des Distrikts Warschau
Amtsblatt des Generalkommissars in Minsk
Amtsblatt des Reichsministers für die besetzten Ostgebiete
Anordnungsblatt des Leiters der Deutschen Post Osten
Brücke zur Heimat
Das Generalgouvernement
Das Vorfeld
Deutsche Gemeinschaft
Deutsche Post Osten
Deutsche Zeitung im Ostland
Die Burg

Haushalt des Reichskommissars für das Ostland
Haushaltsplan des Generalgouvernements
Krakauer Zeitung
Ministerialblatt der inneren Verwaltung
Minsker Zeitung
Mitteilungsblatt der Stadt Warschau
Mitteilungsblatt des Reichskommissars für das Ostland
Ostland
Ostpolitische Informationen des Reichsministers für die besetzten Ostgebiete
Propaganda-Dienst. Informationsorgan für die Propaganda-Dienststelle im Osten
Reichsgesetzblatt
Reichshaushaltsplan
Statistische Berichte für das Ostland
Verordnungsblatt der NSDAP, Arbeitsbereich Generalgouvernement
Verordnungsblatt des Generalgouverneurs für die besetzten polnischen Gebiete
Verordnungsblatt des Reichskommissars für das Ostland
Verordnungsblatt des Reichsministers für die besetzten Ostgebiete
Verordnungsblatt für das Generalgouvernement
Verordnungsblatt für die besetzten Gebiete (Militärbefehlshaber Polen)
Warschauer Kulturblätter
Warschauer Zeitung

Published Sources

Bibliography

Adamska, Jolanta. "Organizacja niemieckich urzędów nadzorczych w Warszawie w latach 1939–1944." In *Warszawa—Lat wojny i okupacji 1939–1944*, vol. 4, edited by Instytut Historii Polskiej Akademii Nauk, 365–384. Warsaw: Państwowe Wydawnictwo Naukowe, 1974.

Adler, Hans Günther. *Der verwaltete Mensch: Studien zur Deportation der Juden aus Deutschland.* Tübingen: Mohr, 1974.

Alberti, Michael. *Die Verfolgung und Vernichtung der Juden im Reichsgau Wartheland 1939–1945.* Wiesbaden: Harrassowitz, 2006.

Albrecht, Karl I. *Sie aber werden die Welt zerstören.* Munich: Herbert Neuner, 1954.

Alvensleben, Udo von, *Lauter Abschiede: Tagebuch im Kriege*, edited by Harald von Koenigswald. Frankfurt: Ullstein, 1971.

Aly, Götz. *Hitlers Volksstaat: Raub, Rassenkrieg und nationaler Sozialismus.* Frankfurt: Fischer, 2005.

Aly, Götz, and Susanne Heim. *Vordenker der Vernichtung: Auschwitz und die deutschen Pläne für eine neue europäische Ordnung.* Hamburg: Hoffmann und Campe, 1991.

Angrick, Andrej, Martina Voigt, Silke Ammerschubert, Peter Klein, Christa Alheit, and Michael Tycher. "'Da hätte man schon ein Tagebuch führen müssen'. Das Polizeibataillon 322 und die Judenmorde im Bereich der Heeresgruppe Mitte während des Sommers und Herbstes 1941. Mit einer Auseinandersetzung über die rechtlichen Konsequenzen." In *Die Normalität des Verbrechens: Bilanz und Perspektiven der Forschung zu den nationalsozialistischen Gewaltverbrechen. Festschrift für Wolfgang Scheffler zum 65. Geburtstag*, edited by Wolfgang Scheffler, Helge Grabitz, Klaus Bästlein, Johannes Tuchel, 325–385. Berlin: Edition Hentrich, 1994.

Arani, Miriam Y. "Aus den Augen, in dem Sinn? Publizierte Fotografien aus dem besetzten Warschau 1939 bis 1945." *Fotogeschichte* 65 and 66 (1997): 33–58 and 33–50.

Bald, Detlef. *Die 'Weiße Rose': Von der Front in den Widerstand*. Berlin: Aufbau-Taschenbuch, 2004.

Banken, Ralf. "National Socialist Plundering of Precious Metals, 1933–1945. The Role of Degussa and the Case of Poland." http://repositories.cdlib.org/ies/060402.

Bartoszewski, Władysław. *Der Todesring um Warschau 1939–1944*. Warsaw: Interpress, 1968.

Bartov, Omer. *Hitlers Wehrmacht: Soldaten, Fanatismus und die Brutalisierung des Krieges*. Hamburg: Rowohlt-Taschenbuch, 1999.

Bartov, Omer. "Killing Space. The Final Solution as Population Policy." In *Germany's War and the Holocaust: Disputed Histories*, edited by Omer Bartov, 79–98. Ithaca, NY: Cornell University Press, 2003.

Bartov, Omer, and Phyllis Mack, eds. *In God's Name: Genocide and Religion in the Twentieth Century*. New York: Berghahn, 2001.

Bauer, Yehuda. *Rethinking the Holocaust*. New Haven, CT: Yale University Press, 2001.

Beck, Birgit. *Wehrmacht und sexuelle Gewalt: Sexualverbrechen vor deutschen Militärgerichten 1939–1945*. Paderborn: Schöningh, 2004.

Becker, Maximilian. *Mitstreiter im Volkstumskampf: Deutsche Justiz in den eingegliederten Ostgebieten 1939–1945*. Munich: De Gruyter, 2014.

Benz, Wolfgang, Konrad Kwiet, and Jürgen Matthäus, eds. *Einsatz im 'Reichskommissariat Ostland': Dokumente zum Völkermord im Baltikum und in Weissrussland, 1941–1944*. Berlin: Metropol, 1998.

Berenstein, Tatiana. "Praca przymusowa Żydów w Warszawie w czasie okupacji hitlerowskiej." *Biuletyn Żydowskiego Instytutu Historycznego* 45/46 (1963): 42–93.

Berenstein, Tatiana. "Waldemar Schön—organizator getta w Warszawie." *Biuletyn Żydowskiego Instytutu Historycznego* 49 (1964): 85–90.

Berenstein, Tatiana, and Adam Rutkowski, "Niemiecka administracja wojskowa na okupowanych ziemiach polskich (1 września—25 października 1939 r.)." *Najnowsze Dzieje Polski 1939–1945. Materiały i studia z okresu II wojny światowej* 6 (1962): 45–57.

Berg, Bohan, ed. *Raporty Ludwiga Fischera Gubernatora Dystryktu Warzsawskiego 1939–1944*. Warsaw: Książka i Wiedza, 1987.

Berg, Nicolas. *Der Holocaust und die westdeutschen Historiker: Erforschung und Erinnerung*. Göttingen: Wallstein, 2003.

Bergen, Doris L. "The Nazi Concept of Volksdeutsche and the Exacerbation of Anti-Semitism in Eastern Europe 1939–45." *Journal of Contemporary History* 29 (1994): 569–582.
Bergen, Doris L. "The Volksdeutschen of Eastern Europe, World War II, and the Holocaust. Constructed Ethnicity, Real Genocide." *Yearbook of European Studies* 13 (1999): 70–93.
Bergen, Doris L. "Between God and Hitler. German Military Chaplains and the Crimes of the Third Reich." In *In God's Name: Genocide and Religion in the Twentieth Century*, edited by Omer Bartov and Phyllis Mack, 123–138. New York: Berghahn, 2001.
Biernacki, Stanisław. "Organizacja hitlerowskiego aparatu policyjnego w Warszawie w pierwszym roku okupacji." *Biuletyn Głównej Komisji Badania Zbrodni Hitlerowskich w Polsce* 31 (1982): 289–294.
Birn, Ruth Bettina. *Die höheren SS- und Polizeiführer: Himmlers Vertreter im Reich und in den besetzten Gebieten*. Düsseldorf: Droste, 1986.
Birn, Ruth Bettina. *Die Sicherheitspolizei in Estland 1941–1944: Eine Studie zur Kollaboration im Osten*. Paderborn: Schöningh, 2006.
Blass, Thomas. "Psychological Perspectives on the Perpetrators of the Holocaust. The Role of Situational Pressures, Personal Dispositions, and Their Interactions." *Holocaust and Genocide Studies* 7 (1993): 30–50.
Blättler, Franz. *Warschau 1942: Tatsachenbericht eines Motorfahrers der zweiten schweizerischen Ärztemission 1942 in Warschau*. Zurich: Micha, 1945.
Boberach, Heinz, ed. *Meldungen aus dem Reich 1938–1945: Die geheimen Lageberichte des Sicherheitsdienstes der SS*, 17 vols. Herrsching: Pawlak, 1984.
Boelcke, Willi A. "Der deutsche Überfall auf die Sowjetunion im Spiegel der Verwaltungsgeschichte." *Archivmitteilungen* 7 (1957): 141–150.
Böhler, Jochen. *Auftakt zum Vernichtungskrieg: Die Wehrmacht in Polen 1939*. Frankfurt: Fischer, 2006.
Böhler, Jochen, and Stephan Lehnstaedt, eds. *Gewalt und Alltag im besetzten Polen 1939–1945*. Osnabrück: fibre, 2012.
Borodziej, Włodzimierz. *Terror und Politik: Die deutsche Polizei und die polnische Widerstandsbewegung im Generalgouvernement 1939–1944*. Mainz: Philipp von Zabern, 1999.
Borodziej, Włodzimierz. *Der Warschauer Aufstand 1944*. Frankfurt: Fischer, 2001.
Bourdieu, Pierre. *Entwurf einer Theorie der Praxis: Auf der ethnologischen Grundlage der kabylischen Gesellschaft*. Frankfurt: Suhrkamp, 1976.
Bourdieu, Pierre. *Sozialer Sinn: Kritik der theoretischen Vernunft*. Frankfurt: Suhrkamp, 1987.
Bourdieu, Pierre. *Rede und Antwort*. Frankfurt: Suhrkamp, 1992.
Brakel, Alexander. "'Das allergefährlichste ist die Wut der Bauern'. Die Versorgung der Partisanen und ihr Verhältnis zur Zivilbevölkerung. Eine Fallstudie zum Gebiet Baranowicze 1941–1944." *Vierteljahrshefte für Zeitgeschichte* 55 (2007): 393–424.
Brandt, Hans Jürgen ed. *Priester in Uniform: Seelsorger, Ordensleute und Theologen als Soldaten im Zweiten Weltkrieg*. Augsburg: Pattloch, 1994.

Browning, Christopher. "Bürokratie und Massenmord. Was deutsche Verwaltungsbeamte unter 'Endlösung' verstanden." In *Der Weg zur 'Endlösung': Entscheidungen und Täter*, edited by Christopher Browning, 105–125. Bonn: Dietz, 1998.

Browning, Christopher. "Die nationalsozialistische Ghettoisierungspolitik in Polen 1939–1941." In *Der Weg zur 'Endlösung': Entscheidungen und Täter*, edited by Christopher Browning, 37–66. Bonn: Dietz, 1998.

Browning, Christopher R. *Ganz normale Männer: Das Reserve-Polizeibataillon 101 und die 'Endlösung' in Polen.* Reinbek: Rowohlt, 2002.

Buchbender, Ortwin. and Reinhold Sterz, eds. *Das andere Gesicht des Krieges: Deutsche Feldpostbriefe 1939–1945.* Munich: C. H. Beck, 1982.

Bühler, Josef. ed. *Das Generalgouvernement. Seine Verwaltung und seine Wirtschaft: Sammlung von Vorträgen der ersten wissenschaftlichen Vortragsreihe der Verwaltungsakademie des Generalgouvernements.* Krakow: Burgverlag, 1943.

Caumanns, Ute, and Michael G. Esch, "Fleckfieber und Fleckfieberbekämpfung im Warschauer Ghetto und die Tätigkeit der deutschen Gesundheitsverwaltung 1941/42." In *Geschichte der Gesundheitspolitik in Deutschland: Von der Weimarer Republik bis in die Frühgeschichte der 'doppelten Staatsgründung,'* edited by Wolfgang Woelk, Jörg Vögele and Silke Fehlemann, 225–262. Berlin: Duncker & Humblot, 2002.

Cerovic, Masha. "De la paix à la guerre. Les habitants de Minsk face aux violences d'occupation allemandes (juin 1941–février 1942)." *Relations internationales* 126 (2006): 67–79.

Chiari, Bernhard. *Alltag hinter der Front: Besatzung, Kollaboration und Widerstand in Weißrußland 1941–1944.* Düsseldorf: Droste, 1998.

Chiari, Bernhard, ed. *Die polnische Heimatarmee: Geschichte und Mythos der Armia Krajowa seit dem Zweiten Weltkrieg.* Munich: De Gruyter, 2003.

Cohen, Laurie R. *Smolensk under the Nazis: Everyday Life in Occupied Russia.* Rochester, NY: University of Rochester Press, 2013.

Cüppers, Martin. "'[ellipsis]auf eine so saubere und anständige SS-mäßige Art'. Die Waffen-SS in Polen 1939–1941." In *Genesis des Genozids: Polen 1939–1941*, edited by Klaus-Michael Mallmann and Bogdan Musiał, 90–110. Darmstadt: Wissenschaftliche Buchgesellschaft, 2004.

Cüppers, Martin. *Wegbereiter der Shoah: Die Waffen-SS, der Kommandostab Reichsführer-SS und die Judenvernichtung 1939–1945.* Darmstadt: Wissenschaftliche Buchgesellschaft, 2005.

Curilla, Wolfgang. *Die deutsche Ordnungspolizei und der Holocaust im Baltikum und in Weissrussland 1941–1944.* Paderborn: Schöningh, 2006.

Czocher, Anna. *W okupowanym Krakowie. Codzienność mieszkańców miasta 1939–1945.* Gdańsk: Oskar, 2011.

Danker, Uwe. "Die 'Zivilverwaltung' des Reichskommissariats Ostland und der Holocaust. Wahrnehmung, Rolle und 'Verarbeitung'." In *Collaboration and Resistance during the Holocaust: Belarus, Estonia, Latvia, Lithuania*, edited by David Gaunt, 45–76. Bern: Lang, 2004.

Dean, Martin. *Collaboration in the Holocaust: Crimes of the local police in Belorussia and Ukraine, 1941–1944.* London: Macmillan, 2000.
Dean, Martin. *Robbing the Jews: The Confiscation of Jewish Property in the Holocaust, 1933–1945.* Cambridge: Cambridge UP, 2008.
Domańska, Regina. "Policja bezpieczeństwa dystryktu warszawskiego j jej więzienie 'śledcze' Pawiak." *Biuletyn Głównej Komisji Badania Zbrodni Hitlerowskich w Polsce* 28 (1978): 145–229.
Dörner, Bernward. *Die Deutschen und der Holocaust: Was niemand wissen wollte, aber jeder wissen konnte.* Berlin: Propyläen, 2007.
Du Prel, Max. *Das Generalgouvernement.* Würzburg: Konrad Triltsch, 1942.
Dunin-Wąsowicz, Krzysztof. *Warszawa w latach 1939–1945.* Warsaw: Wydawnictwo Naukowe PWN, 1984.
Echternkamp, Jorg. ed. *Die deutsche Kriegsgesellschaft 1939 bis 1945: Erster Halbband. Politisierung, Vernichtung, Überleben.* Munich: Deutsche Verlags-Anstalt, 2004.
Engelhardt, Eugen von. *Weißruthenien. Volk und Land.* Berlin: Volk und Reich, 1943.
Engelking, Barbara. *'Szanowny panie gistapo'. Donosy do władz niemieckich w Warszawie i skolicach w latach 1940–1941.* Warsaw: IFiS PAN, 2003.
Engelking, Barbara, and Jacek Leociak. *The Warsaw Ghetto: A Guide to the Perished City.* Yale: Yale University Press, 2009.
Festinger, Leon. *Theorie der kognitiven Dissonanz.* Bern: Huber, 1978.
Friedländer, Saul. *Kitsch und Tod: Der Widerschein des Nazismus.* Munich: Hanser, 1986.
Friedrich, Klaus-Peter. "Kollaboration und Antisemitismus in Polen unter deutscher Besatzung (1939–1944/45). Zu verdrängten Aspekten eines schwierigen deutsch-polnisch-jüdischen Verhältnisses." *Zeitschrift für Geschichtswissenschaft* 45 (1997): 818–834.
Friedrich, Klaus-Peter. "Publizistische Kollaboration im sog. Generalgouvernement. Personengeschichtliche Aspekte der deutschen Okkupationsherrschaft in Polen (1939–1945)." *Zeitschrift für Ostmitteleuropa-Forschung* 48 (1999): 50–89.
Friedrich, Klaus-Peter. "Rassistische Seuchenprävention als Voraussetzung nationalsozialistischer Vernichtungspolitik. Vom Warschauer 'Seuchensperrgebiet' zu den 'Getto'-Mauern (1939/40)." *Zeitschrift für Geschichtswissenschaft* 53 (2005): 609–636.
Fuks, Marian. ed. *Im Warschauer Getto: Das Tagebuch des Adam Czerniaków 1939–1942.* Munich: C. H. Beck, 1986.
Furber, David Bruce. *Going East: Colonialism and German life in Nazi-occupied Poland.* PhD diss., State University of New York at Buffalo, 2003.
Füssel, Marian. "Die Kunst der Schwachen. Zum Begriff der 'Aneignung' in der Geschichtswissenschaft." *Sozial. Geschichte* 21 (2006): 7–28.
Gajewski, Marian. "Urządzenia Komunale m. st. Warszawy w latach 1939–1944." In *Warszawa—Lat wojny i okupacji 1939–1944*, vol. 3, edited by Instytut

Historii Polskiej Akademii Nauk, 61–98. Warsaw: Państwowe Wydawnictwo Naukowe, 1974.

Gartenschläger, Uwe. *Die Stadt Minsk während der deutschen Besetzung (1941–1944)*. Dortmund: IBB, 2001.

Gauweiler, Otto, ed. *Berichte der Abteilung Innere Verwaltung im Amt des Chefs des Distrikts Warschau.: Bericht I: Die Abwicklung von ehem. polnischen Ministerien. Bericht II: Die Innere Verwaltung im Distrikt Warschau*. Warsaw: Staatsdruckerei, 1940.

Gerlach, Christian. *Kalkulierte Morde: Die deutsche Wirtschafts- und Vernichtungspolitik in Weißrußland 1941 bis 1944*. Hamburg: Hamburger Edition, 2000.

Gerlach, Christian, ed. *Krieg, Ernährung, Völkermord: Deutsche Vernichtungspolitik im Zweiten Weltkrieg*. Zurich: Pendo, 2001.

Gerlach, Christian. "Kontextualisierung der Aktionen eines Mordkommandos—die Einsatzgruppe B." In *Täter im Vernichtungskrieg: Der Überfall auf die Sowjetunion und der Völkermord an den Juden*, edited by Wolf Kaiser, 85–95. Berlin: Propyläen, 2002.

Gerlach, Christian. "Extremely Violent Societies. An Alternative to the Concept of Genocide." *Journal of Genocide Research* 8 (2006): 455–471.

Geschichtswerkstatt, Berliner. ed. *Alltagskultur, Subjektivität und Geschichte: Zur Theorie und Praxis von Alltagsgeschichte*. Munster: Verlag Westfälisches Dampfboot, 1994.

Getter, Marek. "Zarys organizacji policji niemieckiej w Warszawie i dystrykcie warszawskim w latach 1939–1945." *Rocznik Warszawski* 6 (1967): 249–271.

Getter, Marek. "Środowisko niemieckie w Warszawie w latach 1939–1944." In *Warszawa—Lat wojny i okupacji 1939–1944*, vol. 3, edited by Instytut Historii Polskiej Akademii Nauk, 223–240. Warsaw: Państwowe Wydawnictwo Naukowe, 1974.

Gollert, Friedrich. *Zwei Jahre Aufbauarbeit im Distrikt Warschau*. Krakow: Buchverlag Deutscher Osten, 1941.

Gollert, Friedrich. *Warschau unter deutscher Herrschaft*. Krakow: Burgverlag, 1942.

Goschler, Constantin. and Philipp Ther, eds. *Raub und Restitution: 'Arisierung' und Rückerstattung des jüdischen Eigentums in Europa*. Frankfurt: Fischer, 2003.

Gottwaldt, Alfred Bernd, and Diana Schulle. *Die 'Judendeportationen' aus dem Deutschen Reich 1941–1945*. Wiesbaden: Marix, 2005.

Grabitz, Helge, and Wolfgang Scheffler. *Letzte Spuren: Ghetto Warschau, SS-Arbeitslager Trawniki, Aktion Erntefest: Fotos und Dokumente über Opfer des Endlösungswahns im Spiegel der historischen Ereignisse*. Berlin: Edition Hentrich, 1988.

Grabowski, Jan. *'Ja tego Żyda znam!': Szantażowanie Żydów w Warszawie, 1939–1943*. Warsaw: IFiS PAN, 2004.

Grundmann, Karl. *Führer durch Warschau*. Krakow: Buchverlag Deutscher Osten, 1942.

Gutman, Israel. *The Jews of Warsaw, 1939–1943: Ghetto, Underground, Revolt*. Bloomington: Indiana University Press, 1982.

Gutschow, Niels, and Barbara Klain. *Vernichtung und Utopie: Stadtplanung Warschau 1939–1945*. Hamburg: Junius, 1995.
Hagen, Wilhelm. *Auftrag und Wirklichkeit: Sozialarzt im 20. Jahrhundert*. Munich: Banaschewski, 1978.
Hahn, Karl Eugen. *Eisenbahner in Krieg und Frieden. Ein Lebensschicksal*. Frankfurt: Lanzenreiter, 1954.
Hardtwig, Wolfgang. "Alltagsgeschichte heute. Eine kritische Bilanz." In *Sozialgeschichte, Alltagsgeschichte, Mikro-Historie: Eine Diskussion*, edited by Winfried Schulze, 19–32. Göttingen: Vandenhoeck & Ruprecht, 1994.
Harvey, Elizabeth. *Women and the Nazi East: Agents and Witnesses of Germanization*. New Haven, CT: Yale University Press, 2003.
Hecker, Clara. "Deutsche Juden im Minsker Ghetto." *Zeitschrift für Geschichtswissenschaft* 56 (2008): 823–843.
Heiber, Helm. "Aus den Akten des Gauleiters Kube." *Vierteljahrshefte für Zeitgeschichte* 4 (1956): 65–92.
Heineman, Elizabeth D. *What Difference Does a Husband Make?: Women and Marital Status in Nazi and Postwar Germany*. Berkeley: University of California Press, 1999.
Herbert, Ulrich. "'Generation der Sachlichkeit': Die völkische Studentenbewegung der frühen zwanziger Jahre in Deutschland." In *Arbeit, Volkstum, Weltanschauung: Über Fremde und Deutsche im 20. Jahrhundert*, edited by Ulrich Herbert, 31–58. Frankfurt: Fischer, 1995.
Herbert, Ulrich. "Vernichtungspolitik. Neue Antworten und Fragen zur Geschichte des 'Holocaust'." In *Nationalsozialistische Vernichtungspolitik 1939–1945: Neue Forschungen und Kontroversen*, edited by Ulrich Herbert, 9–66. Frankfurt: Fischer, 2001.
Herbert, Ulrich. "Drei politische Generationen im 20. Jahrhundert." In *Generationalität und Lebensgeschichte im 20. Jahrhundert*, edited by Ulrich Herbert, 95–114. Munich: Oldenbourg, 2003.
Heydecker, Joe Julius. *Das Warschauer Getto: Foto-Dokumente eines deutschen Soldaten aus dem Jahr 1941*. Munich: dtv, 1983.
Heydemann, Günther, and Heinrich Oberreuter, eds. *Diktaturen in Deutschland, Vergleichsaspekte: Strukturen, Institutionen und Verhaltensweisen*. Bonn: Bundeszentrale für Politische Bildung, 2003.
Hilberg, Raul. *Die Quellen des Holocaust: Entschlüsseln und interpretieren*. Frankfurt: Fischer, 2009.
Hilberg, Raul. *Täter, Opfer, Zuschauer: Die Vernichtung der Juden 1933–1945*. Frankfurt: Fischer, 2011.
Hillebrandt, Frank, and Jörg Ebrecht. "Einleitung. Konturen einer soziologischen Theorie der Praxis." In *Bourdieus Theorie der Praxis: Erklärungskraft—Anwendung—Perspektiven*, edited by Frank Hillebrandt and Jörg Ebrecht, 7–18. Wiesbaden: Westdeutscher Verlag, 2004.
Hoffmann-Curtius, Kathrin. "Trophäen und Amulette: Die Wehrmachts- und SS-Verbrechen in den Brieftaschen der Soldaten." *Fotogeschichte*, 20 (2000): 63–76.

Hosenfeld, Wilm. '*Ich versuche jeden zu retten*': *Das Leben eines deutschen Offiziers in Briefen und Tagebüchern.* Munich: Deutsche Verlags-Anstalt, 2004.

Hürter, Johannes, ed. *Ein deutscher General an der Ostfront. Die Briefe und Tagebücher des Gotthard Heinrici 1941/42.* Erfurt: Sutton, 2001.

Hürter, Johannes. *Hitlers Heerführer: Die deutschen Oberbefehlshaber im Krieg gegen die Sowjetunion 1941/42.* Munich: Oldenbourg, 2006.

Jackiewicz, Danuta, and Eugeniusz Cezary Król, *Im Objektiv des Feindes: Die deutschen Bildberichterstatter im besetzten Warschau 1939–1945.* Warsaw: Oficyna Wydawnicza RYTM, 2008.

Jacobmeyer, Wolfgang. "Die polnische Widerstandsbewegung im Generalgouvernement und ihre Beurteilung durch deutsche Dienststellen." *Vierteljahrshefte für Zeitgeschichte* 25 (1977): 658–681.

Jacobsen, Hans-Adolf, ed. *1939–1945. Der Zweite Weltkrieg in Chronik und Dokumenten.* Darmstadt: Wehr und Wissen, 1959.

Jäger, Herbert. *Verbrechen unter totalitärer Herrschaft: Studien zur nationalsozialistischen Gewaltkriminalität.* Frankfurt: Suhrkamp, 1997.

Janning, Frank. "Habitus und Organisation. Ertrag der Bourdieuschen Problemformulierungen und alternative Konzeptualisierungsvorschläge." In *Bourdieus Theorie der Praxis: Erklärungskraft—Anwendung—Perspektiven*, edited by Frank Hillebrandt and Jörg Ebrecht, 97–126. Wiesbaden: Westdeutscher Verlag, 2004.

Jansen, Christian, and Arno Weckbecker. *Der "Volksdeutsche Selbstschutz" in Polen 1939/40.* Munich: Oldenbourg, 1992.

Janusz, Grzegorz. "Die rechtlichen Regelungen Polens zum Status der deutschen Bevölkerung in den Jahren 1938 bis 1950." In *Deutschsprachige Minderheiten 1945: Ein europäischer Vergleich*, edited by Manfred Kittel, Horst Möller, Jirí Pešek, and Oldrich Tuma, 131–251. Munich: Oldenbourg, 2007.

Jaworski, Rudolf, and Florian Peters. *Alltagsperspektiven im besetzten Warschau: Fotografien eines deutschen Postbeamten (1939–1944).* Marburg: Verlag Herder-Institut, 2013.

Jersak, Tobias. "Entscheidungen zu Mord und Lüge. Die deutsche Kriegsgesellschaft und der Holocaust." In *Die deutsche Kriegsgesellschaft 1939 bis 1945: Erster Halbband. Politisierung, Vernichtung, Überleben*, edited by Jorg Echternkamp, 273–355. Munich: Deutsche Verlags-Anstalt, 2004.

Jockheck, Lars. "'Banditen'—'Terroristen'—'Agenten'—'Opfer'. Der polnische Widerstand und die Heimatarmee in der Presse-Propaganda des 'Generalgouvernements'." In *Die polnische Heimatarmee: Geschichte und Mythos der Armia Krajowa seit dem Zweiten Weltkrieg*, edited by Bernhard Chiari, 431–472. Munich: De Gruyter, 2003.

Jockheck, Lars. *Propaganda im Generalgouvernement: Die NS-Besatzungspresse für Deutsche und Polen 1939–1945.* Osnabrück: fibre, 2006.

Jureit, Ulrike. "Motive—Mentalitäten—Handlungsspielräume. Theoretische Anmerkungen zu Handlungsoptionen von Soldaten." In *Verbrechen der Wehrmacht: Bilanz einer Debatte*, edited by Christian Hartmann, Johannes Hürter and Ulrike Jureit, 163–170, 215–216. Munich: Beck, 2005.

Jureit, Ulrike. *Generationenforschung*. Göttingen: Vandenhoeck & Ruprecht, 2006.
Kay, Alex J. *Exploitation, Resettlement, Mass Murder: Political and Economic Planning for German Occupation Policy in the Soviet Union, 1940–1941*. New York: Berghahn Books, 2006.
Kettenacker, Lothar. "Die Chefs der Zivilverwaltung im Zweiten Weltkrieg." In *Verwaltung kontra Menschenführung im Staate Hitlers: Studien zum politisch-administrativen System*, edited by Dieter Rebentisch and Karl Teppe, 396–417. Göttingen: Vandenhoeck & Ruprecht, 1986.
Kittel, Manfred, Horst Möller, Jirí Pešek and Oldrich Tuma, eds. *Deutschsprachige Minderheiten 1945: Ein europäischer Vergleich*. Munich: De Gruyter, 2007.
Klee, Ernst, Willi Dreßen and Volker Rieß, eds. *'Schöne Zeiten'. Judenmord aus der Sicht der Täter und Gaffer*. Frankfurt: Fischer, 1988.
Klein, Peter. *Die Einsatzgruppen in der besetzten Sowjetunion, 1941/42: Die Tätigkeits- und Lageberichte des Chefs der Sicherheitspolizei und des SD*. Berlin: Edition Hentrich, 1997.
Klein, Peter. "Curt von Gottberg—Siedlungsfunktionär und Massenmörder." In *Karrieren der Gewalt: Nationalsozialistische Täterbiographien, vol. 2: Veröffentlichungen der Forschungsstelle Ludwigsburg der Universität Stuttgart*, edited by Klaus-Michael Mallmann and Gerhard Paul, 95–103. Darmstadt: Wissenschaftliche Buchgesellschaft, 2004.
Klemp, Stefan. *'Nicht ermittelt': Polizeibataillone und die Nachkriegsjustiz ; ein Handbuch*. Munster: Klartext, 2005.
Kleßmann, Christoph. *Die Selbstbehauptung einer Nation: Nationalsozialistische Kulturpolitik und polnische Widerstandsbewegung im Generalgouvernement 1939–1945*. Düsseldorf: Bertelsmann, 1971.
Kohl, Paul. *'Ich wundere mich, daß ich noch lebe': Sowjetische Überlebende berichten*. Gütersloh: Guetersloher Verlagshaus, 1990.
Kohl, Paul. *Das Vernichtungslager Trostenez: Augenzeugenberichte und Dokumente*. Dortmund: Internationales Bildungs- u. Begegnungswerk, 2003.
Kohl, Paul. "Verbrannte Erde—verbrannte Menschen. 2. Juli 1944: Die 'Beschleunigte Räumung' von Minsk." In *Schlüsseljahr 1944*, edited by Peter März, 163–172. Munich: Bayerische Landeszentrale für politische Bildungsarbeit, 2007.
Kołtunowski, Piotr. *Strategia propagandy Hitlerowskie w Generalnym Gubernatostwie na podstawie 'Krakauer Zeitung' (1939–1945)*. Lublin: Wydawnictwo UMCS, 1990.
Koselleck, Reinhart. "Zur historisch-politischen Semantik asymmetrischer Gegenbegriffe." In *Vergangene Zukunft: Zur Semantik geschichtlicher Zeiten: Theorie*, edited by Reinhart Koselleck, 211–259. Frankfurt: Suhrkamp, 1979.
Krannhals, Hanns von. *Der Warschauer Aufstand 1944*. Frankfurt: Bernard & Graefe Verlag für Wehrwesen, 1962.
Krausnick, Helmut. and Hans-Heinrich Wilhelm, *Die Truppe des Weltanschauungskrieges: D. Einsatzgruppen d. Sicherheitspolizei und des SD 1938–1942*. Stuttgart: DVA, 1981.

Kühne, Thomas. *Kameradschaft: Die Soldaten des nationalsozialistischen Krieges und das 20. Jahrhundert*. Göttingen: Vandenhoeck & Ruprecht, 2006.
Kulski, Julian. *Zarząd Miejski Warszawy 1939–1944*. Warsaw: Państwowe Wydawnictwo Naukowe, 1964.
Kunert, Andrzej Krzysztof. "Solica Wolności: Refleksje nad stanem i potrzebami historiografii dziejów warszawy 1939–1945." *Rocznik Warszawski* 32 (2004): 47–71.
Kur, Tadeusz. *Sprawiedliwość pobłażliwa: Proces kata Warszawy Ludwiga Hahna w Hamburgu*. Warsaw: Wydawnictwo Ministerstwo Obrony Narodowej, 1975.
Landwehr, Gordian. "So sah ich sie sterben." In *Priester in Uniform: Seelsorger, Ordensleute und Theologen als Soldaten im Zweiten Weltkrieg*, edited by Hans Jürgen Brandt, 339–354. Augsburg: Pattloch, 1994.
Latzel, Klaus. *Deutsche Soldaten—nationalsozialistischer Krieg?: Kriegserlebnis—Kriegserfahrung 1939–1945*. Paderborn: Schöningh, 1998.
Latzel, Klaus. "Feldpostbriefe: Überlegungen zur Aussagekraft einer Quelle." In *Verbrechen der Wehrmacht: Bilanz einer Debatte*, edited by Christian Hartmann, Johannes Hürter and Ulrike Jureit, 171–181, 216–219. Munich: Beck, 2005.
Lehnstaedt, Stephan. "'Ostnieten' oder Vernichtungsexperten? Die Auswahl deutscher Staatsdiener für den Einsatz im Generalgouvernement Polen 1939–1944." *Zeitschrift für Geschichtswissenschaft* 53 (2007): 701–721.
Lehnstaedt, Stephan. "Volksdeutsche in Tschenstochau: Nationalsozialistische Germanisierungspolitik für Täter, Profiteure und Zuschauer des Holocaust." *Zeitschrift für Ostmitteleuropa-Forschung*, 57 (2008): 425–452.
Lehnstaedt, Stephan. "Deutsche in Warschau: Das Alltagsleben der Besatzer 1939–1944." In *Gewalt und Alltag im besetzten Polen 1939–1945*, edited by Jochen Böhler and Stephan Lehnstaedt, 205–228. Osnabrück: fibre, 2012.
Lehnstaedt, Stephan, and Jochen Böhler, eds. *Die Berichte der Einsatzgruppen aus Polen 1939: Vollständige Edition*. Berlin: Metropol, 2013.
Leide, Henry. *NS-Verbrecher und Staatssicherheit: Die geheime Vergangenheitspolitik der DDR*. Göttingen: Vandenhoeck & Ruprecht, 2005.
Leist, Ludwig. ed. *Bericht über die Verwaltung der Stadt Warschau umfassend die Zeit vom 2. Oktober 1939 bis 31. März 1942*. Warsaw: Staatsdruckerei, 1942.
Leszczyński, Kazimierz. "Dziennik wojenny batalionu policji 322: Opracowanie i tłumaczenie dokumentu." *Biuletyn Głównej Komisji Badania Zbrodni Hitlerowskich w Polsce* 17 (1967): 170–232.
Lieb, Peter. "Täter aus Überzeugung? Oberst Carl von Andrian und die Judenmorde der 707. Infanteriedivision 1941/42." *Vierteljahrshefte für Zeitgeschichte* 50 (2002): 523–558.
Lieb, Peter. *Konventioneller Krieg oder NS-Weltanschauungskrieg? Kriegführung und Partisanenbekämpfung in Frankreich 1943/44*. Munich: Oldenbourg, 2007.
Longerich, Peter. *Politik der Vernichtung: Eine Gesamtdarstellung der nationalsozialistischen Judenverfolgung*. Munich: Piper, 1998.
Longerich, Peter. *'Davon haben wir nichts gewusst'! Die Deutschen und die Judenverfolgung 1933–1945*. Munich: Siedler, 2006.

Longerich, Peter. "Tendenzen und Perspektiven der Täterforschung." *Aus Politik und Zeitgeschichte* 14–15 (2007): 3–7.
Loose, Ingo. *Kredite für NS-Verbrechen: Die deutschen Kreditinstitute in Polen und die Ausraubung der polnischen und jüdischen Bevölkerung 1939–1945.* Munich: Oldenbourg, 2007.
Lüdtke, Alf, ed. *Alltagsgeschichte: Zur Rekonstruktion historischer Erfahrungen und Lebensweisen.* Frankfurt: Campus, 1989.
Lüdtke, Alf. "Einleitung: Was ist und wer treibt Alltagsgeschichte?." In *Alltagsgeschichte: Zur Rekonstruktion historischer Erfahrungen und Lebensweisen,* edited by Alf Lüdtke, 9–47. Frankfurt: Campus, 1989.
Lüdtke, Alf. "Stofflichkeit, Macht-Lust und Reiz der Oberflächen: Zu den Perspektiven von Alltagsgeschichte." In *Sozialgeschichte, Alltagsgeschichte, Mikro-Historie: Eine Diskussion,* edited by Winfried Schulze, 65–80. Göttingen: Vandenhoeck & Ruprecht, 1994.
Lüdtke, Alf. "'Fehlgreifen in der Wahl der Mittel': Optionen im Alltag militärischen Handelns." *Mittelweg 36* 12 (2003): 61–75.
Madajczyk, Czesław, *Die Okkupationspolitik Nazideutschlands in Polen 1939–1945.* East Berlin: Akademie, 1987.
Mallmann, Klaus-Michael, Jochen Böhler, and Jürgen Matthäus, eds. *Einsatzgruppen in Polen: Darstellung und Dokumentation.* Darmstadt: Wissenschaftliche Buchgesellschaft, 2008.
Mann, Michael. "Were the Perpetrators of Genocide 'Ordinary Men' or 'Real Nazis'? Results from Fifteen Hundred Biographies." *Holocaust and Genocide Studies* 14 (2000): 331–366.
Matthäus, Jürgen. "What About the 'Ordinary Men'? The German Order Police and the Holocaust in the Occupied Soviet Union." *Holocaust and Genocide Studies* 11 (1996): 134–150.
Matthäus, Jürgen, ed. *Ausbildungsziel Judenmord?: 'Weltanschauliche Erziehung' von SS, Polizei und Waffen-SS im Rahmen der 'Endlösung'.* Frankfurt: Fischer, 2003.
Matthäus, Jürgen. "Die 'Judenfrage' als Schulungsthema von SS und Polizei: 'Inneres Erlebnis' und Handlungsmotivation." In *Ausbildungsziel Judenmord?: 'Weltanschauliche Erziehung' von SS, Polizei und Waffen-SS im Rahmen der 'Endlösung',* edited by Jürgen Matthäus, 35–86. Frankfurt: Fischer, 2003.
Matthäus, Jürgen. "Georg Heuser—Routinier des sicherheitspolizeilichen Osteinsatzes." In *Karrieren der Gewalt: Nationalsozialistische Täterbiographien, vol. 2: Veröffentlichungen der Forschungsstelle Ludwigsburg der Universität Stuttgart,* edited by Klaus-Michael Mallmann and Gerhard Paul, 115–125. Darmstadt: Wissenschaftliche Buchgesellschaft, 2004.
Meier, Kurt. *Kreuz und Hakenkreuz: Die evangelische Kirche im Dritten Reich.* Munich: dtv, 2001.
Meier, Rudolf. *Soldaten-Führer durch Warschau.* Warsaw: Verlag der Deutschen Buchhandlung, 1942.
Mick, Christoph. *Kriegserfahrungen in einer multiethnischen Stadt: Lemberg 1914–1947.* Wiesbaden: Harrassowitz, 2010.

Missalla, Heinrich. *Für Gott, Führer und Vaterland: Die Verstrickung der katholischen Seelsorge in Hitlers Krieg*. Munich: Kösel, 1999.

Mix, Andreas. "Organisatoren und Praktiker der Gewalt: Die SS- und Polizeiführer im Distrikt Warschau." In *Krieg und Verbrechen: Situation und Intention: Fallbeispiele*, edited by Timm C. Richter, 123–134. Munich: Meidenbauer, 2006.

Młynarczyk, Jacek Andrzej. *Judenmord in Zentralpolen: Der Distrikt Radom im Generalgouvernement 1939–1945*. Darmstadt: Wissenschaftliche Buchgesellschaft, 2007.

Młynarczyk, Jacek Andrzej. "Vom Massenmörder zum Lebensversicherer: Dr. Ludwig Hahn und die Mühlen der deutschen Justiz." In *Die Gestapo nach 1945: Karrieren, Konflikte, Konstruktionen: Wolfgang Scheffler zum Gedenken*, edited by Klaus-Michael Mallmann and Andrej Angrick, 136–150. Darmstadt: Wissenschaftliche Buchgesellschaft, 2009.

Moczarski, Kazimierz. *Rozmowy z katem*. Warsaw: Wydawnictwo Naukowe PWN, 1994.

Moeller, Felix. *Der Filmminister: Goebbels und der Film im Dritten Reich*. Berlin: Henschel, 1998.

Moll, Martin. ed. *'Führer-Erlasse' 1939–1945: Edition sämtlicher überlieferter, nicht im Reichsgesetzblatt abgedruckter, von Hitler während des Zweiten Weltkrieges schriftlich erteilter Direktiven aus den Bereichen Staat, Partei, Wirtschaft, Besatzungspolitik und Militärverwaltung*. Stuttgart: Franz Steiner, 1997.

Morawski, Karol, ed. *1939. Warszawa w oczach maturzysty: Fotografie Romana Mazika*. Warsaw: Oddział Muzeum Historycznego m. st. Warszawy, 2005.

Mühlhäuser, Regina. "Sexuelle Gewalt als Kriegsverbrechen. Eine Herausforderung für die Internationale Kriegsgerichtsbarkeit." *Mittelweg 36* 2 (2004): 33–48.

Musiał, Bogdan. "Recht und Wirtschaft im besetzten Polen (1939–1945)." In *Das Europa des 'Dritten Reichs': Recht, Wirtschaft, Besatzung*, edited by Johannes Bähr and Ralf Banken, 31–57. Frankfurt: Klostermann, 2005.

Musiał, Bogdan. *Deutsche Zivilverwaltung und Judenverfolgung im Generalgouvernement: Eine Fallstudie zum Distrikt Lublin 1939–1944*. Wiesbaden: Harrassowitz, 1999.

Musiał, Bogdan. ed. *Sowjetische Partisanen in Weißrußland: Innenansichten aus dem Gebiet Baranoviči 1941–1944: Eine Dokumentation*. Munich: Oldenbourg, 2004.

Nolzen, Armin. "Die Arbeitsbereiche der NSDAP im Generalgouvernement, in den Niederlanden und in der besetzten Sowjetunion." In *Die deutsche Herrschaft in den 'germanischen' Ländern 1940–1945*, edited by Robert Bohn, 247–275. Stuttgart: Steiner, 1997.

Oldenhage, Klaus. "Die Verwaltung der besetzten Gebiete." In *Deutsche Verwaltungsgeschichte, Bd. IV: Das Reich als Republik und in der Zeit des Nationalsozialismus*, edited by Kurt Jeserich, Hans Pohl, and Wilfried Berg, 1131–1169. Stuttgart: DVA, 1985.

Orlowski, Hubert. "'Krakauer Zeitung' 1939–1945: Auch ein Kapitel deutscher Literaturgeschichte im Dritten Reich." *Text & Kontext* 8 (1980): 411–418.

Paul, Gerhard. "Von Psychopathen, Technokraten des Terrors und 'ganz gewöhnlichen' Deutschen: Die Täter der Shoah im Spiegel der Forschung." In *Die Täter der Shoah: Fanatische Nationalsozialisten oder ganz normale Deutsche?*, edited by Gerhard Paul, 13–92. Göttingen: Wallstei, 2002.

Paulsson, Gunnar S. *Secret City: The Hidden Jews of Warsaw, 1940–1945*. New Haven: Yale University Press, 2002.

Pfoch, Hubert. "Dokumentation zur Judendeportation." *Jahrbuch des Dokumentationsarchivs des österreichischen Widerstands* (1989): 62–67.

Pischel, Werner. *Die Generaldirektion der Ostbahn in Krakau 1939–1945: Ein Beitrag zur Geschichte der deutschen Eisenbahnen im Zweiten Weltkrieg*. Berlin: Springer, 1964.

Podolska, Aldona. *Służba porządkowa w getcie warszawskim w latach 1940–1943*. Warsaw: Wydawnictwo Historia Pro Futuro, 1996.

Pohl, Dieter. *Von der 'Judenpolitik' zum Judenmord: Der Distrikt Lublin des Generalgouvernements 1939–1944*. Frankfurt: Peter Lang, 1993.

Pohl, Dieter. *Nationalsozialistische Judenverfolgung in Ostgalizien 1941–1944: Organisation und Durchführung eines staatlichen Massenverbrechens*. Munich: Oldenbourg, 1997.

Pohl, Dieter. "Die Ermordung der Juden im Generalgouvernement" in *Nationalsozialistische Vernichtungspolitik 1939–1945: Neue Forschungen und Kontroversen*, edited by Ulrich Herbert, 98–121. Frankfurt: Fischer, 2001.

Pohl, Dieter. "Die einheimische Forschung und der Mord an den Juden in den besetzten sowjetischen Gebieten." In *Täter im Vernichtungskrieg: Der Überfall auf die Sowjetunion und der Völkermord an den Juden*, edited by Wolf Kaiser, 204–216. Berlin: Propyläen, 2002.

Pohl, Dieter. "Die Wehrmacht und der Mord an den Juden in den besetzten sowjetischen Gebieten." In *Täter im Vernichtungskrieg: Der Überfall auf die Sowjetunion und der Völkermord an den Juden*, edited by Wolf Kaiser, 39–53. Berlin: Propyläen, 2002.

Pohl, Dieter. "Der Raub an den Juden im besetzten Osteuropa 1939–1942." In *Raub und Restitution: 'Arisierung' und Rückerstattung des jüdischen Eigentums*, edited by Constantin Goschler and Philipp Ther, 58–72. Frankfurt: Fischer, 2003.

Pohl, Dieter. *Die Herrschaft der Wehrmacht: Deutsche Militärbesatzung und einheimische Bevölkerung in der Sowjetunion 1941–1944*. Munich: Oldenbourg, 2008.

Polonsky, Antony. "The German Occupation of Poland during the First and Second World War: A Comparison." In *Armies of Occupation*, edited by Roy A. Prete and A. Hamish Ion, 97–142. Waterloo/Ontario: Wilfrid Laurier University Press, 1984.

Pośpieszalski, Karol Marian. "Protest dra Wilhelma Hagena przeciv zamierzonemu wymordowaniu części ludności Zamojszczyny w latach 1942/1943." *Przegląd Zachodni* (1958): 117–129.

Pottgiesser, Hans. *Die Deutsche Reichsbahn im Ostfeldzug, 1939–1944*. Neckargemund: K. Vowinckel, 1975.

Präg, Werner. and Hans Frank, eds. *Das Diensttagebuch des deutschen Generalgouverneurs in Polen: 1939–1945*. Stuttgart: Deutsche Verlags-Anstalt, 1975.

Belarus, Projektgruppe, ed. *'Existiert das Ghetto noch?': Weissrussland jüdisches Überleben gegen nationalsozialistische Herrschaft*. Berlin: Assoziation A, 2003.

Quinkert, Babette. "Terror und Propaganda. Die 'Ostarbeiteranwerbung' im Generalkommissariat Weißruthenien." *Zeitschrift für Geschichtswissenschaft* 47 (1999): 700–721.

Radziszewska, Krystyna. and Jörg Riecke, eds. *Die Germanisierung von Lodz im Spiegel der nazionalsozialistischen [sic] Presse (1939–1943)*. Łódź: Wydawnictwo Literatura, 2004.

Ramme, Alwin. *Der Sicherheitsdienst der SS: Zu seiner Funktion im faschistischen Machtapparat und im Besatzungsregime des sogenannten Generalgouvernements Polen*. East Berlin: Deutscher Militärverlag, 1970.

Rass, Christoph. *'Menschenmaterial': Deutsche Soldaten an der Ostfront: Innenansichten einer Infanteriedivision, 1939–1945*. Paderborn: Schöningh, 2003.

Rebentisch, Dieter. *Führerstaat und Verwaltung im Zweiten Weltkrieg: Verfassungsentwicklung und Verwaltungspolitik 1939–1945*. Stuttgart: Steiner-Verlag, 1989.

Reichel, Peter. *Der schöne Schein des Dritten Reiches: Faszination und Gewalt des Faschismus*. Frankfurt: Fischer, 1996.

Reimer, Michael. and Volkmar Kubitzki, *Eisenbahn in Polen 1939–1945: Die Geschichte der Generaldirektion der Ostbahn*. Stuttgart: Transpress, 2004.

Rein, Leonid. *The Kings and the Pawns: Collaboration in Byelorussia during World War II*. New York: Berghahn Books, 2011.

Requate, Jörg. "Öffentlichkeit und Medien als Gegenstände historischer Analysen." *Geschichte und Gesellschaft*. 25 (1999): 5–32.

Rogall, Joachim. *Die Deutschen im Posener Land und in Mittelpolen*. Munich: Langen-Müller, 2005.

Röger, Maren. "Sexual Contact between German Occupiers and Polish Occupied in World War II Poland." In *Women and men at war: A gender perspective on World War II and its aftermath in Central and Eastern Europe*, edited by Maren Röger and Ruth Leiserowitz, 135–155. Osnabrück: fibre, 2012.

Römer, Felix. *Kameraden: Die Wehrmacht von innen*. Bonn: Bundeszentrale für Politische Bildung, 2012.

Roschke, Carsten. *Der umworbene 'Urfeind': Polen in der nationalsozialistischen Propaganda 1934–1939*. Marburg: Tectum, 2000.

Rossino, Alexander B. *Hitler Strikes Poland: Blitzkrieg, Ideology, and Atrocity*. Kansas City: University Press of Kansas, 2003.

Roth, Markus. *Herrenmenschen: Die deutschen Kreishauptleute im besetzten Polen—Karrierewege, Herrschaftspraxis und Nachgeschichte*. Göttingen: Wallstein, 2009.

Ruck, Michael. *Korpsgeist und Staatsbewusstsein: Beamte im deutschen Südwesten 1928 bis 1972*. Munich: Oldenbourg, 1996.

Rückerl, Adalbert, ed. *NS-Prozesse: Nach 25 Jahren Strafverfolgung Möglichkeiten, Grenzen, Ergebnisse*. Karlsruhe: Müller, 1971.

Rückerl, Adalbert, ed. *Nationalsozialistische Vernichtungslager im Spiegel deutscher Strafprozesse: Belzec, Sobibor, Treblinka, Chelmno*. Munich: dtv, 1977.

Rückerl, Adalbert. *NS-Verbrechen vor Gericht: Versuch einer Vergangenheitsbewältigung*. Heidelberg: Müller, 1982.

Rusinek, Bernd A. "Krieg als Sehnsucht: Militärischer Stil und 'junge Generation' in der Weimarer Republik." In *Generationalität und Lebensgeschichte im 20. Jahrhundert*, edited by Jürgen Reulecke, 127–144. Munich: Oldenbourg, 2003.

Sakowska, Ruta. *Menschen im Ghetto: Die jüdische Bevölkerung im besetzten Warschau 1939–1943*. Osnabrück: fibre, 1999.

Saldern, Adelheid von. "Öffentlichkeiten in Diktaturen. Zu den Herrschaftspraktiken in Deutschland im 20. Jahrhundert." In *Diktaturen in Deutschland, Vergleichsaspekte: Strukturen, Institutionen und Verhaltensweisen*, edited by Günther Heydemann and Heinrich Oberreuter, 442–475. Bonn: Bundeszentrale für Politische Bildung, 2003.

Sawicki, Jerzy. *Vor dem polnischen Staatsanwalt*. East Berlin: Deutscher Militärverlag, 1962.

Scheffler, Wolfgang. "NS-Prozesse als Geschichtsquelle. Bedeutung und Grenzen ihrer Auswertbarkeit durch den Historiker." In *Lerntage des Zentrums für Antisemitismusforschung: V. Lerntag über den Holocaust als Thema im Geschichtsunterricht und in der politischen Bildung*, edited by Wolfgang Scheffler and Werner Bergmann, 13–27. Berlin: Universitätsverlag TU, 1988.

Scheffler, Wolfgang, and Helge Grabitz, eds. *Der Ghetto-Aufstand Warschau 1943 aus der Sicht der Täter und Opfer in Aussagen vor deutschen Gerichten*. Munich: Goldmann, 1993.

Schlootz, Johannes, ed. *Deutsche Propaganda in Weißrußland 1941–1944: Eine Konfrontation von Propaganda und Wirklichkeit: Eine Ausstellung in Berlin und Minsk*. Berlin: Freie Universität, 1996.

Schwarberg, Günther. *Im Ghetto von Warschau: Heinrich Jösts Fotografien*. Göttingen: Steidl, 2001.

Schwarz, Gudrun. *Eine Frau an seiner Seite: Ehefrauen in der 'SS-Sippengemeinschaft'*. Berlin: Aufbau-Taschenbuch, 2001.

Schwingel, Markus. *Pierre Bourdieu zur Einführung*. Hamburg: Junius, 2005.

Seidler, Franz. *Prostitution, Homosexualität, Selbstverstümmelung: Probleme der deutschen Sanitätsführung 1939–1945*. Neckargemünd: Vowinkel, 1977.

Seidel, Robert. *Deutsche Besatzungspolitik in Polen: Der Distrikt Radom 1939–1945*. Paderborn: Schöningh, 2006.

Sloan, Jacob, ed. *Notes from the Warsaw ghetto: The journal of Emmanuel Ringelblum*. New York: McGraw-Hill, 1958.

Snyder, Timothy. *Bloodlands: Europe between Hitler and Stalin*. London: The Bodley Head, 2010.

Sofsky, Wolfgang. *Traktat über die Gewalt*. Frankfurt: Fischer, 2001.

Sofsky, Wolfgang. *Das Prinzip Sicherheit*. Frankfurt: Fischer, 2005.

Statistisches Amt des Generalgouvernements, ed. *Amtliches Gemeinde- und Dorfverzeichnis für das Generalgouvernement auf Grund der summarischen Bevölkerungsbestandsaufnahme am 1. März 1943*. Krakow: Burgverlag, 1943.

Stawarz, Andrzej. ed. *Pawiak 1835–1944*. Warsaw: Muzeum Niepodległości, 2002.
Steber, Martina, and Bernhard Gotto, eds. *Visions of Community in Nazi Germany: Social Engineering and Private Lives*. Oxford: Oxford UP, 2014.
Steber, Martina, and Bernhard Gotto. "*Volksgemeinschaft*: Writing the Social History of the Nazi Regime." In *Visions of Community in Nazi Germany: Social Engineering and Private Lives*, edited by Martina Steber and Bernhard Gotto, 1–25. Oxford: Oxford UP, 2014.
Steber, Martina. and Bernhard Gotto, "Volksgemeinschaft und die Gesellschaftsgeschichte des NS-Regimes." *Vierteljahrshefte für Zeitgeschichte* 62 (2014): 433–467.
Stephan, Anke. "'Banditen' oder 'Helden'? Der Warschauer Aufstand in der Wahrnehmung deutscher Mannschaftssoldaten." In *Die polnische Heimatarmee: Geschichte und Mythos der Armia Krajowa seit dem Zweiten Weltkrieg*, edited by Bernhard Chiari, 473–496. Munich: De Gruyter, 2003.
Strippel, Andreas. *NS-Volkstumspolitik und die Neuordnung Europas: Rassenpolitische Selektion der Einwandererzentralstelle des Chefs der Sicherheitspolizei und des SD 1939–1945*. Paderborn: Schöningh, 2011.
Stroop, Jürgen. *Es gibt keinen jüdischen Wohnbezirk in Warschau mehr*. Neuwied: Luchterhand, 1960.
Strzembosz, Tomasz. *Akcje zbrojne podziemnej Warszawy 1939–1944*. Warsaw: Państwowy Instytut Wydawniczy, 1983.
Szarota, Tomasz. *Warschau unter dem Hakenkreuz: Leben und Alltag im besetzten Warschau 1.10.1939 bis 31.7.1944*. Paderborn: Schöningh, 1985.
Szarota, Tomasz. "Die Luftangriffe auf Warschau im Zweiten Weltkrieg." *Acta Poloniae Historica* 69 (1994): 133–145.
Sziling, Jan. "Die Kirchen im Generalgouvernement." *Miscellanea Historiae Ecclesiasticae* 9 (1984): 277–288.
Thieme, Hans. "Erinnerungen eines deutschen Stabsoffiziers an den Warschauer Aufstand." In *Der Warschauer Aufstand 1944*, edited by Bernd Martin and Stanisława Lewandowska, 301–307. Warsaw: Deutsch-Polnischer Verlag, 1999.
Trunk, Isaiah. *Judenrat: The Jewish Councils in Eastern Europe under Nazi Occupation*. Lincoln: University of Nebraska Press, 1996 [first 1972].
Tucker, Erica L. *Remembering Occupied Warsaw: Polish Narratives of World War II*. DeKalb: Northern Illinois University Press, 2011.
Tusk-Scheinwechslerowa, Franciska. "Fabryka Waltera C. Többensa w getcie warszawskim." *Biuletyn Żydowskiego Instytutu Historycznego* 23 (1957): 63–70.
Umbreit, Hans. *Deutsche Militärverwaltungen 1938/39: Die militärische Besetzung der Tschechoslowakei und Polens*. Stuttgart: DVA, 1977.
van Laak, Dirk. "Alltagsgeschichte." In *Aufriß der historischen Wissenschaften: Bd. 7. Neue Themen und Methoden der Geschichtswissenschaft*, edited by Michael Maurer, 14–80. Stuttgart: Philipp Reclam jun, 2003.
Villinger, Tanja. "Der Aufstand in der Berichterstattung der deutschen Medien." In *Der Warschauer Aufstand 1944*, edited by Bernd Martin and Stanisława Lewandowska, 271–280. Warsaw: Deutsch-Polnischer Verlag, 1999.

Vossler, Frank. *Propaganda in die eigene Truppe: Die Truppenbetreuung in der Wehrmacht 1939–1945.* Paderborn: Schöningh, 2005.
Walichnowski, Tadeusz. *Rozmowy z Leistem: Hitlerowskim starosta Warszawy.* Warsaw: Państwowe Wydawnictwo Naukowe, 1986.
Wankewitsch, Alla Georgijewna. *'Fahrt nach Trostenez'. Dokumentation über das Vernichtungslager.* Minsk, 1986.
Welzer, Harald, and Michaela Christ. *Täter: Wie aus ganz normalen Menschen Massenmörder werden.* Frankfurt: Fischer, 2005.
Westerbarkey, Joachim. *Das Geheimnis: Zur funktionalen Ambivalenz von Kommunikationsstrukturen.* Opladen: Westdeutscher Verlag, 1991.
Wette, Wolfram. *Die Wehrmacht: Feindbilder, Vernichtungskrieg, Legenden.* Frankfurt: Fischer, 2002.
Wildt, Michael. "Die politische Ordnung der Volksgemeinschaft. Ernst Fraenkels 'Doppelstaat' neu betrachtet." *Mittelweg 36* 12 (2003): 45–61.
Wildt, Michael. *Generation des Unbedingten: Das Führungskorps des Reichssicherheitshauptamtes.* Hamburg: Hamburger Ed, 2003.
Witte, Peter, Michael Wildt, Martina Voigt, Dieter Pohl et al., eds. *Der Dienstkalender Heinrich Himmlers 1941/42.* Hamburg: Christians, 1999.
Wolf, Gerhard. *Ideologie und Herrschaftsrationalität: Nationalsozialistische Germanisierungspolitik in Polen.* Hamburg: Hamburger Ed, 2012.
Wulf, Josef. *Das Dritte Reich und seine Vollstrecker: Die Liquidation von 500000 Juden im Ghetto Warschau.* Berlin-Grunewald: Arani, 1961.
Yahil, Leni. *The Holocaust: The Fate of European Jewry, 1932–1945.* New York: Oxford UP, 1991.
Zankel, Sönke. *Mit Flugblättern gegen Hitler: Der Widerstandskreis um Hans Scholl und Alexander Schmorell.* Cologne: Böhlau, 2008.
Zarząd Miejski m.st. Warszawy, ed. *Rocznik Statystycyny Warszawy 1936 i 1937.* Warsaw: Zakład Wydawnictw Statystycznych, 1938.
Zellhuber, Andreas. *'Unsere Verwaltung treibt einer Katastrophe zu[ellipsis]': Das Reichsministerium für die besetzten Ostgebiete und die deutsche Besatzungsherrschaft in der Sowjetunion 1941–1945.* Stamsried: Vögel, 2006.
Zimmerer, Jürgen. "Die Geburt des 'Ostlandes' aus dem Geiste des Kolonialismus. Die nationalsozialistische Eroberungs- und Beherrschungspolitik in (post-)kolonialer Perspektive." *Sozial. Geschichte* 19 (2004): 1–43.
Zimmermann, Volker. "'Volksgenossen' erster und zweiter Klasse? Reichs- und Sudetendeutsche in Böhmen und Mähren 1938–1945." In *Die 'Volksdeutschen' in Polen, Frankreich, Ungarn und der Tschechoslowakei: Mythos und Realität*, edited by Jerzy Kochanowski and Maike Sach, 257–272. Osnabrück: fibre, 2006.
Zimmermann, Wilhelm. "Der Ehrenbürger: Aus der politischen Biographie des NSDAP-Gauleiters der 'Kurmark' und Oberpräsidenten der Provinz Brandenburg Wilhelm Kube." *Uckermärkische Hefte* 1 and 2 (1989 and 1995): 245–260 and 215–247.

Index

A

Albers, Hans, 88
alcohol consumption, 144–9, 153, 165, 167, 234
Alvensleben, Udo von, 62, 100, 176, 194
Andrian, Carl von, 17, 77, 83, 91, 125, 130, 173, 212, 217, 229, 231, 249
Asid Instytut Serologiczny, 52
Aubin, Hermann, 110
Auerswald, Heinz, 41, 63, 184
Auschwitz, 237, 250–1
Auswärtiges Amt Berlin, 235

B

Bach-Zelewski, Erich von dem, 242, 244
Balley, Adalbert, 257
Bechtolsheim, Gustav von, 25
Belarus, 1, 124
Belorusssians
    contacts with, 61–63, 85
    food rationing, 42, 210–11
    forced labor, 214–5
    prejudices against, 172–3, 182, 194, 197, 257
    sexual contacts with, 189–91
    see also resistance
    see also violence
Bergengruen, Werner, 92
Berlin, 131, 142, 179, 228–9
Beutel, Lothar, 67
Beyerlein, Hermann, 4, 82, 184
Bielefeld, 228
Bischof, Max, 179, 225, 248
black market, 136–40, 154, 212
Blobel, Paul, 252
Bonk, Eitel-Friedrich, 52
bookshop for Germans (Warsaw), 93–94
Borisov, 248–9, 252

Böttcher, Herbert, 67
Bourdieu, Pierre, 10, 161
Bremen, 229
Breyer, Albert, 49
Brückner, Heinz, 188
Brünn, 229
Bund Deutscher Mädel (BDM) see Hitler Youth
Bursche, Juliusz, 142

C

Calderon, Pedro, 98
children, German, 49–50, 108, 128, 184, 188, 238
    births in Warsaw, 49, 184
    Kindergarten, 49
    see also Hitler youth
    see also schools
churches
    Catholic, 141–143
    Lutheran, 141
Chwastek, Karl, 136
Cieciora, Antoni, 177
civil administration, 34–43, 51, 235–6
    accommodation of personnel, 40–41, 45, 79, 133
    bribery, 140–1, 169–70
    canteens, 80
    female personnel, 44–45
    heads of, 37–38, 41–43
    leave for Germany, 128–30
    local personnel, 40
    offices and institutions, 38–39
        office duty, 76–78
    recruitment of personnel, 34–36, 193–4
    salary, 132–133
    supply of personnel, 83
civilians (Reich Germans), 43–45, 51–53
    accomodation, 45
    business opportunities in the East, 51

Index

wives, 128, 183–4, 187
women, 43–45, 83–84, 126, 200–1, 272
   see also residential quarter
   see also Volksdeutsche
Claudius, Erich, 98
Cochenhausen, Conrad von, 65
Cologne, 229
colonialism, 131, 200–1
comradeship, 78, 87, 135, 145, 148–54, 166, 197–9, 271
   see also society of occupiers
conflicts among Germans, 148, 150–4
Conti, Leonardo, 247
cultural activities
   concerts and music, 91, 96–101
   operetta, opera and theatre, 52, 96–101
   see also leisure activities
Czerniaków, Adam, 63

D

Dauthendey, Max, 97
De Molina, Tirso, 98
Decker, Willi, 111
Dengel, Oskar, 68
Deutsche Industrie- und Handelskammer Warsaw, 52
Deutsches Haus (Warsaw), 85–86
Dirksen textile company, 51
Distrikt Radom, 47
Distrikt Warschau, 38–39, 47, 55, 79, 150
Düsseldorf, 229

E

Eitner, Albrecht, 51
Epstein, Johanna, 188

F

Fabrika Kabli Ożarów, 52
Fabryka Silników i Traktorów URSUS, 52
Fausthammer, Rudolf, 124
Fischer, Ludwig, 37–38, 41, 43, 55, 80, 93, 96, 98–99, 102, 105, 107–10, 132, 134, 142, 145, 172, 195, 222
Förster, Arthur, 146
France, 124, 173, 195
Frank, Hans, 1, 9, 24, 34, 37, 41, 43, 47, 50, 76, 86, 90, 93, 96, 106–7, 111, 123, 145–6, 181–2, 193, 195, 217, 239
Frankfurt, 229
Freter, Wilhelm, 25
Freudenthal, Carl Ludwig, 149
Freythag-Loringhofen, Axel von, 94
Frick, Wilhelm, 36
Friedrichs, Hermann, 189

G

Garwolin, 149
Gauweiler, Otto, 42–43
Gdańsk, 51
Geibel, Otto, 67
Gelsenkirchen, 228
Generalgouvernement (Polen), 1, 34
Generalkommissariat Weißruthenien, 1, 39, 45
Germanization
   Generalplan Ost, 123
   of Warsaw, 57–59
ghetto
   in Minsk, 30, 55, 221–3, 227–30, 234–5
   in Warsaw, 28, 31, 33, 37, 41–42, 48, 125, 133–4, 139–40, 177, 198, 212–213, 222–31, 235, 239–40, 258
   see also resistance
Goebbels, Joseph, 92–93, 126, 224
Goethe, Johann Wolfgang, 98
Gollert, Friedrich, 42–43, 58
Gottberg, Curt von, 32, 38, 217
Graf, Karl, 257
Grodzisk, 165
Groh, Otto Ernst, 97
Gunst, Wilhelm, 48

H

habitus
   theoretical concept, 10–11, 161–2
   of the German occupiers, 162–171, 194, 197, 200–1, 256–8, 271, 275–7, 279
Hagen, Wilhelm, 213, 230, 237, 247–8
Hahn, Ludwig, 28–29, 183, 185
Hamburg, 228–9
Hannover, 228
Hasse, Senior Lieutenant, 255
Hebbel, Friedrich, 96
Heinrici, Gotthard, 131
Hennig, Johannes, 238
Hesse, Hermann, 92
Heuser, Georg, 27–28, 257
Heydecker, Joe, 231
Hilgers, Hans, 91
Himmler, Heinrich, 29, 46, 145, 182, 189, 232, 242, 246
history of daily life (concept), 2–3, 8–10
Hitler youth, 23, 50, 113
   Bund Deutscher Mädel (BDM), 44, 50
   see also children
Hitler, Adolf, 1, 22, 34, 109–10, 141, 149, 242, 244, 247
Hofmann, Walter, 67
Hornig, Herbert, 149
Hosenfeld, Wilm, 62, 77, 87, 94–95, 98–99, 104–5, 128–9, 143–4, 177, 180, 192, 198, 213, 215, 220, 222, 227, 232, 237, 240, 244, 247, 251, 255–6

Hotel Bristol (Warsaw), 41 51, 54, 150, 152, 190
Huber, Kurt, 253

J

Janetzke, Wilhelm, 37–38, 55
Jesuiter, Max, 255
Jews, 220–238
    contact with, 176
    deportation, 25, 42, 143, 224, 226, 234–7, 239, 255
    expropriation, 133–5, 137, 139, 176, 235
    forced labor, 213, 221–2, 226, 236
    from Germany, 228–30
    help for, 177, 230, 237
    in hiding, 249–50
    prejudices against, 125, 173, 176, 178, 194–5, 197, 231, 257
    Judenrat, 63, 135, 176
    Ordnungsdienst, 62, 224
    sexual contacts with, 188, 222
    starvation, 42, 198, 209–13, 230
    see also ghettos
    see also resistance
    see also violence
Jonas, Franz, 77, 257
Julius Meinl (company), 52, 140
Junkers (company), 52

K

Kern, Anderl, 100
Koderisch, Günter, 90
Kojdanow, 228
Königsberg, 229
Kostrzewa, Peter Paul, 94
Krakauer Philharmoniker, 98
Krakow, 1, 29, 32, 34, 90, 92, 96, 110, 147, 153, 174, 182, 215, 247
Krause, Ernst Hermann, 105
Krüger, Friedrich Wilhelm, 247
Krusche, Waldemar, 142
Kube, Wilhelm, 1, 32, 37–38, 55, 58, 96, 101, 106, 113, 125–7, 129, 132, 140, 145, 163, 178, 191, 193–4, 212, 217, 232, 235
Künneke, Eduard, 97
Kutschera, Franz, 180–2

L

Landwehr, Gordian, 142–3, 252
Leist, Ludwig, 37–38, 96
leisure activities
    books, 93–95
    cinema, 87–90, 99
    radio, 90–91

    see also cultural activities
    see also sport
Ley, Robert, 180
Lida, 165
Lieschke, Konrad, 94, 101, 125, 127, 129–31, 146, 173, 176, 196, 203, 212–3, 229–30, 265
Łódz, 227
Lohse, Hinrich, 37
Lublin, 226

M

Magdeburg, 228
Małkinia, 104
Maly Trostenets camp, 30, 228, 234, 252
marriages of Germans, 183–7
Mechanische Werkstätten Neubrandenburg, 221
Meisinger, Josef, 28–29
Morsbach, Elisabeth, 83, 113
Müller, Gerhard, 189
Munich, 124
Münster, 228

N

Nahlmann, Otto, 78, 210
National Socialism (ideology), 21, 109–110, 113–114, 153–4, 174, 193, 198, 200–1, 221, 224, 244, 272
    criticism of, 149, 244, 274
    moral questions in the East, 163–4, 232, 254–8
    propaganda, 29, 58, 76–77, 82, 89–93, 109, 111, 126–7, 127, 173, 182, 194, 197, 200–1, 217, 224, 230–1, 241, 245, 254, 257, 272
Nationalsozialistische Volkswohlfahrt, 43, 49, 134, 136, 169, 188
Nazi Party (NSDAP), 35, 43, 46, 56, 103–104, 106–111, 113, 195
    ideological schooling, 91, 107–111, 113
    Nazi Party Chancellory, 35, 191
    party organization in Warsaw, 106–7
    see also Hitler youth
Nelkel, Franz, 77
Neuhauser, Hermine, 154
Neumann, Rudolf, 231
Neumann-Neurode, Karl-Ulrich, 65
newspapers, 91–93
    Generalgouvernement (journal), 93
    Krakauer Zeitung see Warschauer Zeitung
    Minsker Zeitung, 53, 91–93, 135, 146, 179, 218, 225
    Völkischer Beobachter, 245
    Warschauer Kulturblätter, 93
    Warschauer Zeitung, 15, 47, 92–93, 96, 103, 221, 224–7, 237
Noak, Curt, 101

O

Ohle, Walter, 146
Okęcie, 102–103
Organisation Todt, 52, 170, 175, 180, 221
Ostbahn see Reichsbahn

P

Paderborn, 228
Paersch, Fritz, 215
Palmiry, 26
Paris, 131, 243, 280
Pawiak prison, 30–32, 151, 186, 219
Pilder, Hans, 248
Piłsudski, Józef, 58
Pohle, Helgo, 84
Poland, 124
Polanski, Roman, 62
Poles
    Catholic church, 141–2
    contacts with, 61–63, 150, 175–7
    expropriation, 176
    resettlement, 57–58, 222
    forced labor, 213–4
    Lutheran church, 142
    prejudices against, 125–126, 172–3, 176–8, 182, 194–5, 197, 257
    sexual contacts with, 61, 128, 186, 188, 190–1, 199
    starvation, 42, 177, 210–11, 213
    police. *See* SS
    see also resistance
    see also violence
Polski Bank Przemyslowy, 52
Potsdam, 228
prisoners of war
    after the Warsaw Uprising, 242
    help for, 177
    Soviet soldiers, 24, 177, 211–12, 258
    Stalag no. 352, 24, 30

R

Red Army, 1, 242
    bombing of Warsaw, 196
Reich Germans *see* civilians
Reich Interior Ministry, 34–36, 68
Reich Ministry for the Occupied Eastern Territories, 36, 126, 173
Reichsbahn, 20, 35, 39–40, 45, 60, 77, 83, 111, 128, 194, 228–9, 235–6, 243
    local personnel, 174–5
Reichspost, 20, 35, 39–40, 45, 81, 127, 243, 250
    quarters in Warsaw, 82
religion *see* churches
reputation of Germans in the East *see* habitus

residential quarter for Germans
    in Minsk, 55, 60
    in Warsaw, 38, 40, 54–64
    shops for Germans, 59
resistance, 178–82, 239–45
    Armia Krajowa, 56, 242, 244–5
    Bandenkampf, 25, 216–8
    Soviet partisans, 178, 196, 215–6
    uprising in the Warsaw ghetto, 31, 33, 58, 134, 233, 239–42
    Warsaw Uprising 1944, 233, 242–5
    Weiße Rose, 253
robbery, 133–136, 138–9, 154, 165–6, 168–9
Rohrweder, Max, 98, 105, 143, 248
Rosenberg, Alfred, 36–37, 68, 123, 129, 165, 188
Rossum, Fritz von, 65

S

SA, 167–8, 182
Sammern-Frankenegg, Ferdinand von, 67, 247
Schartow, Werner, 65
Scheiermann, Hugo, 138
Schenk, Richard, 180
Schild, Fritz, 179
Schlosser, Heinrich, 150
Schmeling, Max, 104
Schmid, Kurt, 178, 217
Schön, Waldemar, 41
schools for Germans, 49–50
Schultz, Fritz, 52, 226
Schützeicher, Josef, 177
Schweikart, Hans, 97
Schwerin, 228
Seel, Kurt, 173
Seifert, Werner, 107
Siedlce, 238
Siemens, 52
Sierck, Detlef, 88
Sirk, Douglas. *See* Sierck, Detlef
Sluzk, 163
society of occupiers, 20, 26, 196–201, 248, 253–6, 269–70, 272–4, 277–8
    see also comradeship
Sondergericht Minsk, 165, 167
Sondergericht Warsaw, 16, 42, 53, 138, 140, 149, 165–71, 192, 196, 199–200, 251
Soviet Union, 1, 36, 45, 85, 91, 123, 125–6, 137, 171, 245
Spilker, Alfred, 31
sport, 101–106
    Nazi party and, 103–104
    Schalke 04, 103
SS, 26–34, 231
    barber shop in Warsaw, 81
    brothels for, 189–90
    daily routine, 78–79
    Einsatzgruppen, 25, 30
    female employees, 184–5

ideology, 29–30
leadership personnel in Warsaw and Minsk, 27–29, 32–33
local police auxiliaries, 33–34, 173–4, 224, 249–50
Police Battalion 11, 163
Police Battalion 61, 131, 232, 251–2
Police Battalion 309, 223
Police Battalion 322, 233
Police Regiment 23, 179
porcelain manufacturer in Munich-Allach, 132
quarters in Warsaw, 31–32, 78, 81
quarters in Minsk, 33
recruitment and training, 27, 30
Reichskommissar für die Festigung des Deutschen Volkstums, 46, 50
Sicherheitsdienst, 25, 245
Sicherheitspolizei, 24, 26, 31–32, 50, 111, 147–8, 183, 234, 241
Sonderkommando 1005, 252–3
SS court, 147, 153, 174
Waffen-SS, 242–3
Stahel, Rainer, 65
Stampe, Friedrichfranz, 96
Steyr Daimler Puch, 52
Strauch, Eduard, 27–28, 145, 191
Stroop, Jürgen, 28–29, 58, 67, 134, 240
Szpilman, Władysław, 62, 177

T

Theresienstadt, 228–9
Toebbens, Walter, 52, 226, 231, 237, 250
Transawia Waffen, 138
Treblinka camp, 25, 42, 143, 224, 226, 234–7, 239, 250, 255

U

Unruh, Heinz, 136
Unruh, Walter von, 65

V

Vienna, 131, 229
violence
  against Belorusssians, 216–9
  against Jews, 30, 150, 163, 176, 198, 209, 217–8, 221, 224, 232–4, 238–40
  against partisans, 215–9
  against Poles, 189, 192, 195–6, 218–20, 233, 242–5
  disapproval of, 214–7, 220, 224, 227, 230, 238–40, 253, 255
  extermination of Jews, 226–42, 246, 248–53
  legitimation of, 209–10, 230–1, 233–4, 238–9, 241–2, 244, 249, 252–8, 276–8
  public nature of, 217–20, 222, 224–33, 235–8, 240–1, 245–258, 277
Vistula river, 102, 105, 109, 180–181, 242
Volga Germans, 55
Volksdeutsche, 3, 20, 45–51, 174–5, 272–3
  contacts with Reich Germans, 62, 175, 187
  crimes of, 136, 138–40, 167–70, 192, 196, 251
  membership in Nazi party, 46
  Reich Germans' prejudices against, 50, 273
  Selbstschutz, 28, 48, 90
  see also civilians
Volksgemeinschaft, 3, 148, 273

W

Warsaw Uprising, 33, 56
  see also ghetto, uprising
Wehrmacht, 1, 21–26, 111–112, 215–6, 223–4, 231, 236–7, 243, 246
  286th Security Division, 25
  354th Infantry Regiment, 24
  707th Infantry Division, 25, 216, 224
  brothels for, 189–90
  Chef der Zivilverwaltung, 34
  daily routine, 77
  Feldgendarmerie, 24
  Feldkommandantur Warsaw, 147, 230
  hospitals in Warsaw, 22
  quarters in Minsk, 82–84, 125
  quarters in Warsaw, 59, 130
  recruitment and training, 22–23,
  relationship to other German institutions, 24
  Rüstungskommando Warschau, 25
  soldiers, 20, 22–23, 122
Weirauch, Lothar, 247
Wiesmann, Franz, 80
Wigand, Arpad, 67
Winterhilfswerk, 112–113, 149, 200
Witte, Georg, 136
Witte, Karl, 134
World War I, 21, 29, 125, 270, 279

Z

Zakopane, 104, 129
Zamość, 123
Zerkaulen, Heinrich, 97

www.ingramcontent.com/pod-product-compliance
Lightning Source LLC
Chambersburg PA
CBHW072145100526
44589CB00015B/2095